Research and Global Perspectives in Learning Disabilities

Essays in Honor of William M. Cruickshank

The LEA Series on Special Education and Disability
John Wills Lloyd, Series Editor

Research and Global Perspectives in Learning Disabilities

Essays in Honor of William M. Cruickshank

Edited by

Daniel P. Hallahan
University of Virginia, USA

Barbara K. Keogh
UCLA, USA

LEA

LAWRENCE ERLBAUM ASSOCIATES, PUBLISHERS
2001   Mahwah, New Jersey   London

Lawrence Erlbaum Associates, Inc., Publishers
10 Industrial Avenue
Mahwah, NJ 07430

Cover design by Kathryn Houghtaling Lacey

Library of Congress Cataloging-in-Publication Data

Research and global perspectives in learning disabilities :
    essays in honor of William M. Cruickshank / edited by
    Daniel P. Hallahan, Barbara K. Keogh.
    p.   cm.—(The LEA series on special education and disability)
The executive committee of the International Academy for
    Research in Learning Disabilities planned this volume on
    the occasion of its 25th anniversary to honor the founder of
    the Academy, William M. Cruickshank.
    Includes bibliographical references and indexes.
ISBN 0-8058-3617-9 (cloth : alk. paper)
1. Learning disabilities—Cross-cultural studies.   2. Learning
    disabled children—Education—Cross-cultural studies.
    I. Hallahan, Daniel P., 1944–   II. Keogh, Barbara K.
    III. Cruickshank, William M.   IV. Series.

LC4704 .R48   2000
371.9—dc21   00-069933

Books published by Lawrence Erlbaum Associates are printed
on acid-free paper, and their bindings are chosen for strength
and durability.

Printed in the United States of America
10   9   8   7   6   5   4   3   2   1

Contents

Chapter 1

Introduction

Daniel P. Hallahan
University of Virginia

Barbara K. Keogh
University of California at Los Angeles

The executive committee of the International Academy for Research in Learning Disabilities (IARLD) planned this volume to honor the founder of the Academy, William M. Cruickshank, and his many accomplishments. The Academy thought it appropriate that a volume be published on the occasion of the Academy's 25th anniversary. Bill's influence on special education in general, and learning disabilities in specific, is evident throughout the world. Consistent with his international activities, the contributors to this book represent eight different countries in addition to the United States. The chapters reflect a range of perspectives on "the state of the art" in learning disabilities, documenting both commonalities and differences across countries. Taken together, the chapters provide a comprehensive and informative picture of learning disabilities. We are confident Bill Cruickshank would be pleased to see how broad and deep his influence has been. We are hopeful that he would be pleased with how we chose to organize this book.

A BRIEF HISTORY OF LEARNING DISABILITIES

The term *learning disabilities* is credited to Samuel Kirk, who used the term in 1963 at a conference focused on children with perceptual handicaps (Kirk, 1963). However, specific learning disabilities have a long history, although under different, and sometimes quite exotic, names.

Kirk, for example, relied heavily on the earlier work of the clinician Marion Monroe, as well as Grace Fernald (1943) and James Hinshelwood (1907, 1917). In 1907, Hinshelwood, a Scottish ophthalmologist, reported on four cases of what he referred to as "congenital word blindness." Because all the cases occurred in the same family, he theorized a genetic component to the condition. Hinshelwood also conjectured that the word blindness was caused by damage to particular areas of the brain.

Another influential early figure was Samuel Orton, a neurologist, who studied and worked clinically with children with reading disabilities. Orton (1937) attributed these childrens' reading failures to lack of hemispheric dominance resulting in a condition he termed "strephosymbolia." Although Orton's theory of hemispheric dominance has not withstood empirical validation, his theory, and that of Hinshelwood, that reading disabilities might have a genetic basis has received considerable research support (DeFries, Gillis, & Wadsworth, 1993; Pennington, 1995; Reynolds et al., 1996). Orton's multisensory educational approach for children with reading disabilities, known as the Orton–Gillingham Approach (Anna Gillingham was a psychologist and educator with whom he collaborated), is used widely although evidence of its effectiveness is limited (Hallahan, Kauffman, & Lloyd, 1999).

The idea that reading or specific learning problems were due to underlying neurological damage was consistent with the work of Kurt Goldstein, who documented the learning and behavior problems of German soldiers wounded in World War I (Goldstein, 1936, 1939). Through clinical case studies of these soldiers, Goldstein concluded that brain injury results, among other things, in distractibility, perseveration, and perceptual problems (e.g., figure–background confusion).

Goldstein's work had a strong influence on researchers in the United States, including Heinz Werner, Alfred Strauss, Newell Kephart, Laura Lehtinen, and William Cruickshank, all of whom worked at the Wayne County Training School, a school for children with mental retardation, located in Michigan. Werner and Strauss, through a series of studies, attempted to determine whether some of the characteristics of Goldstein's soldiers, in particular the figure–background problems, could be replicated in children who were mentally retarded and presumably brain injured (Strauss & Werner, 1942; Werner & Strauss, 1941). Although these studies were aptly criticized because of flaws in how brain injury status was determined (see Hallahan & Cruickshank, 1973, for a review), they were historically important because they were some of the first demonstrations that children with mental retardation are not all alike in their behavioral profiles. More important, the recognition of behavioral differences led Werner and Strauss to the significant conclusion that educational programming for children with mental retardation should not all be the same. Although they were still talking about differentiating *groups* of children for educational purposes, we can view these efforts as the embryonic stages of the principle of individualization of instruction that is at the heart of today's individualized educational programs dictated by the Individuals with Disabilities Education Act (IDEA).

In collaboration with Laura Lehtinen, Strauss developed an educational program for children with mental retardation whom they considered to be distractible and to have perceptual–motor disturbances (Strauss & Lehtinen, 1947). Among other things, the program emphasized a distraction-free environment and highly structured, teacher-directed activities.

Cruickshank was the important link between Werner, Strauss, and Lehtinen's work with children who were retarded to work with children of normal intelligence. Cruickshank and his colleagues used essentially the same figure–background measures that Werner and Strauss had used, but the population they chose to study, children with cerebral palsy, had bona fide brain injury (Cruickshank, Bice, & Wallen, 1957; Dolphin & Cruickshank, 1951). In addition, the children were of near average, average, or above average intelligence. Cruickshank and his colleagues found that these students with cerebral palsy were more likely to be distracted by the background than nondisabled peers, thus replicating Werner and Strauss' findings.

Following his studies of children with cerebral palsy, Cruickshank was funded for 1 year to establish demonstration classrooms for students of normal intelligence with the behavioral characteristics that Werner and Strauss had found in children with mental retardation (e.g., distractibility, hyperactivity, perseveration, and perceptual–motor problems). Many of the students in the program had diagnoses of *minimal brain injury*, a then popular term for children who exhibited behavioral but not neurological signs of brain injury. Today, it is highly likely that most of these children would have been identified as learning disabled and/or as having attention deficit hyperactivity disorder (ADHD). Cruickshank and his colleagues designed the environment and the curriculum along the lines recommended by the theories of Strauss and Lehtinen (Cruickshank, Bentzen, Ratzeburg, & Tannhauser, 1961). The program emphasized a nonstimulating environment. Students worked in separate cubicles, the classrooms were plain with little or no decoration, and the classroom routine was the same every day. Teachers were encouraged to minimize distractions of all kinds, including their personal appearance and behavior.

At the end of the year, results of the effectiveness of the program were mixed, with gains evident for measures of perceptual–motor skills and distractibility but not for standardized tests of achievement. The impact of Cruickshank's educational program, however, was felt for several years. And today, although few teachers still use cubicles to shield students from external distractions, many theorists and practitioners still espouse a highly structured, teacher-directed curriculum for students with learning, behavioral, and/or attention problems.

Other contemporaries of Cruickshank instrumental in establishing some of the founding principles of the learning disabilities field were Marianne Frostig, Newell Kephart, Doris Johnson, Helmer Myklebust, and Samuel Kirk. Frostig and Kephart emphasized the remediation of perceptual and perceptual–motor problems whereas Johnson, Myklebust, and Kirk focused on language processing as the root of learning disabilities. Johnson and Myklebust (1967) linked problems in auditory comprehension to aspects of learning disabilities. Kirk (Kirk, McCarthy, & Kirk, 1968) developed a test of psycholinguistic abilities aimed at documenting patterns of children's language processing skills.

Over the years, the research evidence has been much kinder to the language theorists than to the perceptual–motor theorists. Concern for the role of language in learning disabilities is a major focus in both research and remediation today. The National Institute of Child Health and Human Development (NICHD) has been a major force in research on early reading, and this work has led to a number of language-based programs for young and/or disabled readers (Lyon & Moats, 1997). The importance of phonological processing in learning to read is widely accepted in the United States and abroad, and instruction in phonological skills is now widely implemented in early reading programs and with children with learning disabilities.

LEARNING DISABILITIES AS A SPECIAL EDUCATION CATEGORY

In 1969 the U.S. Congress passed legislation authorizing the U.S. Office of Education to initiate programs for students with learning disabilities. Further legislation followed (the Education of All Handicapped Children Act of 1975 and IDEA in 1990 and 1997) confirming that learning disabilities was a legitimate category of special education. Learning Disabilities is now the largest category of special education under IDEA. In the 1997–1998 school year, 2,699,491 students ages 6 to 21 were served in programs for learning disabilities. This represents almost 52% of the 5,224,328 students served in all categories of special education. Overall, 10.83% of all students in the United States are provided special education services; 5.53% receive services as learning disabled (U.S. Department of Education, 1998). Examination of programs confirms that there is wide variation in content, methods, intensity, and breadth of services. There is increasing movement toward placement in inclusive settings. A number of professional organizations have influenced the development of the field and provide advocacy and support. These include the Learning Disabilities Association of America (LDA), the Division of Learning Disabilities (DLD) of the Council for Exceptional Children, the Council for Learning Disabilities (CLD), the National Joint Committee on Learning Disabilities (NJCLD), and the International Academy for Research in Learning Disabilities (IARLD).

DEFINITIONS OF LEARNING DISABILITIES

Samuel Kirk, in the first edition of his introductory text in special education, defined learning disabilities as follows:

> A learning disability refers to a retardation, disorder, or delayed development in one or more of the processes of speech, language, reading, writing, arithmetic, or other school subject resulting from a psychological handicap caused by a possible cerebral dysfunction and/or emotional or behavioral disturbances. It is not the result of mental retardation, sensory deprivation, or cultural and instructional factors. (Kirk, 1962, p. 263)

There have been at least seven or eight definitions since Kirk's that have enjoyed a relatively high degree of acceptance by virtue of being promulgated by a government agency or an influential professional or parent organization.

In 1967 the National Advisory Committee on the Handicapped proposed a definition that, although often criticized, has essentially been the basis for subsequent legislation. The current federal legislative definition, which is used by the majority of states, reads:

A. GENERAL—The term "specific learning disability" means a disorder in one or more of the basic psychological processes involved in understanding or in using language, spoken or written, which disorder may manifest itself in an imperfect ability to listen, think, speak, read, write, spell, or do mathematical calculations.

B. DISORDERS INCLUDED—Such term includes such conditions as perceptual disabilities, brain injury, minimal brain dysfunction, dyslexia, and developmental aphasia.

C. DISORDERS NOT INCLUDED—Such term does not include a learning problem that is primarily the result of visual, hearing, or motor handicaps, of mental retardation, or emotional disturbance, or of environmental, cultural, or economic disadvantage. (Individuals with Disabilities Education Act Amendments of 1997, Sec. 602(26), p. 13)

More recently the NJCLD proposed a definition that stressed the heterogeneity of the condition and that added social skills to the list of problems covered. The latter has not been incorporated into formal legislation.

CHALLENGES TO LEARNING DISABILITIES AS A CONDITION

Despite the large numbers of students identified as having specific learning disabilities, there are many challenges to the reality of the condition. The two central notions in most definitions are that individuals with learning disabilities are characterized by a discrepancy between their general ability and their academic achievement and by an uneven profile in performance across academic content areas. Although defensible on a conceptual level, there have been continuing challenges to how the definition should be operationalized (Siegel, 1989; Stanovich, 1989). How should the ability and achievement components of the definition be measured? What about the known correlations between IQ and measures of academic achievement? What constitutes a meaningful discrepancy? Can learning disabilities be reliably differentiated from other problem conditions? What about possible cultural and economic bias in assessment techniques? The exclusionary aspects of the definitions have been particularly controversial, critics arguing that they in effect restrict learning disabilities to a select socioeconomic group.

THE REALITY OF LEARNING DISABILITIES

Clearly, there are many aspects of learning disabilities that require further study and refinement. Yet both clinical and research evidence argues for the reality of the condition. Current work using neuroimaging techniques provides evidence of individual differences in the organization and patterning of brain activities in learning and in response to different types of stimuli (Hynd, Marshall, & Gonzalez, 1991; Shaywitz et al., 1998). There also appear to be gender differences and age differences in how the brain functions. This area of research holds real promise for untangling some of the complexities observed in individuals with learning disabilities. An extensive clinical and educational literature also argues for the reality of learning disabilities. The learning characteristics of young children have been shown to persist into adulthood, suggesting that learning disabilities is not developmentally specific. Educational programs aimed at improving the achievement of young problem readers achieve success with the majority of those enrolled. Yet such programs also have 2–6% of nonresponders, children who may be truly learning disabled (Torgesen, 2000).

It is likely that significant numbers of individuals are misdiagnosed as learning disabled and that many of the students receiving services as learning disabilities are poor learners for other reasons. School and other service systems must deal with struggling learners whatever the diagnosis or category. Thus, school- and clinic-identified individuals represent a range of conditions that is frequently served under the learning disabilities rubric (MacMillan, Gresham, & Bocian, 1988). That the numbers of students with learning disabilities are likely overestimated and that diagnoses are imprecise does not negate the reality of learning disabilities as a problem condition.

Gerber (2000–2001) has likened the "birth" of learning disabilities to the discovery of blue-green algae in the biological realm. Because it did not fit the taxonomy of the time, the discovery of blue-green algae forced scientists to come up with a more complex system of categorizing species of living things. For Gerber, learning disabilities is the blue-green algae of human learner differences. Prior to the acknowledgment of learning disabilities, special education taxonomy consisted of the relatively straightforward disabilities of blindness, deafness, mental retardation, and so forth. But when parents began to point to their children who scored in the normal range of intelligence (therefore, not mentally retarded), had good vision (therefore, not blind), and had good hearing (therefore, not deaf), a new "species" of individual difference, or disability, was identified. And just like the blue-green algae, the entrance of learning disabilities to the taxonomical system has expanded the complexity of how scientists consider individual differences:

> Identifying LD did more than launch a search for useful and valid information about variations in human beings as they relate to academic and life success. The more difficult it was to create this new taxon of disability, the more the received taxonomy describing able and disabled began to unravel. It became clear we needed better understanding of intelligence beyond IQ.... We needed to understand more about how cognitive capacities and functions, like attention, memory, and metacognition, subserve learning and performing in academic domains.... We needed better componential analyses of the specific cognitive operations that permit word decoding and prose comprehension.... The detailed experiments and analyses required for reading were needed in all other suspect domains as well, and so a literature was developed that investigated other

aspects of language development and use, writing, mathematics, content study, and social cognition. (Gerber, 2000–2001, p. 38)

The important point is that the puzzles surrounding learning disabilities do not argue against the existence of the condition. Ten, 20, or 50 years from now we may have a more valid and reliable operational definition for these children, but that does not mean that their learning problems are not real.

ORGANIZATION OF THIS BOOK

Our goal for this book has been to organize it thematically around the major ideas that Bill Cruickshank espoused over his career. Because Bill's professional legacy is so extensive and varied, with his ideas spanning several disciplines and categories of special education, it was difficult to narrow the field of possible themes to a manageable number. Given that we were doing the volume under the auspices of the International Academy for Research in Learning Disabilities, our first decision—to limit the topics to those related to learning disabilities—was easy. The second decision, which was almost as easy as the first, was to be sure to have a major portion of the book devoted to global perspectives on learning disabilities. Of all the pioneers in learning disabilities, Bill Cruickshank was undoubtedly the one most interested in fostering an *international* community of scholars. His founding of the Academy is testimony to his international focus.

However, Bill's thinking was so broad, and his writing was so prolific, that we could only hope to cover the main ideas he championed. Although we both knew Bill very well, these are themes based only on *our* impressions of Bill's major contributions. Others, undoubtedly, can think of topics we could have included. After this introductory chapter, and prior to chapters devoted to ideas linked to Bill's major philosophical positions, is Chapter 2, "The Lives and Careers of Bill and Dorothy Cruickshank," written by Doris Johnson and Barbara Keogh, with the assistance of Dorothy Cruickshank. We include such a chapter to recognize the intimate connection between Bill's professional and personal lives. Those who had the pleasure of socializing with the Cruickshanks know the grace and aplomb they displayed as a team.

Chapter 3, written by Michelle Kibby and George Hynd, is entitled, "Neurological Basis of Learning Disabilities." A major portion of Bill's rationale for the authenticity of the learning disabilities category was his firm belief in the neurological basis of the condition. Bill recognized the tenuous scientific credibility of the evidence for causal factors at the level of the central nervous system, but he was visionary in believing that some day technology would uncover neurological factors as key etiological agents in learning disabilities. Although a believer in the importance of the environment, he frequently remarked that, ultimately, all behavior was understandable as a neurological act.

As we noted above, one of the primary characteristics of the students Bill studied was distractibility. In fact, many of the children in the research demonstration classrooms he established would today be diagnosed as having ADHD, as well as learning disabilities. Research since that time has confirmed the high level of comorbidity between learning disabilities and ADHD. For these reasons, Ronald Kotkin, Steven Forness, and Kenneth Kavale have co-authored Chapter 4, "Comorbid ADHD and Learning Disabilities: Diagnosis, Special Education, and Intervention."

Chapter 5, by Dheepa Sridhar and Sharon Vaughn, is entitled, "Social Functioning of Students with Learning Disabilities." Bill was always adamant about the interplay of social development and learning. He often opined that learning disabilities rarely come without some emotional overlay. As so much research has subsequently demonstrated, Bill was once again on target.

Bill also held strong opinions (Indeed, some might ask, "What didn't Bill hold strong opinions about?") about assessment. Although not the only one to hold this view, Bill was certainly one of the most vocal critics of using only standardized testing in the diagnosis of learning disabilities. He argued that testing should be prescriptive. That is, childrens' performance on tests should be, first and foremost, useful for educational purposes. Results of tests should also be useful for teachers in designing instruction. Lynn and Doug Fuchs address this in Chapter 6, "Using Assessment to Account for and Promote Strong Outcomes for Students with Learning Disabilities."

Chapter 7, "Strategic Learning in Students with Learning Disabilities: What Have We Learned?" is co-authored by Lynn Meltzer and Marjorie Montague. Bill was a strong proponent of the need for teachers to base their instruction on an understanding of the psychological processes of their students. He believed that, with this knowledge, teachers would truly be able to *individualize* their instruction, a conceptual cornerstone of *special* education.

Bill was also one of the first to speak out on the misuse of the concept of the least restrictive environment. In an article (Cruickshank, 1977) entitled, "Least-Restrictive Placement: Administrative Wishful Thinking," Bill pointed out that least restrictive did not always translate into a regular classroom placement. In Chapter 9, "The Concept of the Least Restrictive Environment and Learning Disabilities: Least Restrictive of What?" Jean Crockett and James Kauffman expand on Bill's ideas.

The idea that many students with learning disabilities require highly structured and teacher-directed instruction is arguably Bill's most important contribution to the special education literature. It was the cornerstone of his educational program for such students. Margaret Weiss and John Lloyd expand on the idea of structure and teacher direction in Chapter 8, "Structure and Effective Teaching."

Bill was one of the first advocates for the notion that learning disabilities do not usually cease after childhood. For far too many adults, learning disabilities continue to present significant educational, vocational, and social problems. Paul Gerber, a former student of Bill's, addresses this topic in Chapter 10, "Learning Disabilities: A Life-Span Approach."

Consistent with Bill's international perspective, we invited outstanding professionals in eight different parts of the world to write about learning disabilities in their countries. We asked each to provide a brief description of the "state of the art" of learning disabilities in his or her country. The different chapters (11–18) provide an international picture of learning disabilities, how learning disabilities is defined, the relationship of learning disabilities to general and special education systems, the types provided, and particular issues, problems, and trends. It is a credit to Bill's international activities that all of the authors invited accepted without hesitation. Many had known Bill and Dorothy personally, some had worked with Bill, and all had been influenced by his thinking. Following are the countries and authors represented: Australia (John Elkins), Canada (Bernice Wong and Nancy Hutchinson), Germany (Günther Opp), Great Britain (Klaus Wedell), Japan (Masayoshi Tsuge), the Netherlands (Luc Stevens and Wim van Werkhoven), Scandinavia (Ingvar Lundberg and Torleiv Höien), and South America (Luis Bravo-Valdivieso and Neva Milicic Müller). The final chapter in this section, by Susan A. Vogel, is entitled, "The challenge of International Research in Learning Disabilities."

Bill's influence on the field of special education and its ultimate impact on the lives of persons with learning disabilities have been enormous. We recognize that no one volume of this length could capture all that he achieved, but we are hopeful that this book at least comes close to doing justice to Bill Cruickshank's legacy.

REFERENCES

Cruickshank, W. M. (1977). Least-restrictive placement: Administrative wishful thinking. *Journal of Learning Disabilities, 10,* 5–6.

Cruickshank, W. M., Bentzen, F. A., Ratzeburg, F. H., & Tannhauser, M. T. (1961). *A teaching method for brain-injured and hyperactive children.* Syracuse: Syracuse University Press.

Cruickshank, W. M., Bice, H. V., & Wallen, N. E. (1957). *Perception and Cerebral Palsy.* Syracuse: Syracuse University Press.

DeFries, J. C., Gillis, J. J., & Wadsworth, S. J. (1993). Genes and genders: A twin study of reading disability. In A. M. Galaburda (Ed.), *Dyslexia and development: Neurological aspects of extra-ordinary brains* (pp. 187–204). Cambridge, MA: Harvard University Press.

Dolphin, J. E., & Cruickshank, W. M. (1951). Visuo-motor perception of children with cerebral palsy. *Quarterly Journal of Child Behavior, 3,* 198–209.

Fernald, G. M. (1943). *Remedial techniques in basic school subjects.* New York: McGraw-Hill.

Gerber, M. M. (2000–2001). An appreciation of learning disabilities: The value of blue-green algae. *Exceptionality, 8,* 29–42.

Goldstein, K. (1936). The modifications of behavior consequent to cerebral lesions. *Psychiatric Quarterly, 10,* 586–610.

Goldstein, K. (1939). *The organism.* New York: American Books.

Hallahan, D. P., & Cruickshank, W. M. (1973). *Psychoeducational foundations of learning disabilities.* Englewood Cliffs, NJ: Prentice-Hall.

Hallahan, D. P., Kauffman, J. M., & Lloyd, J. W. (1999). *Introduction to learning disabilities* (2nd ed.). Boston: Allyn & Bacon.

Hinshelwood, J. (1907). Four cases of congenital word-blindness occurring in the same family. *British Medical Journal, 2,* 1229–1232.

Hinshelwood, J. (1917). *Congenital word blindness.* London: Lewis.

Hynd, G. W., Marshall, R., & Gonzalez, J. (1991). Learning disabilities and presumed central nervous system dysfunction. *Learning Disability Quarterly, 14,* 283–296.

Individuals with Disabilities Education Act Amendments (IDEA) of 1997, Public Law 105–17.

Johnson, D. J., & Myklebust, H. R. (1967). *Learning disabilities: Educational principles and practices.* New York: Grune & Stratton.

Kirk, S. A. (1962). *Educating exceptional children.* Boston: Houghton Mifflin.

Kirk, S. A. (1963, April 6). Behavioral diagnosis and remediation of learning disabilities. *Proceedings of the Conference on Exploration into the Problems of the Perceptually Handicapped Child,* First Annual Meeting, Chicago.

Kirk, S. A., McCarthy, J., & Kirk, W. E. (1968). *Illinois Test of Psycholinguistic Abilities.* Urbana, IL: University of Illinois Press.

Lyon, G. R., & Moats, L. C. (1997). Critical conceptual and methodological considerations in reading intervention research. *Journal of Learning Disabilities, 30,* 578–588.

MacMillan, D. L., Gresham, F. M., & Bocian, K. M. (1988). Discrepancy between definitions of learning disabilities and what schools use: An empirical investigation. *Journal of Learning Disabilities, 31,* 314–326.

Orton, S. (1937). *Reading, writing, and speech problems in children.* New York: Norton.

Pennington, B. F. (1995). Genetics of learning disabilities. *Journal of Child Neurology, 10* (Suppl. No. 1), S69–S77.

Reynolds, C. A., Hewitt, J. K., Erickson, M. T., Silberg, J. L., Rutter, M., Simonoff, E., Meyer, J., & Eaves, L. J. (1996). The genetics of children's oral reading performance. *Journal of Child Psychology & Psychiatry & Allied Disciplines, 37,* 425–434.

Shaywitz, S. E., Shaywitz, B. A., Pugh, K. R., Fulbright, R. K., Constable, R. T., Mencl, W. E., Shankweiler, D. P., Liberman, A. M., Skudlarski, P., Fletcher, J. M., Katz, L., Marchione, K. E., Lacadie, C., Gatenby, C., & Gore, J. C. (1998). Functional disruption in the organization of the brain for reading in dyslexia. *Neurobiology, 95,* 2636–2641.

Siegel, L. S. (1989). IQ is irrelevant to the definition of learning disabilities. *Journal of Learning Disabilities, 22,* 469–478.

Stanovich, K. E. (1989). Has the learning disabilities field lost its intelligence? *Journal of Learning Disabilities, 22,* 487–492.

Strauss, A. A., & Lehtinen, L. E. (1947). *Psychopathology and education of the brain-injured child.* New York: Grune and Stratton.

Strauss, A. A., & Werner, H. (1942). Disorders of conceptual thinking in the brain-injured child. *Journal of Nervous and Mental Disease, 96,* 153–172.

Torgesen, J. K. (2000). Individual differences in response to early interventions in reading: The lingering problem of treatment resisters. *Learning Disabilities Research and Practice, 15,* 55–64.

U.S. Department of Education. (1998). *Twentieth Annual Report to Congress on the Implementation of the Individuals with Disabilities Education Act.* Washington, DC: Author.

Werner, H., & Strauss, A. A. (1941). Pathology of figure-background relation in the child. *Journal of Abnormal and Social Psychology, 36,* 236–248.

Chapter 2

The Lives and Careers of Bill and Dorothy Cruickshank

Doris Johnson
Barbara Keogh

Bill Cruickshank was a complex man with many talents. One of the dominant themes in his lectures, teaching, and writing was a quest for excellence. He expected the best possible performance from students, teachers, researchers, and the field in general. At the same time, he was a very caring, generous person. In order to capture the many sides of Bill, we consider his roles in life from several perspectives.

BILL, THE STUDENT

Bill was born March 25, 1915, in Detroit, Michigan. His preschool, elementary, and high school years were all spent in Michigan. He completed his undergraduate degree at Eastern Michigan University in 1937, his M.A. at the University of Chicago in 1938, and his Ph.D. in Psychology at the University of Michigan in 1945.

His first position was instructor at the Horace Rackham School of Special Education at Eastern Michigan University in Ypsilanti, from 1939 to 1941. During World War II he was a clinical psychologist in the U.S. Armed Forces, and from 1943 to 1944, he was an instructor at the American Army University in Shrivenham, England. Like many of the leaders in our field, he observed learning and communication problems associated with various types of injuries and traumatic conditions.

When Bill returned from overseas service, he became the Special Education Executive at the Boys' Vocational School in Lansing, Michigan He was intrigued with the study of exceptional learners and never lost interest in cognitive processes, particularly perception. He was concerned with a wide range of handicapping conditions, including cerebral palsy, exogenous mental retardation, and epilepsy, especially the neurobiological bases for these conditions. During the late 1940s Bill was influenced by the research of Alfred Strauss and Heinz Werner as well as others who were at the Wayne County Training Center in Michigan. Many of the early leaders in the field of learning disabilities were stimulated by the questions and hypotheses related to brain–behavior relationships in that Center. Bill was also interested in the most appropriate procedures for measuring overall cognitive ability among people who could not always respond to traditional tests. This interest was evident in many of his publications (Cruickshank, 1947a, 1976a, 1977; Cruickshank & Qualtere, 1950; Cruickshank, Hallahan, & Bice, 1976).

Bill was interested in more than testing, however. He was deeply committed to the educational and mental health needs of exceptional learners (Cruickshank, 1947b, 1948, 1971). He thought that education was a universal human need, and that differential aptitudes were characteristic of the species. He also believed that some children required unusual instructional methods. Bill remained a student throughout his life, always wanting to learn more about cognitive processes and the latest findings regarding atypical learners.

BILL, THE TEACHER/MENTOR

Between 1946 and 1966, Bill was professor of psychology and education and director of the Division of Special Education and Rehabilitation at Syracuse University in Syracuse, New York. He was dean of the summer sessions & special services, and was appointed the Margaret O. Slocum Distinguished Professor of Psychology & Education at Syracuse in 1952.

In 1966, Bill joined the faculty at the University of Michigan where he was director of the Institute for the Study of Mental Retardation and Related Disabilities until 1980. During that time he was also professor of psychology, professor of education, and from 1977 to 1979 was chairman of Special Education and the Speech and Hearing Sciences Program at the University of Michigan. Following his retirement, he was appointed Professor Emeritus of Child and Family Health in the School of Public Health at Michigan. He was twice a Fulbright Lecturer to the Ministries of Health and Education in Peru, and held five honorary doctoral degrees from American universities and one from a major university in Peru. The honorary degrees in the United States were from the State University of New York at Albany, Syracuse University, Central Michigan University, Cardinal Stritch College in Milwaukee, and Eastern Michigan University. He spent time in England as a Priorsfield Fellow at the University of Birmingham. At various times in his career he was a consultant to almost 30 foreign ministries of education and nearly every state and province in the United States and Canada.

After Bill retired from the University of Michigan he spent a year or more teaching and consulting at several universities, including the University of New Orleans, University of North Carolina at Chapel Hill, Cardinal Stritch College in Milwaukee, Wisconsin, Virginia Commonwealth University in Richmond, California State University at Los Angeles, UCLA, the University of South Florida, and Duke. While on the faculty at Duke, he also worked in the Netherlands.

It is a testament to the impact of Bill's role as teacher and mentor that many of his students are now leaders in the field. Conversations with several of those people indicated he was a demanding but supportive teacher. According to reports from former students, the high point for doctoral candidates came during the final defense of their thesis. If the committee agreed on a "pass," Bill said nothing, but quietly went to a cupboard and brought out a bottle of champagne.

As a teacher/mentor, Bill always mentioned the contributions of his students. In his articles and books, one sees the names of Haring, Hallahan, Kaufman, Bice, Dolphin, Gerber, and many others.

BILL, THE RESEARCHER

Bill was heavily influenced by the work of Werner and Strauss, who studied the behavior and cognitive skills of people with mental retardation due to brain damage. Problems related to perception, conceptualization, and behavior were of interest to many of the investigators at the Wayne County Training Center. One can only imagine the lively discussions with Strauss, Lehtinen, Kephart, Cruickshank, and others. Much of their work was based on Gestalt psychology; thus, there was considerable emphasis on part–whole and figure–ground relationships (Dolphin & Cruickshank, 1951).

Although Bill was always interested in perception, a review of his vita indicated broad interests. His first article, published in 1946, was on the arithmetic ability of mentally retarded boys (Cruickshank, 1946). He was also very interested in the mental health of handicapped learners, as evident in numerous publications related to their emotional needs and social adjustment (Cruickshank, 1947b, 1948; Cruickshank & Medve, 1948; Cruickshank & Dolphin, 1949; Cruickshank & Haring, 1955).

As indicated earlier, many of his articles focused on the use of intelligence tests with retarded and physically handicapped children. Cruickshank and his students conducted studies that indicated that cerebral palsied children of near average, average, and above average intelligence differed from their nonhandicapped peers in discrimination of figure from ground, in concept formation, in visual-motor performance, and in tactual-motor performance (see Hallahan & Cruickshank, 1973, p. 66). These studies led Cruickshank to call for better assessment of children with cerebral palsy, exogenous mental retardation, and epilepsy.

Bill maintained his interest in the perceptual problems of brain-injured children, but defined perception relatively broadly so it included other cognitive processes such as memory. He contended that perceptual disturbances were present among many children with neurological impairments and thought that it was unnecessary, if not incorrect, to rule out children with mental retardation in the definition of learning disabilities (Cruickshank, 1983). In 1977 Cruickshank said that learning disabilities, and specifically perceptual processing deficits, can be found in children of every intellectual level. In fact, he said much of what was known about perceptual processing deficits came from the study of exogenous mentally retarded children of educable levels. Consequently, he argued against arbitrary cut off points in definitions and eligibility criteria for learning disabilities.

Bill and his colleagues were among the first to conduct a demonstration pilot study of brain injured children in a special class (Cruickshank, Bentzen, Ratzeburg, & Tannhauser, 1961). Using many of the theories that had been generated by Strauss, Lehtinen, and Werner, the group planned an instructional program, which was carried out in Maryland. Emphasis was given to structure, control of extraneous variables, and perceptual training. The book, which was published at the conclusion of the project, included suggestions for materials and management of brain-injured children in the classroom. The concept of structure was extended by Norris Haring, a former student, with the use of behavior modification principles. Cruickshank, Haring, and Stern (1958) were also interested in the attitudes of educators toward exceptional children. Bill thought that the lives of people with handicaps could be improved if those around them gained a better understanding of their strengths and weaknesses.

BILL, THE LEADER

The image that is perhaps the most vivid is Bill, the leader. As such, he initiated many large-scale projects and brought professionals from many disciplines together to investigate the nature of various neurological and educational disorders, discuss issues, synthesize findings, and present challenges to the field. For example, in the 1960s, shortly after the term *learning disabilities* became more widely used, he brought together 27 professionals from many disciplines to grapple with definitions, concepts, and state-of-the-art procedures for teaching perceptual motor skills, reading, arithmetic, and other areas of achievement. He said that the meeting was unlike any before or since in the field. Many issues were discussed regarding terminology and the use of etiological, behavioral, or educational terms (e.g., "brain damage" versus learning disability). Problems related to attention, behavior management, and instruction were addressed by the participants. The conference proceedings were intended to give teachers up-to-date information they could use to help children with specific needs (Cruickshank, 1966).

Bill's role as a leader was very evident when he directed a major interdisciplinary institute at the University of Michigan where professionals from many disciplines worked together to explore the bases of neurological disorders as well as to develop effective treatments. According to John Hagen, who predated Bill at Michigan, the University Board of Regents approved the establishment of the Institute for the Study of Mental Retardation (later renamed Institute for the Study of Mental Retardation and Related Disabilities) in 1967. When Bill took over the leadership, he became professor of education, psychology, and public health. Hagen noted that Bill worked hard to make the Center truly interdisciplinary. It flourished for several years and was strong because at least ten disciplines were represented. After several successful years, funding was reduced and the core support diminished. Nevertheless, it was a model training center and provided preparation for leadership. Dan Hallahan, who did undergraduate work in psychology with Hagen, was one of Bill Cruickshank's first doctoral students in the Institute at Michigan. Dan did some of his research in the Plymouth State Home and Training School where Bill was a consultant.

Bill held strong opinions about many issues in learning disabilities and special education and he was never afraid to express his ideas, concerns, and challenges. Some of these ideas were expressed in his article "Myths and Realities in Learning Disabilities" (Cruickshank, 1977). In this article and elsewhere he raised many concerns about "ill-prepared teachers." He decried the fact that people had minimal preparation to work with handicapped children who had complex needs. At one time he said it might be worth letting one generation of children go with little or no help until a cadre of highly skilled university professors could assist in the preparation of special educators. Bill was also concerned about the professional preparation of physicians, psychologists, educators, and others who worked with exceptional children (Cruickshank, Junkala, & Paul, 1968). He disliked what Kirk called "the cafeteria" approach with a "little of this" and a "little of that." In a 1981 article in the *Journal of Learning Disabilities,* he said that the status of learning disabilities in the public schools of this country was an educational catastrophe. He argued for the preparation of well-qualified university teachers, and suggested a new perspective or area of specialization called a neuroeducator (1981b). He also challenged every school superintendent, principal, psychologist, and educator to enroll in courses in special education.

Bill continued this general theme in an article called "Learning disabilities: A series of challenges" in *Learning Disabilities Focus,* 1985. In this article he challenged the field to adopt an honest and accurate definition of learning disabilities, and challenged the U.S. Department of Education to initiate a comprehensive epidemiological research program based on a minimum of 100,000 children. He also challenged the Department to undertake longitudinal studies to investigate various intervention methods.

Bill felt strongly about the quality of education that children were getting in mainstream classrooms. He considered it a myth that children with specific learning disabilities can and ought to be educated in the regular grades of the community and challenged the concept of the least restrictive environment.

> Children with perceptual processing deficits resulting in specific learning disabilities have needs which the general elementary or secondary educator cannot meet in the normal classroom setting. Probably some integration for short periods each day might be valuable, but until genuine success experiences are integrated into the child's self-perception, either through the medium of well-prepared teachers working in resource rooms or in special clinical teaching stations, the capacity of the child with anything short of a very mild learning disability is going to be less than that needed to function in a normal or ordinary classroom situation.

> Unless general elementary educators understand the nature and needs of the problems of processing deficits and know how to adapt the learning situation and teaching materials to the child's needs, the potential for continued failure on the part of the child is present. It is unlikely that preparation of elementary general educators will include this emphasis in the foreseeable future. In the meantime, what of the children who are physically, but neither educationally or psychologically, integrated? (Cruickshank, 1977, p. 301)

In many of his writings Bill emphasized that learning disabilities is a developmental problem that required individual attention. He said, "the essence of the problem . . . is one of clinical diagnosis that required careful study." He thought that categories per se were unnecessary. He thought that the focus should be on the psychological processing problems . . . inherent in the definition. As these are identified, they must be matched with carefully considered teaching techniques so that new learning will result (Cruickshank, 1976b, 1977, 1980, 1981a). Bill considered learning disabilities, as well as other handicaps, developmental problems, and thought that the term "remediation" was inappropriate.

The needs of families and the exceptional child at home were also of concern to Bill. His book on the brain-injured child at home, school, and community has been used by many parents to understand their special needs and to provide appropriate support (Cruickshank, 1967). Later he wrote about the special problems of adolescents and the transition to work.

Bill was concerned about the proliferation of commercial companies and materials that were presumed to be beneficial to learning disabled children. He urged editors and consulting editors to produce journals that were accurate and useful to practicing educators, thereby benefiting children.

Because of Bill's leadership qualities he was asked to consult in many agencies, schools, and government projects in the United States and abroad. During some of those journeys he saw the pressing need to bring professionals together from around the world. Hence, in conversations with Jacob Valk from the Netherlands, the International Academy on Research in Learning Disabilities (IARLD) was established in 1976. The goal was and is to provide a forum for the exchange of information and the advancement of knowledge regarding learning disabilities. He gave generously of his time and money to foster communication among physicians, psychologists, and educators from many countries. During the 1970s and 80s he made every effort to help professionals from the Eastern bloc countries to obtain information about IARLD, and he encouraged members who could do so to pay dues and support those people who had limited resources. With the newsletter *Thalamus* and the monograph series, the research conducted by IARLD members was made more visible and available to professionals around the world. Whenever things were not going as well as he expected, Bill called upon the membership to act and become involved. At one time he assigned every member in the group to one or more committees in order to foster more participation. He sought countless ways to generate funds for interdisciplinary activities.

Bill's efforts and commitment to exceptional children were recognized by many people in this country and abroad. In addition to his honorary degrees, he received many awards including the distinguished alumnus award from Eastern Michigan University, an award of merit from the Quebec Association for Children with Learning Disabilities, the distinguished service award from the Louisiana Division for Children with Learning Disabilities CEC, the American Association on Mental Deficiency Education Award, and the distinguished professional service award from the Association for Children with Learning Disabilities.

Bill would be pleased and honored to see the growth of the field, the status of the IARLD, and the publication of this book in his honor. He also would be pleased to hear the series of William Cruickshank lectures that have been given in his memory at each IARLD conference since his death on August 13, 1992.

BEYOND WORK

Finally, a word about Bill, the man. He could be tough (as many leaders are), but he was kind and generous to many students and colleagues in need. It was not unusual for him to invite a student to live with his family or to have foreign colleagues as house guests for extended periods of time. Together, he and Dorothy opened their home to countless visitors and friends.

Bill had boundless energy—even with a relatively serious heart condition. At the IARLD meeting in Greece, despite the heat, he always joined the group for a hike, a hearty meal, or an evening boat ride. At the meeting in the Netherlands he required medical attention, but he did not really stop his activities. And at Northwestern, when Doris Johnson went to unlock the building at 7:30 on a Saturday morning, Bill was already inside working (having flagged a public safety official to open the buildings). Dorothy said he always carried a typewriter with him and spent hours in airports working on manuscripts.

Bill and Dorothy spent their leisure-time hours during the academic year at the symphony and opera in Detroit and Ann Arbor. During the summer, they went to their Georgian Bay home in Lake Huron to be with family and friends. They had a separate cabin for special, invited friends. Dorothy said no one could reach Bill by phone in that quiet setting. At the lake, he spent time writing, but not just professional writing. He loved to write poetry and had one collection published.

It is evident that Bill's legacy is huge and that he will not be forgotten. He was a man of many talents who held strong opinions. Indeed, he was sometimes opinionated, even contentious. He argued his views eloquently and well, and moved the field of learning disabilities to value evidence, rather than belief. All of us involved with the IARLD are grateful to him for giving us the opportunity for the professional and personal relationships we now enjoy.

DOROTHY CRUICKSHANK

It is difficult to think of Bill Cruickshank without thinking of Dorothy. She is that gentle and gracious lady who accompanied him to conferences and speaking engagements around the world. She is the one who listened to hundreds, perhaps thousands, of lectures, discussions, arguments, and opinions expressed in many languages and from many national and professional perspectives. She is the one who made the Cruickshank lives run smoothly, who made colleagues and students feel welcome and valued. As we honor Bill, we also honor Dorothy.

Dorothy Wager was born in Detroit, Michigan, on August 28, 1913. Detroit and the Highland Park neighborhood were her home for most of her early years. Her father and mother worked for the Ford Motor Company. Dorothy describes her early years with her twin brother as a "fun life" with good schools and many friends. Dorothy was an avid swimmer during elementary school and swam competitively as a member of her high school and community college teams. Her enthusiasm for swimming also led her to leave Detroit for Stetson University in Florida. "It was warm there and I loved it. I could swim all year long." Today she still swims, but now in Lake Washington in Seattle where the temperature is notably cooler! At Stetson she was a Physical Education major specializing in Health and Dance, subjects she taught in elementary school after returning to Detroit.

Her return to Detroit marked a new period in her life as she became reacquainted with Bill. Reacquainted is the correct verb, as each remembered the other as children in the Presbyterian Preschool in Detroit. They dated, became engaged, and were married in 1938. Their first daughter was born in 1943, followed by sisters in 1944 and 1950. There are now six grandchildren in the Cruickshank family. While raising their young family, Dorothy completed a master's degree at Wayne State University and Bill finished his Ph.D. at the University of Michigan.

After Bill's return from overseas duties in Germany and England during World War II, the family moved to Syracuse University. Syracuse was home for 22 years before Bill and Dorothy moved to Ann Arbor and the University of Michigan. Dorothy recalls their time together on both campuses with great fondness. Their lives were full with their own

children and their professional and personal activities. They also wel-
comed and nurtured dozens of students from many countries, some
from the American Field Service Program. They provided an open and
hospitable home complete with plenty of good food and lots of attention. Former students who are well established professionals in their
own right attest to the important roles Dorothy and Bill played in their
academic and personal lives.

After Bill's death in 1992, Dorothy moved to a retirement community
in Seattle, Washington, where she is near one of her daughters. She has
already been elected president of the residents association (which comes
as no surprise to those of us who know her). She says this job keeps her
busy listening to people and being a voice for the residents. She has
maintained her interest in people, in flowers, in reading and learning,
and especially in art.

Dorothy and Bill traveled a great deal over the years, and she became
increasingly interested in art, pursuing this interest in major galleries
around the world. She is a serious student of a number of forms of
art, including impressionist painting and tapestries. Her current focus
is on womens' art, and she has studied women artists from the few in the
fifteenth century to a large number of well known contemporary women
artists such as Georgia O'Keefe and Judy Chicago. In addition to art, she
is an avid reader, her recent favorites Zukiaz' "Dancing Wuli Masters" and
Katherine Graham's autobiography. To date she has avoided computers,
but acknowledges she "probably could learn if she tried." No doubt.

Dorothy's interests and understanding of learning disabilities continue. Although she thinks her views were influenced by Bill's, she has
some special concerns of her own. She emphasizes the importance of
framing a problem condition in a positive way. "If people can face up to
a problem they can be helped." She is strongly in support of parents' involvement in their children's lives, and commends parents for the efforts
they make on behalf of their children with problems. In her words, "parents need help not blame." She expresses some concern about the notion that one educational program fits all, suggesting that some children
need specialized teaching that may not be possible in a single placement.
She is also concerned about the widespread use of stimulant medication
for children. Overall, she is optimistic that there will be changes and
improved services in the future.

Dorothy's life was intertwined with Bill's in many ways. She provided
a secure and stable life for them both, which allowed him to pursue
his many interests. She was a constant traveling companion, making
a "home" in many diverse places. She was also a sounding board, a
reasoned voice, and on occasion, a gentle critic. Importantly, she is
an interesting and talented person in her own right. She has a deep

understanding of learning disabilities and of children's development, and is committed to improving the social good. On a personal note, one of the joys of having known Bill Cruickshank is that we have become friends of Dorothy's.

REFERENCES

Cruickshank, W. M. (1946). Arithmetic vocabulary of mentally retarded boys. *Journal of Exceptional Children, 13,* 65–69.

Cruickshank, W. (1947a). Qualitative analysis of intelligence test responses. *Journal of Clinical Psychology, 3,* 381–386.

Cruickshank, W. M. (1947b). Mental hygiene approach to the handicapped child. *American Journal of Occupational Therapy, 3,* 215–221.

Cruickshank, W. M. (1948). The impact of physical disability on social adjustment. *Journal of Social Issues, 4,* 78–83.

Cruickshank, W. (Ed.). (1966). *The teacher of brain-injured children.* Syracuse: Syracuse University Press.

Cruickshank, W. M. (1967). *The brain-injured child in home, school, and community.* Syracuse: Syracuse University Press.

Cruickshank, W. (Ed.). (1971). *Psychology of exceptional children and youth* (3rd ed.). Englewood Cliffs, NJ: Prentice-Hall.

Cruickshank, W. (1972). Some issues facing the field of learning disabilities. *Journal of Learning Disabilities, 5*(7), 380–388.

Cruickshank, W. (Ed.). (1976a). *Cerebral palsy: A developmental disability* (3rd rev. ed.). Syracuse: Syracuse University Press.

Cruickshank, W. M. (1976b). Personal perspectives. In J. Kauffman & D. Hallahan (Eds.), *Teaching children with learning disabilities: Personal perspectives.* Columbus: Charles Merrill Publishers.

Cruickshank, W. (1977 January). Myths and realities in learning disabilities. *Journal of Learning Disabilities, 10*(1), 57–64.

Cruickshank, W. M. (Ed.). (1980). *Psychology of exceptional children and youth* (4th rev. ed.). Englewood Cliffs, NJ: Prentice Hall, Inc.

Cruickshank, W. (1981a). *Concepts in special education: Learning Disabilities* Vol. 2. Syracuse: Syracuse University Press.

Cruickshank, W. (1981b). A new perspective in teacher education. The neuro-educator. *Journal of Learning Disabilities 14*(6), 337–341, 367.

Cruickshank, W. M. (1983 February). Learning disabilities: A neuropsychological dysfunction. *Journal of Learning Disabilities.*

Cruickshank, W. (1985). Learning disabilities: A series of challenges. *Learning Disabilities Focus, 1*(1), 5–8.

Cruickshank, W. M., & Dolphin, J. E. (1949). The emotional needs of crippled and non-crippled children. *Journal of Exceptional Children, 16,* 33–40.

Cruickshank, W. M., & Haring, N. G. (1955). Adjustment of physically handicapped adolescent youth. *Exceptional Children, 21,* 282–288.

Cruickshank, W. M., & Medve, J. (1948). Social relationships of physically handicapped children. *Journal of Exceptional Children, 14,* 100–106.

Cruickshank, W. M., & Qualtere, T. J. (1950). The use of intelligence tests with children of retarded mental development II: Clinical considerations. *American Journal of Mental Deficiency, 54,* 370–381.

Cruickshank, W. M., Haring, N. J., & Stern, G. G. (1958). Attitudes of educators toward exceptional children. *Special Education and Rehabilitation Research Monograph Series No. 3*. Syracuse: Syracuse University Press.

Cruickshank, W., Bentzen, D., Ratzeburg, F., & Tannhauser, M. (1961). *A teaching method for brain-injured and hyperactive children: A demonstration-pilot study*. Syracuse: Syracuse University Press.

Cruickshank, W. M., Junkala, J. B., & Paul, J. L. (1968). *The preparation of teachers of brain-injured children*. Syracuse: Syracuse University Press.

Cruickshank, W. M., Hallahan, D. P., & Bice, H. V. (1976). The evaluation of intelligence. In W. M. Cruickshank (Ed.), *Cerebral palsy: A developmental disability* (3rd rev. ed.). Syracuse: Syracuse University Press.

Dolphin, J. E., & Cruickshank, W. M. (1951). Figure-background relationships in children with cerebral palsy. *Journal of Clinical Psychology, 7*, 228–231.

Hallahan, D. P., & Cruickshank, W. M. (1973). *Psychoeducational foundations of learning disabilities*. Englewood Cliffs, NJ: Prentice-Hall, Inc.

Chapter 3

Neurobiological Basis of Learning Disabilities[1]

Michelle Y. Kibby
George W. Hynd
University of Georgia & Medical College of Georgia

It is generally accepted that learning disabilities impact the lives of an estimated 3%–6% of all school-aged children, although some would suggest that the percentage of affected children exceeds this estimated incidence (Shaywitz, Fletcher, & Shaywitz, 1995). In this behaviorally diagnosed disorder, it is generally presumed that difficulty in learning in school exists in the presence of adequate intelligence and cannot be attributed to inadequate instruction, environmental factors, or other handicapping conditions (American Psychiatric Association, 1994).

Although there are likely many different cognitive and social domains in which learning disabilities may be evident (e.g., language, mathematics, social skills), it is in the area of specific reading disabilities (also referred to as developmental dyslexia in the medical literature[2]) that researchers have made progress in trying to understand the presumed neurobiological basis. The suspicion that some damage or developmental variation in brain ontogeny must underlie reading disabilities was first discussed over a century ago by Hinshelwood (1900),

---

[1] Preparation of this chapter was supported in part by a grant (RO1-HD26890-05) awarded to GWH from the National Institute of Health and Human Development (NICHHD) of the National Institutes of Health (NIH).
[2] The term *reading disability* will be used throughout this chapter as it is more reflective of the tradition found in the learning disability literature. It should be recognized, however, that in the medical literature the term *dyslexia* is used because of the rich history of investigations by those convinced that a neurobiological basis existed for severe reading disability.

Kussmaul (1877), and Morgan (1896). What encouraged discussion was the observation that children with severe reading disability evidenced behaviors commonly associated with those of individuals with subtle brain damage. They were also encouraged by the work of other scholars of this era who provided clinical evidence as to the organization of the central language zones (Kral, Nielsen, & Hynd, 1998). With considerable specificity Hinshelwood suggested that "I have shown ... that there is a definite cerebral area within which these visual memories of words and letters are registered - viz., the angular and supra-marginal gyri on the left side of the brain in right-handed people. If there be any abnormality within this area, due whether to disease, to injury at birth, or to defective development, it is easily conceivable how such an individual should experience great difficulty in learning to read" (1900, p. 1507).

What is remarkable about Hinshelwood's (1900) hypothesis, and that of others (e.g., Bastian, 1898), is that the brain regions they implicated are still being studied by those interested in how the behavioral deficits we observe in persons with severe reading disability relate to brain structure and function. Hence, there is an increasingly better understanding of the relationship between functioning of the brain and behavioral and cognitive difficulties experienced by persons with reading disability. Neuropathological, structural imaging procedures, and functional brain imaging techniques have advanced our state of knowledge regarding the neurobiological basis of the most common form of learning disabilities, reading disabilities. In the remainder of this chapter we provide an overview of this literature.

NEUROBIOLOGICAL RESEARCH

As the organization of the cortex and its associated systems became better understood in the early half of the last century, it became evident that some regions of the brain in humans had evolved certain asymmetries that were believed due to the specialization required for language. Geschwind and Levitsky (1968) documented that in 100 normal brains the region of the planum temporale (see Figure 3.1) was larger on the left side in 65% of brains while it was larger on the right in only 11% of brains. The remainder of brains were characterized by symmetry in this region. The planum temporale was believed to be essential for linguistic comprehension, and therefore was thought to be central to rapid whole word comprehension in reading (Hynd & Hynd, 1984; Hynd & Semrud-Clikeman, 1989). Specifically, a left-sided asymmetry of the planum temporale was thought to represent a more well

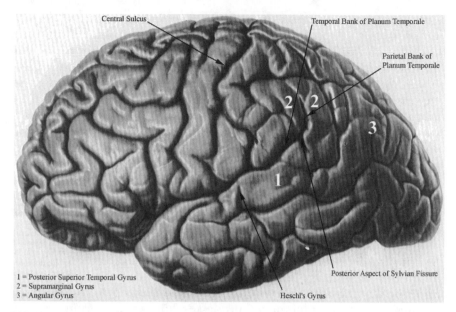

FIG. 3.1. This brain shows the major landmarks associated with various structures discussed in the chapter. In particular, the extent of the planum temporale is noted.

developed language cortex, which in turn would support the higher-order cognitive processes essential for linguistically related processes, such as those involved in fluent reading. While other asymmetries exist in the human brain, including the right frontal cortex (R > L, Weinberger, Luchins, Morihisa, & Wyatt, 1982), it was this noted asymmetry favoring the left hemisphere that captured the attention of those seeking some evidence of the neurobiological basis of severe reading disabilities.

Neuropathological Studies

Based on the neurobiological work and ideas developed by Geschwind and Levitsky (1968), Galaburda and his colleagues published a series of seminal studies (e.g., Galaburda & Kemper, 1979; Galaburda, Sherman, Rosen, Aboitiz, & Geschwind, 1985) in which the microstructure of the cortex and asymmetry patterns of the planum temporale were examined in the brains of individuals with a documented history of severe reading disabilities. The findings of these studies were quite remarkable.

Although the brains examined were small in number, the consistencies across the deviations noted in these brains highlighted a neurodevelopmental origin. In all of their studies, Galaburda and his colleagues noted symmetry of the planum temporale and focal cellular abnormalities (dysplasias) widely distributed in the frontal and central language cortex in the left hemisphere of the brain. Other abnormalities were also noted and included abnormally small gyri (polymicrogyria) and other subtle deviations in brain development. All of these abnormalities, however, were located in regions of the brain essential for language and other cognitive processes involved in reading. Galaburda and his colleagues believed that symmetry of the planum temporale was not sufficient cause for reading disabilities to manifest but that reading disabilities may be potentiated by the presence of both symmetry of the planum temporale and these focal brain abnormalities in the language cortex (Galaburda et al., 1985). It was also postulated that interactions occurred among the presence of left-handedness, the presence of autoimmune disorders, male gender differentiation, and the presence of reading disorders. Genetic influences seemed likely (Galaburda, 1990). Although aspects of this theory remain controversial, there can be no doubt that these neuropathological studies provided the first concrete evidence that the brains of persons with severe reading disability may be affected by neurodevelopmental processes that can only occur between the fifth to the seventh month of fetal gestation. It is during the middle trimester of pregnancy that these deviations in brain structure can occur.

Although the neuropathological studies were truly exceptional in providing evidence for a neurobiological basis to severe reading disabilities, the small number of brains available for study, difficulty in consistent retrospective diagnostic procedures, and the expense all suggested that other methods of investigation might be worthwhile. Studies employing brain neuroimaging procedures could potentially support these findings, or reveal other deviations in the brain that might be associated with difficulty in the acquisition of fluent reading ability.

Structural Imaging Studies

The first structural neuroimaging studies of the brains of individuals with severe reading disability were reported by Hier and his colleagues using Computed Tomography (CT) (Hier, LeMay, Rosenberger, & Perlo, 1978). These investigators found that in contrast to nondisabled children, children with severe reading disability had reversed asymmetry (R > L) of the posterior cortex. It was suggested that reversed asymmetry of the posterior cortex of the brain increased the risk of severe reading disability significantly. In a follow-up study, Rosenberger and Hier (1980) reported that reversed posterior asymmetry was associated with lower verbal IQ.

Encouraged by these studies and the postmortem studies reported by Galaburda and his colleagues, Hynd, Semrud-Clikeman, Lorys, Novey, and Eliopulos (1990) used Magnetic Resonance Imaging to examine brain asymmetries in nondisabled children, reading disabled children, and in children with Attention Deficit Disorder (ADD). One significant advantage of MRI over CT procedures is that with MRI there is no exposure to radiation. Rather, images of the brain are derived by recording subtle changes in radio frequency emissions from the brain due to alterations in the magnetic field surrounding the head. In addition to reporting that both the children with reading disability and ADD had symmetry of the frontal lobes and that the children with reading disability had a smaller bilateral insular cortex, they reported a very significant incidence of symmetry or reversed asymmetry of the planum temporale among the children with reading disability. These findings highlighted the general conclusion that the brains of children with reading disability are morphologically different from those of normal reading children, and specifically so in the posterior language area, the planum temporale. Figure 3.2 graphically illustrates the patterns of asymmetry in the region of the planum temorale in normal children, in children with ADD, and in children with reading disability. As can be seen, there exists a dramatic shift in the normal patterns of asymmetry only among the children with severe reading disability. In a follow-up study, Semrud-Clikeman and Hynd (1990) demonstrated, similar to the findings reported by Rosenberger and Hier (1980), that these shifts in patterns of normal brain morphology are related to deficient neurolinguistic processes (e.g., receptive language, rapid naming) and reading abilities (reading comprehension). In fact, when one examines plana asymmetry according to whether one scores below average (achievement < 85 standard score), or average or above (achievement > 85 standard score) on a standardized reading test of passage comprehension, one finds that the incidence of L > R plana asymmetry increases significantly (see Figure 3.3) when achievement scores on this reading test are average or better. This suggests some lawful relationship between having a larger left planum temporale, in contrast to the right, and reading ability.

Other investigations targeted the morphology of the corpus callosum, a large pathway of fibers interconnecting the right and left hemispheres (Hynd et al., 1995; Jernigan, Hesselink, Stowell, & Tallal, 1991), while others examined larger aspects of the temporal lobe, which likely included the planum temporale (Kushch, Gross-Glenn, & Jallad, 1993). Generally, these studies reported variation in normal patterns of brain development in those areas believed to be important to reading and learning.

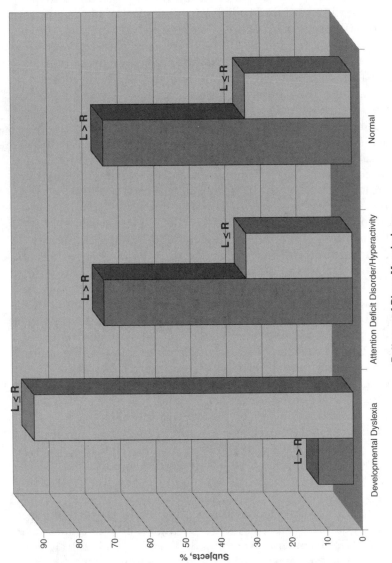

Patterns of Plana Morphology

FIG. 3.2.   Percent of subjects by group with left-right asymmetry or symmetry of the plana length. L > R indicates left greater than right; L ≤ R, left less than or equal to right. (From Hynd et al., 1990, used with permission).

Temporal Bank Asymmetry
– Passage Comprehension –

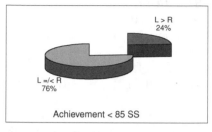
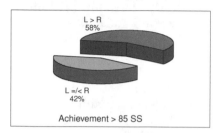

FIG. 3.3. Pie chart showing that when achievement is below average (Achievement < 85 SS) on a test of Passage Comprehension that only 24% of children showed the more typical L > R pattern of plana asymmetry. However, when achievement is average or better (Achievement > 85 SS), the percentage of typical L > R plana asymmetry increases to 58%.

Neuroanatomically, it was beginning to be appreciated that the morphology of the planum temporale normally extended into the parietal region. Thus, Leonard and colleagues examined both the temporal and parietal banks of the planum temporale in the brains of adults with severe reading disability (Leonard et al., 1993). These investigators reported two findings of interest. First, most nondisabled adults evidenced a left-sided asymmetry of the temporal bank and a right-sided asymmetry for the parietal bank of the planum temporale. However, the adults with a reported history of reading disability showed increased asymmetry of the right planum temporale due to a shift of tissue from the temporal to the parietal bank on the right side of the brain. Second, the brains of adults with reading disability displayed more cortical abnormalities in the region of the planum temporale. These cortical abnormalities, polymicrogyri, are similar to those observed in the first postmortem case reported by Galaburda & Kemper (1979).

Two more recent structural neuroimaging MRI studies deserve note. Based on research that suggested variation may exist in the region of the temporoparietal cortex in the nondisabled population, Hiemenz and Hynd (2000) examined gyral morphology patterns in children with reading disability. Essentially, they found that a specific gyral morphology pattern was associated with lower verbal intelligence, language, and reading ability than another gyral pattern in this region of interest. Gyral patterns did not discriminate nondisabled from reading disabled children, however. Second, Pennington et al. (1999) used MRI to examine brain structural differences in nondisabled and reading disabled children. They found subtle brain differences between the two groups of children, most notably in the superior frontal and insular cortex. No structural differences were found for subcortical regions, including the corpus callosum. However, the finding of a small insular cortex in the children with reading disability did confirm the previously reported finding by Hynd and colleagues nine years earlier (Hynd et al., 1990). The insular cortex is deep within the central language area, and aspects of this cortex have long been thought to be associated with receptive and expressive language processes (Kral, Nielsen, & Hynd, 1998).

The results of studies employing structural MRI procedures have been interesting and continue to provide evidence that subtle deviations in brain morphology likely are associated with the behavioral and cognitive difficulties observed in reading disability. Despite serious differences in diagnostic criteria among these studies, small numbers of subjects, methodological and measurement limitations, and sometimes conflicting results (Filipek, 1999), four tentative conclusions seem justified based on these structural neuroimaging studies. First, these studies collectively suggest that the trajectory of brain development, especially in those areas subserving language and reading abilities, is often at variance from that expected in the brains of those without reading disability. Second, based on what is known about cortical and gyral differentiation, these differences in brain morphology most likely first manifest during the middle trimester of pregnancy (Hynd & Hiemenz, 1997). Third, evidence from several studies suggests that these variations in brain structure, particularly those in the region of the planum temporale and its surrounding area, are correlated with reading ability/disability and verbal intelligence. And fourth, consistent with the observations of scholars over a century ago (Bastian, 1898; Hinshelwood, 1900), these subtle differences in the development of the brain in persons with reading disability are potentially under the influence of genetic factors (Galaburda, 1990; Pennington et al., 1999). In fact, genetic markers for reading disability have been identified on the short arm of chromosome 6 (Cardon et al., 1994) and on chromosome 15 (Grigorenko, Wood, & Meyer, 1997).

However, as was pointed out some time ago regarding the proposed link between the existence of neurological soft signs in reading disabled persons and hypothesized neurological dysfunction (Taylor & Fletcher, 1983), the results of the structural imaging studies are correlative in nature. Although the deviations in normal patterns of brain morphology among the brains of persons with reading disability seem to correlate with structures thought to be involved in language and reading, it cannot conclusively be stated that this is indeed the case. It is for this reason that the functional brain imaging studies are so very important, even though they are accompanied by their own theoretical and methodological challenges. The functional brain imaging studies are informative because they provide better linkage among cognitive processes, brain structural organization, and functional activation of the brain.

Functional Imaging Studies

As opposed to structural imaging such as with CT and MRI, functional imaging allows direct assessment of the neural networks involved in a particular cognitive task. Most studies to date have used the subtraction technique as a means to isolate specific language and reading processes. This technique entails having individuals perform a task in the scanner that requires the specific cognitive process of interest, as well as other cognitive processes. In order to meet these processing demands, various neural systems are metabolically activated, changes occur in brain metabolic activity, and this results in accompanying changes in cerebral blood flow that are measured through various techniques including Positron Emission Tomography (PET) and functional Magnetic Resonance Imaging (f MRI). In the subtraction technique, individuals also perform a control task(s) that shares as many cognitive operations as possible with the experimental task except for the cognitive process of interest. Modalities used and response demands would generally be the same across tasks. By subtracting the activation resulting from a control task from that of the experimental task, brain regions associated with a specific cognitive process are identified. Hence, through functional imaging it is possible to discern specific neural networks involved in reading and neurolinguistic functioning.

During the past decade several studies have used PET to investigate the processes involved in reading using adults who read normally. For a thorough review of this literature, the reader is referred to Rumsey (1996). Studies using persons with reading disability (regardless of how the reading disability was defined) deserve consideration.

Early studies of individuals with severe reading disability typically used xenon-inhalation techniques with adults. In the first of such studies, Rumsey et al. (1987) studied right-handed men on tasks designed to activate the left or right hemisphere preferentially. On these tasks controls demonstrated greater blood flow on the left side of the brain during a semantic classification task and on the right side during a line orientation task. Although individuals with reading disability displayed similar patterns of activation, they presented with exaggerated blood flow on the left or right, respectively, as compared to controls on both tasks. It was concluded that the findings may represent poor bihemispheric integration or inefficient allocation of cognitive resources in the brains of persons with reading disability. In addition to exaggerated blood flow findings in the left and right hemisphere, individuals with reading disability presented with reduced blood flow in the frontal region during the difficult line orientation task. Flowers and colleagues (Flowers, Wood, & Naylor, 1991) measured regional blood flow in adults, including many who had a childhood history of reading impairment, while they listened to concrete nouns and identified those containing four letters. In all persons, accuracy of performance was positively correlated with blood flow in Wernicke's area, an area encompassing the planum temporale, but those with a history of reading problems showed reduced flow in Wernicke's area in accordance with reduced performance. In contrast, childhood reading level was inversely correlated with greater activation at the temporoparietal juncture. These investigators hypothesized that their findings may reflect atypical connectivity, in which axons normally targeted for Wernicke's area instead synapse in the temporoparietal cortex, resulting in inefficiency related to reading. Other authors suggested elevated lingual (a brain region between the visual and language association cortices) activity may be indicative of dysfunction. For example, Gross-Glenn et al. (1991) found men with reading disabilities displayed greater symmetry in prefrontal regions, increased activation in lingual regions, and reversed asymmetry in lingual regions.

Subsequent research typically has used PET technology, employing various tracers to measure changes in blood flow. Hagman et al. (1992) studied adults with reading disability, primarily men, while they performed a speech discrimination task. Individuals with reading disability showed higher metabolism in the medial temporal lobe bilaterally, which was hypothesized to reflect either inefficient processing or activation of compensatory brain pathways. Wood and colleagues (1991) also used a similar phoneme detection task to study individuals with reading disabilities. Although the authors did not report differences in activation level, they found different correlation patterns between normal and impaired readers. In normal readers task accuracy was related to decreased activation of the left superior temporal region, whereas in poor readers task accuracy was related to increased left temporal activation. The task used in this study was relatively easy for normal readers, but it was not easy for those with reading disabilities. Hence, phoneme detection appeared to be inefficient in persons with reading disabilities in this study as well.

Rumsey used PET to study right-handed, severely reading disabled men and well-matched control subjects on a variety of tasks (Rumsey et al., 1992; Rumsey, Andreason et al., 1994; Rumsey, Zametkin et al., 1994). All tasks involved auditory stimuli and a button-press response. Reliable differences were found between reading disabled and nondisabled adults in the pattern of cortical activation during a phonological rhyme detection task in which the adults were presented with word pairs and had to judge whether they rhymed. Those persons with reading disability showed less activation in left temporoparietal regions near the angular gyrus, with activation of this region being related to verbal intelligence. In contrast, individuals with reading disability showed activation in left anterior temporal and right temporal regions, perhaps reflecting use of compensatory activities for a malfunctioning left temporoparietal region. Supporting this hypothesis was the finding that activation occurred in the anterior temporal lobe only in individuals with reading disability during a nonverbal tone detection task, suggesting that this activation is abnormal. In contrast to the above findings, men with reading disability did not differ from controls in their activation of left inferior frontal and middle to anterior temporal cortex during a syntactic task in which participants listened to pairs of sentences and judged whether they differed in meaning. These results suggest that deficits in the brains of persons with reading disability are limited to specific aspects of neurolinguistic functioning (phonological processing), rather than being global in nature.

Paulesu et al. (1996) also used PET technology to study phonological processing in individuals with reading disability. Similar to the work of Rumsey and colleagues, they found reduced activity in the left temporoparietal region in individuals with reading disability during a phonological memory task. In contrast to the work of Rumsey et al., they found reduced activity in Broca's region and surrounding areas during a rhyming task. They also found regions activate independently, rather than sequentially as expected, in individuals with reading disability. Given that individuals with reading disability showed no activation in the insular region, the authors hypothesized that dyslexia is a disconnection syndrome resulting from a dysfunctional left insula. The implication of the insular cortex supports the morphological deviations noted in this area by Hynd et al. (1990) and Pennington et al. (1999).

Even though the majority of researchers hypothesize that the core deficit in reading disabilities is poor phonological processing, some researchers have found that individuals with reading disability have various nonverbal deficits as well. Using a tonal memory task, Rumsey, Andreason et al. (1994) found reduced activation in the right middle temporal lobe and in the right inferior frontal region, homologous to Broca's area, in individuals with reading disability. This finding should be interpreted cautiously, however, because persons with reading disability showed highly significant impairments in performance. Given the neuropathological findings of bilateral cortical anomalies and an enlarged planum temporale on the right by Galaburda and colleagues (which contributed to symmetry of the planum temporale), this reduction in activation might be expected as the tonal task was designed to preferentially activate right temporal cortex (Rumsey, 1996). Alternatively, this finding may reflect a severity issue, as many individuals with reading disability learn to compensate over time, and Rumsey and colleagues only studied adults with severe reading disability. Hence, deficits in severe cases of reading disability may be more encompassing than just reduced phonological processing, and may be associated with involvement of widely distributed neural circuits, affecting bilateral temporal, and possibly, other brain regions (Rumsey, 1996).

In addition to auditory processing deficits, visual processing deficits have been found in the brains of persons with reading disability. Galaburda and Livingstone (1993) hypothesized that individuals with reading disability have difficulties with rapid visual processing secondary to a malfunctioning magnocellular visual system. Consistent with this, using f MRI, Eden and colleagues found that presentation of moving stimuli failed to produce activation in the magnocellular visual subsystem in persons with reading disability, but presentation of stationary stimuli resulted in activation patterns comparable to controls (Eden, Van Meter, Maisog, Rumsey, & Zeffiro, 1995).

Although PET technology has led to many informative discoveries, it has significant limitations, including the necessity of using radiation and the logistics of generating short-lived isotopes. In contrast to PET, f MRI does not require radiation, so numerous scans can be performed on the same individual to achieve an adequate signal-to-noise ratio. Rather than measuring blood flow changes through use of an injected isotope, differences in f MRI signal are determined by measuring differences in the magnetic properties of oxygenated and unoxygenated blood (Shaywitz et al., 1996). At least two laboratories are using f MRI in the study of reading impairment.

Bookheimer and colleagues (unpublished data, Bookheimer & Dapretto, 1996) used f MRI to study regions involved with two processes, rhyming and spelling. In a normal adult, activation was found in the inferior frontal cortex during the rhyming task and in the left superior temporal and angular gyri for both tasks. An older child with reading disabilities demonstrated similar activation in the left inferior frontal lobe during both tasks. However, lack of activation was found in left superior temporal and angular regions, whereas homologous right hemisphere regions were active during both tasks. These findings do not appear to be due to age differences between the child with reading disabilities and the control because a child without reading problems displayed similar activation patterns to that of the adult control. Hence, the findings of Bookheimer et al. are consistent with structural MRI findings that found reduced symmetry of the planum temporale, or greater size of the right planum temporale in individuals with reading disability (Bookheimer & Dapretto, 1996). They also are generally consistent with the work of Rumsey and colleagues (Rumsey et al., 1992; Rumsey, Zametkin et al., 1994).

Shaywitz and colleagues have designed a series of tasks in order to investigate the major components of the reading process: orthography, phonology, and semantics (Shaywitz et al., 1996). In their 1995 study, nonimpaired, right-handed adults (19 men and 19 women) were examined (Shaywitz et al., 1995). Results indicated that the extrastriate was uniquely associated with orthographic processing. The superior aspect of the inferior frontal gyrus (IFG), previously shown to be activated in speech tasks when phonetic decisions are required (Demonet et al., 1992; Demonet, Price, Wise, & Frackowiak, 1994), was found to be uniquely associated with phonological processing on a rhyme judgment task. Rhyme judgment also was associated with activation in the superior temporal gyrus and middle temporal gyrus, but the semantic task activated both of these regions significantly more than the rhyme task. This suggests that the superior and middle temporal gyri subserve both phonological and lexical semantic processing. The IFG, in contrast, was uniquely associated with rhyming. In a subsequent study examining adults with reading disability using a similar paradigm, Shaywitz et al. (1998) found participants with reading disability to have underactivation of left posterior perisylvian and occipital regions (Wernicke's, angular gyrus, striate cortex) and overactivation in left anterior (inferior frontal gyrus) and right posterior perisylvian regions during phonological processing.

DISCUSSION & CONCLUSIONS

Although an overview of the literature reveals somewhat discrepant findings, the majority of the imaging studies point to anomalous structure and function in traditional language regions of the brain in the presence of reading disabilities. These include superior temporal lobe, often implicated to be an auditory association cortex, and posterior parietal regions, often implicated in grapheme–phoneme correspondence. Some studies also have found anomalous structure and function in the left inferior frontal region, as well as in various right hemisphere regions analogous to language areas. In addition, the magnocellular visual system has been shown to be deficient in some individuals with reading disability.

There are many factors that could be leading to what appear to be discrepant findings. One factor is task selection and design. Selection

of tasks has differed across laboratories and occasionally within laboratories. MRI acquisition protocols also vary across sites. Other possible
confounds include secondary factors such as rate of stimulation and
practice effects. There also may be factors related to differences in task
difficulty and performance when research is comparing controls and
individuals with reading disability. Further, research groups frequently
vary in their operational definition of reading disabilities, resulting in
potentially different populations of reading disabled being studied. Gender effects are an additional confound (Pennington et al., 1999). The
laboratories at Yale (Shaywitz et al., 1995) have demonstrated significant gender differences in their measures of language functioning, yet
gender composition varies widely across studies. Presence of comorbid
ADHD has not been well-controlled either, despite anomalous structural
and functional patterns being demonstrated in individuals with ADHD
(Filipek, 1999; Hynd et al., 1990, Hynd et al., 1993), a disorder that frequently co-occurs with dyslexia. Another possible confound that has not
been well-controlled is handedness, which has been shown by some to
play a significant role in the extent of language lateralization (Rumsey,
1996). Alternatively, discrepant findings may reflect different cognitive
strategies employed by the participants in these studies, whether reading
disabled or nondisabled readers (Rumsey, 1996).

An equivalent explanation of such discrepant findings is that reading
is a highly complex skill involving many neural structures and systems.
In fact, individuals with reading disability present with heterogeneity
in their neuropsychological deficits. In addition to core phonological
deficits, reading disabilities are often associated with multifaceted language deficits, comorbid academic skill deficits in spelling, writing, and
math, and comorbid attentional disorders (Lombardino, Riccio, & Hynd,
1997). Hence, variably distributed subtle developmental anomalies may
constitute the substrate of this disorder, rather than a localized deficit
in a small portion of the cortex (Rumsey, 1996). If reading disability
is a manifestation of deficits in the connectivity of a widely distributed
neural network, then variability of findings is reasonable; deficits in any
part of network may produce symptoms of reading disability (Hynd,
Hooper, & Takahashi, 1998). This explanation also can help to explain
the inconsistent results of morphological studies discussed previously.

So, what can be projected for the future? First and foremost, evidence
will continue to document that subtle deviations in brain development,
likely under genetic control, underlie the manifestation of severe problems in learning to read. One can only presume that these neurobiological approaches to research will be extended to the study of mathematics
and social skills learning disabilities as well. Further, evidence will continue to mount that these subtle deviations in brain development are

tied directly to the behavioral deficiencies we observe in children with learning disability. Study of these deviations also may lead to a better understanding of the frequent patterns of psychiatric disturbance (e.g., ADHD, depression, anxiety) seen in these children during their later development in adolescence and adulthood. Finally, as these studies are already underway, we should expect to see these functional neuroimaging procedures employed in documenting the impact of educational remediation on brain functional organization in children with reading disability. It is in this latter arena that scholars from the neurological, psychological, and educational sciences may find their collaborative research most meaningful and productive in improving the lives of children with severe learning disability.

REFERENCES

American Psychiatric Association. (1994). *Diagnostic and statistical manual of mental disorders (Fourth Edition)*. Washington, D.C.: American Psychiatric Association.

Bastian, H. C. (1898). *A treatise on aphasia and other speech defects*. London: H. K. Lewis.

Bookheimer, S. Y., & Dapretto, M. (1996). Functional neuroimaging of language in children: Current directions and future challenges. In R. W. Thatcher, G. R. Lyon, J. Rumsey, & N. Krasnegor (Eds.), *Developmental neuroimaging: Mapping the development of brain and behavior*. (pp. 143–155). San Diego, CA: Academic Press, Inc.

Cardon, L. R., Smith, S. D., Fulker, D. W., Kimberling, W. J., Pennington, B. F., & DeFries, J. C. (1994). Quantitative trait locus for reading disability on chromosome 6. *Science, 266,* 276–279.

Demonet, J. F., Chollet, F., Ramay, S., Cardeloat, D., Nespoulous, J. L., Wise, R., Rascol, A., & Frackowiak, R. (1992). The anatomy of phonological and semantic processing in normal subjects. *Brain, 115,* 1753–1768.

Demonet, J. F., Price, C., Wise, R., & Frackowiak, R. S. J. (1994). A PET study of cognitive strategies in normal subjects during language tasks; Influence of phonetic ambiguity and sequence processing on phoneme monitoring. *Brain, 117,* 671–682.

Eden, G. F., Van Meter, J. W., Maisog, J. M., Rumsey, J., & Zeffiro, T. A. (1995). Abnormal visual motion processing in dyslexic subjects demonstrated with functional magnetic imaging. *Society for Neuroscience Abstracts, 21,* 268.1.

Filipek, P. A. (1999). Neuroimaging in the developmental disorders: The state of the science. *Journal of Child Psychology and Psychiatry, 40,* 113–128.

Flowers, D. L., Wood, F. B., & Naylor, C. E. (1991). Regional cerebral blood flow correlates of language processes in reading disability. *Archives of Neurology, 48,* 637–643.

Galaburda, A. (1990). The testosterone hypothesis: Assessment since Geschwind and Behan, 1982. *Annals of Dyslexia, 40,* 18–38.

Galaburda, A., & Kemper, T. L. (1979). Cytoarchitectonic abnormalities in developmental dyslexia: A case study. *Annals of Neurology, 6,* 94–100.

Galaburda A. M., & Livingstone, M. (1993). Evidence for a magnocellular defect in developmental dyslexia. *Annals of the New York Academy of Sciences, 682,* 70–82.

Galaburda, A., Sherman, G., Rosen, G., Aboitiz, F., & Geschwind, N. (1985). Developmental dyslexia: Four consecutive patients with cortical abnormalities. *Annals of Neurology, 18,* 222–233.

Geschwind, N., & Levitsky, W. (1968). Human brain: Left-right asymmetries in temporal speech region. *Science, 161*, 186–187.

Grigorenko, E. L., Wood, F. B., & Meyer, M. S. (1997). Susceptibility loci for distinct components of developmental dyslexia on chromosome 6 and 15. *American Journal of Human Genetics, 60*, 27–39.

Gross-Glenn, K., Duara, R., Barker, W. W., Loewenstein, D., Chang, J. Y., Yoshii, F., Apicella, A. M., Pascal, S., Boothe, T., Sevush, S., Jallad, B. J., Novoa, L., & Lubs, H. A. (1991). Positron emission tomographic studies during serial word reading by normal and dyslexic adults. *Journal of Clinical and Experimental Neuropsychology, 13*, 531–544.

Hagman, J. O., Wood, F., Buchsbaum, M. S., Tallal, P., Flowers, L., & Katz, W. (1992). Cerebral brain metabolism in adult dyslexic subjects assessed with positron emission tomography during performance of an auditory task. *Archives of Neurology, 49*, 734–739.

Hiemenz, J. R., & Hynd, G. W. (2000). Sulcal/gyral pattern morphology of the perisylvian language region in developmental dyslexia. *Brain and Language, 74*, 113–133

Hier, D., LeMay, M., Rosenberger, P., & Perlo, V. (1978). Developmental dyslexia: Evidence for a subgroup with a reversal of cerebral asymmetry. *Archives of Neurology, 35*, 90–92.

Hinshelwood, J. (1900). Congenital word-blindness. *The Lancet, 1*, 1506–1508.

Hynd, G. W., Hall, J., Novey, E. S., Eliopulos, D., Black, K., Gonzalez, J., Edmonds, J., Riccio, C., & Cohen, M. (1995). Dyslexia and corpus callosum morphology. *Archives of Neurology, 52*, 32–38.

Hynd, G. W., & Hiemenz, J. R. (1997). Dyslexia and gyral morphology variation. In C. Hulme & M. Snowling (Eds.), *Dyslexia: Biology, cognition and intervention.* (pp. 38–58). London: Whurr Publishers, Ltd.

Hynd, G. W., Hern, K., Novey, E., Eliopulos, D., Marshall, R., Gonzalez, J., & Voeller, K. (1993). Attention Deficit Hyperactivity Disorder (ADHD) and asymmetry of the caudate nucleus. *Journal of Child Neurology, 8*, 339–347.

Hynd, G. W., Hooper, S. R., & Takahashi, T. (1998). Dyslexia and language-based learning disabilities. In C. E. Coffey & R. A. Brumback (Eds.), *Textbook of pediatric neuropsychiatry* (pp. 691–717). Washington, D.C.: American Psychiatric Press, Inc.

Hynd, G. W., & Hynd, C. R. (1984). Dyslexia: Neuroanatomical/neurolinguistic perspectives. *Reading Research Quarterly, 19*, 482–498.

Hynd, G. W., & Semrud-Clikeman, M. (1989). Dyslexia and brain morphology. *Psychological Bulletin, 106*, 447–482.

Hynd, G.W., Semrud-Clikeman, M., Lorys, A., Novey, E., & Eliopulos, D. (1990). Brain morphology in developmental dyslexia and Attention Deficit Hyperactivity Disorder. *Archives of Neurology, 47*, 919–926.

Jernigan, T. L., Hesselink, J. P., Stowell, E., & Tallal, P. (1991). Cerebral structure on magnetic resonance imaging in language- and learning-impaired children. *Archives of Neurology, 48*, 539–545.

Kral, M., Nielsen, K., & Hynd, G. W. (1998). Historical conceptualization of developmental dyslexia: Neurolinguistic contributions from the 19th and early 20th centuries. In R. Licht, A. Bouma, W. Slot, & W. Koops (Eds.), *Child Neuropsychology,* (pp. 1–16). Delft: The Netherlands, Eburon Publishers.

Kushch, A., Gross-Glenn, K., & Jallad, B. (1993). Temporal lobe surface area measurements on MRI in normal and dyslexic readers. *Neuropsychologia, 31*, 811–821.

Kussmaul, A. (1877). Disturbances of speech. *Cyclopedia of the practice of medicine, 14*, 581, 875.

Leonard, C., Voeller, K., Lombardino, L., Morris, M., Hynd, G. W., Alexander, A., Andersen, H., Garofalakis, M., Honeyman, J., Mao, J., Agee, H. & Staab, E. (1993). Anomalous cerebral structure in dyslexia revealed with magnetic resonance imaging. *Archives of Neurology, 50*, 461–469.

Lombardino, L., Riccio, C. A., & Hynd, G. W. (1997). Linguistic and associated phonological deficits in children with reading disabilities. *American Journal of Speech-Language Pathology, 6,* 71–78.

Morgan, W. P. (1896). A case of congenital word-blindness. *British Medical Journal, 2,* 1378.

Paulesu, E., Frith, U., Snowling, M., Gallagher, A., Morton, J., Frackowiak, R. S. J., & Frith, C. D. (1996). Is developmental dyslexia a disconnection syndrome? Evidence from PET. *Brain, 119,* 143–157.

Pennington, B. F., Filipek, P. A., Lefly, D., Churchwell, J., Kennedy, D. N., Simon, J. H., Filley, C. M., Galaburda, A., Alarcon, M., & DeFries, J. C. (1999). Brain morphometry in reading-disabled twins. *Neurology, 53,* 723–729.

Rosenberger, P., & Hier, D. (1980). Cerebral asymmetry and verbal intellectual deficits. *Annals of Neurology, 8,* 300–304.

Rumsey, J. M. (1996). Neuroimaging in developmental dyslexia: A review and conceptualization. In G. R. Lyon & J. M. Rumsey (Eds.), *Neuroimaging: A window to the neurological foundations of learning and behavior in children* (pp. 57–77). Baltimore, MD: Paul H. Brookes Publishing Co.

Rumsey, J. M., Andreason, P., Zametkin, A. J., Aquino, T., King, A. C., Hamburger, S. D., Pikus, A., Rapoport, J. L., & Cohen, R. M. (1992). Failure to activate the left temporoparietal cortex in dyslexia: An oxygen 15 positron emission tomography study. *Archives of Neurology, 49,* 527–534.

Rumsey, J. M., Andreason, P., Zametkin, A. J., King, A. C., Hamburger, S. D., Aquino, T., Hanahan, A. P., Pikus, A., & Cohen, R. M. (1994). Right frontotemporal activation by tonal memory in dyslexia, an O^{15} PET study. *Biological Psychiatry, 36,* 171–180.

Rumsey, J. M., Berman, K. F., Denckla, M. B., Hamburger, S. D., Kruesi, M. J., & Weinberger, D. R. (1987). Regional blood flow in severe developmental dyslexia. *Archives of Neurology, 44,* 1144–1150.

Rumsey, J., Zametkin, A., Andreason, P., Hanahan, A., Hamburger, S., Aquino, T., King, A., Pikus, A., & Cohen, R. (1994). Normal activation of frontotemporal language cortex in dyslexia, as measured with oxygen 15 positron emission tomography. *Archives of Neurology, 51,* 27–38.

Semrud-Clikeman, M., & Hynd, G. W. (1990). Dyslexia and brain morphology: Relationships between neuroanatomical variation and neurolinguistic tasks. *Learning and Individual Differences, 3,* 225–242.

Shaywitz, B. A., Fletcher, J. M., & Shaywitz, S. E. (1995). Defining and classifying learning disabilities and attention-deficit/hyperactivity disorder. *Journal of Child Neurology, 10(suppl 1),* 50–57.

Shaywitz, B. A., Shaywitz, S. E., Pugh, K. R., Constable, R. T., Skudlarski, P., Fulbright, R. K., Bronen, R. T., Fletcher, J. M., Shankweiler, D. P., Katz, L., & Gore, J. D. (1995). Sex differences in the functional organization of the brain for language. *Nature, 373,* 607–609.

Shaywitz, B. A., Shaywitz, S. E., Pugh, K. R., Skudlarski, P., Fulbright, R. K., Constable, R. T., Bronen, R. A., Fletcher, J. M., Liberman, A. M., Shankweiler, D. P., Katz, L., Lacadie, C., Marchione, K. E., & Gore, J. C. (1996). Functional magnetic resonance imaging as a tool to understand reading and reading disability. In R. W. Thatcher, G. R. Lyon, J. Rumsey, & N. Krasnegor (Eds.), *Developmental neuroimaging: Mapping the development of brain and behavior* (pp. 157–167). San Diego, CA: Academic Press, Inc.

Shaywitz S. E., Shaywitz, B. A., Pugh, K. R., Fulbright, R. K., Constable, R. T., Mencl, W. E., Shankweiler, D. P., Liberman, A. M., Skudlarski, P., Fletcher, J. M., Katz, L., Marchione, K. E., Lacadie, C., Gatenby, C., & Gore, J. C. (1998). Functional disruption in the organization of the brain for reading in dyslexia. *Proceedings of the National Academy of Sciences, USA, 95,* 2636–2641.

Taylor, H. G., & Fletcher, J. M. (1983). Biological foundations of "specific developmental disorders": Methods, findings, and future directions. *Journal of Clinical Child Psychology, 12,* 46–65.

Weinberger, D., Luchins, D., Morihisa, J., & Wyatt, R. (1982). Asymmetrical volumes of the right and left frontal and occipital regions of the human brain. *Neurology, 11,* 97–100.

Wood F., Flowers, L., Buchsbaum, M., et al. (1991). Investigation of abnormal left temporal functioning in dyslexia through rCBF, auditory evoked potentials, and positron emission tomography. *Reading and Writing, 3,* 379–393.

Chapter 4

Comorbid ADHD and Learning Disabilities: Diagnosis, Special Education, and Intervention

Ronald A. Kotkin, Ph.D.
UCI Child Development Center

Steven R. Forness, Ed.D.
UCLA Nueropsychiatric Hospital

Kenneth A. Kavale, Ph.D.
University of Iowa, Iowa City

Learning disabilities (LD) and Attention Deficit Hyperactivity Disorder (ADHD) often co-occur in children. This has led clinicians and researchers to question whether one disorder leads to the other or whether they are related to one another because of a common underlying factor. Differential diagnosis, which does not recognize co-occurring disorders, often leads to partial treatment of only one of the disorders in children with comorbid ADHD and learning disabilities. Categorical placement of children in special education that does not take into account co-occurring problems of ADHD and learning disabilities often leads to individual educational plans that only partially address a child's academic, social emotional, or behavioral needs. Children with co-occurring ADHD and learning disabilities are sometimes placed in settings where teachers are not trained or skilled in using strategies to remediate learning disabilities or intervene with behavioral problems. The failure to recognize and treat both disorders, when they co-occur, may prevent the child from realizing the maximum benefit of intervention by focusing on only one of the disabilities. Many such children become frustrated and develop secondary emotional problems (Silver, 1981). In this chapter we briefly trace the origin of the link between ADHD and LD, outline the difficulties in diagnosing the disorders, discuss the co-occurrence of ADHD and learning disabilities, and discuss the implications for school-based interventions and placement in special education. Among the "new" behavioral disorders, Attention Deficit Hyperactivity Disorder (ADHD) is perhaps the most problematic and is a prime illustration of the difficulties encountered in creating special education categories and how the issue of co-occurrence tends to be a confounding factor (Kavale & Forness, 1998).

THE LINK BETWEEN ADHD AND LD

Although the disorders of ADHD and LD evolved from a common focus on symptoms of brain damage, they have emerged into separate but often overlapping disorders. The ADHD concept emanated from the study of brain damage in which sequelae of an insult to the brain might include inattention, hyperactivity, and impulsivity (see Shaywitz & Shaywitz, 1988). Over time, there was the recognition that such symptoms could occur when there was no history or evidence of brain insult and resulted in the condition of minimal brain damage, whereby neurological involvement was slight but still an adverse influence. By the 1960s it became clear that the large majority of cases revealed no evidence of brain injury but rather it was a case in which the brain did not function the way it should. To reflect a problem in functioning rather than structure, Clements (1966) formalized the term *minimal brain dysfunction (MBD)*, which included among its most cited characteristics hyperactivity, disorders of attention, impulsivity (placing MBD in the ADHD realm), and specific learning disabilities. Thus the co-joining of ADHD and learning disabilities was established within the MBD framework. There was increasing recognition, however, that MBD was a flawed concept, and this resulted in confusion in the diagnosis of both learning disabilities and ADHD (Kavale & Forness, 1998).

Over time, the ADHD concept has seen substantial changes in nomenclature and criteria. Currently, DSM-IV diagnostic criteria for ADHD (American Psychiatric Association, 1994) require the demonstration of at least six symptoms of either inattention or hyperactivity-impulsivity that were present before age 7 years, have persisted for at least six months, manifested in two or more settings, and impair academic, social, or occupational functioning. The prevalence estimates for ADHD in the school-age population are 3% to 5% (Barkley, 1990; Szatmari, Offord, & Boyle, 1989).

Although refinements have been attempted, the ADHD concept remains an ill-defined constellation of behaviors that was not based on an empirical foundation (Shaywitz & Shaywitz, 1988). Consequently, the rationale for making discrete behaviors into mental disorders has been questioned (e.g., Schacht & Nathan, 1977) as well as the validity of ADHD as a distinct diagnostic entity (Prior & Sanson, 1986; Rutter, 1983). Additionally, the wisdom of making ADHD a special education disability category has been challenged (Reid, Maag, & Vasa, 1993). The validity question surrounds a number of issues, including postdictive validity (no common etiology), predictive validity (outcomes differ significantly), and concurrent validity (the term does not describe current status and does not allow clear differentiation from other disorders) (Shaffer & Greenhill, 1979). These vagaries have led to the suggestion that ADHD, rather than a clearly circumscribed syndrome, is really an acronym for "*Any Dysfunction or Difficulty*" (Goodman & Poillion, 1992).

DIFFICULTIES IN DIAGNOSING THE DISORDERS

Attention Deficit Hyperactivity Disorder (ADHD) and Learning Disorders (LD) are described in the *DSM IV* (American Psychiatric Association, 1994). Educational criteria are used to identify similar but not identical conditions in the Individuals with Disabilities Educational Act (IDEA) (U.S. Department of Education, 1998). In IDEA the term *disability* is used rather than disorder. ADHD is included under the category of Other Health Impaired (OHI) and learning disabilities is a separate category termed Specific Learning Disabilities. ADHD was included as part of the OHI category based on part B of the IDEA and section 504 of the Rehabilitation Act of 1973 if ADHD produced "limited alertness" that seriously impaired school performance. Limited alertness has since been defined to include heightened alertness to environmental stimuli resulting in limited alertness to relevant stimuli in the educational setting (amendments to IDEA, 1997). If it is determined that the severity of the impairment is not sufficient to qualify for the OHI category under educational laws, then "504" accommodations for the ADHD can be developed in the regular classroom under civil rights laws.

In clinical practice, ADHD is typically assessed using psychiatric interviews and symptom rating scales (Richters, Arnold, Jensen, et al., 1995). The diagnosis is subjective based on ratings by caregivers. Although psychometric and psychological tests may suggest problems of attention, they are not generally accepted for diagnosis (Baren & Swanson, 1996). In the National Institute of Health (NIH) consensus conference (Forness & Kavale, in press) on ADHD, it was noted that the use of subjective measures of ADHD (rating scales) from varying sources may lead to a "disconnect," in which the ratings from one setting may differ greatly from the other source. For example, the rating of symptoms of ADHD in the home may not indicate impairment even though the ratings in the school are extreme, or the rating of symptoms in the home may be extreme with low ratings at school. This may be due to a variety of subjective variables that influence the rating of severity for items on the rating scales. Raters may have an agenda for rating the child more or less severely; there may be a difference in the tolerance level for certain behaviors by individuals rating the child; or the rating may reflect only the most recent experience with the child prior to completion of the rating scale and not reflect typical performance. For this reason, collaborators in the national multisite multimodality treatment study of an ADHD cooperative group (MTA) (1999) suggest the use of structured interviews to examine the apparent discrepancies between raters (Richters et al., 1995). Richters et al. (1995) give specific examples of structured interviews used to follow up discrepant rating scales. They suggest that structured interviews should always be used to clarify discrepancies before a diagnosis is made.

Professionals do use psychometric and psychological tests of potential and achievement to diagnose learning disabilities. They base the diagnosis on a discrepancy between potential as measured by an intelligence test and achievement based on a standardized measure of academic performance. Professionals commonly use two methods to determine a significant discrepancy, the simple-difference method and the predicted-achievement method. Using the simple-difference method, scores on a standardized achievement test are subtracted from a measure of ability (such as the full-scale IQ). In the predicted-achievement method, IQ scores are replaced with estimated achievement scores predicted by the IQ scores. Predictions are made based on correlations between the ability–achievement measures. There is considerable controversy over the validity of the discrepancy approach. The choice of method carries a bias that favors individuals with low or high IQ (Swanson et al., in press). Swanson (in press) have pointed out that both methods have different statistical assumptions and formulas used to establish cutoffs for "significant discrepancy," and depending on which method is used the number of cases identified may be very different. Therefore, the number of students identified with comorbid ADHD and learning disabilities is dependent on the method used to determine the discrepancy.

CO-OCCURRENCE OF ADHD AND LEARNING DISABILITIES

Estimated prevalence of learning disabilities in the general population is approximately 5%. Studies of children with ADHD suggest a prevalence of comorbid learning disabilities ranging from 10% to 92% (Biederman, Newcorn, & Sprich, 1991); but, when appropriate diagnostic criteria for learning disabilities are applied, the prevalence of comorbid learning disabilities appears to be in the range of 10% to 25% (Richters et al., 1995). In the MTA study of children with ADHD (MTA Cooperative Group, 1999), children were diagnosed with learning disabilities according to the two criteria involving discrepancy between measured intelligence and academic achievement discussed in the previous section. The simple-difference method produced a rate of comorbid learning disabilities of approximately 35%, and the predicted-achievement method produced a rate of approximately 18%. The latter method is probably more appropriate in that it accounts more fully for overlap between the particular combination of IQ and achievement tests used.

The difficulty in the differential diagnosis of ADHD (e.g., Werry, Reeves, & Elkind, 1987) creates the possibility of considerable overlap between ADHD and related conditions. The association, for example, between ADHD and learning disabilities is a matter of debate (e.g., Silver, 1990) that is most clearly evidenced in prevalence rates of learning disabilities in ADHD cited above that range from 10%–92% (Biederman, Newcorn, & Sprich, 1991) while the prevalence rates of ADHD in learning disabilities is found to range from 40%–80% (e.g., Halperin, Gittelman, Klein, & Rudel, 1984; Holborrow & Berry, 1986; Safer & Allen, 1976; Silver, 1981). The variability in estimates is due not only to different definitions of learning disabilities and ADHD used in investigations but also to differences in selection criteria, sampling methods, and measurement procedures used to study each.

In examining the co-occurrence of disorders, the nature of the association becomes an important consideration. When two conditions (e.g., X and Y) are found associated with each other, the association may be conceptualized in three ways: (a) X may lead to Y, (b) Y may lead to X, and (c) both X and Y are independent manifestations of a common underlying factor. Consequently, questions about the nature of the association arise. Are they both subtypes of the same disorder? Does one predispose an individual to the other? Do they share a common etiology that produces two distinct syndromes? Until answers are forthcoming, difficulties are likely to be encountered in providing precise definitions for particular conditions (Kavale & Forness, 1998).

The example of the association between learning disabilities and ADHD provides an illustration. The assumption that ADHD would lead to learning disabilities possesses intuitive appeal. Students with difficulties in sustaining attention, selectively attending, responding impulsively, and demonstrating fidgeting and restlessness behavior that are core symptoms of ADHD would probably be expected to have academic problems (Dykman & Ackerman, 1992). The difficulty is that no evidence exists that ADHD itself leads directly to learning disabilities (McGee & Share, 1988). First, many students with ADHD do not have learning disabilities; and even when both are present, group comparisons (ADHD versus ADHD/LD) have revealed minimal differences on behavioral and neuropsychological measures (Halperin et al., 1984). Second, the fact that ADHD overlaps with other problems e.g., Conduct Disorder (CD) raises the possibility that the concurrent disorder, not ADHD itself, is the primary factor responsible for learning disabilities (Cantwell & Baker, 1992). The nature of the relationship between ADHD and CD has been differentiated into subtypes of either (a) purely inattentive, purely aggressive, and mixed inattentive-aggressive (Loney & Milich, 1982) or (b) pure hyperactivity, pure conduct problem, and mixed hyperactivity-conduct problem (Trites & LaPrade, 1983). These delineations have not received unequivocal support (e.g., Reeves, Werry, Elkind, & Zametkin, 1987). Thus, although it appears that ADHD, learning disabilities, or CD can occur independently, it also appears that they can co-occur.

The reverse scenario in which learning disabilities leads to ADHD has been suggested (e.g., Cunningham & Barkley, 1978), but again, no evidence is available to substantiate the relationship (Cantwell & Baker, 1992). Although there is evidence to suggest that reading disability results in increased risk for behavior problems (e.g., McGee, Share, Anderson, & Silva, 1986), the behavior problem might be ADHD, but also commonly associated were CD and anxiety disorders. The association with learning disabilities is thus not specific to ADHD.

The possibility that learning disabilities and ADHD are related to each other because of common underlying factors is plausible, but the range of possible factors (e.g., environmental, organic, cognitive) makes it difficult to isolate a single factor (Cantwell & Baker, 1992). Although there is the suggestion that the mechanism may reside in cognitive functioning (e.g., Douglas, 1980), specification about the nature of cognitive functioning and academic performance among samples with learning disabilities, ADHD, and LD/ADHD has been complicated by theoretical and measurement complexities (McGee & Share, 1988).

The possibility also exists that associations exist only between certain subtypes of the primary disorders. A number of investigations have attempted to divide heterogeneous samples of students with learning disabilities into homeogeneous groups based on a pattern of performance across a variety of tasks related to learning disabilities and across a variety of tasks related to ADHD (Kavale & Forness, 1987). One suggested subtyping scheme describes learning disabilities subtypes based on deficits in adaptive behavior that impair social functioning (Weller & Strawser, 1987). Based on the perceived social difficulties present in 3 of the 5 subtypes, it is possible that students with learning disabilities in these subtypes would also qualify for diagnosis of ADHD, CD, or depressive disorder (Forness, 1990). Similarly, it appears that ADHD can be subtyped into components based on facets of attention and behavior (Lahey, Schaughency, Hynd, Carlson, & Nieves, 1987; Loney & Milich, 1982). Such findings led August and Garfinkel (1989) to identify two subtypes of ADHD that were termed "behavioral" and "cognitive." In addition to inattention, overactivity, and impulsivity, the cognitive subtype of ADHD was also characterized by academic underachievement and neuropsychological skill deficits (i.e., learning disabilities). It thus appears that learning disabilities and ADHD are not unitary phenomena, and subtyping efforts may provide enhanced understanding about the exact degree and nature of the interrelationship between learning disabilities and ADHD.

Shaywitz and Shaywitz (1991) reviewed the interrelationship between ADHD, learning disabilities, and conduct and oppositional disorders concluding that naming and linguistic fluency deficits reflect reading disability, whereas verbal learning and memory deficits are linked to ADHD. Their review supports the finding that ADHD and learning disabilities are distinct disorders that often co-occur in a significant number of children. In another study Shaywitz, Fletcher, and Holahan (1995) compared children with only reading disability, only ADHD, and both reading disability and ADHD. They found that children with reading disabilities have problems only with language (phonologic awareness, rapid naming, lexical/vocabulary) whereas children with ADHD and no reading disability have problems with problem solving. Children with both disorders (reading and ADHD) have problems in all cognitive domains measured. They concluded that reading disability and ADHD appear to have distinctly different characteristics in isolation but have characteristics of both disorders when presenting together. Although they frequently co-occur in the same child they represent separate disorders.

Standford and Hynd (1994) compared the differences among children with ADD without hyperactivity (ADD/WO), children with ADD with hyperactivity (ADD/H), and children with learning disabilities. They studied whether the behavioral characteristics of children with ADD/WO more closely resembled the profiles of children with learning disabilities than children with ADD/H in a population of 77 outpatients between the ages of 5 and 16. The group was divided into ADD/WO, ADD/H, and learning-disabled children. Self, parent, and teacher reports were obtained for each child. Children with ADD/H were viewed by parents and teachers as more disruptive and impulsive than ADD/WO or learning disabled children. ADD/WO and learning-disabled children were seen as more lethargic, shy, and daydreaming than children with ADD/H. The two ADD groups (ADD/WO, ADD/H) were seen as more similar on measures of attention than the children with learning disabilities. The learning disabilities and ADD/WO groups were also not similar in patterns of impulsivity as a result of disorganization. The results indicate that ADHD and learning disabilities children have some behaviors that are similar, but the two disorders do not represent the same diagnosis. Although all three groups are susceptible to learning problems, the causes may be different (i.e., behavioral versus inattention versus processing).

Although children with ADHD may not have co-occuring learning disabilities, they still have significant problems with school behavior and performance. These negative school outcomes occur even in the absence of a specific learning disability (Wells et al., in press).

IMPLICATIONS FOR SCHOOL-BASED INTERVENTIONS AND PLACEMENT IN SPECIAL EDUCATION

In special education, the learning disabilities category is generally reserved for a student who has intelligence in the normal range, no primary emotional disorder or visual or hearing impairments, and at least a reasonable period of instruction in the regular grades, but who still remains unable to read, write, do math, or use language at an acceptable level. As noted earlier, what constitutes an acceptable level of academic performance, however, depends on whether the child has a significant discrepancy between his or her intelligence and academic skill level A child with ADHD may do poorly only on certain IQ subtests because he or she has difficulty paying attention, which artificially lowers the entire IQ score. When this happens, the child may not show a significant discrepancy between IQ and achievement test scores and therefore not qualify for special education services for learning disabilities (Forness et al., 1992).

Eligibility determinations, however, must be placed in the context of the learning disabilities definition problem. As suggested earlier, learning disabilities has not been defined with precision, and that has led to reliance on a single factor, discrepancy, in making a diagnosis. With such a unidimensional view, learning disabilities classification becomes contingent on the presence or absence of an aptitude–achievement discrepancy, and learning disabilities becomes the equivalent of underachievement. This is a narrow view and does not provide a comprehensive view of the symptom complex surrounding learning disabilities (Kavale & Forness, 1995). With school learning problems being an expected consequence for most psychiatric disorders, the learning disorders present may not actually be learning disabilities in the special education sense but are labeled as such because of the ease in which that designation is applied. For example, Forness, Kavale, and Lopez (1993) reviewed the intellectual and academic test findings for 55 students with a primary diagnosis of ADHD. Twenty-seven of the ADHD group were found to have concurrent CD or ODD. This resulted in either a pure or mixed ADHD group. These groups were very similar with respect to intellectual performance, but the ADHD group with CD/ODD was more impaired academically. Under these circumstances, the ADHD group with CD/ODD would more likely be given a learning disabilities diagnosis because of the greater likelihood of finding an aptitude–achievement discrepancy. The concurrent learning disabilities diagnosis would also give the student an enhanced chance of being found eligible for special education. The co-occurrence of learning disabilities with other psychiatric disorders, especially because of the way learning disabilities has come to be defined, may lead to special education service for students who would not usually be found eligible. This scenario multiplied many times over may account partially for the large number of students served under the learning disabilities rubric in special education (Kavale & Forness, 1998).

The situation may, in fact, be reversed for emotional disturbance. The current special education criteria for emotional disturbance contains five different areas, including inability to learn, which cannot be explained by intellectual, sensory, or health factors; inability to build and maintain satisfactory interpersonal relationships with peers and teachers; inappropriate types of behavior or feelings under normal circumstances; general mood of unhappiness or depression; and tendency to develop physical symptoms or fears associated with personal or school problems. To be eligible for the emotional disturbance category, a child must have a problem in one of these areas and exhibit this problem over a long period of time, to a marked degree, and to a point that it adversely affects educational performance. A child is excluded from eligibility in this category if his or her problems are considered to be merely "social maladjustment." ADHD symptoms are not specifically referred to in the criteria for any of the five areas.

Through archival analysis and parent interviews of 85 students with emotional disturbance, Duncan, Forness, and Hartsough (1995) found a significant delay before the emotional disturbance diagnosis was established. Most parents appeared to know that something was seriously amiss in their child's social or emotional development, and a professional (e.g., family physician) typically identified a problem during the preschool years. The children with emotional or behavior disorders initially received intervention at a mean age of 6.4 years, mainly a specified and isolated treatment (e.g., therapy for child abuse). Identification for special education did not occur until 7.8 years, on average, and this was primarily for learning disabilities (53%). What might be considered the appropriate placement in an emotional disturbance program did not occur until the mean age was 10.4 years. Thus, the Duncan, Forness, and Hartsough (1995) investigation shows that initial school action for an emotionally disturbed sample was usually for problems other than emotional and behavioral, and perhaps five or more years passed until there was appropriate special education recognition of the problem (i.e., ED).

In another investigation of 204 students referred to study teams, Del'Homme, Kasari, Forness, and Bagley (1996) focused on the initial complaints supplied by regular classroom teachers that were categorized by academic, behavioral, or combined problems (academic + behavioral). Only about one-quarter of the sample were referred primarily for behavioral problems or for behavioral problems with some minor academic difficulties, with another one-fifth having behavioral and academic problems in about equal proportion. The rate of subsequent referral to special education, however, was much lower proportionally for students with primary behavioral problems. This rate suggests that potential emotional and behavioral disorder was underidentified, possibly because of either a focus on CD or ODD (that would lead to exclusion) or a focus on academic difficulties (e.g., learning disabilities) rather than on potential emotional and behavioral disorders.

The potential for disregarding the significance of emotional and behavioral disorders was also confirmed in a study of 150 students in second to fourth grade (Lopez, Forness, MacMillan, Bocian, & Gresham, 1996). Strict research-based diagnostic criteria were used to identify students with ADHD, emotional and behavioral disorders, and other disabilities (e.g., MR and learning disabilities), and school personnel were not informed of diagnoses established in the investigation. Over time, all 150 students were tracked to determine if they had either been placed in special education, were found not eligible for special education, were still being considered by a study team, or had moved out of the district.

About 37% of ADHD and 50% of emotional and behavioral disordered students were placed in a learning disabilities program, but only about 9% of ADHD and one of the emotional and behavioral disordered students were considered for emotional disturbance programs. In fact, only one student out of the total of 55 with ADHD or emotional and behavioral disorder who might reasonably be expected to receive services for emotional disturbance actually ended up doing so. That the remaining 54 students who might be appropriately expected to profit from services for emotional disturbance were not placed there should be a source of concern. Why were they placed in a seemingly inappropriate program? The social maladjustment exclusion for emotional disturbance may mean that school personnel place such students in learning disabilities programs in order to provide at least some special education without the stigma of an emotional or behavior disorder. The difficulty, however, is that learning disabilties programs may be inappropriate because such programs may not be equipped to remedy the behavior problems associated with ADHD or emotional and behavioral disorder and thus not likely to change the major contributor to academic difficulties (Forness, Kavale, MacMillan, Asarnow, & Duncan, 1996). Nevertheless, such students are counted in the learning disabilities and not emotional disturbance category, and may account partially for the overidentification and underidentification, respectively, associated with these special education classifications.

These findings are consistent with those of Duncan, Forness, and Hartsough (1995), who also found that a large percentage of emotionally disturbed children initially received services under the category of learning disabilities. There is an obvious reluctance of schools to initially place behavior-disordered children in emotional disturbance programs. Because of the social maladjustment exclusion, students having disruptive behavior disorders such as oppositional and defiant disorder, conduct disorder, and ADHD may thus be found ineligible for special education under the emotional disturbance category (Forness & Knitzer, 1992). Hence, children with such disorders may have problems severe enough to cause failure in regular education; however, because they are deemed socially maladjusted, they do not qualify for emotional disturbance programs. Concerned school personnel may therefore place them in the learning disabilties category in order for them to receive at least some special education assistance, misidentifying the behavior disorder as a learning disability.

It has been pointed out that placing children with behavior disorders into learning disabilities classrooms or attempting to serve them in regular classrooms with resource specialist support may be inappropriate because such classrooms are not equipped to control the behavior problems of ADHD and emotional and behavioral disordered children. Lopez et al. (1996) found that ADHD and emotional and behavioral disordered children are more socially incompetent and have more problem behaviors than other nonbehavior disordered children identified as at-risk. Even more interesting are the findings that ADHD and emotional- and behavioral-disordered children who qualified for learning disabilities programs are more socially incompetent and have more problem behaviors than nonbehavior-disordered children who qualified for learning disabilities programs. The behavior-disordered students are even rated by teachers as less academically competent than other children classified as learning disabled. Although there is a large literature on social skills deficits in students with learning disabilities, the results of this study tend to confirm the hypothesis that these deficits may be a result of emotional or behavior disorders rather than of learning disabilities itself (Lopez et al., 1996).

Estimates of learning disabilities in children with ADHD, however, are not the same as estimates of children with ADHD who are actually found eligible for learning disabilities in the schools (Forness & Kavale, in press). Few studies have specifically examined the latter issue because special education research traditionally focuses on existing categories of disability as defined in the Individuals with Disabilities Education Act (IDEA). Therefore, we selected only three studies from 1990 to the present for review here because changes in reauthorization of IDEA and in public awareness of ADHD issues in school render previous studies less relevant to present policy and practice. MacMillan, Gresham, and Bocian (1998) studied children in grades two to four across several school districts who were currently being referred for special education. They found that, of 61 children classified as learning disabled by the schools during that period, 19 (31.1%) had been diagnosed by research diagnostic criteria as ADHD. Although these diagnoses were not confirmed by structured interview, extensive behavioral and social skill ratings were used to establish diagnoses. Bussing, Zima, Belin and Forness (1998) screened for ADHD in 499 children in both learning disabilities and emotional disturbance classrooms, also in grades two to four, and found that 90 who screened positive for ADHD were in learning disabilities and 58 in emotional disturbance programs. However, only 59 of those in learning disabilities programs were subsequently confirmed as ADHD on structured interview. Extrapolating from the total number of children with learning disabilities in the school district involved, these 59 children with ADHD accounted for 16.2% of children in learning disabilities classrooms. McConaughy, Mattison, and Peterson (1994) used the borderline clinical cutoff point for attention problems on the teacher version of the Child Behavior Checklist (CBCL) with 366 children in learning disabilities programs and 366 children in emotional disturbance programs across samples in three different states. They found 28.1% of children with presumed ADHD in learning disabilities programs.

Although the MTA study has examined special education placements of children with ADHD, data are not available on what proportion children with ADHD represent in special education programs. Several studies on comorbidity of ADHD in learning disabilities samples are available but only the three studies reviewed above contain data on specific special education eligibility. Although the Bussing et al. study is probably the most definitive in terms of ADHD ascertainment, the MacMillan and McConaughy studies have somewhat more representative samples and cannot be discounted, so no particular rationale for weighing among these three studies presents itself. The average percentage of children across these three studies is approximately 25% of children in learning disabilities programs who have ADHD.

Eligibility category cannot, according to IDEA, be linked to classroom placement. One might nonetheless predict that children with ADHD who have higher rates of psychiatric comorbidity would be placed in the emotional disturbance category and thus be more frequently found in segregated settings based on their level of need. Such is not necessarily the case. Bussing, Zima, Belin, and Forness (1998) found no significant differences in levels of comorbid conduct or oppositional disorders, depression, or anxiety disorders between two groups of children with ADHD who were in learning disabilities versus emotional disturbance programs, although presence of comorbid learning disabilities in either group was not available. In another study (Lopez et al., 1996), no IQ or achievement differences were found between two groups of children within learning disabilities programs; one group had ADHD and the other were presumably free of emotional or behavioral disorders. Measured social skills were significantly lower, however, in the ADHD group. These data reflect the complexity of issues regarding academic versus behavioral issues in placement of children with ADHD.

Presence of comorbid psychiatric disorders may nonetheless distinguish between children with ADHD who are eligible for special education and those who are not. Comorbid conduct or oppositional disorders appear to distinguish elementary school boys with ADHD or related disorders who were eligible for the emotional disturbance category from those who were not (Mattison & Forness, 1995). In another study, children with ADHD + CD were generally lower across several areas of academic achievement than those with "pure" ADHD, although both groups were quite similar on measures of intelligence (Forness, Youpa, Hanna et al., 1992). School children with ADHD + CD have likewise been found not only to be significantly lower on a variety of academic and social interaction measures than nondisabled children; but, on most of these measures, they were also significantly lower than children with other emotional or behavioral disorders (Gresham, MacMillan, Bocian, Ward, and Forness, in press).

The point here is that the impact on segregated classrooms by children with ADHD who are eligible for special education is likely to be significant. Such children may be more likely to have comorbid academic or behavioral problems that distinguish them even from non-ADHD children in the same special education classrooms. Such children also seem equally likely to appear in either learning disabilities or emotional disturbance programs. Teachers in learning disabilities classrooms may be less prepared to deal with their emotional or behavioral problems, and teachers in emotional disturbance classrooms may be less prepared to deal with their academic deficiencies. The nature of children with ADHD who find themselves in segregated special education classrooms may thus push the outer limits of such classrooms as effective special education resources.

Thorough diagnosis that identifies co-occurring conditions may offer the opportunity for collateral therapies to support the school and home settings. For example, children with ADHD often benefit from stimulant medication. In a "review of reviews" synthesizing the literature on the effects of stimulant medication on the diagnostic symptoms and associated features of ADHD, Swanson et al. (1993) noted that stimulant medication provides temporary management of the diagnostic symptoms (overactivity, inattention, impulsivity) and associated features (deportment, aggression, social interaction, and academic productivity) of ADHD. Forness, Kavale, & Crenshaw (1999) found similar results in their meta-analysis with the largest effect of stimulant medication on core components of ADHD. Academic outcome variables did not show as robust an effect as behavioral variables, but demonstrated better results when measured with classroom measures (e.g., percentage of work completed, accuracy on classroom assignments) as opposed to academic achievement tests. A large (579 children with ADHD beween the ages of 7-9.9 years), long-term (14 mos.) multimodality treatment (MTA) study of children with ADHD sponsored by the National Institute of Mental Health and co-sponsored by the Department of Education compared four treatment groups: medication management, psychosocial treatment, combined treatment, and community treatment/assessment and referral (MTA Cooperative Group, 1999). Results on the 14-month follow-up showed that combined treatment was superior to behavioral treatment in benefiting ADHD symptoms of inattention, hyperactivity/impulsivity, (MTA Cooperative Group, 1999). Combined treatment also had a greater effect than behavioral treatment on ratings of oppositional/aggressive behaviors, reported internalizing problems, and individual achievement scores in reading. There are clear benefits for children who are positive responders to medication. Recognizing co-occurring ADHD and providing information to parents on the potential benefits of medication may offer parents an opportunity to enhance school and home interventions.

Forness and Kavale, in press reviewed the types of special interventions that teachers report using with children with ADHD. These interventions include changing seating, behavior modification, time out, shortened assignments, one-to-one instruction, special consultation, peer tutoring, frequent breaks, and assignment format (Reid, Maag, & Vasa, 1993). Teachers in general education rank one-to-one instruction and consultation with colleagues much lower than teachers in special education. In fact, only one intervention, changing seating, was reportedly used by more than 40% of teachers in general education settings. Teachers in special education, on the other hand, reported much higher rates of use in that the first seven interventions were reportedly used by 44% to 72% of these teachers.

Meta-analysis of interventions for ADHD reveal only 63 studies of which all but 25 were single-subject research (Dupaul & Eckert, 1997). Only eight studies in this meta-analysis employed a control group, and 17 studies were pre–post designs. Effect sizes were .45 and .64, respectively, for effectiveness of ADHD interventions from these two groups of studies. Note that effect size (ES) is similar to a standard deviation unit, usually ranging from 0 to 1 or greater, and that an ES of .40 indicates moderate effectiveness while ESs above .50 are considered to be much more substantial (Forness & Kavale, 1994). Comparisons between those interventions done in special education settings versus those used in general education classes suggested a clear advantage for interventions done in special (ES = 1.24) over general education (ES = .49) settings.

DISCUSSION

Current delivery systems within general education for providing intervention to students with comorbid ADHD and learning disabilities have limitations in effectively meeting the range of behavioral, academic, social, and emotional needs presented by these children. The range of identified needs of children with ADHD and learning disabilities are on an academic and a behavioral continuum. Children with ADHD fall on the extreme end of the continuum with behavior problems of hyperactivity, impulsivity, and attention. Children with learning disabilities have greater difficulty in acquiring academic skills using traditional methods of instruction. However, implementation of strategies both for managing classroom behaviors and for individualizing instruction increase the range of children who can be served effectively in the general education classroom. The "positive side effect" of learning strategies to assist children with ADHD and learning disabilities is that all children can benefit.

Many children who do not technically meet the criteria necessary to qualify for a diagnosis of ADHD and special education under "OHI" or section 504 accommodations may nonetheless benefit from a structured behavioral program. Children who do not meet the discrepancy criteria for learning disabilities may still require specialized remedial strategies to allow them to meet their potential. If children with ADHD and co-occuring learning disabilities are to be routinely served in general education, changes in teacher training programs, district inservice training programs, school psychology training programs, and schoolwide behavior management programs that translate research into practice need to be explored.

As stated above, the behavioral symptoms of children with ADHD are common behaviors that all children at some time exhibit. Although children with ADHD emit these behaviors at a higher rate and to a greater extent than their non-ADHD peers, they are not unique behaviors. For example, non-ADHD children sometimes interrupt, make noises that disrupt the class, have difficulty completing academic tasks, and get out of their seats without permission. Training in the use of behavior modification strategies has not been an integral a part of teacher training (Andersen, Kratochwill, & Bergen, 1986; Kotkin, 1995). Teachers who develop skills in behavior modification to address the problem behaviors of students with ADHD are better equipped to manage the less frequent and extreme problem behaviors of non-ADHD students that routinely occur in general education classrooms. This would serve to improve general classroom management, provide early effective intervention for students with ADHD, and reduce the impact of disruptive behavior on the classroom.

To address the fact that the majority of teachers currently teaching are not trained in behavior modification, alternative training programs that provide on-the-job training should be explored. School psychologists or other trained support staff can supervise teachers in the implementation of behavioral interventions in the classroom. Instructional aides can be trained in the use of behavioral strategies to support the teacher in providing more intensive behavioral interventions to students with ADHD (Kotkin, 1995, Kotkin, 1998; Swanson, 1992). Faculty can design training programs in community colleges, and undergraduate programs can be designed to certificate instructional aides as specially trained paraprofessional behavioral specialists. Trained paraprofessionals can intervene directly with targeted students under the supervision of the teacher and school psychologist.

The Irvine Paraprofessional Program (IPP) is an example of such a model (Kotkin, 1995, Kotkin, 1998, Swanson, 1992). Students with behavioral problems are identified for intervention by the student study team. In this model, a trained paraprofessional is assigned to the teachers classroom for a 12–16-week period to provide direct intervention to the targeted student while providing assistance to the teacher in general classroom management. Every other week the teacher is provided behavioral consultation by the school psychologist in 45–60-minute consultations. The school psychologist assists the teacher in making modifications to the classroom to strengthen the existing behavior management program in order to take over the intervention at the end of the 12–16-week period. The goal is to fade the initially intensive program of frequent feedback and reinforcement to a level the teacher can implement alone. In addition to providing direct intervention with the targeted student, the paraprofessional models behavioral strategies and provides objective data on the effectiveness of intervention. The teacher learns behavior management strategies through consultation and supervision by the school psychologist and observation of the paraprofessional. Through on-the-job training, the teacher learns behavioral strategies that can benefit all students. The recognition of comorbidity in children with learning disabilities and ADHD has underscored the need for changes in education to broaden the training of teachers and support staff in skills previously thought to be only in the realm of special education. As stated earlier, the positive side effect of developing effective programs for children with co-occurring learning disabilities and ADHD is a more effective program for all children.

REFERENCES

Abikoff, H., Gittleman-Kein, R., & Klein, D. (1997). Validation of a classroom observation code for hyperactive children. *Journal of Consulting and Clinical Psychology, 45*, 772–783.

American Psychiatric Association. (1968). *Diagnostic and Statistical Manual of Mental Disorders (2nd ed.).* Washington, DC: author.

American Psychiatric Association. (1980). *Diagnostic and Statistical Manual of Mental Disorders (3rd ed.).* Washington, DC: author.

American Psychiatric Association. (1994). *Diagnostic and Statistical Manual of Mental Disorders (4th ed.).* Washington, DC: author.

Andersen, T. K., Kratochwill, T. R., & Bergan, J. R. (1986). Training teachers in behavioral consultation and therapy: An analysis of verbal behaviors. *Jounal of School Psychology, 24*, 229–241.

Anderson, J. C., Williams, S., Mcgee, R., & Silva, P. A. (1987). DSM-III disorders in preadolescent children. *Archives of General Psychiatry, 44*, 69–76.

August, G. L., & Garfinkel, B. D. (1989). Behavioral and cognitive subtypes of ADHD. *Journal of the American Academy of Child and Adolescent Psychiatry, 28*, 739–748.

Baren, M., & Swanson, J. M. (1996). How not to diagnose ADHD. *Contemporary Pediatrics, 13*, 53–64.

Barkley, R. A. (1990). *Attention Deficit Hyperactivity Disorder: A handbook for diagnosis and treatment.* New York: Guildford Press.

Barkley, R. A., Dupaul, G. J., & McMurray, M. B. (1990). Attention deficit disorder with and without hyperactivity: Clinical response to three dose levels of methylphenidate. *Pediatrics, 87,* 519–531.

Barkley, R. A., Fischer, M., Edelbrock, C. S., & Smallish, L. (1991). The adolescent outcome of hyperactive children diagnoses by research criteria: Mother-child interactions, family conflicts and maternal psychopathology. *Journal of Child Psychology and Psychiatry, 32,* 233–256.

Biederman, J., Farone, S., Mick, E., & Lelone, E. (1995). Psychiatric comorbidity among referred juveniles with major depression: Facts or artifact ? *Journal of the American Academy of Child and Adolescent Psychiatry, 34,* 579–590.

Biederman, J., Newcorn, J., & Sprich, S. (1991). Comorbidity of attention deficit hyperactivity disorder with conduct, depressive, anxiety, and other disorders. *American Journal of Psychiatry, 148,* 564–577.

Bussing, R., Zima, B. T., Belin, T. R., & Forness, S. R. (1998). Children who qualify for and SED programs: Do they differ in level of ADHD symptoms and comorbid psychiatric conditions? *Journal of Emotional Disorders, 22,* 85–97.

Cantwell, D. P., & Baker, L. (1992). Association between attention deficit-hyperactivity disorder and learning disorders. In S. E. Shaywitz & B. E. Shaywitz (Eds.), *Attention deficit disorder comes of age* (pp. 145–164). Austin, TX: Pro-ED.

Cantwell, D. P., & Satterfield, J. H. (1978). Prevalence of academic achievement in hyperactive childern. *Journal of Pediatric Psychology, 3,* 168–171.

Clements, S. D. (1966). *Minimal brain dysfunction in children: Terminology and identification.* (Public Health Service Publication no. 1415). Washington, DC: U.S. Department of Health, Education, and Welfare.

Cunningham, C. E., & Barkley, R. A. (1978). The role of academic failure in hyperactive behavior. *Jounal of Learning Disabilities, 11,* 15–21.

Del'Homme, M., Kasari, C., Forness, S.R., & Bagley, R. (1996). Pre-referral intervention and children at risk for emotional or behavioral disorders. *Education and Treatment of Children, 19,* 272–285.

Diagnostic and Statistical Manual of Mental Disorders. (3rd ed. rev.). Washington DC: Author.

Douglas, V. I. (1980). Higher mental processes in hyperactive children: Implications for training. In R. M. Knights & D. J. Baker (Eds.), *Treatment of hyperactive and learning disordered children* (pp. 65–91). Baltimore, MD: University Park Press.

Duncan, B. B., Forness, S. R., & Hartsough, C. (1995). Student identified as seriously emotionally disturbed in day treatment classroom: Cognitive, psychiatric and special education characteristics. *Behavioral Disorder, 20,* 238–252.

Dupaul, G. J., & Eckert, T. Z. (1997). The effects of school-based interventions for attention deficit hyperactivity disorder: A meta analysis. *School Psychology Review,* 26:1, 5–27.

Dykman, R. A., & Ackerman, P. T. (1992). Attention deficit disorder and specific reading disability: separate but often overlapping disorders. In S. E. Shaywitz & B. A. Shaywitz (Eds.), *Attention deficit disorder comes of age* (pp.165–183). Austin, TX: PRO-ED.

Forness, S. R. (1990). Resolving the definitional and diagnositic issues of serious emotional disturbance in the schools. In S. Braaten & G. Wrobel (Eds.), *Perspectives on the diagnosis and treatmen of students with emotional behavioral disorders* (pp. 1–15). Minneapolis, MN: CCBD.

Forness, S. R., Kavale, K. A., and Crenshaw, T. M. (1999). Stimulant medicated revisited: Effective treatment of children with ADHD. Journal of emotional and behavioral problems vol. 7, 230–235.

Forness, S. R., Kavale, K. A. (1994). Meta-analysis in intervention research: Methods and implications. In J. Rothman & J. Thomas (Eds.), *Intervention research; effective methods for professional practice* (pp. 117–131). Chicago, IL: Haworth Press.

Forness, S. R., & Kavale, K. (In press). Impact of ADHD on school systems. In P. Jensen & J. R. Cooper (Eds.), *NIH Consensus Conference*, Bethesda, MD.

Forness, S. R., Kavale, K. A., & Lopez, M. (1993). Conduct disorders in school: Special education eligibility and co-morbidity. *Journal of Emotional and Behavioral Disorders, 1*, 101–108.

Forness, S. R., Kavale, K. A., MacMillan, D. L., Asarnow, J. R., & Duncan, B. R. (1996). Early detection and prevention of emotional or behavioral disorders: Developmental aspects of systems of care. *Behavioral Disorder, 21*, 226–240.

Forness, S. R., & Knitzers, J. (1992). A new proposed definition and terminology to replace "Serious Emotional Disturbance" In individuals with Disabilities Education Act. School Psychology Review, 21, 12–20.

Forness, S. R., Youpa, D., Hanna, G. L., Cantwell, D. P., & Swanson, J. M. (1992). Classroom instructional characteristics in attention deficit hyperactivity disorder: Comparison of pure and mixed subgroups. *Behavior Disorders, 17*, 115–125.

Goodman, G., & Poillion, M. J. (1992). ADD: Acronym for any dysfunction or difficulty. *Journal of Special Education, 26*, 37–56.

Gresham, F. M., MacMillan, D. L., Bocian, K., Ward, S. L., & Forness, S. R. (In press). Comorbidity of hyperactivity impulsivity − inattention + conduct problems: risk factors in social, affective, and academic domains. *Journal of Abnormal Child Psychology*.

Halperin, J., Gittleman, R., Klein, D., & Rudel, R. (1984). Reading disabled hyperactive children: A distinct subgroup of attention deficit disorder with hyperactivity? *Journal of Abnormal Child Psychology, 12*, 1–14.

Hinshaw, S. P. Academic underachievement, attention deficits, and aggression: Comorbidity and implications for intervention. *Journal Of Consulting and Clincal Psychology, 60*, 893–903.

Holborrow, P. L., & Berry, P. S. (1986). Hyperactivity and learning difficulties. *Journal of Learning Disabilities, 19*, 426–431.

Kavale, K., & Forness, S. (1987). The far side of heterogeneity: A cortical analysis of empirical subtyping research in learning disabilities. *Journal of Learning Disabilities, 20*, 374–382.

Kavale, K., & Forness, S. R. (1998). Covariance in learning disabilities and behavior disorders: An examination of classification and placement. In T. Scruggs & M. Mastropieri (Eds.), *Advances in Learning and Behavioral Disabilities: Vol. 12* (pp. 1–14). Greenwich, CT: JAI Press.

Kavale, K. A., & Forness, S. (1995). *The nature of learning disabilities*. Mahwah, NJ: Erlbaum.

Kotkin, R. A. (1995). The Irvine Paraprofessional Program; using paraprofessionals in serving students with ADHD. *Intervention in School and Clinic, 30*, 235–240.

Kotkin, R. A. (1998). Irvine Paraprofessional Program (IPP): A promising practice for serving students with ADHD. *Journal of Learning Disabilities, 31*:6, 556–564.

Lahey, B. B., Schaughency, E. A., Hynd, G. W., Carlson, C. C., & Nieves, N. (1987). Attention deficit disorder with and without hyperactvity: Comparison of behavioral characteristics of clinic referred children. *Journal of the American Academy of Child and Adolescent Psychiatry, 19*, 611–622.

Lambert, N. M., & Sandoval, J. (1980). The prevalence of learning disabilities in a in a sample of children considered hyperactive. *Journal of Abnormal Child Psychology, 8*, 33–50.

Lloyd, M., Forness, S. R., & Kavale, K. (1996). Some methods are more effective than others. *Intervention in School and Clinic, 19*, 286–299.

Loney, J., & Milich, R. (1982). Hyperactivity, inattention, and aggression in clinical practice. In M. Wolraich & D. K. Routh (Eds.), *Advances in behavioral pediatrics*. Vol. 2. (pp. 113–145). Greenwich, CT: JAI Press.

Lopez, M., Forness, S. R., MacMillan, D. L., Bocian, K., & Gresham, F. M. (1996). Children with attention deficit hyperactivity disorder and emotional of behavioral disorders in the primary grades: Inappropriate placement in the learning disabilities category. *Education and Treatment of Children, 19*, 286–299.

MacMillan, D. L., Gresham, F. M., & Bocian, K. (1998). Discrepancy between definition of learning disabilities and school practices: An empirical investigation. *Journal of Learning Disabilities, 31,* 314–326.

Mattison, R. E., & Forness, S. R. (1995). The role of psychiatric and other mental health services in special education placement decisions for children with emotional or behavioral disorders. In J. M. Kaufman, J. W. Lloyd, D. Hallahan, & T. A. Astuto. (Eds.), *Issues in Educational Placement of Children with Emotional or Behavioral Disorders* (pp. 119–160). Hillsdale, NJ: Lawrence Erlbaum Associates, Publishers.

McConaughy, J. H., Mattison, R. E., & Peterson, R. (1994). Behavioral / emotional problems of children with serious emotional disturbance and learning disabilities. *School Psychology Review, 23,* 81–98.

McGee, R., & Share, D. L., (1988). Attention deficit-hyperactivity disorder and academic failure: Which comes first and what should be treated? *Journal of the American Academy of Child and Adolescent Psychiatry, 27,* 318–325.

McGee, R., Share, R. L., Anderson, J., & Silva, P. A. (1986). The relationship between specific reading retardation, general reading backwardness, and behavioral problems in a large sample of Dunedin boys. *Journal of Child Psychology and Psychiatry, 27,* 597–610.

Mercer, C. D., Jordan, L., Allsopp, D. H., Mercer, A. R. (1996). Learning disabilities definitions and criteria used by state educationa departments. *Learning Disabilities Quarterly, 19,* 217–232.

MTA Cooperative Group. (1999). A 14-month randomized clinical trial of treatment strategies for attention-deficit/hyperactivity disorder. *Archives of General Psychiatry, 56,* 1073–1086.

National Institutes of Health. *Consensus Development Conference on Diagnosis and Treatment of Attention Deficit Disorder (ADHD).* Bethseda, MD: National Institutes of Health.

Pfiffner, L. J., & Barkley, R. A. (1998). Educational placement and classroom management. In R. A. Barkley (Ed.), *Attention Deficit Hyperactivity Disorder: A handbook for diagnosis and treatment* (2nd ed.) (pp. 458–490). New York: Guildford Press.

Prior, M., & Sanson, A. (1986). Attention deficit disorder with hyperactivity: A critique. *Journal of Othopsychiatry, 27,* 307–319.

Reeves, J. C., Werry, J. S., Elkind, G. S., & Zametkin, A. (1987). Attention deficit, conduct, oppositional, and anxiety disorders in children: II. Clinical characteristics. *Journal of the American Academy or Child and Adolescent Psychiatry, 26,* 144–155.

Reid, R., Maag, J. W., & Vasa, S. F. (1993). Attention deficit hyperactivity disorder as a disabiltiy category: A critique. *Exceptional Children, 60,* 198–214.

Reschly, D. J., & McMaster-Beyer, M. (1991). Influences of degree level, affiliation and accreditation status on school psychology graduate education. *Professional Psychology: Research and Practice, 22,* 368–374.

Richters, J. E., Arnold, L. D., Jensen, P. S., Abbikoff, H., Conners, C. K., Greenhill, L. L., Hechtman, L., Hinshaw, S. P., Pelham, W. E., & Swanson, J. M. (1995). NIMH collaborative multisite multimodal treatment study of children with ADHD: I. Background and rationale. *Journal of American Academy of Child Adolescent Psychiatry, 34,* 987–1000.

Rutter, M. (1983). Behavioral studies: Questions and findings on the concept of a distinctive syndrome. In M. Rutter (Ed.), *Developmental Neuropsychology,* (pp. 259–279). New York: Guildford Press.

Safer, D. J., & Allen, R. D. (1976). *Hyperactive children: diagnosis and management.* Baltimore, MD: University Park Press.

Schacht, T., & Nathan, P. E. (1977). But is it good for psychologists? Appraisal and status of DSM-III. *American Psychologist, 32,* 1017–1025.

Shaffer, D. & Greenhill, L. (1979). A critical note on the predictive validity of "the hyperkinetic syndrome." *Journal of Child Psychology and Psychiatry, 20,* 61–72.

Shaywitz, B. A., Fletcher, J. M., & Holahan, J. M. (1995). Cognitive profiles of reading disability: Interrelationships between reading disability and attention hyperactivity disorder. *Child Neuropsychology*, 1, 170.

Shaywitz, S. E., & Shaywitz, B. A. (1988). Attention deficit disorder: Current perspectives. In J. F. Kavanagh & T. J. Truss (Eds.), *Learning disabilities: Proceedings of the national conference* (pp. 368–523). Parkton, MD:York Press.

Shaywitz, S. E., & Shaywitz, B. A. (1991). Introduction to the special series on attention deficit disorder. *Journal of Learning Disabilities*, 24, 68–72.

Silver, L. B. (1981). The relationship between learning disabilities, hyperactivity, distractibility, and behavioral problems: A clinical analysis. *Journal of the American Academy of Child Psychiatry*, 20, 385–397.

Silver, L. B. (1990). Attention deficit-hyperactivity disorder: Is it a learning disability or a related disorder? *Journal of Learning Disabilities*, 23, 394–397.

Standford, L. D., & Hynd, G. W. (1994). Congruence of behavioral symptomatology in children with ADD/H, ADD/WO, and learning disabilities. *Journal of Learning Disabilities*, 27, 243–253.

Swanson, J. M. (1992). *School-based assessment and interventions for ADD students.* Irvine, CA: K. C. Publishing.

Swanson, J. M., Hanley, T., Simpson, S., Davies, M., Shulte, A., Wells, K., Hinshaw, S., Abikoff, H., Hechtman, L., Pelham, B., Hoza, B., Severe, J., Forness, S., Gresham, F., Arnold, E.L. (In press). Evaluation of learning disorders in children with a psychiatric disorder: An example from the multimodality treatment study of ADHD (MTA). In *Learning Disabilities: Implications for Psychiatric Treatment.* Washington, DC: American Psychiatric Press Inc.

Swanson, J. M., McBurnett, K., Wigal, T., Pfiffner, L. J., Lerner, M. A., Williams, L., Christian, D. L., Tam, L., Willicutt, E., Crowley, K., Clevenger, W., Khouzam, N., Woo, C., Crinella, F. M., & Fischer, T. (1993). Effect of stimulation medication on children with attention deficit disorder: A "review of reviews." *Exceptional Children*, 60:2, 154–162.

Szatmari, P., Offord, D. R., & Boyle, M. H. (1989). Ontario child health study: Prevalence of attention deficit disorder with hyperactivity. *Journal of Child Psychology and Psychiatry*, 30, 205–218.

Trites, R. J., & LaPrade, K. (1983). Evidence for an independent syndrome of hyperactivity. *Journal of Child Psychology and Psychiatry*, 24, 573–586.

U. S. Department of Education. (1990–1997). *Twelfth through Nineteenth Annual Congress on the implementation of The Individuals with Disabilities Act.* Washington, DC: U.S. Office of Special Education Programs.

U. S. Department of Education. (1998). *Twentieth Annual Report to Congress on the Implementation of the Individuals with Disabilities Education Act.* Washington, DC: U.S. Office of Special Education Programs.

Weller, C., & Strawser, S. (1987). Adaptive behavior of subtypes of learning disabled of learning disabled individuals. *Journal of Special Education*, 21, 101–115.

Wells, K., Pelham, W. E., Kotkin, R. A., Hoza, B., Abikoff, H., Arnold, L. E., Abramowitz, A., Cantwell, D. P., Conner, C. K., Del Carmen, R., Elliot, G., Greenhill, L. L., Hechtman, L. T., Hinshaw, S. P., Jensen, P. S., March, J. S., Schiller, E., Severe, J., & Swanson, J. M. (in press). Psychosocial treatment strategies in the MTA study: Rationale methods, and critical issues in design and implementation. *Journal of Abnormal Child Psychology*.

Werry, J. S., Reeves, J. C., & Elkind, G. S. (1987). Attention deficit, conduct, oppositional and anxiety disorder in children: I. A review of research on differentiating characteristics. *Journal of the American Academy of Child and Adolescent Psychiatry*, 26, 133–143.

Whalen, C. K., Henker, B., & Dotemoto, S. (1980). Methylphenidate and hyperactivity: Effects on teacher behaviors. *Science*, 208, 1280–1282.

Chapter 5

Social Functioning of Students with Learning Disabilities

Dheepa Sridhar
Sharon Vaughn
The University of Texas at Austin

INTRODUCTION

When the definition of learning disabilities was established about 25 years ago, it was in response to the needs expressed by parents and teachers advocating for children who were not mentally retarded but exhibited unexpected underachievement (Keogh, 1970). However, it soon became apparent that the needs of individuals with learning disabilities (LD) extended beyond the academic domain (Cruickshank, 1981b). The same difficulties that cause learning problems in students with LD are believed by some to cause difficulties in social functioning.

Although the fact that many students with learning disabilities demonstrate poor social functioning is no longer questioned, the characteristic social functioning of students with LD, the cause of such social functioning, and the features of effective interventions in this domain are still being studied (Forness & Kavale, 1991; Gresham, 1992; McIntosh, Vaughn, & Zaragoza, 1991). This chapter presents the prevalence and social characteristics of students with LD, causes of these deficits, their long-term implications, and interventions used to enhance social functioning.

Considering the negative consequences of poor social functioning (Parker & Asher, 1987; Sabornie, Marshall, & Ellis, 1990; Vaughn, Hogan, Kouzekanani, & Shapiro, 1990; Wiener, Harris, & Shirer, 1990), and the long-term effects of these consequences to the well-being of individuals (Alexander & Entwisle, 1988; Dalley, Bolocofsky, Alcorn, & Baker, 1992;

Health & Wiener, 1996; Seidel & Vaughn, 1991), interest in social functioning and in interventions that enhance social functioning is increasing.

PREVALENCE AND SOCIAL CHARACTERISTICS OF STUDENTS WITH LD

Findings from several studies suggest that while not all students with LD demonstrate deficits in social functioning, many of them differ significantly from their peers in this area (Foss, 1991; Jarvis & Justice, 1992; Merrell, 1991; Swanson & Malone, 1992). However, this should not be interpreted to suggest that there are converging findings regarding the social functioning of students with LD. This is likely a function of the range of social behaviors exhibited by students with LD, including students with LD who demonstrate very poor social behaviors and those for whom social functioning is a strength.

The social functioning of students with LD has been the subject of research for more than a decade. Findings from initial research suggest that almost 50% of students with LD are not well accepted by their peers and are at risk for social isolation (Stone & La Greca, 1990; Vaughn, McIntosh, & Spencer-Rowe, 1991). A quantitative synthesis of research conducted on the social skill deficits among students with LD indicates that approximately 75% of students with LD manifest social skill deficits that distinguish them from comparison samples of non-LD students (Kavale & Forness, 1996). It is important to note that while many students with LD can be distinguished from their non-LD peers by their level of social functioning, this does not mean that their social functioning is so dysfunctional as to warrant intervention. For many students with LD, lower social functioning than their peers does not mean highly problematic social behavior.

Studies indicate that students with learning disabilities demonstrate social difficulties that are recognized by parents (McConaughy & Ritter, 1986), teachers (Seidel & Vaughn, 1991; Vaughn, Hogan, Kouzekanani, & Shapiro, 1990), and peers (Seidel & Vaughn, 1991; Stone & La Greca, 1990).

When compared to non-LD peers, students with LD appear to display appropriate conversational skills less frequently and inconsistently (Hartas & Donahue, 1997; Mathinos, 1991), and demonstrate lower levels of social competence and behavioral adjustment (Merrell, 1991), fewer social problem-solving skills (Hartas & Donahue, 1997; Shondrick, Serafica, Clark, & Miller 1992; Toro, Weissberg, Guare, & Liebenstein, 1990), and fewer social skills (Bramlett, Smith, & Edmonds, 1994). For example, in the study conducted by Shondrick, Serafica, Clark, and Miller (1992), third- and fourth-grade boys with and without LD were assessed using the Test of Interpersonal Problem Solving (TIPS). Students were presented with vignettes depicting an age-appropriate dilemma followed by a series of standard questions. Examination of student responses indicated that students with LD scored below average in defining a problem and generating effective solutions when compared to their non-LD peers (Shondrick et al., 1992).

Furthermore, students with LD appear to be disproportionately rejected by peers (Stone & La Greca, 1990), both prior to and after identification (Vaughn & Hogan, 1990; Vaughn, Hogan, Kouzekanani, & Shapiro, 1990). Peer acceptance appeared to decline with time (Vaughn et al., 1990) suggesting that peer rejection persisted over time. A study of middle school students with LD suggests that students with LD were more lonely, received more threats, had personal items stolen more often, and participated less in within-school and out-of-school activities when compared to their non-LD peers. Students with LD were also rated by regular classroom teachers as demonstrating lower social competence than non-LD peers (Sabornie, 1994).

CAUSES OF POOR SOCIAL FUNCTIONING

The academic challenges faced by students with learning disabilities may contribute to their poor social functioning (Vogel & Forness, 1992). Some studies suggest social functioning to be caused by neurological dysfunction while others suggest information-processing deficits are associated with both the academic and social difficulties experienced by students with LD.

Neurological Dysfunction

Attempts to study the neurological basis of LD have been a major area of research over the last three decades. Research indicates that LD may be due to a congenital neurological deficit (Marshall & Hynd, 1993), and that this deficit may also be the cause of various social difficulties (Vogel & Forness, 1992). According to Cruickshank (1981a), learning disabilities, when correctly identified, are neurological in nature (p. 339). The modified definition of LD embodies this neurological impairment hypothesis by stating: "These disorders are intrinsic to the individual and presumed to be due to central nervous system dysfunction" (Interagency Committee on Learning Disabilities [ICLD], 1987, p. 550).

Research conducted within a neurodevelopment model suggests the emergence of specific subtypes of LD (Rourke & Fuerst, 1992; Shapiro, Lipton, & Krivit, 1992). One such subtype is nonverbal learning disabilities (NVLD). Students with NVLD appear to demonstrate a characteristic cluster of assets such as auditory perception and deficits such as tactile perception (Little, 1993; Rourke & Fuerst, 1992). These primary neurological assets and deficits are thought to lead to certain secondary neurological assets such as auditory attention and deficits such as visual attention/tactile attention. According to Rourke and Fuerst (1992), students with LD who possess the assets of auditory perception, simple motor functioning, and memorizing of rote material also demonstrate deficits in tactile and visual perception, complex psychomotor functioning, and responding appropriately to novel material. These primary neurological deficits are suggested to lead to secondary assets involving auditory/verbal attention and deficits involving tactile attention, visual attention, and exploratory behavior (Rourke & Fuerst, 1992). A study conducted by Ozols and Rourke (1985) focused on the psychosocial functioning of students with NVLD and students with typical LD. Performance of the two groups of students were compared on four exploratory measures of responsiveness and social judgment. The results indicated that students with typical LD outperformed students with NVLD on tasks requiring nonverbal responses. However, students with NVLD outperformed students with typical LD on tasks requiring verbal responses. Loveland, Fletcher, and Bailey (1990) studied the nonverbal communication of events in students with various subtypes of LD. Their results regarding the social perception and social judgment of students with NVLD support the results obtained through earlier studies. The psychopathological manifestation of these neurological deficits and the discrepancies between assets and deficits exhibited by students with NVLD appear to progress with time (Rourke & Fuerst, 1992).

A review of NVLD conducted by Semrud-Clikeman and Hynd (1990) indicates that deficits in social skills of some students with LD may be caused by right hemispheric dysfunction (Gresham, 1992). Injury to the head and particularly to the right hemisphere seems to increase the risk of NVLD (Rourke, 1987). Right hemispheric dysfunction has been implicated in difficulties in maintaining social relationships, interpreting the intentions of others, and self-help skills (Gresham, 1992). Although research investigating the neurological basis of LD is extensive, neurological deficits have not been demonstrated to be the cause of LD.

Information-Processing Deficits

A review of social difficulties experienced by students with LD indicates that many students with LD demonstrate difficulties involving their ability to perceive, interpret, and process social information (Rudolph & Luckner, 1991). This impaired perception usually exerts a significant impact on accurate interpretation of social situations, which further leads to inappropriate responses, and ultimately social isolation (Foss, 1991).

A study investigating students' ability to accurately interpret social situations was conducted with students with LD in secondary schools and a community college (Jarvis & Justice, 1992). Students in this study were presented with a series of four audiotaped stories depicting adult actors in happy, angry, anxious, and sad situations. After the tape was played for the first time, students were asked how the actor felt. The tape was then replayed and students were asked why the actor felt the way he did. Students' responses were recorded and scored for accuracy of interpretation. Results indicated that students with LD were significantly less accurate at interpreting social situations than were their non-LD peers (Jarvis & Justice, 1992).

A similar study conducted by Pearl, Bryan, Fallon, and Herzog (1991) noted that students with LD experienced difficulty in identifying deceptive ments when compared to students without LD. In this study, students in seventh and eighth grades were presented with audiotapes depicting 12 stories. Each story contained sincere, deceptive, sarcastic, and neutral versions. The stories were presented randomly and only one version was presented at a time. Following presentation of each story, students were asked a series of questions to determine the student's recall of the story, understanding of the facts in the story, assessment of the speaker's belief, assessment of the speaker's intent, and the evidence used to determine the speaker's belief and intent. This study indicated that students with LD were more likely to believe that the speaker was sincere but wrong while students without LD were more likely to detect that the speaker was insincere (Pearl et al., 1991).

When compared to non-LD peers, students with LD appear to be less accurate in interpreting emotions, social situations, and predicting consequences (Holder & Kirkpatrick, 1991; Jackson, Enright, & Murdock, 1987; Saloner & Gettinger, 1985). In a study conducted by Pearl and Cosden (1982), students with LD exhibited difficulties in understanding social interactions in vignettes from television soap operas. Specific research involving the nature of the social information-processing by students with LD indicates that compared to low-achieving and average-achieving students, students with LD display a distinct pattern of processing social information inaccurately (Tur-Kaspa & Bryan, 1994). In this study students with LD demonstrated a unique difficulty in the encoding of social information and in their tendency to select incompetent self-generated solutions to social situations (Tur-Kaspa & Bryan, 1994). This impairment of perception may contribute to the poor social functioning of students with LD, which when untreated ultimately may lead to social isolation, peer rejection, depression, and social isolation (Health & Wiener, 1996; Parker & Asher, 1987).

Students with LD are often described as demonstrating deficits in social perception and visual imagery (Cruickshank, 1985; Foss, 1991).

Early studies indicate that compared to non-LD peers, students with LD performed poorly on social perception tasks (Creasey & Jarvis, 1987; Pearl & Cosden, 1982), and were less accurate in understanding others' thoughts and feelings when these conflicted with their own (Dickstein & Warren, 1980; Wong & Wong, 1980). Dickstein and Warren compared role-taking skills of students with LD aged five to eight with non-LD peers. Results indicated that students with LD demonstrated significantly lower role-taking skills. Further investigation of 20 additional students with LD aged nine to twelve years was conducted to determine whether role-taking skills improved in older students with LD. Results indicated that the older students with LD demonstrated similar role-taking skills as eight-year-old students with LD. Deficits in social perception and cognition are situation-specific and not characteristic of all students with LD (Pearl, Bryan, Fallon, & Herzog, 1991).

LONG-TERM SOCIAL IMPLICATIONS

Neurological and perceptional difficulties are associated with a myriad of sociobehavioral difficulties that have important implications for the social and emotional well-being of students with LD. Studies indicate that most students with LD in all grades are less likely to be rated as popular and more likely to be rejected by peers (Wiener, Harris, & Shirer, 1990). Consequently these students receive higher ratings on measures of loneliness and view themselves as deficient in social skills across grades and cultures (Margalit & Levin-Alyagon, 1994). Students with LD who demonstrate social problems tend to exhibit increasing levels of social withdrawal as they grow older and appear to be at a higher risk for developing "internalized" psychopathology, such as anxiety and depression (Rourke, 1989). A good indicator of the problems in social functioning experienced by many students with LD is the nature of their relationships with others and the students' self-perceptions. Self-perception or self-concept is one of the variables influencing social functioning and has been extensively studied (Vaughn & Elbaum, 1999). We are unable to adequately address self-concept within the scope of this chapter, thus the focus is on the relations of students with others.

Relations with Others

As already noted, many students with LD experience difficulty making and maintaining positive relations with others, including peers and adults such as parents and teachers (McConaughy & Ritter, 1986; Seidel &

Vaughn 1991; Stone & La Greca, 1990; Vaughn, Hogan, Kouzekanani, & Shapiro, 1990). A brief summary of the social relations of students with LD with both peers and adults follows.

Peers

Successful social interactions with peers are associated with social success in school, at work, and in the community. Approximately 16% of students with LD appear to demonstrate the required social skills to be as well-accepted by their peers as students without LD (Gresham & Reschly, 1986). However, 50% to 75% of students with LD (Kavale & Forness, 1996; Stone & La Greca, 1990; Vaughn, McIntosh, & Spencer-Rowe, 1991) seem to lack this skill and are rejected by their peers. Numerous studies indicate that students with LD, as a group, are often rejected by their mainstream peers (Parker & Asher, 1987; Sabornie, Marshall, & Ellis, 1990; Vaughn et al., 1990; Wiener, Harris, & Shirer, 1990). Research suggests that students with LD are likely to be rejected by non-LD peers as early as kindergarten, both prior and subsequent to identification (Vaughn et al., 1990). Studies of peer status of students with LD suggest that few classmates indicate high levels of liking and, in fact, many classmates indicate active dislike for students with LD (Forness & Kavale, 1991; Landau & Milich, 1990). Longitudinal studies of students with LD note that they are less well-accepted by their peers than average-achieving peers over time (Vaughn & Haager, 1994). A study of second-, third-, fourth-, and sixth-grade students with LD suggests that participants were less well-accepted by peers than their low-achieving and high-achieving non-LD peers. In addition, students with LD were viewed by low-achieving and high-achieving non-LD peers as significantly more disruptive and less cooperative (Bursuck, 1989).

Other than the immediate consequences of low peer liking, students experiencing peer rejection are at risk for a variety of negative consequences (Alexander & Entwisle, 1988; Parker & Asher, 1987). Studies suggest peer rejection in the early years to be associated with school dropout (Finn, 1989; Zigmond & Thornton, 1985), social isolation (Seidel & Vaughn, 1991), and later adjustment problems. The social functioning of students with LD that predisposes them for peer rejection is also believed to influence their relations with significant adults.

Adults

Parents and teachers have long known that many students with LD display difficulties in social interaction. However, the specific nature of the social relations between students with LD and significant adults, particularly parents, has not been widely studied. Many of the studies that do exist address teacher–student relations.

Several studies suggest that many teachers hold negative perceptions of students with LD. As early as kindergarten, students with LD are perceived by their teachers as having attention problems and social skill deficits (Vaughn et al., 1990). Students with LD also seem to experience low teacher acceptance (Vaughn et al., 1990), which could be the result of negative perceptions by teachers (Garrett & Crump, 1980). These low perceptions of teachers may also influence the academic performance of students. A study conducted by Juvonen and Bear (1992) indicated that teachers perceived socially adjusted students with LD as less competent than similarly adjusted students without LD. Teachers' perceptions in this study remained stable even in light of the finding that there were no significant differences between students with and without LD in the proportions of students accepted and rejected by peers. A study conducted by Dalley et al. (1992) reveals that teachers recognized the lack of social competency in students with LD and perceived them to exhibit increased depressive symptomatology, depressogenic attributional style, and dysfunctional attitude. Considering that teachers' expectations can become self-fulfilling prophecies, and that teacher and student perceptions of the social acceptance of other students is highly related (Garrett & Crump, 1980), this area of social functioning warrants further research.

Teacher and peer rejection of students with LD appears to start as early as kindergarten (Vaughn et al., 1990) and remains relatively stable (Vaughn & Haager, 1994). Considering the long-term impact of peer rejection (Alexander & Entwisle, 1988; Parker & Asher, 1987) and the contribution of peer rejection to depression (Health & Wiener, 1996), school dropout (Seidel & Vaughn, 1991) and overall social functioning, there has been considerable focus on developing interventions to improve social functioning and peer acceptance. The next section examines interventions used to enhance social functioning of students with LD.

INTERVENTIONS

Significantly greater numbers of students with LD are rejected by peers than non-LD students. A popular assumption regarding the social rejection of students with LD is that it is a result of poor social skills. Considering the long-term negative consequences of peer rejection and social isolation a variety of instructional approaches has been designed to enhance the social skills of students with LD. However, how the interventions are provided often varies. While some studies use peers or adults (a general or special education teacher, researcher, or parent) to provide the intervention, some have investigated the use of technology and differential placements of students as an intervention to improve social functioning. Only studies investigating the effectiveness of interventions in enhancing social functioning of students through interventions involving peers or adults as mediators were examined and are presented according to: (a) who provided the intervention, and (b) intervention effectiveness.

Who Provided the Intervention

The following section examines the various methods by which social interventions are typically provided to students with LD such as by peers and adults. Table 5.1 presents peer interventions investigating the enhancement of social functioning of students with LD.

Peers

An examination of interventions provided by peers reveals that only one of the eight peer-mediated interventions failed to produce a significant effect (Cosden, Goldman, & Hine, 1990). Probable reason for lack of improvement in social functioning of students in the Cosden, Goldman, and Hine (1990) study could be the use of pairing students with LD with each other. Participants may have served as inappropriate models to each other thus not able to decrease the rate of inappropriate social behaviors. In addition, the students did not receive any training in social behavior, but were observed while they worked with a peer with LD on a microcomputer-based writing activity.

However, all of the effective interventions that included a peer component also included an adult component, typically with the adult providing training in social skills. Although this review suggests that pairing of a well-accepted student with a low-accepted student with LD appears to increase the social status of students with LD, the results are confounded by the inclusion of social skills training in the intervention package. The effects of the studies reviewed here could have been due to the social skills training rather than the inclusion of a peer component. Though research on peer models with young students has yielded positive social effects (Fox, 1989; Larson & Gerber, 1987), the direct effect of peers on the social functioning and acceptance of students with LD requires further investigation.

TABLE 5.1

Peer-Mediated Interventions That Investigated Social Functioning of Students with LD

Author/Year	Participants	Duration	Content	Measures	Effects
Cosden, Golden, & Hine (1990)	11 third to seventh graders with LD	One and a half hours, five days a week, for four weeks	Students worked alone as well as in dyads with two different partners during microcomputer-based writing. Paired students with LD with each other.	Sequential analysis of initiations and responses within the dyads. Quantitative measures of story production focussing on measures of fluency. Qualitative measures of story production focusing on the quality/complexity of story.	Student interactions had a negative impact on story production. Students demonstrated higher levels of assertive, demanding behavior than requests for peer information or collaboration.
Fox (1989)	86 fourth to fifth graders with LD	40-minute weekly sessions for eight weeks	Paired each student with LD with a non-LD, same-sex, highly accepted peer. Dyads were divided into four groups; each group received a different instruction. Discovery group engaged in activities to promote discussion of mutual interest. Academic group completed class assignments. Hawthorne effects group met in the treatment setting but engaged in no specific activity. The control group received no specific intervention.	Friendship Rating Instrument (FRI) by peers	The students with LD in the discovery and academic groups increased in peer-acceptance ratings. Students with LD in the Hawthorne effects and control groups did not change in peer-acceptance ratings.

| Larson & Gerber (1987) | Thirty four 16–19 year-old students with LD | A total of 22 30-minute sessions over seven weeks | Students from resource rooms paired with low-achieving non-LD peers. Pairs were assigned to either a full treatment, attention control, or a test control group. Treatment included social metacognitive training on impulse control, and metacognitive awareness and control. | Observations and school-level promotions for appropriate behaviors. | Full treatment group improved significantly when compared to other groups. Students with LD made significantly greater gains than non-LD students. |
| McMahon, Wacker, Sasso, & Melloy, (1994) | Three 3-to-9-year-olds with behavioral and learning disorders | Duration of intervention not reported | Social skills training in the special education classroom provided by an adult focusing on social initiations and sustained responses. Training occurred in three phases: Individual behavioral contracts and social skills training; tangible reinforcements were provided & a peer with a disability was assigned by the teacher to assist in the training of target skills to students during recess. Tangible reinforcements for the pair were contingent on the students' interacting together on the playground. Withdrawal: All training components were removed. | Observations in classrooms and on the playground. Teacher ratings of student behavior. | All three students displayed increased trained behaviors on the playground during training and increases in the duration of peer interactions. Two students maintained high duration of cooperative play. One student did not demonstrate generalization of training effects. All students demonstrated decreased levels of inappropriate behavior and increased levels of appropriate behavior. |

(Continued)

TABLE 5.1
(Continued)

Author/Year	Participants	Duration	Content	Measures	Effects
Mesch, Lew, Johnson, & Johnson (1986)	Five eighth-grade, socially isolated students with LD	Twice a week for 25 weeks	Students grouped into three learning conditions across two content areas. Treatment conditions: cooperative learning with group academic contingencies; cooperative learning with social skills group contingencies; cooperative learning with academic and social skills group contingencies; cooperative learning, no contingencies.	Teacher-made achievement tests. Sociometric measure. Self-assessment. Observations of the nature of verbal interactions.	Students in both content areas improved significantly in the third condition.
Omizo & Omizo (1988)	31 fourth to sixth graders with LD in each group	50-to-60-minute sessions once a week for 10 weeks	Intervention provided in group sessions including working with relaxation training, discussing feelings, and demonstrating nonverbal communication and role-playing.	The Piers-Harris Children's Self-Concept Scale. Social Behavior Assessment.	Students in group counseling sessions scored significantly higher than controls on self-concept and treatment group members were rated by teachers as demonstrating better social skills relative to interpersonal and task-related behaviors.

Trapani (1987)	20 elementary students with LD	Social skills training for seven consecutive school days. Tutoring for 15 days in 20-minute sessions, three times a week	Treatment and comparison groups received direct instruction in five social skills. Treatment group members rehearsed their skills by training nonhandicapped second-grade boys in spelling. Experimental group received feedback from the researcher about the social and academic aspects of the tutoring interaction immediately after each session. Comparison group was not involved in the second phase of the intervention, while the control group had no contact with the researchers.	Classroom observations. Test of Written Spelling. Problem Behavior Identification Checklist.	Significant differences between experimental and control students on use of greetings and answering questions. Treatment group scored significantly higher than the control group on the Test of Written Spelling.
Vaughn, Lancelotta, & Minnis (1988)	One fourth grader with LD	25-minute sessions, three days a week, for 10 weeks	Paired the lowest-accepted student with LD with a same-sex, highly accepted peer and provided social skills training, Mnemonic strategy training, and regular classroom involvement using cognitive behavioral approaches.	Pre/postclassroom social ratings and nominations.	Peer nominations of the target student changed from a status of rejected to popular.
Vaughn, McIntosh, & Spencer-Rowe (1991)	10 third to sixth graders with LD	30-minute sessions, two to three times a week for 20 weeks	Training done in groups of two to four students and included strategies related to making friends and solving interpersonal problems; practicing those skills and teaching those skills to classmates.	Classroom peer ratings and nominations.	Target students received an increased number of peer nominations following intervention.

Adult

The majority of the adult-mediated interventions focused on specific skills to be taught and appear to be effective in enhancing social functioning of students with LD (see Table 5.2). While most interventions involved primarily the teacher and the student, we identified one study in which parents provided a significant component of the intervention (Northcutt, 1986). In this study, third-, fourth-, and fifth-grade students with LD and one parent participated in a nine-week social skills program. The focus of the training was to encourage teacher-pleasing behaviors to enhance teacher–student relationships. However, following treatment, the treatment group did not change relative to the control group on measures of conduct disorder, attention problems, and immaturity as indicated by parents and teachers. In contrast, anecdotal reports and a questionnaire completed by parents reported improvements in behavior for 8 of the 11 students at home.

Although many studies in this review suggest that social skills training enhances social functioning, a synthesis of studies by Kelly (1993) provides results to the contrary. Students with LD in grades one through six were provided a structured learning social skills training program for 50 minutes a week for four weeks. All students received the intervention, which included training in specific social skills, student reports of practicing the social skills learnt at home, and praise and encouragement from the parent. Students were also praised as a group, and each student received a certificate of good performance as a member of a team. The results of the study indicated that the intervention did not influence the rate of positive social behavior in students. However, it raised the social competence and self-efficacy of most students, and these effects were maintained during a follow-up test after five weeks. A possible reason for the lack of change in behavior could be the relatively short duration of the intervention (once a week for four weeks) while the duration of the intervention for other studies ranged from five weeks to six months.

A study conducted by Wiener and Harris (1997) investigated the effects of varying durations of a social skills intervention. Students with LD between ages 9 and 12 years were divided into three groups. Group 1 received a social skills program involving coaching and problem solving for six weeks. Group 2 received the same intervention for 12 weeks, and group 3 served as a no-contact control group. The results indicated that group 1 improved after the intervention while group 2 showed no change and group 3 showed an increase in problem behaviors. Although some studies have suggested that extended interventions may not be as effective as shorter more focused interventions (Schneider & Byrne, 1985), the assignment of students to the various groups could be a factor that influenced the intervention outcomes in this study. Since this study assigned randomly intact classrooms to the various groups as opposed to students, results may be confounded by class dynamics specific to each classroom. Furthermore, pretest scores revealed group 2 to be different from the other two groups on peer nominations for disruptive behavior and aggressiveness. Although this difference was accounted for in the analysis, it is a difference that could help explain the lack of intervention effects on this group. Furthermore, follow-up data for group 1 was collected about a year after the intervention to assess maintenance of the treatment. This data suggests that the group maintained treatment effects.

Three studies were identified that investigated the effects of therapy focusing on specific behaviors on the self-concept and behaviors of students with LD (Abrams, 1985; Lo, 1986; Todd, 1990). Todd (1990) investigated the effects of group problem solving and group therapy on the self-concept and behavior of students with LD. Participants were divided into two treatment groups. Both groups received a week of academic social skills training following which one group received group problem-solving training while the other group received group therapy focussing on feelings. Results indicated that both groups made similar gains on self-concept and decreased inappropriate behavior. Abrams (1985) provided group counseling to students. The counseling included the identification of self-defeating behaviors and feelings and overcoming them through guided imagery. The intervention had a problem-solving component that may have influenced the outcome of enhanced self-concept. Lo (1986) studied the effects of rational emotive education on the self-concept and perception of locus of control orientation of participants. Results indicated that the treatment group increased significantly on dimensions of self-concept and perception of locus of control. It should be noted that the intervention also included training in problem-solving skills, which was correlated with social functioning. Hence, the effects of counseling on behavior warrants further investigation since present studies are confounded by inclusion of social skills and problem-solving skills in the treatment.

Three studies investigated the effects of social skills training combined with coaching, problem solving, and practice or role-playing (Blackbourn, 1989; Conte, Andrews, Loomer, & Hutton, 1995; Wiener & Harris, 1997). Results indicated that students in all the studies who received the treatment acquired specific target skills, improved their sociometric status, or demonstrated a decrease in problem behaviors. It should be noted that all three studies included a coaching component. A follow-up evaluation of the students in the study conducted

TABLE 5.2

Adult-Mediated Interventions That Investigated Social Functioning of Students with LD

Author/Year	Participants	Duration	Content	Measures	Effects
Abrams (1985)	60 sixth to ninth graders with LD	60–90-minute sessions, once a week for 7 weeks	Intervention delivered through the group by school counselor and included group experience designed to eliminate self-defeating behaviors; realization of learnt helplessness; and guided imagery of overcoming barriers to eliminate self-defeating behaviors.	Dimensions of self-concept. Nowicki-Strickland scale.	Intervention improved the self-concept and locus of control orientation in students who received treatment.
Blackbourn (1989)	Four elementary students with LD	Intervention implemented during spring of 1985 and follow-up conducted in fall of 1985	Social skills training provided in the resource room and included the following: discussion, explanation, prompting, corrective feedback, verbal rehearsal, and positive attention with opportunities to practice target behavior under teacher.	Observations	Target students acquired specific behaviors across each of the training environments. Behaviors generalized to environments other than those they were trained in.

Study	Participants	Duration	Intervention	Measures	Results
Conte, Andrews, & Loomer, & Hutton (1995)	Twelve 12-year-old students with LD	Six months	Classroom-based social skills program consisting of coaching, role-playing, and information sharing.	Abbreviated Conners Questionnaire by teachers, Taxonomy of Problem Situations by teachers. Oral solutions to hypothetical situations by students.	Students who received intervention improved their sociometric status and increased problem-solving skills in an interview situation.
Houchens-Nichols (1987)	46 tenth graders with emotional impairments and LD	55-minute sessions, every day for 20 weeks	A personal adjustment curriculum was implemented in small groups to enhance the affective–social skills.	Piers-Harris Children's Self-Concept Scale. Interpersonal Communication Inventory.	Significant differences found between treatment and control groups on both the Interpersonal Communication Inventory and the Piers-Harris Children's Self-Concept Scale. Control group indicated greater awareness of nonverbal aspects of conversation than treatment group.

(Continued)

TABLE 5.2
(Continued)

Author/Year	Participants	Duration	Content	Measures	Effects
Kelly (1993)	12 first to sixth graders	Once a week, 50 minutes for four weeks. Follow-up after five weeks.	Social skills tutoring included self-report homework, parent support system, group praise, and weekly token reinforcement system.	Child Behavior Checklist. Student and Teacher Skill Checklists. Children's Self-Efficacy for Peer Interaction Scale.	Intervention did not influence rate of positive social behavior, but raised social competence and self-efficacy for most students. Effects were maintained during a follow-up after five weeks.
Lo (1986)	60 ninth to twelfth graders	Two 60-minute lessons a week for six weeks.	Treatment included learning about feelings, disputing irrational thoughts, accepting mistakes, and learning self-help and problem-solving skills, as well as guided imagery. Control group watched National Geographic films as a group while the treatment group engaged in treatment.	Dimensions of Self-Concept. Rotter Internal-External Scale.	Posttest scores of the treatment group increased significantly on Dimensions of Self-Concept and perception of locus of control orientation.

Northcutt (1986)	30 third to fifth graders	Students and parents participated in a nine-week social skills program	Social skills training program to improve the teacher–student relationship. Treatment group and their parents participated in a nine-week social skills training program and 18 students participated in a nine-week control academic program.	Teachers and parents completed the Revised Behavior Problem Checklist. Students completed the Bronfenbrenner Parent and Teacher Behavior Questionnaires.	Experimental and control groups did not differ on the Revised Behavior Problem Checklist. Anecdotal reports and a questionnaire completed by 11 parents indicated changes in behavior at home for eight of the children who received treatment.
Obradovich (1991)	53 sixth graders	Once a week for eight months.	Program focused on saying thank-you, giving compliments, apologizing, accepting criticism, and resisting peer pressure.	Awareness quiz for each skill. Survey of detentions. Survey of satisfaction of program by parents.	More than 90% of the students had generalized skills to mainstream environment. Fewer students served detentions during the target year as opposed to the previous year.

(Continued)

TABLE 5.2
(Continued)

Author/Year	Participants	Duration	Content	Measures	Effects
Smilon (1985)	39 sixth to twelfth graders	45-minute sessions once a week for 12 weeks	Treatment group was encouraged to use the skills learnt during social skills training in school and the community, and report the incidents to the group. Treatment group engaged in role-play. First control group received academic remedial instruction. Second control group received remedial math or reading instruction.	Coppersmith Self-Esteem Inventory. Teacher ratings of relevant behaviors on a modified Coppersmith Behavior Rating Form.	Treatment group did not gain in total self-esteem when compared to control groups. Treatment group made significant gains in social self-esteem and on teacher ratings of positive and assertive behavior.
Todd (1990)	Thirty four 9 to 12 year olds	Both groups received eight sessions of specific interventions. Follow-up three weeks after posttest.	Treatment group received problem-solving group counseling. Control group received group therapy focusing on feelings. Both the groups initially received academic social skills training.	Classroom observations between posttest and follow-up. Conners' Teacher Rating Scale (CTRS).	Both groups increased significantly on measures of self-concept and decreased in terms of inappropriate classroom behaviors. A significant difference from pretest to posttest for all students on the CTRS.

| Wiener & Harris (1997) | Forty five 9 to 12 year olds | Group 1 received six weeks of intervention, group 2 received 12 weeks of intervention, and group 3 received no intervention. Follow-up was conducted after one year | Classroom-based social skills program consisting of coaching and problem solving. | Teacher records. Weekly videotapes of sessions. Classroom and playground observations. Social Skills Rating System by teachers and students. Child Behavior Checklist by teacher. Self-Perception Profile for Learning Disabled Students. Student status through peer nominations. | Treatment group 1 decreased in problem behaviors and increased in social skills and peer acceptance, and generalized the skills across settings. Control group decreased in peer acceptance. Groups 1 and 2 did not improve relative to control group. Results could not be replicated in another classroom, possibly due to dynamics specific to that classroom. |

by Blackbourn (1989) indicated that the students had generalized the target behaviors to environments other than those in which they were trained.

A study conducted by Smilon (1985) indicated that students who received social skills training did not demonstrate an increase in overall self-concept when compared to students who had received academic remedial instruction or remedial math or reading instruction. However, the group that received social skills training gained in social self-concept and on teacher ratings of positive and assertive behavior (Smilon, 1985). The studies reviewed suggest adult-mediated social skills interventions to be most effective when they target specific skills to be taught, include coaching, and provide opportunities for practice of the skill.

CONCLUSION

The literature on the social functioning of students with LD suggests that many students with LD demonstrate deficits in social functioning (e.g., Foss, 1991; Jarvis & Justice, 1992; Kavale & Forness, 1996; Merrell, 1991). Although the causes of these deficits are still being investigated, the results of social interventions for these students provide some common findings. Most studies included in this cursory review indicate specific social skills interventions produce an increase in appropriate social behavior and positive peer ratings. However, a meta-analysis of the positive effects of social skills training found effects of the training were about two-tenths of a standard deviation. Moreover, the control groups responded better in 10% of the studies, thus providing little support for the positive effects of social skills training (Kavale & Forness, 1996).

Research is required to isolate the specific effects of the various components of social skills training such as coaching, problem solving, and practice, and to determine which features are associated with positive outcomes in social functioning. Effects of including a peer component in the intervention also warrant further investigation.

Further research is required to determine the effects of various levels of placement on the social functioning of students with LD, and to determine best practices to promote social functioning and acceptance of students with LD in general education classrooms. Future studies should focus on the characteristics of the target students to help determine student features that may increase effectiveness of specific interventions. From the studies examined, it appears that although peer acceptance and rejection are relatively stable, specific training in social skills may facilitate change in the social status of students with LD.

REFERENCES

Abrams, B. C. (1985). The effects of participation in a group to eliminate self-defeating behaviors on self-concept and locus of control of learning disabled adolescents. *Dissertation Abstracts*, AAT 8508999.

Alexander, K. L., & Entwisle, D. R. (1988). Achievement in the first 2 years of school: Patterns and processes. *Monographs of the Society for the Research in Child Development, 53*(2), 157.

Blackbourn, J. (1989). Acquisition and generalization of social skills in elementary aged children with learning disabilities. *Journal of Learning Disabilities, 22,* 28–34.

Bramlett, R. K., Smith, B. L., & Edmonds, J. (1994). A comparison of nonreferred, learning-disabled, and midly mentally retarded students utilizing the social skills rating system. *Psychology in the Schools, 31,* 13–19.

Bursuck, W. (1989). A comparison of students with learning disabilities to low achieving and high achieving students on three dimensions of social acceptance. *Journal of Learning Disabilities, 22*(3), 188–194.

Canfield, J., & Wells, H. C. (1994). *100 ways to enhance self-concept in the classroom.* Boston: Allyn & Bacon.

Cartledge, G., Stupay, D., & Kaezala, C. (1986). Social skills and social perception of LD and nonhandicapped elementary-school students. *Learning Disability Quarterly, 9,* 226–233.

Coleman, J. M. (1983). Self-concept and the midley handicapped: The role of social comparisons. *The Journal of Special Education, 17,* 37–45.

Conte, R., Andrews, J. W., Loomer, M., & Hutton, G. (1995). A classroom-based social skills intervention for children with learning disabilities. *The Alberta Journal of Educational Research, 41*(1), 84–102.

Cooley, E. J., & Ayers, R. R. (1988). Self-concept and success-failure attributions of nonhandicapped students and students with learning disabilities. *Journal of Learning Disabilities, 21*(3), 174–178.

Cosden, M. A., Goldman, S. R., & Hine, M. S. (1990). Learning handicapped students' interactions during a microcomputer-based group writing activity. *Journal of Special Education Technology, 10*(4), 220–232.

Creasey, G. L., & Jarvis, P. A. (1987). Sensitivity to nonverbal communication among male learning disabled adolescents. *Perceptual and Motor Skills, 64,* 873–874.

Cruickshank, W. M. (1981a). A new perspective in teacher education: The neuroeducator. *Journal of Learning Disabilities, 14*(6), 337–341.

Cruickshank, W. M. (1981b). Learning disabilities: A definitional statement. In *W. M. Cruickshank, selected writings* (pp. xx–xx). Syracuse: Syracuse University.

Cruickshank, W. M. (1985). Learning disabilities: Educational and assessment considerations. *Studies in Educational Evaluation, 11,* 31–41.

Dalley, B. M., Bolocofsky, N. D., Alcorn, B. M., & Baker, C. (1992). Depressive symptomology, attributional style, dysfunctional attitude, and social competency in adolescents with and without learning disabilities. *School Psychology Review, 21*(3), 444–458.

Dickstein, E. B., & Warren, D. R. (1980). Roletaking deficits in learning disabled children. *Journal of Learning Disabilities, 13,* 378–382.

Finn, J. D. (1989). Withdrawing from school. *Review of Educational Research, 59,* 117–142.

Forness, S., & Kavale, K. (1991). Social skills deficits as primary learning disabilities: A note on problems with the ICLD diagnostic criteria. *Learning Disabilities Research and Practice, 6,* 44–49.

Foss, J. M. (1991). Nonverbal learning disabilities and remedial interventions. *Annals of Dyslexia, 41,* 128–140.

Fox, C. L. (1989). Peer acceptance of learning disabled children in the regular classroom. *Exceptional Children, 56*(1), 50–59.

Garrett, M. K., & Crump, W. D.(1980). Peer acceptance, teacher preference, and self-appraisal of social status among learning disabled students. *Learning Disability quarterly, 3*(3), 42–48.

Gresham, F. M. (1992). Social skills and learning disabilities: Causal, concomitant, or correlational? *School Psychology Review, 21*(3), 348–360.

Gresham, F. M., & Reschly, D. J. (1986). Social skill deficits and low peer acceptance of mainstreamed learning disabled children. *Learning Disability Quarterby, 9*(1), 23–32.

Grolnick, W. S., & Ryan, R. M. (1990). Self-perceptions, motivation, and adjustment in children with learning disabilities: A multiple group comparison. *Journal of Learning Disabilities, 23*, 177–184.

Hartas, D., & Donahue, L. M. (1997). Conversational and social problem-solving skills in adolescents with learning disabilities. *Learning Disabilities Research and Practice, 12*(4), 213–220.

Health, N. L., & Wiener, J. (1996). Depression and nonacademic self-perceptions in children with and without learning disabilities. *Learning Disability Quarterly, 19*(1), 34–44.

Holder, H. B., & Kirkpatrick, S. W. (1991). Interpretation of emotion from facial expressions in children with and without learning disabilities. *Journal of Learning Disabilities, 24*, 170–177.

Houchens-Nichols, C. (1987). The effects of a personal growth curriculum on the communication skills and self-concept in secondary learning disabled and emotionally impaired students. *Dissertation Abstracts International, 8706168 AAT.*

Interagency Committee on Learning Disabilities. (1987). *Learning Disabilities: A report to the U.S. Congress.* Washington, DC: U.S. Department of Health and Human Services.

Jackson, S. C., Enright, R. D., & Murdock, J. Y. (1987). Social perception problems in learning disabled youth: Developmental lag versus perceptual deficit. *Journal of Learning Disabilities, 20*, 361–364.

Jarvis, P. A., & Justice, E. M. (1992). Social sensitivity in adolescents and adults with learning disabilities. *Adolescence, 27*(108), 977–988.

Juvonen, J., & Bear, G. (1992). Social adjusment of children with and without learning disabilities in integrated classrooms. *Journal of Educational Psychology, 84*(3), 322–330.

Kavale, K., & Forness, S. R. (1996). Social skill deficits and learning disabilities: A meta-analysis. *Journal of Learning Disabilities, 29*(3), 226–237.

Kelly, J. A. (1993). Social skills training with learning disabled children. *Dissertation Abstracts,* AAT MM 77174.

Keogh, B. K. (1970). Early identification of children with potential learning problems. *Journal of Special Education, 4*(3), 307–363.

Keogh, B. K., Juvonen, J., & Bernheimer, L. P. (1989). Assessing children's competence: Mothers' and teachers' ratings of competent behavior. *Psychological Assessment: A Journal of Consulting and Clinical Psychology, 1*(3), 224–229.

Landau, S., & Milich, R. (1990). Assessment of children's social status and peer relations. In N A. M. La Greca (Ed.), *Through the eyes of the child: Obtaining self-reports from children and adolescents* (pp. 259–291). Boston: Allyn & Bacon.

Larson, K. A., & Gerber, M. M. (1987). Effects of social metacognitive training for enhancing overt behavior in learning disabled and low achieving delinquents. *Exceptional Children, 54*(3), 201–211.

Little, S. S. (1993). Nonverbal learning disabilities and socioemotional functioning: A review of recent literature. *Journal of Learning Disabilities, 26*(10), 653–665.

Lo, F. G. (1986). The effects of a rational-emotive education program on self-concept and locus of control among learning disabled adolescents (social, emotional, self-concept). *Dissertation Abstracts International, 8706168 AAA.*

Loveland, K. A., Fletcher, J. M., & Bailey, V. (1990). Nonverbal communication of events in learning disability subtypes. *Journal of Clinical and Experimental Neuropsychology, 12*, 433–447.

Margalit, M., & Levin-Alyagon, M. (1994). Learning disability subtyping, loneliness, and classroom adjustment. *Learning Disability Quarterly, 17*(4), 297–310.

Marshall, R. M., & Hynd, W. G. (1993). Neurological basis of learning disabilities. In W. N. Bender (Ed.), *Professional Issues in Learning Disabilities: Practical Strategies and Relevant Research Findings* (pp. 3–25). Austin, TX: Pro-Ed.

Mathinos, D. A. (1991). Conversational engagement of children with learning disabilities. *Journal of Learning Disabilities, 24*(7), 439–446.

McConaughy, S. H., & Ritter, D. R. (1986). Social competence and behavioral problems of learning disabled boys ages 6–11. *Journal of Learning Disabilities, 19*(1), 39–45.

McIntosh, R., Vaughn, S., & Zaragoza, N. (1991). A review of social interventions for students with learning disabilities. *Journal of Learning Disabilities, 24*(8), 451–458.

McMahon, C. M., Wacker, D. P., Sasso, G. M., & Melloy, K. J. (1994). Evaluation of the multiple effects of a social skill intervention. *Behavior Disorders, 20*(1), 35–50.

Merrell, K. W. (1991). Teacher ratings of social competence and behavioral adjustment: Differences between learning-disabled, low-achieving, and typical students. *Journal of School Psychology, 29*(3), 207–217.

Merz, M. A. (1985). Social skills training with learning disabled children (therapy, socialization). *Dissertation Abstracts,* AAT 8514145.

Mesch, D., Lew, M., Johnson, D. W., & Johnson, R. (1985). Isolated teenagers, cooperative learning, and training of social skills. *The Journal of Psychology, 120*(4), 323–334.

Montgomery, M. S. (1994). Self-concept and children with learning disabilities: Observer-child concordance across six context-dependent domains. *Journal of Learning Disabilities, 27*(4), 254–262.

Northcutt, T. E. (1986). The impact of a social skills training program on the teacher-student relationship (learning disabled). *Dissertation Abstracts,* 0525.

Obradovich, L. (1991). Improving sixth grade students' social skills through the implementation of the social skills for daily living program. ERIC Document Reproduction Service Number (ED NO: 336692).

Omizo, M. M., & Omizo, S. A. (1988). Group counseling's effects on self- concept and social behavior among children with learning disabilities. *Journal of Humanistic Education and Development, 26,* 109–117.

Ozols, E. J., & Rourke, B. P. (1985). Dimensions of social sensitivity in two types of learning-disabled children. In B. P. Rourke (Ed.), *Neuropsychology of learning disabilities: Essentials of subtype analysis* (pp. 281–301). New York: Guilford Press.

Parker, J. G., & Asher, S. R. (1987). Peer relations and later personal adjustment: Are low-accepted children at risk? *Psychological Bulletin, 102,* 357–389.

Pearl, R., Bryan, T., Fallon, P., & Herzog, A. (1991). Learning disabled students' detection of deception. *Learning Disabilities Research and Practice, 6,* 12–16.

Pearl, R., & Cosden, M. (1982). Sizing up a situation: Learning disabled children's understanding of social interactions. *Learning Disability Quarterly, 5,* 371–373.

Renick, M. J., & Harter, S. (1989). Impact of social comparisons on the developing self-perceptions of learning disabled students. *Journal of Educational Psychology, 81,* 631–638.

Rothman, H. R., & Cosden, M. (1995). The relationship between self-perception of a learning disability and achievement, self-concept, and social support. *Learning Disability Quarterly, 18*(3), 203–212.

Rourke, B. P. (1987). Syndrome of nonverbal learning disabilities: The final common pathway of white-matter disease/dysfunction? *The Clinical Neuropsychologist, 1,* 209–234.

Rourke, B. P. (1989). *Nonverbal Learning Disabilities.* New York: Guilford Press.

Rourke, B. P., & Fuerst, D. R. (1992). Psychological dimensions of learning disability subtypes: Neuropsychological studies in the windsor laboratory. *School Psychology Review, 21*(3), 361–374.

Rudolph, S., & Luckner, J. L. (1991). Social skills training for students with learning disabilities. *Journal of Humanistic Education and Development, 29*(4), 163–171.

Sabornie, E. J. (1994). Social-affective characteristics in early adolescents identified as learning disabled and nondisabled. *Learning Disabilities Quarterly, 17*(4), 268–279.

Sabornie, E. J., Marshall, K. K., & Ellis, E. S. (1990). Restructuring of mainstream sociometry with learning disabled and nonhandicapped students. *Exceptional Children, 56*(4), 314–323.

Saloner, M. R., & Gettinger, M. (1985). Social inference skills in learning disabled and nondisabled children. *Psychology in the Schools, 22,* 201–207.

Schneider, B. H., & Byrne, B. M. (1985). Children's social skills training: A meta-analysis. In B. H. Schneider, K. H. Rubin, & J. E. Ledingham (Eds.), *Children's peer relations: Issues in assessment and intervention* (pp. 175–192). New York: Springer-Verlag.

Semrud-Clikeman, M., & Hynd, G. (1990). Right hemisphere dysfunction in nonverbal learning disabilities: Social, academic, and adaptive functioning in adults and children. *Psychological Bulletin, 107,* 196–209.

Shapiro, E. G., Lipton, M. E., & Krivit, W. (1992). White matter dysfunction and its neuropsychological correlates: A longitudinal study of a case of metachromatic leukodystrophy. *Journal of Clinical and Experimental Neuropsychology, 14.*

Shondrick, D. D., Serafica, F. C., Clark, P., & Miller, K. G. (1992). *Learning Disability Quarterly, 15*(2), 95–102.

Seidel, J. F., & Vaughn, S. (1991). Social alienation and the LD school dropout. *Learning Disabilities Research, 6*(3), 152–157.

Smilon, R. (1985). The effect of social skills training of self-concept and teacher ratings of adolescents. *Dissertation Abstracts,* AAT 8502523.

Stone, W. L., & La Greca, A. M. (1990). *Journal of Learning Disabilities, 23*(1), 32–37.

Swanson, H. L., & Malone, S. (1992). Social skills and learning disabilities: A meta-analysis of the literature. *School Psychology Review, 21*(3), 427–443.

Todd, J. F. (1990). The effects of problem-solving group counseling on academic social skills training for learning disabled children. *Dissertation Abstracts,* AAT 9005682.

Toro, P. A., Weissberg, R. P., Guare, J., & Liebenstein, N. L. (1990). A comparison of children with and without learning disabilities on social problem-solving skill, school behavior, and family background. *Journal of Learning Disabilities, 23*(2), 115–120.

Trapani, C. (1987). The effect of social skills training on the use of social skills by LD boys. *Dissertation Abstracts International, 47,* 3398A.

Tur-Kaspa, H., & Bryan, T. (1994). Social information-processing skills of students with learning disabilities. *Learning Disabilities Research and Practice, 9*(1), 12–23.

Vaughn, S., & Elbaum, B. E. (1999). The self concept and friendships of students with learning disabilities: A developmental perspective. In R. Gallimore, L. Bernheimer, D. L. MacMillan, D. L. Speece, & S. Vaughn (Eds.), *Developmental perspective on children with high incidence disabilities* (pp. 81–110). Mahwah, NJ: Erlbaum.

Vaughn, S., & Haager, D. (1994). Social competence as a multifaceted construct: How do students with learning disabilities fare? *Learning Disability Quarterly, 17*(4), 253–266.

Vaughn, S., & Hogan, A. (1990). Social competence and learning disabilities: A prospective study. In H. L. Swanson & B. Keogh (Eds.), *Learning disabilities: Theoretical and research issues* (pp. 175–194). Hillsdale, NJ: Lawrence Erlbaum, Inc.

Vaughn, S., Hogan, A., Kouzekanani, K., & Shapiro, S. (1990). Peer acceptance, self-perceptions, and social skills of learning disabled students prior to identification. *Journal of Educational Psychology, 82*(1), 101–106.

Vaughn, S., & Lancelotta, G. X. (1990). Teaching interpersonal social skills to low accepted students: peer-pairing versus no peer-pairing. *Journal of School Psychology, 28*(3), 181–188.

Vaughn, S., Lancelotta, G. X., & Minnis, S. (1988). Social strategy training and peer involvement: Increasing peer acceptance of a female, LD student. *Learning Disabilities Focus, 4*(1), 32–37.

Vaughn, S., McIntosh, R., & Spencer-Rowe, J. (1991). Peer rejection is a stubborn thing: Increasing peer acceptance of rejected students with learning disabilities. *Learning Disabilities Research and Practice, 6*(2), 65–132.

Vogel, S. A., & Forness, S. R. (1992). Social functioning in adults with learning disabilities. *School Psychology Review, 21*(3), 375–386.

Wiener, J., & Harris, P. J. (1997). Evaluation of an individualized, context-based social skills training program for children with learning disabilities. *Learning Disabilities Research and Practice, 12*(1), 40–53.

Wiener, J., Harris, P. J., & Shirer, C. (1990). Achievement and social-behavioral correlates of peer status in LD children. *Learning Disability Quarterly, 13,* 114–127.

Wong, B. Y., & Wong, R. (1980). Role-taking skills in normal achieving and learning disabled children. *Learning Disability Quarterly, 3,* 11–18.

Zigmond, N., & Thornton, H. (1985). Follow up of postsecondary age learning disabled graduates and dropouts. *Learning Disabilities Research, 1*(1), 50–55.

Chapter 6

Using Assessment to Account for and Promote Strong Outcomes for Students with Learning Disabilities

Lynn S. Fuchs and Douglas Fuchs
Peabody College of Vanderbilt University

Education reform in this country is dominated by standards-based reform, which seeks to use assessment to upgrade student learning. Within general and special education alike, the history and phenomenon run similar paths. Historically, accountability has focused on documenting the processes or inputs to education; today, by contrast, the press is to demonstrate that students are learning large amounts of challenging content. In special education, for example, accountability used to require that Individual Education Programs (IEPs) were complete and internally consistent descriptions of the services students receive; now schools are expected to demonstrate that students with disabilities are mastering important goals so they will succeed after school. This press on accountability for student outcomes has created many technical and conceptual challenges for special as well as general systems (for discussion of a broader set of issues, see Fuchs & Fuchs, 2000; McDonnell, McLaughlin, & Morison, 1997). In this chapter, we limit our discussion to two related questions: How can we ensure the participation of students with LD within general education's standards-based reform accountability programs? and Is participation in general education's system adequate to accomplish better outcomes for students with LD?

MEANINGFUL PARTICIPATION IN GENERAL EDUCATION'S ACCOUNTABILITY PROGRAMS

Rates of Participation

Prior to passage of Individuals with Disabilities Education Act 1997, participation rates of students with LD in state assessments were dismal. As recently as 1995–1996, when the first tests of some accommodations occurred, only 45%–75% of students with disabilities participated in the National Assessment of Educational Progress, and states' and districts' annual testing programs excluded large numbers of students with LD. In addition, even when students with LD were permitted to take high-stakes assessments, some states or districts excluded their scores from public reports (Thurlow, Scott, & Ysseldyke, 1995). Even following passage of IDEA 1997, when participation was mandated, the rates with which students with disabilities have been included in accountability databases continue to be disappointing. In the most recent reports (Ysseldyke, 2000), nearly two years following the federal deadline for full participation, some states continue to exclude 50% of students with disabilities from their accountability databases, and participation rates in some states are declining rather than increasing.

This is problematic. If schools are to consider the needs of students with LD deliberately and proactively in reform and improvement activities, the outcomes of these students must be represented in public accountability systems. Only with representation in assessment databases will schools be held accountable for the learning of students with LD, be encouraged to establish challenging goals for students with LD, and be prompted to identify more effective instructional approaches for these students. Unfortunately, before meaningful participation can be accomplished, several critical technical problems must be addressed.

Technical Challenge to Meaningful Participation: Lack of Methods for Determining Accommodations

The biggest technical problem to meaningful participation in accountability programs is the absence of standard methods for determining which testing accommodations preserve the meaningfulness of scores. Accommodations are changes in standardized assessment conditions introduced to "level the playing field" for students with disabilities by removing the construct-irrelevant variance (or barriers to performance) created by the disability. Valid accommodations produce scores for students with disabilities that reflect the same attributes as standard assessments measure in nondisabled individuals (McDonnell et al., 1997). On one hand, disallowing valid accommodations prevents students with disabilities from demonstrating their abilities. On the other hand, overly permissive accommodation policies inflate scores and inadvertently reduce pressure on schools to increase expectations and outcomes for students with disabilities.

The primary strategy for identifying which test accommodations are valid relies on the notion of differential effects; that is, an accommodation is valid if it boosts the scores of students with disabilities more than it benefits students without disabilities. This principle is evident in the logic behind the use of a Braille accommodation for students with visual disabilities. One can predict that Braille will make a reading test accessible for students with visual disabilities and thereby boost students' scores over what we might expect with a standard administration. By contrast, for students without disabilities, we would expect a Braille accommodation to depress scores. This illustrates the principle of differential boost.

As states have developed accommodation policies over the past two years, it has become clear that tremendous variability in these policies exists (Ysseldyke, 2000). In fact, some states prohibit the same accommodations that other states recommend. Moreover, decisions for individual students with disabilities are typically formulated idiosyncratically with vague decision-making rules that often focus on superficial variables. Without well-agreed upon criteria for determining whether and if so which accommodations are allowed, comparisons among schools, districts, or states with varying accommodation policies are unfair and meaningless.

And some of the stickiest questions about the meaningfulness of accommodations occur for students with LD. Questions are particularly difficult for these students for two reasons. First, this population of learners is heterogeneous. It is well-known that school-identified LD can be subtyped into clusters with varying underlying problems (Morris et al., 1998). This makes conceptual analysis of meaningful accommodations impossible (as it might be, for example, with students with visual disabilities). Instead, heterogeneity within the population of learners with LD dictates empirical study with a strong focus on individual differences.

The second problem raising important questions for students with LD is the nature of the cognitive problems these students experience. The most distinguishing characteristic of LD is reading and math deficits (Kavale & Reece, 1992), and most high-stakes assessments directly measure or rely heavily on those very skills. Therefore, many accommodations popular for students with LD (such as extended time, decoding questions, encoding responses) may distort the meaning and interpretation of scores. In essence, because the disability is intertwined with the constructs being measured, allowing accommodations may effectively exempt these students with LD from demonstrating the cognitive skills the assessments are designed to index.

An Absence of Research Guidelines

Unfortunately, research provides little guidance for determining which accommodations preserve the meaningfulness of test accommodation for students with LD. In a recent comprehensive literature review, we (Fuchs & Fuchs, 2000) identified all studies that (a) compared accommodation effects for students with and without disabilities (to get at the notion of differential boost), (b) focused on reading and mathematics tests, (c) considered accommodations that preserved the reading or mathematics construct assessed, and (d) examined one single rather than multiple accommodations. We identified only 19 studies that met these criteria, many of which investigated effects for postsecondary students. Moreover, results were often contradictory, and varying definitions of accommodations across studies made it difficult to identify reasons for inconsistent findings. At this time, in light of the paucity of well-controlled research on testing accommodations, the only conclusion to draw is that additional research must be conducted. This research should examine differential effects by including students with and without LD within the same designs; by testing the effects of accommodations separately (rather than using a set of accommodations as a "package"); by focusing on school-age populations; by carefully equating alternate forms; by specifically operationalizing accommodations; and by counterbalancing the order in which conditions and alternate forms are administered.

An Innovative Approach to Identifying Fair, Appropriate Accommodations for Students with LD

Consequently, at this time, it is not possible to formulate conclusions about the validity of testing accommodations for the group of students labeled as LD. Of course, even if we could point to a well-established literature that documented differential effects for students with LD, the research would represent average performances. And because students with LD demonstrate a variety of underlying deficits, there is tremendous heterogeneity in the population. This means that many students with LD do not conform to "average" findings in the research literature. In fact, although some accommodations may ultimately reveal differential average effects, some students with LD will fail to benefit from those accommodations. In the same way, although some accommodations may eventually fail to demonstrate differential average effects, some students with LD undoubtedly will profit from those very accommodations substantially more than nondisabled students. For this reason, individual diagnosis of appropriate accommodations is necessary for students with LD.

To address this problem, we have been developing and studying an assessment tool that teachers can use to supplement their judgments about whether an individual student with LD should be awarded a specific accommodation. We call this tool the Dynamic Assessment of Test Accommodations, or DATA. With DATA, teachers administer alternate forms of short tests under varying conditions in math computation, standard and extended time; in math concepts and applications, standard, extended time, calculator, and an adult reading text; in math problem solving, standard, extended time, calculator, an adult reading text, and an adult writing students' nonmathematical responses upon request; in reading, standard, extended time, large print, and students reading aloud. For each student with LD, within each domain (i.e., math computation, math concepts and applications, math problem solving, and reading), the teacher calculates the size of the accommodation boost (i.e., the score earned using the accommodation minus the score earned in the standard format). Then, the teacher compares the individual student's boosts with normative information on nondisabled students. When a student with LD derives an accommodation boost that substantially exceeds the boost expected for nondisabled students, DATA recommends that the teacher and IEP team consider the accommodation for use during classroom tests and for the statewide assessment.

Research we have conducted with DATA is promising. Results for math and reading are similar. This chapter provides an overview of the reading study (Fuchs, Fuchs, Eaton, Hamlett, Binkley, & Crouch, 2000). (See Fuchs, Fuchs, Eaton, Hamlett, & Karns, 2000 for the math study.) Participants in the reading study were 365 students; most were in the fourth grade. Approximately half of these students had no identified disability; the other half had an LD. To each student, we administered four brief reading assessments; each testing required students to read three passages and, for each passage, to answer six literal and two inferential questions. These four assessments were completed under varying conditions: standard (four minutes per passage, regular-size print, student reads silently), extended time (eight minutes per passage), large print, and student reads aloud. Test forms and condition orders were counterbalanced. Scores were corrected for guessing (number correct minus [number incorrect/3]) and then averaged across the three passages. Interscorer agreement on 15% of protocols was 98.4%. Alternate form/test-retest reliability averaged .82; the correlation with the Iowa Test of Basic Skills–Reading Comprehension was .80.

We used the scores on these brief assessments, which constitute DATA, for three purposes. First, we explored whether students with LD benefited differentially from the test accommodations. Second, we used the sample of students without LD to estimate the "typical" boost we might expect for each accommodation from nondisabled students. Third, we compared the accommodation boost of each individual student with LD to the "typical" boost to determine whether the individual demonstrated a greater-than-expected boost and therefore qualified for that accommodation on the large-scale assessment. We compared accommodation decisions based on DATA to the decisions teachers had formulated using their judgment.

Finally, to each student with LD, we administered two forms of a large-scale reading assessment (the Iowa Test of Basic Skills) under standard and accommodated conditions, with test forms and administration orders counterbalanced. We examined how well teacher and DATA decisions corresponded to the accommodation boosts students experienced on the Iowa.

Do Students with LD Benefit Differentially from Test Accommodations?

For two of three accommodations, extended time and large print, students with LD did not benefit more than non-LD students. In fact, the effect sizes for these accommodations were almost identical for students without and with LD (.36 and .38 for extended time and .03 and .08 for large print). These findings are notable. Extended time may be the accommodation most frequently awarded to students with LD. Yet results showed that extended time may not serve to level the playing field for students with LD. Rather, extended time may provide students with LD an advantage from which most students would derive benefit. In this way, extended time does not speak to something essential about the nature of learning disabilities. In fact, instead of making test scores more valid, the use of extended time may serve to inflate the scores of students with LD. Similar conclusions apply to the use of large print.

By contrast, results for permitting students to read tests aloud illustrate how some accommodations may in fact level the playing field for students with and without LD. The interaction was statistically significant. The combined effect size across students with and without LD summed to .18 standard deviations. Results showed how this accommodation increases scores of students with LD, even as it depresses scores of students without LD. In this way, the accommodation appears to speak to something essential about the disability and serves to level the playing field. This finding is consistent with previous work showing that although poor readers increase their text comprehension when they read aloud, more skilled readers benefit more from silent reading. It suggests that having students read reading tests aloud may represent a valid test accommodation, which permits students with LD the opportunity to demonstrate the reading competence they actually possess.

How Well do Teacher Judgments about Accommodations Correspond to DATA Decisions?

As discussed, mean group differences represent only one yardstick by which the validity of test accommodations should be assessed. Whenever groups differ along any dimension, the populations inevitably overlap. This means that, despite group patterns, some individuals with LD will profit differentially from extended time or large print; others will fail to profit from reading aloud. This is why decisions must be formulated individually to limit accommodation awards to the subset of students who realize greater boosts than are expected for students without LD. An individualized test accommodation perspective is especially important for learning disabilities, where the underlying deficits are heterogeneous and where the nature of the cognitive disability is intertwined with the constructs tests measure. We, therefore, used DATA to formulate individual decisions about test accommodations, and we compared the DATA-based decisions to those of teachers.

We found poor correspondence. Teachers awarded many more accommodations (73% versus 41% for DATA). Moreover, students to whom teachers had awarded accommodations failed to earn greater accommodation boosts than did students to whom teachers had denied accommodations. In fact, effect sizes were minimal, ranging from −.07 to .06 standard deviations, with boosts larger for teacher denials than for teacher awards for two of three accommodations.

This calls into question the accuracy of teacher judgments in specifying testing accommodations. And the accuracy of teacher judgments is especially important in light of the demographic markers and performance variables associated with teachers' decisions. Specifically, in our research, the students whom teachers had selected for accommodations had been retained in school more years, disproportionately were African American and received reduced or free lunch, and had lower IQs and reading instructional levels. Importantly, no such differences were associated with the decisions formulated with the DATA-based method.

Did DATA Enhance Teachers' Accommodation Decisions?

Which method for identifying accommodations better predicted the boosts students earned on the large-scale assessment? We dedicated the final phase of our study to answering this question. This final study phase was limited to students with LD with whom we conducted two forms of a commercial test used for large-scale assessments: the Iowa Test of Basic Skills. Students completed one form in standard format. For the other form, they received the accommodation(s) specified by DATA or, if DATA had ruled out all accommodations, they received a randomly assigned accommodation.

The accommodation boosts on this commercial test revealed the potential for DATA to supplement and enhance teacher judgments. Accommodation boosts did not correspond to teachers' judgments about whether students did or did not warrant accommodations. The main effect for teacher judgment failed to achieve statistical significance. In fact, students to whom teachers had *denied* accommodations actually earned somewhat *larger* accommodation boosts than did the students to whom teachers had awarded accommodations.

By contrast, the main effect sorting students into DATA-based decisions did achieve statistical significance. Students to whom DATA had awarded accommodations earned larger boosts as a function of having those accommodations, compared to the subset to whom DATA had denied accommodations. The effect size was .34 standard deviations.

Consequently, teachers granted accommodations to large numbers of students with LD who failed to profit from those accommodations more than would be expected among nondisabled students. DATA was, however, helpful in sorting students into those who did and those who did not profit differentially from accommodations.

When we looked solely at the group of students to whom teachers had awarded accommodations, we found the following patterns. Accommodation boosts of students to whom DATA had awarded accommodations were 2.81 times higher than those to whom DATA had denied accommodations. This substantial benefit illustrates how DATA differentiated true from false positives. Of course, reducing false positive accommodation decisions is critical. One important goal of including students with LD in accountability databases is to prompt schools to use their resources to enhance outcomes for these children. If this is to occur, test scores must provide realistic, not inflated, estimates of student capacity so that schools can use accountability databases to identify which students with LD require additional attention. In fact, when accommodations produce spuriously high scores, schools experience reduced pressure to intervene on behalf of students with LD.

In a similar way, if we take the subgroup of students to whom teachers had denied accommodations and we further divide those students into the ones to whom DATA had and had not awarded accommodations, we see a 17.52-fold increase in accommodation boost between DATA-based decisions. Therefore, DATA was useful in sorting the group of students to whom teachers had denied accommodations into two subsets: those who did and those who did not benefit differentially. The implications of denying accommodations to students, when those accommodations are warranted, are serious. Without accommodations, these students may be disallowed the opportunity to demonstrate the mathematical problem-solving competence they possess. And, when high-stakes consequences for individual students are associated with participation in accountability systems, it is essential for students with LD be permitted the test accommodations their disability warrants.

Summary

This study, as does a parallel investigation in math (Fuchs, Fuchs, Eaton, Hamlett, & Karns, 2000), calls into question teacher judgment about test accommodations. Teachers' decisions do not correspond to students' actual accommodation boosts on the brief assessments or on the longer, large-scale, commercial test. Moreover, teachers' decisions appeared to be influenced by demographic and performance variables that were not associated with more objective methods for determining accommodation decisions.

These findings may not be surprising. After all, federal legislation requiring test accommodations to facilitate student participation in large-scale testing programs is new, and teachers have limited experience in formulating these decisions. They also have little conceptual background about the function of test accommodations, no formal opportunities to compare the actual effects of test accommodations for students with and without disabilities, and a scant literature base to consult as they seek information to help inform their decisions.

Although the shortcomings of teacher judgment may be understandable, findings do nevertheless provide the basis for concern. Fortunately, this study also demonstrates how objective data sources, such as DATA, can supplement teacher judgments to enhance accommodation decisions. The findings of this research are promising and provide the basis for replication and extension of research on DATA. Results also provide support for investigators as they develop and study other objective methods for supplementing teachers' accommodation decisions.

Until additional information is available, however, teachers will continue to face the challenge of formulating accommodation decisions. As they engage in this decision-making process, teachers may consider DATA as one objective data source for helping them supplement their judgments. In addition, as teachers use DATA, their understanding of accommodations and effects should increase.

IS PARTICIPATION IN GENERAL EDUCATION'S SYSTEM ADEQUATE TO ACCOMPLISH BETTER OUTCOMES?: BROADENING THE CONCEPTUALIZATION OF ACCOUNTABILITY FOR STUDENTS WITH LD

Our discussion has focused on issues related to the participation of students with LD within the general education accountability system. So far, we have avoided a larger question about whether participation in these accountability testing programs is adequate to accomplish the goals of standards-based reform for students with LD: higher expectations and more successful outcomes.

Although we believe that broad participation in these assessment programs activities is necessary, we strongly suspect that such participation is unlikely to represent a sufficient condition for promoting more challenging goals and stronger learning for students with LD. This is due to the enormous gap between the level of achievement required in most testing programs and the actual performance levels of most students with LD. Research documents that such distal goals may not serve to motivate students and teachers and may not enhance student learning (Locke, Shaw, Saari, & Latham, 1981).

Consequently, for many students with LD, it may be necessary to supplement the general education, high-stakes assessment programs with a supplementary assessment and accountability system, which provides a more proximal framework for assessing and monitoring individual student learning. In fact, for students with LD, a second approach to accountability currently does exist. Special education has a supplementary accountability system with the explicit purpose of increasing expectations and learning. Whereas the general education strategy involves annual (or even less frequent) large-scale assessments and sets uniform standards without considering individual differences, the special education strategy requires frequent assessment and sets flexible standards that allow for individual differences. This special education perspective is codified in the IEP process.

Unfortunately, the IEP assessment and accountability process to date has been shown to operate ineffectively (McDonnell et al., 1997). Nevertheless, the potential for a greatly revised IEP process to increase expectations and learning has been demonstrated. Researchers have developed systems that structure a more effective process for setting ambitious goals for individual students and provide reliable and valid assessment information about progress toward attaining those goals. Research illustrates how increases in teacher and student expectations as well as student learning can be achieved when practitioners use these individually referenced assessment systems. A revised IEP framework, built on strong measurement systems for monitoring students' acquisition of fundamental skills, would correct many of the ills associated with current, common IEP practice. These revised systems focus on student outcomes rather than procedural inputs; they help teachers attend to broad, important, but realistic goals, rather than long lists of short-term objectives; and they correspond directly with the skills necessary to promote successful postschool adjustments for students with LD. Moreover, for students with LD, they provide a mechanism for supplementing the broader, more distal standards-based reform assessment activities. The best-developed system, in terms of research on reliability, validity, and instructional utility, is curriculum-based measurement (CBM).

What is CBM?

CBM (Deno, 1985) is a set of standardized methods for indexing academic competence and progress. Based on a program of research conducted at multiple sites since 1977 (Deno, 1985; Shinn, 1989), CBM specifies procedures for sampling test stimuli from local curricula, for administering and scoring those assessments, and for summarizing and interpreting the resulting database (Deno & Fuchs, 1987). Research has documented that CBM produces reliable and valid information about a student's academic standing at a given point in time (Marston, 1989). In addition, when performance is measured routinely on alternate forms, CBM models academic progress reasonably well (Good, Deno, & Fuchs, 1995).

CBM deliberately integrates key concepts from traditional measurement theory and from the conventions of classroom-based observational methodology to forge an innovative approach to assessment. As with traditional measurement, each CBM samples a relatively broad range of skills: Each dimension of the annual curriculum is represented on each weekly test. Consequently, each repeated measurement is an alternate form, of equivalent difficulty, assessing the same constructs. This principle is illustrated in CBM's spelling assessment, which samples the same relatively large domain of spelling words in the same way, to include multiple phonetic patterns and irregular spellings and to represent the same constructs and difficulty level (Fuchs, Allinder, Hamlett, & Fuchs, 1990). This sampling strategy differs markedly from typical classroom-based assessment methods, where teachers assess mastery on a list of 10–20 words and after mastery is demonstrated, move on to a different set of words (see Fuchs & Deno, 1991). CBM also relies on a traditional psychometric framework by incorporating conventional notions of reliability and validity so that the standardized test administration and scoring methods yield accurate and meaningful information (Deno, Mirkin, Lowry, & Kuehnle, 1980).

By sampling broadly and relying on standardized administration and scoring procedures, the total CBM score can be viewed as a "performance indicator." It produces a broad dispersion of scores across individuals of the same age (i.e., spelling scores typically range from 15 to 180 letter sequences correct), with rank orderings that correspond to important external criteria. CBM thereby represents an individual's global level of competence in the domain (e.g., Deno et al., 1980). Practitioners can use this performance indicator to identify discrepancies in performance levels between individuals and peer groups, which can inform decisions about the need for special services or the point at which disability decertification might occur.

At the same time, however, CBM departs from conventional psychometric applications by integrating the concepts of standardized measurement and traditional reliability and validity with key features from classroom-based observational methodology: repeated performance sampling, fixed time recording, graphic displays of time-series data, and qualitative descriptions of student performance. Reliance on these classroom-based observational methods permits estimates of slope for different time periods and for alternative interventions for the same individual. This creates the necessary data for testing the effectiveness of different treatments for a given student and permits schools to quantify students' rates of academic progress. Research also suggests that, when combined with prescriptive decision rules, these time-series analytic methods result in better instruction and learning. Teachers raise goals more often and develop higher expectations (Fuchs, Fuchs, & Hamlett, 1989a), introduce more revisions to their instructional programs (Fuchs, Fuchs, & Hamlett, 1989b), and effect better achievement (Fuchs, Fuchs, Hamlett, & Stecker, 1991).

In addition, because each assessment simultaneously samples the multiple skills embedded in the annual curriculum, CBM can yield rich, qualitative descriptions of student performance to supplement the graphed, quantitative analysis of performance. These diagnostic profiles demonstrate adequate reliability and validity (see Fuchs, Fuchs, Hamlett, & Allinder, 1989; Fuchs, Fuchs, Hamlett, Thompson, Roberts, Kubec, & Stecker, 1994); offer the advantage of being rooted in the local curriculum; provide a framework for determining strategies for improving student programs (see Fuchs, Fuchs, & Hamlett, 1994); and result in teachers planning more varied, specific, and responsive instruction to meet individual student needs (Fuchs, Fuchs, Hamlett, & Allinder, 1991).

Consequently, CBM bridges traditional psychometric and classroom-based observational assessment paradigms to forge an innovative approach to measurement. Through this bridging of frameworks, CBM simultaneously yields information about standing and change in global competence as well as skill-by-skill mastery. It can, therefore, be used to answer questions about interindividual differences (e.g., How different is Henry's academic level from that of other students in the class, school, or district?); questions about intraindividual improvement (e.g., How successful is an adapted regular classroom in producing better academic growth for Henry?); and questions about how to strengthen individual students' programs (e.g., On which skills in the annual curriculum does Henry require instruction?).

A well-established, long-standing research program documents CBM's capacity to help teachers plan better instructional programs and effect superior achievement. Studies have examined the specific effects of alternative data-utilization strategies, as well as CBM's overall contribution to instructional planning and student achievement. CBM has been shown to enhance teacher planning and student outcomes in three ways: by helping teachers maintain appropriately ambitious student goals (Fuchs, Fuchs, & Hamlett, 1989a), assisting teachers in determining when revisions to their instructional programs are necessary to prompt better student growth (Fuchs, Fuchs, & Hamlett, 1989b; Stecker & Fuchs, in press; Wesson, 1991; Wesson, Skiba, Sevcik, King, & Deno, 1984), and providing ideas for potentially effective instructional adjustments (Fuchs, Fuchs, Hamlett, & Allinder, 1991; Fuchs, Fuchs, & Hamlett, 1989c; Fuchs, Fuchs, Hamlett, & Stecker, 1991). In these ways, CBM provides a strong framework for accomplishing standards-based reform's objectives: Teachers can use CBM to monitor student learning, to increase expectations for student learning, and to effect stronger outcomes.

What Are The Challenges to Using CBM as a Supplement to a General Education Accountability System?

Therefore, CBM represents a well-developed assessment system that can be used in a routine way to quantify students' academic progress, to prompt teachers to adopt high expectations for students with LD, and to help educators plan more responsively to individual needs so that learning increases. Because of the strength of the research base, CBM is used in many states, districts, and classrooms across the country (e.g., Swain & Allinder, 1997). But, why is CBM not used even more broadly? And, what are the impediments to using CBM as an accountability tool? We offer three possibilities.

Unifying Standards

Before CBM can achieve status as a universally accepted and implemented accountability tool, which is used to formulate comparisons among states, districts, schools, and teachers about program effectiveness for students with LD, national normative information must be collected. The provision of nationally representative norms would permit teachers to identify how much progress typically developing children at different grade levels manifest within an academic year. With such information, teachers could establish IEP goals, which specify "acceptable" rates of academic progress. With CBM norms, teachers, administrators, and policy makers could have the necessary yardstick by which to judge the adequacy of an individual student's progress.

Teacher Training and Support for Use

Another impediment to broad implementation of CBM is teacher training. Although an increasing number of special education textbooks present information about CBM, those discussions typically are superficial. CBM represents the most technically advanced classroom-based assessment methodology, which can be used effectively within an IEP framework. Consequently, the Council for Exceptional Children and other teacher-accrediting bodies need to incorporate competence in this research-based assessment practice as a standard for teacher certification. In a related way, professional organizations and school districts need to allocate attention to providing professional development opportunities to help teachers gain competence in using CBM. And, importantly, state departments of education need to organize efforts to provide leadership to school districts in supporting teachers' routine use of CBM, which has been demonstrated to increase goal ambitiousness and improve learning outcomes for students with LD.

Expanding CBM's Focus

Most work conducted on CBM concerns the acquisition of basic skills in reading, mathematics, spelling, and written expression. With standards-based reform's focus on more complex skills and knowledge application, CBM must expand its focus. Our work on mathematical problem solving illustrates this type of extension (see, for example, Fuchs, Fuchs, Karns, Hamlett, Dutka, & Katzaroff, 2000; Fuchs, Fuchs, Karns, Hamlett, & Katzaroff, 1999). With the CBM problem-solving framework, teachers measure students' incoming levels of mathematical problem-solving competence. With an estimate of baseline performance, teachers set individual student goals for the level of performance they expect by year's end. Each month, students complete a problem-solving assessment. Students receive feedback along with tips for improving their performance; teachers receive reports that include recommendations for how to structure instruction to effect better student progress. These reports describe the student's current performance levels along several dimensions; they also quantify student progress over time in terms of slope. Teachers can compare slopes with alternative instructional components in place to determine effective program features for an individual child. They can also aggregate student slopes to determine how groups of students are progressing. Teachers can use the CBM problem-solving system to establish ambitious goals and to effect superior outcomes on challenging content. This is the purpose of standards-based reform. In a similar way, analogous development can occur to extend CBM from basic skills to more complex curriculum at the elementary and secondary levels.

CONCLUSIONS

CBM literature illustrates how a technically strong measurement system can provide schools with an effective tool for monitoring student progress toward achieving important goals, how teachers can use this information to enhance the quality of their instructional programs, and how increased expectations and superior student outcomes may result. This literature is well-developed; it provides the basis for clear conclusions. Moreover, strong potential exists for developing national CBM norms by which teachers and IEP teams might standardize and raise expectations for how quickly students with LD acquire the basic skills necessary for high school graduation and for successful outcomes after they leave secondary school. Moreover, research illustrates how CBM can be extended to more complex academic domains of knowledge.

At the same time, federal law mandates the participation of students with LD in a second accountability framework: general education annual testing programs. Unfortunately, research examining the means for effecting participation is scarce. For students with LD to participate in general education accountability systems in ways that promote potential benefits, additional research on testing accommodations is necessary. Moreover, research is needed to explore methods for standardizing accommodation decisions and to investigate the effects of requiring IEP teams to adopt standardized protocols for formulating accommodation decisions.

ACKNOWLEDGMENT

This chapter was prepared with support in part by Grant #H324V980001 from the U.S. Department of Education, Office of Special Education Programs, and Core Grant HD15052 from the National Institute of Child

Health and Human Services to Vanderbilt University. Statements do not reflect official policy of any agency.

REFERENCES

Deno, S. L. (1985). Curriculum-based measurement: The emerging alternative. *Exceptional Children, 52,* 219–232.

Deno, S. L., & Fuchs, L. S. (1987). Developing curriculum-based measurement systems for data-based decision making. *Focus on Exceptional Children, 19*(8), 1–16.

Deno, S. L., Mirkin, P. M., Lowry, L., & Kuehnle, K. (1980). *Relationships among simple measures of spelling and performance on standardized achievement tests* (Research Report No. 22). Minneapolis: University of Minnesota Institute for Research on Learning Disabilities.

Fuchs, L. S., Allinder, R. M., Hamlett, C. L., & Fuchs, D. (1990). An analysis of spelling curricula and teachers' skills in identifying error types. *Remedial and Special Education, 11*(1), 42–53.

Fuchs, L. S., & Deno, S. L. (1991). Paradigmatic distinctions between instructionally relevant measurement models. *Exceptional Children, 57,* 488–501.

Fuchs, L. S., & Fuchs, D. (2000). *Accountability and assessment in the 21ˢᵗ century: Implications for students with LD.* Unpublished manuscript. Available from the Pew Charitable Trusts.

Fuchs, L. S., Fuchs, D., Eaton, S., Hamlett, C. L., Binkley, E., & Crouch, R. (2000). Using objective data sources to supplement teacher judgment about reading test accommodations. *Exceptional Children, 67,* 67–82.

Fuchs, L. S., Fuchs, D., Eaton, S., Hamlett, C. L., & Karns, K. (2000). Supplementing teachers' judgments of mathematics test accommodations with objective data sources. *School Psychology Review, 29,* 65–85.

Fuchs, L. S., Fuchs, D., & Hamlett, C. L. (1989a). Effects of alternative goal structures within curriculum-based measurement. *Exceptional Children, 55,* 429–438.

Fuchs, L. S., Fuchs, D., & Hamlett, C. L. (1989b). Instrumental use of curriculum-based measurement to enhance instructional programs. *Remedial and Special Education, 10*(2), 43–52.

Fuchs, L. S., Fuchs, D., & Hamlett, C. L. (1989c). Monitoring reading growth using student recalls: Effects of two teacher feedback systems. *Journal of Educational Research, 83,* 103–111.

Fuchs, L. S., Fuchs, D., & Hamlett, C. L. (1994). Strengthening the connection between assessment and instructional planning with expert systems. *Exceptional Children, 61,* 138–146.

Fuchs, L. S., Fuchs, D., Hamlett, C. L., & Allinder, R. M. (1989). The reliability and validity of skills analysis within curriculum-based measurement. *Diagnostique, 14,* 203–221.

Fuchs, L. S., Fuchs, D., Hamlett, C. L., & Allinder, R. M. (1991). Effects of expert system advice within curriculum-based measurement on teacher planning and student achievement in spelling. *School Psychology Review, 20,* 49–66.

Fuchs, L. S., Fuchs, D., Hamlett, C. L., & Stecker, P. M. (1990). The role of skills analysis in curriculum-based measurement in math. *School Psychology Review, 19,* 6–22.

Fuchs, L. S., Fuchs, D., Hamlett, C. L., & Stecker, P. M. (1991). Effects of curriculum-based measurement and consultation on teacher planning and student achievement in mathematics operations. *American Educational Research Journal, 28,* 617–641.

Fuchs, L. S., Fuchs, D., Hamlett, C. L., Thompson, A., Roberts, P. H., Kubec, P., & Stecker, P. M. (1994). Technical features of a mathematics concepts and applications curriculum-based measurement system. *Diagnostique, 19*(4), 23–49.

Fuchs, L. S., Fuchs, D., Hamlett, C. L., Walz, L., & Germann, G. (1993). Formative evaluation of academic progress: How much growth can we expect? *School Psychology Review, 22,* 27–48.

Fuchs, L. S., Fuchs, D., Karns, K., Hamlett, C. L., Dutka, S., & Katzaroff, M. (2000). The importance of providing background information on the structure and scoring of performance assessments. *Applied Measurement in Education, 13,* 1–34.

Fuchs, L. S., Fuchs, D., Karns, K., Hamlett, C. L., & Katzaroff, M. (1999). Mathematics performance assessment in the classroom: Effects on teacher planning and student learning. *American Educational Research Journal, 36,* 609–646.

Fuchs, L. S., Fuchs, D., Karns, K., Hamlett, C. L., Katzaroff, M., & Dutka, S. (1997). Effects of task-focused goals on low-achieving students with and without learning disabilities. *American Educational Research Journal, 34,* 513–544.

Fuchs, L. S., Fuchs, D., & Maxwell, L. (1988). The validity of informal reading comprehension measures. *Remedial and Special Education, 9*(2), 20–29.

Good, R., Deno, S. L., & Fuchs, L. S. (1995, February). *Modeling academic growth within and across years for students with and without disabilities.* Paper presented at the third annual Pacific Coast Research Conference, Laguna Beach, CA.

Kavale, K. A., & Reece, J. H. (1992). The character of learning disabilities. *Learning Disability Quarter, 15,* 74–94.

Locke, E. A., Shaw, K. N., Saari, L. M., & Latham, G. P. (1981). Goal-setting and task performance: 1969–1980. *Psychological Bulletin, 90,* 125–152.

Marston, D. (1989). A curriculum-based measurement approach to assessing academic performance: What is it and why do it? In M. R. Shinn (Ed.), *Curriculum-based measurement: Assessing special children* (pp. ××–××). New York: Guilford.

McDonnell, L. M., McLaughlin, M. J., & Morison, P. (Eds.). (1997). *Educating one and all: Students with disabilities and standards-based reform.* Washington, DC: National Academic Press.

Morris, R. D., Stuebing, K. K., Fletcher, J. M., Shaywitz, S. E., Lyon, G. R., Shankweiler, D. P., Katz, L., Francis, D. J., & Shaywitz, B. A. (1998). Subtypes of reading disability: Variability and a phonological core. *Journal of Educational Psychology, 80,* 347–373.

Phillips, S. E. (1994). High-stakes testing accommodations: Validity versus disabled rights. *Applied Measurement in Education, 7*(2), 93–120.

Shinn, M. R. (1989). (Ed.). *Curriculum-based measurement: Assessing special children.* New York: Guilford.

Speece, D. L., & Cooper, D. H. (1990). Ontogeny of school failure: Classification of first-grade children. *American Educational Research Journal, 27,* 119–140.

Stecker, P. M., & Fuchs, L. S. (In press). Effecting superior achievement using curriculum-based measurement: The importance of individual program monitoring. *Learning Disabilities Research and Practice.*

Swain, K. D., & Allinder, R. M. (1997). An exploration of the use of curriculum-based measurement by elementary special educators. *Diagnostique, 23,* 87–104.

Thurlow, M., Scott, D., & Ysseldyke, J. (1995). *A compilation of states' guidelines for including students with disabilities in assessments* (Synthesis Report No. 17). Minneapolis, MN: University of Minnesota, National Center on Educational Outcomes.

Wesson, C. L. (1991). Curriculum-based measurement and two models of follow-up consultation. *Exceptional Children, 57,* 246–257.

Wesson, C., Skiba, R., Sevcik, B., King, R., & Deno, S. L. (1984). The effects of technically adequate instructional data on achievement. *Remedial and Special Education, 5,* 17–22.

Ysseldyke, J. E. (2000, January). *Issues in the participation of students with disabilities within accountability systems.* Invited presentation at Vanderbilt University, Nashville.

Ysseldyke, J., Thurlow, M., McGrew, K. S., & Shriner, J. (1994). *Recommendations for making decisions about the participation of students with disabilities in statewide assessment programs* (Synthesis Report No. 15). Minneapolis, MN: University of Minnesota, National Center on Educational Outcomes.

Chapter 7

Strategic Learning in Students with Learning Disabilities: What Have We Learned?

Lynn Meltzer
Research Institute for Learning and Development and Tufts University

Marjorie Montague
University of Miami

INTRODUCTION

Over the past 40 years, conceptualizations of learning disabilities have changed from unitary approaches that emphasize isolated processes toward multidimensional approaches that focus on the interactions between neurologically based characteristics and environmentally transmitted influences. There has also been increasing recognition of the complex array of processes that contribute to learning including cognition, processing speed, background knowledge, and motivation. There is a growing understanding that learning problems are influenced by the complexity of the curriculum and the style of teaching. Consequently, the nature and severity of students' difficulties in learning may change over time as a function of the interactions among their developmental strengths and weaknesses on the one hand, and the curriculum complexity and volume on the other. The impact of learning disabilities is also affected by students' motivation and determination and the effort they are able or willing to expend in order to overcome and compensate for their difficulties in learning.

The past two decades have witnessed an increasing awareness of the importance of strategic learning as well as the range of difficulties that students with learning disabilities experience with strategy selection and strategy execution (Pressley, Symons, Snyder, & Cariglia-Bull, 1989; Stone & Conca, 1993; Swanson, Hoskyn, & Lee, 1999; Wong, 1986, 1987).

These students often do not know when to access strategies or which strategies to select. They are inefficient in abandoning ineffective strategies, and they do not readily adapt previously used strategies (Meltzer, 1993a, 1993b; Montague & Applegate, 1993a, 1993b; Stone and Conca, 1993). Research over the past 20 years has provided some explanations for these difficulties and a broad range of intervention strategies has been developed to address some of these deficits (Deshler, Warner, Schumaker, & Alley, 1983; Harris & Graham, 1992; Meltzer, 1993a, 1993b; Montague & Applegate, 1993b; Swanson et al., 1999; Wong, 1987). However, we have not yet found an answer to the question of how to teach and empower students to use strategies on a consistent basis in order to compensate for their learning difficulties.

DEFINITIONAL ISSUES

Before we discuss the research on strategic learning, it seems necessary to clarify what we mean by the term. Defining strategic learning has been somewhat difficult given the variation in terminology used by researchers. Alexander (2000), in her recent discussion of academic development and knowledge acquisition, suggests that knowledge reflects a broad range of processes and outcomes. These include the individual's perspectives and perceptions, degree of attention directed toward a task, comprehension, memory, motivation, strategic processing, problem solving, ability to consider alternative perspectives, and judgment of the importance of the information or task. Flavell (1985) uses the terms *metamemory* and *metacognition* in a similar vein to describe "any knowledge or cognitive activity that takes as its object, or regulates, any aspect of any cognitive enterprise" (p. 104). Sternberg (1985) described metacomponents as mechanisms that interact with knowledge acquisition and performance components. Thus, the terms *knowledge* and *metacognition* are not mutually exclusive and are commonly used in lieu of strategies or are construed as encompassing them. To further complicate the issue, executive functioning has been discussed at length (e.g., Lyon & Krasnegor, 1996) as being nearly synonymous with metacognition or mental control processes.

One of the most widely accepted definitions of strategies reflects the metacognitive and self-regulatory role they play and considers strategies as processes that are consciously devised to achieve particular goals (Paris, Wasik, & Turner, 1990). These researchers differentiate strategies from skills, which are viewed as unconscious, more automatic processes. However, they maintain that a close relationship exists between skills and strategies and that strategies are "skills under consideration" and can become skills when they "go underground" (Paris et al., 1990). Most recently, Swanson et al. (1999) used the term *strategy* to describe a range of specific processes including rehearsal, outlining, and memorizing as well as broader cognitive activities such as planning and comprehension. He views strategies as directed toward higher-order thinking such as problem solving, self-monitoring, and rule learning. Regardless of the variations in defining strategies, however, there seems to be consensus that strategies are cognitive and/or metacognitive processes or mental activities that facilitate learning and may be relatively simple or complex as a function of the level of the task. For example, a simple strategy might be a rhyme for memorizing a math fact (6 and 7 were mighty blue until they met 42) and a more complex strategy might be a mnemonic for remembering the critical steps involved in checking (STOPS = Check for Sentence structure, Tenses, Organization of the writing, Punctuation and paragraphs, and Spelling; Meltzer et al., 1996a)

This chapter addresses the role of strategies in the academic performance of students with learning disabilities from late elementary school onward. First, we provide an overview of strategy development and use in students with learning disabilities. Then, we review procedures for assessing strategic learning. Finally, we describe approaches to strategy instruction that have been effective with these students and issues surrounding strategy instruction in inclusive classrooms.

STRATEGY USE IN STUDENTS WITH LEARNING DISABILITIES

Deficits in strategic learning characterize many students with learning disabilities to the extent that their performance is often adversely affected across a broad range of content areas and their many strengths are masked (Meltzer, 1993a, 1993b; Pressley et al., 1989; Swanson, 1991). As a result, many of these students process information differently and use inefficient routes to access information, which compromises their accuracy and efficiency. Students with learning disabilities have been characterized as "actively inefficient learners" (Swanson, 1989) because of their weaknesses in a number of executive and self-regulatory strategies. They frequently have problems accessing, organizing, and coordinating multiple processes and strategies simultaneously or in close succession. Higher-level academic tasks such as reading comprehension, writing and composition, studying, and note taking can be particularly challenging because students may find it difficult to shift flexibly from the global themes to the details and back to the themes. They may also struggle to identify the salient attributes in different situations while ignoring irrelevant details (Meltzer, 1993a; Meltzer & Reid, 1994; Meltzer, Solomon,

Fenton, & Levine, 1989; Swanson, 1989, 1991). More often than not, these students neglect to use self-regulatory strategies such as checking, planning, monitoring, and revising (Short & Ryan, 1984; Swanson, 1989) and may fail to make efficient use of feedback concerning the relevance of their choices.

These strategic weaknesses do not uniformly characterize all students with learning disabilities, nor do they manifest across all learning situations in the same student. Students' success or failure is often governed by the complexity and volume of the task demands and the extent to which tasks require the rapid integration and coordination of multiple processes. For instance, students may display flexibility in their approach to structured verbal or nonverbal reasoning tasks, yet may be inflexible in an academic situation that demands the integrated use of a broad range of skills and strategies. Similarly, students may actively use learning strategies on tasks with which they are familiar but may not access strategies on other tasks that are perceived as too difficult or that require the simultaneous mobilization of multiple processes and strategies. They may also inappropriately rely on strategies that were previously helpful but are inadequate for meeting the increased complexity of new tasks.

SELF-AWARENESS, MOTIVATION, AND STRATEGY USE

Cognitive psychologists have long recognized the interrelationship of the cognitive and affective domains in the learning process. Studies of the interactions of these variables, however, have been relatively limited with respect to students with learning disabilities (e.g., Borkowski & Burke, 1996). Although intuitively we know that motivation to learn has a direct impact on students' attention, memory, and ability to recall information, the role that self-awareness and motivation play in the learning process is not sufficiently understood. Furthermore, these important affective attributes have been emphasized in instructional programs for students with learning disabilities. Research findings on these aspects of strategic learning have been somewhat equivocal, particularly with respect to students' self-perceptions of their academic performance.

The motivation to use strategic approaches in the learning situation is heavily dependent on students' self-awareness and self-understanding (Deshler et al., 1983; Deshler & Schumaker, 1986; Meltzer, 1995; Meltzer et al., 1998a; Paris and Winograd, 1990; Pressley et al., 1989). An underlying component of effective strategic learning is students' awareness of their own strengths and weaknesses and their understanding of the impact that strategies can have on their performance. In other words, they need to recognize and accept that their performance can be improved through effective strategy use and that strategy use can result in success. Their willingness to make the effort to use strategies is also affected by their self-concept and self-confidence in the learning situation, particularly when they have experienced considerable frustration and failure in school.

The question that seems most important here is whether the global and academic self-concepts of students with learning disabilities are positive enough to give them the impetus to use strategies. Findings have varied across studies and according to the form of self-concept that has been measured (see reviews by Chapman, 1988; McPhail & Stone, 1995; Meltzer, 1995). Investigations of global self-concept have shown positive feelings of self-worth in these students who have perceived themselves as equally capable and effective as their normally achieving peers (Renick & Harter, 1988, 1989; Winne, Woodlands, & Wong, 1982; McPhail & Stone, 1995). However, when academic self-concept has been the focus of the study, findings regarding students with learning disabilities have varied.

One group of studies has shown that students with learning disabilities often rate their academic abilities and achievement as lower than their normally achieving peers although they maintain positive feelings of overall self-worth (Grolnick & Ryan, 1990; Licht, 1993; Rogers & Saklofske, 1985; review by McPhail & Stone, 1995). Specifically, investigations have demonstrated that many of these students have negative self-perceptions of their ability as students and little confidence in their ability to learn. They often find themselves caught in a cycle of failure that begins with negative early school experiences, creating a sense of helplessness, low self-worth, and maladaptive attributional beliefs (Groteluschen, Borkowski, & Hale, 1990). In contrast, another group of studies has shown that many students with learning disabilities show positive academic self-concepts and that their academic self-ratings are higher than external ratings such as teacher evaluations, standardized achievement tests, and sociometric measures (Graham, Schwartz & McArthur, 1993; Grolnick & Ryan, 1990; Meltzer, Roditi, Houser, & Perlman, 1998a,b; Priel & Leshem, 1990; Schunk, 1989a, 1989b; Vaughn, Hogan, Kouzekanani, & Shapiro, 1990).

Similar findings were obtained in a large-scale study of a group of 663 students and their 57 teachers (Meltzer, Roditi, Houser, & Perlman, 1996, 1998a). Students with learning disabilities displayed very positive self-perceptions and rated themselves as appropriately strategic and competent in the domains of reading, writing, spelling, math, and organization. They also rated their level of effort and their use of strategies as average to above average. Students' self-ratings were more positive than their teachers' ratings in all the academic and organizational domains. Teachers rated the students with learning disabilities as weak in their strategy use and below average in their performance in all domains. These findings have added to the increasing body of research that students with learning disabilities frequently perceive themselves as capable and effective. Indeed, they often judge themselves as more strategic and academically stronger than their teachers judge them to be.

EFFORT AND STRATEGY USE

Another important concern has to do with the impact that effort, persistence, and determination have on strategy use and academic performance in students with learning disabilities. Because of their processing and skill deficits, students with learning disabilities must exert strong motivation, effort, and persistence in order to access the strategies they need to bypass their areas of weakness and to succeed academically. Until the 1990s, theories of learned helplessness postulated that students with learning disabilities may make less effort in the learning situation because of numerous and early school failures (Grolnick & Ryan, 1990; Licht, 1993). The basic tenet of these theories was that early school difficulties lead to learned helplessness and reduced effort in the learning situation. More recent research has shown, however, that students with learning disabilities exert considerable effort in the learning process and that their global self-concepts are positive enough to give them the impetus to expend the effort needed to learn (McPhail & Stone, 1995; Meltzer et al., 1998a,b). Nevertheless, investigations of students' self-perceptions, strategy use, and academic performance have only recently begun to include an analysis of the role of effort in the learning process (McPhail & Stone, 1995; Meltzer, Roditi et al., 1996; Montague & Applegate, in press; Sawyer, Nelson, Jayanthi, Bursuck, Epstein, 1996). Of interest is the finding by Sawyer et al. (1996) that students with learning disabilities who experienced success as a result of their effort felt more personal responsibility for their achievements, expressed a stronger intent to succeed, and were therefore more likely to continue to work hard.

A similar finding was obtained in a series of studies on the contribution of strategy use and effort toward academic achievement (Katzir-Cohen, Miller, Houser, & Meltzer, 2000; Meltzer, Katzir-Cohen, Miller, & Roditi, 2000). These studies were part of the *Strategies for Success* project, a two-year strategy intervention project in general education classrooms (Meltzer et al., 1998a,b). The investigation focused on students' perceptions of their level of effort, strategy use, and academic performance in the domains of reading, writing, spelling, math, and organization. The major objective was to compare students' perceptions with their teachers' ratings and to contrast high- and low-achieving students with and without learning disabilities. Findings showed that students' ratings were slightly discrepant from their teachers' judgments. Students viewed effort as the most important factor associated with their academic performance whereas their teachers viewed strategy use as the most important predictor of their students' academic achievement. Students with learning disabilities viewed themselves as motivated, appropriately strategic, and academically competent. In contrast, teachers rated these students as lower than they rated themselves in all these domains.

Of greatest interest was a comparison of teacher ratings of high-achieving students with learning disabilities and high achievers with no learning issues (Meltzer et al., 2000). Findings showed that teachers rated the effort and strategy use of both groups similarly. In other words, teachers' judgments of students' effort, hard work, and strategy use were influenced by the overall levels of academic performance attained by the students, and the existence of a learning disability did not interfere negatively with this perception. These findings suggest that students with learning disabilities who succeed academically when they work hard and make the effort are able to use the appropriate strategies in their reading, written language, and math work. When students are successful academically as a result of their hard work and strategy use, they feel empowered to take more responsibility for their work, to value the strategies they have used, and to continue to work hard. In other words, the positive outcome of their hard work and strategy use feeds self-concept and motivates them to continue to work hard and to make the effort to use the appropriate strategies. These findings further support the notion of a reciprocal strategy–effort interaction. Students must believe that making the effort to use strategies is worthwhile because these strategies lead to efficient and accurate academic performance. In other words, effort is central to strategy use, which, in turn, results in improved academic performance. These findings have important implications for assessment and intervention and for the prediction of the long-term outcomes of a learning disability.

ASSESSMENT OF STRATEGY USE

A core principle of process and strategy-oriented approaches to assessment is the belief that "individuals with comparable scores on static tests may have taken different paths to these scores, and [that] consideration of these differences can provide information of additional diagnostic value" (Campione, 1989). Over the past decade, there has been greater acceptance of the importance of holistic and interactive assessment paradigms that account for the strategies as well as the skills that students use in the learning situation and that contain specific implications for teaching and treatment (Campione, 1989; Haywood & Tzuriel, 1992; Lidz, 1987; Meltzer, 1993a, 1993b; Montague, 1996). Nevertheless, there is still a dearth of process and strategy assessment methods available for the diagnosis of learning disabilities. These measures are particularly critical for evaluating the performance of students from the fourth grade onward when the task demands shift toward an emphasis on the rapid integration of multiple subskills and strategies. The curriculum emphasis on independent work, study skills, summarizing, note taking, and multiple choice tests often exposes the weaknesses of students with learning disabilities. These academic tasks require students to access knowledge automatically and to coordinate and integrate multiple subskills and strategies. These skills are not typically assessed on traditional psychometric measures. Without appropriate assessment related specifically to strategic learning, the learning disability could easily be overlooked and students may instead be viewed as lazy or stubborn.

As the goal of assessment is to improve instruction, it is important to consider the specific objectives of instructional assessment, which Lloyd and Blandford (1991) have conceptualized as follows: (a) To identify those areas where instruction is needed, (b) To determine a starting point for instruction, (c) To determine what instructional method to use, and (d) To evaluate the success of instruction. These four goals can only be achieved if assessment and instruction are interconnected and are viewed as evolving processes that need constant refinement. One paradigm, which connects process-oriented assessment with classroom-based teaching, is the Assessment for Teaching model (AFT) (Meltzer, 1991; Meltzer & Roditi, 1989). Assessment is viewed as an ongoing process that is constantly modified and that, in turn, modifies teaching through follow-up and monitoring of student progress. Within the framework of the AFT model, assessment of each student's unique profile of strengths and weaknesses in cognitive and educational areas allows instruction to be targeted to each student's areas of strength and to address his or her areas of weakness. Assessment is conceptualized as a systematic process, which emphasizes the interactions among the child's developmental, cognitive, and educational skills and strategies as well as the overall curriculum expectations.

The AFT model incorporates the Surveys of Problem-Solving and Educational Skills (SPES), which merge dynamic and process approaches to assessment with strategy-oriented views of learning disabilities (Meltzer, 1987, 1993a, 1993b; Meltzer et al., 1989). The problem-solving and educational tasks incorporated in the SPES are anchored theoretically in a paradigm of strategic learning emphasizing the major components of strategy use that are essential for learning: efficiency, flexibility, methods, styles, and the ability to justify the solutions provided. These components of strategic learning focus on identification of students' understanding of task instructions, their ease in formulating strategies, their ability to identify salient details, and the flexibility with which they shift problem-solving approaches. The SPES emphasizes the importance of systematic, strategy-oriented assessment and addresses the close connections among automaticity, problem-solving strategies, and educational performance. The tasks identify how students solve problems as well as their strategic planning, monitoring of errors, and self-corrections. The SPES incorporates two equally important components: the Survey of Problem-Solving Skills (SPRS) and the Survey of Educational Skills (SEDS). The SPRS is a process measure that provides information about the strategies that the student uses to solve nonacademic problem-solving tasks; their impact on educational performance in the reading, writing, and math areas is explored during administration of the SEDS. The two inventories are used together to evaluate the connections among problem-solving strategies, learning processes, and educational outcomes, thus ensuring continuity between assessment and teaching practices. This criterion-referenced assessment system emphasizes the importance of identifying how students solve problems, not just how they come to their final solutions. Strategic planning, monitoring of errors, and self-corrections are also assessed. Students' profiles on both these surveys are used to generate educational recommendations that take account of their strengths and weaknesses in problem-solving and educational areas. It should be noted that strategy assessment methods such as the SPES can constitute one component of performance-based assessment and can provide teachers with an additional lens for understanding their students' strengths and weaknesses as they manifest in the classroom.

Questionnaires and Rating Systems

Questionnaires, rating systems, and think-aloud methods have been useful for informally assessing students' self-perceptions as well as their knowledge and use of strategies (Harris & Graham, 1999; Meltzer et al., 1998a; Montague, 1996). One example is Montague's (1993a) Mathematical Problem-Solving Assessment (MPSA), (Montague, 1993; Montague & Applegate, 1993a) which is a two-part interview for middle school students. First, students solve six word problems and then are interviewed about what they did as they solved the problems. Part One has

20 items measuring perceptions of mathematical achievement and the importance of mathematical problem solving, attitudes toward mathematics, and general strategy knowledge. Part Two has 56 objective and open-ended items measuring students' knowledge and use of cognitive and metacognitive strategies specific to mathematical problem solving. Research indicates that the MPSA differentiates between average and above-average achievers and students with learning disabilities in the number and type of problem-solving strategies they know about and use. The instrument has been modified into a shorter version, the MPSA-Short Form (Montague, 1996) and is recommended as a quick, informal measure of students' perceptions as well as their strategy knowledge and use.

Another example of a classroom-based strategy rating system is the Strategy Observation System (SOS). This is anchored in a strategic learning paradigm (Meltzer, 1993a) and was developed as part of a three-year strategy intervention program, *Strategies for Success* (Meltzer et al., 1996a, 1998a,b; Meltzer, Roditi, & Stein, 1998c). This consists of three questionnaires, one for students and two for teachers. The first measure, the Student Self-Report System (SSRS), is a 50-item questionnaire evaluating students' perceptions of the extent to which they use strategies in five academic areas: reading, written language, spelling, math, and organization. Students rate themselves on a 5-point scale on items such as: "When I read, I ask myself questions to help me remember," "Before I write, I plan my ideas on paper." The second measure, the Teacher Observation System (TOS), is a 20-item questionnaire that provides teachers with a brief, systematic method for observing and analyzing students' efficiency and flexibility in strategic learning and self-monitoring strategies. Teachers observe students' learning strategies and work habits in the same domains that are evaluated on the SSRS and they rate students' strategy use on a 5-point scale on items such as the following: Uses outlines to organize writing, Uses strategies (e.g., pictures) to solve word problems. Finally, the Survey of Strategy Awareness (SOSA) emphasizes teachers' understanding of the importance of learning strategies and encourages them to reflect on their students' learning profiles and their own teaching methods.

In summary, although a few measures are available for assessing strategy use, the situation has not improved significantly since Wong (1991) discussed the problems experienced by teachers and practitioners who did not have appropriate assessment techniques available for evaluating their students' metacognitive strategies. It is clear that more evaluation systems need to be developed for assessing the interactions among strategic learning, self-awareness, and motivation.

STRATEGY INSTRUCTION FOR STUDENTS WITH LEARNING DISABILITIES

Cognitive strategy research has focused primarily on identifying the types of process and strategic difficulties experienced by students with learning disabilities and providing systematic strategy instruction to ameliorate the processing problems (e.g., Harris & Graham, 1999; Meltzer, 1995; Montague & Applegate, in press). The theoretical basis for cognitive strategy intervention is that effective and efficient use of strategies will improve students' information processing, thus having a positive effect on comprehension, problem solving, and learning in general. This section first describes the components of effective strategy instruction as empirically determined by Swanson et al. (1999). Second, examples are presented that indicate how effective approaches incorporate these principles and procedures into academic instruction for students with learning disabilities.

Swanson and his colleagues (1999) reported the results of comprehensive meta-analyses of both single-subject and group intervention studies conducted over the past 20 years with students with learning disabilities. The most salient finding from their analyses was that strategy instruction and direct instruction models were the most effective of the myriad of interventions studied. They identified studies as representative of the direct instruction model if they focused on skill development and included some of these components: (a) drills and probes, (b) ongoing feedback, (c) fast-paced instruction, (d) individualization, (e) task analysis, (f) pictures and diagrams, (g) small-group instruction, and (h) directed questions. In contrast, studies reflecting the strategy instruction model focused on processes (like metacognition) and included some of these components: (a) descriptions, elaborations, and explanations of the task and how to perform the task; (b) cognitive modeling by the teacher; (c) cues, prompts, and reminders to use the strategy being taught; and (d) probes, questions, and ongoing demonstrations. For the purposes of delineating the most effective instructional procedures, Swanson et al. (1999) went beyond the initial analyses to identify the most important components of these instructional models. The components that emerged as most important to the academic success of students were sequencing, drill/practice/feedback, task analysis, technology, task difficulty, control, modeling, cues and prompts, supplemental support, small-group instruction, and directed questions/responses. The following examples of effective strategy instruction focus on techniques for teaching students a process for writing compositions, solving mathematical problems, and comprehending what they read.

Harris and Graham (1999) have conducted over 20 studies to improve the composition skills of students using an approach titled "Self-Regulated Strategy Development." The self-regulation component includes explicitly teaching students how to give themselves instructions, set goals, and monitor their own performance. Their program for improving writing in students with learning disabilities contains the following components: (a) developing students' background knowledge; (b) discussing the purpose of strategy instruction and students' pretest performance; (c) presenting and explaining the strategy; (d) modeling and discussing how to use self-instructions; (e) describing how to use goal-setting and self-monitoring; (f) modeling the writing process using all elements; (f) having students memorize the strategy steps and self-instructions; (g) providing practice and support; and (h) finally moving to independent performance with feedback, goal-setting, and self-monitoring procedures. This approach teaches students strategies specific to the writing process for understanding and incorporating the rules and mechanics of writing into compositions, formulating and organizing ideas, adhering to the form and structure of the composition, setting a purpose and goals for writing, and evaluating what they write.

Another example of effective strategy instruction is Montague's "Solve It!," a comprehensive instructional routine for improving students' mathematical problem solving (Montague & Warger, 2000). This routine teaches students strategies for deciding what to do when they solve problems. Students learn how to understand the mathematical problems, analyze the information presented, develop logical plans to solve problems, and evaluate their solutions. Students are taught specifically how to read the problem for understanding, paraphrase by putting the problem into their own words, visualize the problem by drawing a picture or making a mental image, set up a plan for solving the problem, estimate the answer, and compute and verify the solution. Students are also taught self-regulation strategies needed for effective problem solving, which include giving themselves instructions, asking themselves questions, and monitoring their performance. Self-regulation strategies such as self-instruction, self-questioning, and self-monitoring assist students in comprehension and problem solving by developing their strategic knowledge, guiding them as they apply that knowledge, and regulating their use of strategies and their performance during complex academic tasks. These strategies help problem solvers gain access to strategic knowledge, guide learners as they apply strategies, and regulate learners' use of strategies and their overall performance as they solve problems.

Other strategy instruction researchers have also focused on addressing noncognitive factors related to academic performance of students with learning disabilities. Implementing what they refer to as "achievement change programs," Borkowski and colleagues have integrated attribution retraining with strategy instruction that includes training in self-control and self-regulation (Borkowski & Burke, 1996; Borkowski, Reid, & Kurtz, 1984). In one of these studies, students with learning disabilities received attribution retraining that focused on the importance of effort in addition to strategy instruction to improve reading comprehension. These students outperformed other students with learning disabilities who received only attribution training or only strategy training (Borkowski, Weyhing, & Carr, 1988). Thus, there appears to be an important connection between effort-related attribution, motivation, strategy use, and achievement.

In sum, there are elements or components of strategy instruction that seem essential to its effectiveness for students with learning disabilities. Additionally, it is necessary to assess student performance and identify students for whom strategy instruction is appropriate. It is particularly important to instruct students in the acquisition and application of strategies in the context of domain-specific tasks, and to evaluate student outcomes systematically to ensure that the strategies are maintained and generalized. It seems essential that teachers address the noncognitive factors as well and provide students with activities to improve their academic self-perceptions, to develop their ability to understand the complexity levels of problems and to judge their level of difficulty.

STRATEGY INSTRUCTION IN INCLUSIVE CLASSROOMS

The recent trend toward inclusive classrooms means that increasing numbers of students with learning disabilities receive the majority of their instruction in the context of the general education program. Because we know from the research base that students with learning disabilities more closely approximate the performance of normally achieving students when educational programming includes strategy instruction, it is critical to incorporate strategy instruction into their academic programs (Swanson et al., 1999). There are two major considerations when programming for students with learning disabilities in inclusive classrooms. First, how, where, and by whom should explicit domain-specific instruction be provided for these students? Second, what instructional practice methods can general education classroom teachers use without much effort to enhance academic learning for students with learning disabilities in inclusive classrooms?

To address the first question, research-based strategy instruction needs to be provided by expert remedial teachers who understand the characteristics of students with learning disabilities and the principles associated with assisting students in learning, applying, and generalizing strategies (Montague, 1993). Strategy instruction is generally intense and time-limited and needs to be provided to small groups of students to ensure an optimal outcome. Both general and special education teachers need to collaborate in planning how students will receive strategy instruction and how they will be given opportunities to apply and generalize these strategies. Most importantly, students need opportunities to succeed as a result of using a strategy and to recognize the link between their use of a specific strategy and their academic improvement.

To address the second question regarding specific instructional practices for general education teachers, there are several research-based strategy instruction methods that have been shown to enhance learning for students with learning disabilities. These methods can be easily incorporated into daily instruction by general education classroom teachers (Swanson et al., 1999, p. 218). These include (a) sequencing (breaking the task into component subtasks, short activities, step-by-step prompts that are eventually faded); (b) drill and repetition, review, and distributed practice; (c) segmentation (task analysis and synthesis of component parts); (d) skilled and multilevel directed questions and responses; (e) adjusting the difficulty level and processing demands of the task; (f) using technology to enhance and supplement learning; (g) cognitive or think-aloud modeling of successful task completion; (h) interactive, small-group instruction; (i) enlisting peers, tutors, or parents to supplement instruction; and (j) cueing students to use the strategies they have learned. After carefully analyzing and synthesizing the intervention research, Swanson et al. (1999) concluded that strategy instruction needs to be systematic, explicit, and recursive and should occur in both the special and general education settings. Because most of the instructional programs that were effective for these students occurred in special education settings, there seems to be strong support for provision of strategy instruction in small-group remedial settings.

The remaining question regards the effectiveness of classroom-based strategy instruction and how classroom teachers can provide strategy instruction that generalizes to academic performance. In a study of 72 classroom teachers and their 625 students from grades four through nine, significant improvements were identified in the strategy use, organization, and academic performance of students with learning disabilities (Meltzer et al., 1996b; Meltzer et al., 1998a,b). In this study, teachers were assigned to one of two intervention groups that received different levels of strategy instruction or they were assigned to a control group that received no intervention. Teachers were trained through in-service sessions and classroom consultations to embed strategies in the context of the curriculum. Findings indicated that students with learning disabilities used strategies more consistently and effectively as a result of the classroom-based strategy instruction. Students were viewed by their teachers as more strategic in reading, writing, spelling, math, and organization as well as planning and self-monitoring. Their increased strategy use was also reflected in their significantly improved academic performance in all these domains. Most importantly, these strategies benefited the average-achieving students with no learning disabilities who also became more strategic and more effective in their classroom work. In contrast, in the control classrooms where teachers did not receive strategy training, students did not show increased strategy use nor did they show academic improvements. Notwithstanding these gains, the students with learning disabilities still used strategies less often than the average achievers even after the intervention program. This reflected their need for more intense strategy instruction in a small-group, special education setting.

These results were consistent with the conclusions of Swanson et al. (1999) that a continuum of services provides the most effective instructional opportunities for students with learning disabilities. In other words, students with learning disabilities need a "double dose" of strategy instruction (Meltzer et al., 1998c) to be provided in the large-group classroom setting as well as the more structured and individualized remedial setting, often over a number of years. Use of strategies in both settings allows for consolidation and generalization and ensures that students learn to use strategies flexibly in different domains and with different tasks. Small-group instruction provides opportunities for practice and mastery of strategies while classroom-based instruction ensures that generalization occurs.

CONCLUSION

Now that we have strong evidence for the effectiveness of strategy instruction for students with learning disabilities, researchers can begin to examine the combinations and components that are most effective and for whom they are most effective. Given the limited instructional time that students spend in the classroom, it is crucial that researchers identify the most parsimonious approach to strategy instruction, the conditions under which strategy instruction works best, and the techniques and procedures that will help students to maintain and generalize strategy use. Intervention research must continue to be a priority. The past 20 years of research offers considerable insight into the instructional approaches that are most effective for students with learning disabilities. The next

20 years should provide even more solid evidence to support the critical role of strategic teaching and learning for these students.

ACKNOWLEDGMENTS

A special thanks from Lynn Meltzer to Bethany Roditi, Ph.D., Joan Steinberg, M.Ed, Lynne Miller, M.A., and Irene Papadopoulos, M.A. for their support and many helpful comments during the preparation of this manuscript.

REFERENCES

Alexander, P. A. (2000). Toward a model of academic development: Schooling and the acquisition of knowledge. *Educational Researcher, 29,* 28–33.

Borkowski, J. G., & Burke, J. E. (1996). Theories, models, and measurements of executive functioning. In G. R. Lyon & N. A. Krasnegor (Eds.), *Attention, memory, and executive function* (pp. 235–262). Baltimore, MD: Paul Brooks.

Borkowski, J. G., Reid, M. K., & Kurtz, B. E. (1984). Metacognition and mental retardation: Paradigmatic, theoretical, and applied perspectives. In M. McCawly & B. Broods (Eds.), *Learning and cognition in the mentally retarded* (pp. 33–57). Hillsdale, NJ: Lawrence Erlbaum.

Borkowski, J. G., Weyhing, R. S., & Carr, M. (1988). Effects of attributional training on strategy based reading comprehension in learning-disabled students. *Journal of Educational Psychology, 80,* 46–53.

Campione, J. C. (1989). Assisted assessment: A taxonomy of approaches and an outline of strengths and weaknesses. *Journal of Learning Disabilities, 22,* 151–165.

Chapman, J. W. (1988). Learning disabled children's self-concepts. *Review of Educational Research, 58,* 347–371.

Deshler, D. D., & Schumaker, J. B. (1986). Learning strategies: An instructional alternative for low achieving adolescents. *Exceptional Children, 52*(6), 583–590.

Deshler, D. D., Warner, M. M., Schumaker, J. B., & Alley, G. R. (1983). Learning strategies intervention model: Key components and current status. In J. D. McKinney & L. Feagans (Eds.), *Current topics in learning disabilities* (pp. 245–283). Norwood, NJ: Ablex.

Dykman, R. A., Ackerman, P. T., & Ogelby, D. M. (1979). Selective and sustained attention in hyperactive, learning disabled, and normal boys. *Journal of Nervous and Mental Disease, 167,* 288–297.

Flavell, J. H. (1985). *Cognitive development* (2nd ed.). Englewood Cliffs, NJ: Prentice-Hall.

Graham, S., & Harris, K. (1993). Teaching writing strategies to students with learning disabilities: Issues and recommendations. In L. J. Meltzer (Ed.), *Strategy assessment and instruction for students with learning disabilities: From theory to practice* (pp. 271–292). Austin, TX: Pro-Ed.

Graham, S., Schwartz, S., & McArthur, C. (1993). Knowledge of writing and the composing process, attitude toward writing, self-efficacy for students with and without learning disabilities. *Journal of Learning Disabilities, 26*(4), 237–249.

Grolnick, W. S., & Ryan, R. M. (1990). Self perceptions, motivation, and adjustment in children with learning disabilities: A multiple group comparison study. *Journal of Learning Disabilities, 23*(3), 177–184.

Groteluschen, A., Borkowski, J., & Hale, C. (1990). Strategy instruction is often insufficient: Addressing the interdependency of executive and attributional processes. In T. E. Scruggs & B. Y. L. Wong (Eds.), *Intervention research in learning disabilities* (pp. 81–101). New York: Springer-Verlag.

Harris, K. R., & Graham, S. (1992). *Helping young writers master the craft: strategy instruction and self regulation in the writing process.* Cambridge, MA: Brookline Press.

Harris, K. R., & Graham, S. (1999). Programmatic intervention research: Illustrations from the evolution of self-regulated strategy development. *Learning Disability Quarterly, 22,* 251–263.

Haywood, H. C., & Tzuriel, D. (1992). *Interactive Assessment.* New York: Springer-Verlag.

Katzir-Cohen, Miller, Houser, R. F., & Meltzer. L. J. (2000). *Self-perceptions of effort, strategy use and achievement in students with learning disabilities.* Paper to be presented at the International Academy for Research in Learning Disabilities, British Columbia, Canada.

Licht, B. (1993). Achievement-related beliefs in children with learning disabilities: Impact on motivation and strategic learning. In L. J. Meltzer (Ed.), *Strategy assessment and instruction for students with learning disabilities: From theory to practice* (pp. 195–220). Austin, TX: Pro-Ed.

Lidz, C. (1987). *Dynamic assessment.* New York: Guilford Press.

Lloyd, J. W., & Blandford, B. J. (1991). Assessment for instruction. In H. L. Swanson (Ed.), *Handbook on the assessment of learning disabilities: Theory, research, and practice.* TX: Pro-Ed.

Lyon, G. R., & Krasnegor, N. A. (1996). *Attention, memory, and executive function.* Baltimore, MD: Paul H. Brookes.

Mastropieri, M. A., & Scruggs, T. E. (1991). *Teaching students ways to remember: Strategies for learning mnemonically.* Cambridge, MA: Brookline Books.

McPhail, J. C., & Stone, C. A. (1995). The self-concept of adolescents with learning disabilities: A review of the literature and a call for theoretical elaboration. *Advances in Learning and Behavioral Disabilities, 9,* 193–226.

Meltzer, L. J. (1987). *The surveys of problem-solving and educational skills.* Cambridge, MA: Educator's Publishing Service.

Meltzer, L. J. (1990). Problem-solving strategies and academic performance in learning disabled students: Do subtypes exist? In L. Feagans, E. J. Short, & L. Meltzer (Eds.), *Learning disability subtypes.* Hillsdale, NJ: Erlbaum.

Meltzer, L. J. (1991). Problem-solving strategies and academic performance in learning disabled students: Do subtypes exist? In L. V. Feagans, E. J. Short, & L. J. Meltzer (Eds.), *Subtypes of learning disabilities* (pp. 163–188). Hillsdale, NJ: Lawrence.

Meltzer, L. J. (1993). Strategy use in learning disabled students: The challenge of assessment. In L. Meltzer (Ed.), *Strategy assessment and instruction for students with learning disabilities: From theory to practice* (pp. 93–136). Austin, TX: Pro-Ed.

Meltzer, L. J. (1993a). Strategy use in children with learning disabilities: The challenge of assessment. In L. J. Meltzer (Ed.), *Strategy assessment and instruction for students with learning disabilities: From theory to practice* (pp. 93–136). Austin, TX: Pro-Ed.

Meltzer, L. J. (1993b). *Are LD students' self perceptions of their academic strategies and competence realistic?* Paper presented at the International Academy for Research in Learning Disabilities, Boston, MA.

Meltzer, L. J. (1995). Strategic learning in students with learning disabilities: The role of students' self-awareness and self-perceptions. In T. E. Scruggs & M. Mastropieri (Eds.), *Advances in learning and behavioral disabilities* (pp. 181–199). Greenwich, CT: JAI.

Meltzer, L. J. Katzir-Cohen, Miller, & Roditi. B. (2000). *Effort, strategy use and academic performance: Student and teacher perspectives.* Paper to be presented at the International Academy for Research in Learning Disabilities, British Columbia, Canada.

Meltzer, L., & Reid, D. (1994). New directions in the assessment of students with special needs: The shift toward a constructivist perspective. *The Journal of Special Education, 28*(3), 338–355.

Meltzer, L. J., Roditi, B., Haynes, D., Biddle, L., Paster, M., & Taber, S. (1996). *Strategies for success: Classroom teaching techniques for students with learning problems.* Austin, TX: Pro-Ed.

Meltzer, L. J., Roditi, B., Houser, R. F., & Perlman, M. (1996). *The strategies for success program: Helping classroom teachers to address the needs of students with learning and attentional difficulties.* Paper presented at the International Academy for Research in Learning Disabilities, Dearborn, Michigan, 1996.

Meltzer, L. J., Roditi, B., Houser, R. F., & Perlman, M. (1998a). Perceptions of academic strategies and competence in students with learning disabilities. *Journal of Learning Disabilities, 31*(5), 437–451.

Meltzer, L. J., Roditi, B., Houser, R. F., & Perlman, M. (1998b). The strategies for success program: Helping classroom teachers to address the needs of students with learning and attentional difficulties. *Thalamus, 16*(1), 25–26.

Meltzer, L. J., Roditi, B. N., & Stein, J. (1998c) Strategy Instruction: The Heartbeat of Successful Inclusion. *Perspectives,* 11–13.

Meltzer, L. J., Solomon, B., Fenton, T., & Levine, M. D. (1989). A developmental study of problem-solving strategies in children with and without learning difficulties. *Journal of Applied Developmental Psychology, 10,* 171–193.

Meyers, J., Pfeffer, J., & Erlbaum, V. (1985). Process assessment: A model for broadening assessment. *Journal of Special Education, 19*(1), 73–87.

Montague, M. (1992). The effects of cognitive and metacognitive strategy instruction on mathematical problem solving of middle school students with learning disabilities. *Journal of Learning Disabilities, 25,* 230–248.

Montague, M. (1993). Student-centered or strategy centered instruction: What is our purpose? *Journal of Learning Disabilities, 26,* 433–437.

Montague, M. (1996). Assessing mathematical problem solving. *Learning Disabilities Research and Practice, 11,* 228–238.

Montague, M. (1997a). Student perception, mathematical problem solving, and learning disabilities. *Remedial and Special Education, 18,* 46–53.

Montague, M. (1997b). Cognitive strategy training in mathematics instruction for students with learning disabilities. *Journal of Learning Disabilities, 30,* 164–177.

Montague, M., & Applegate, B. (In press). Middle school students' perceptions, persistence, and performance in mathematical problem solving. *Learning Disability Quarterly.*

Montague, M., & Applegate, B. (1993a). Mathematical problem-solving characteristics of middle school students with learning disabilities. *The Journal of Special Education, 27,* 175–201.

Montague, M., & Applegate, B. (1993b). Middle school students' mathematical problem solving: An analysis of think-aloud protocols. *Learning Disability Quarterly, 16,* 19–32.

Montague, M., Applegate, B., & Marquard, K. (1993). Cognitive strategy instruction and mathematical problem-solving performance of students with learning disabilities. *Learning Disabilities Research and Practice, 29,* 251–261.

Montague, M., & Bos, C. (1986). The effect of cognitive strategy training on verbal math problem solving performance of learning disabled adolescents. *Journal of Learning Disabilities, 19,* 26–33.

Montague, M., Bos, C., & Doucette, M. (1991). Affective, cognitive, and metacognitive attributes of eighth-grade mathematical problem solvers. *Learning Disabilities Research and Practice, 6,* 145–151.

Montague, M., & Warger, C. (2000). Solve it! Strategy instruction to improve mathematical problem solving. *Learning Disabilities Research and Practice, 15,* 110–116.

Paris, S. G., Wasik, B. A., & Turner, J. C. (1990). The development of strategic readers. In P. D. Pearson (Ed.), *Handbook of reading research,* 2nd ed. (pp. 609–640). New York: Longman.

Paris, S. G., & Winograd, P. (1990). How metacognition can promote academic learning and instruction. In B. Jones & L. Idol (Eds.), *Dimensions of thinking and cognitive instruction* (pp. xx–xx). Hillsdale, NJ: Erlbaum.

Pressley, M., Borkowski, J. G., Forrest-Pressley, D., Gaskins I., & Wile, D. (1993). Closing thoughts in strategy instruction for individuals with learning disabilities: The good information processing perspective. In L. J. Meltzer (Ed.), *Strategy assessment and instruction for students with learning disabilities: From theory to practice* (pp. 355–377). Austin, TX: Pro-Ed.

Pressley, M., Symons, S., Snyder, B. L., & Cariglia-Bull, T. (1989). Strategy instruction research comes of age. *Learning Disabilities Quarterly, 12,* 16–30.

Priel, B., & Leshem, T. (1990). Self-perceptions of first and second grade children with learning disabilities. *Journal of Learning Disabilities, 23*(10), 637–642.

Putnam, M., Deshler, D., & Schumaker, J. (1993). The investigation of setting demands: A missing link in learning strategy instruction. In L. J. Meltzer (Ed.), *Strategy assessment and instruction for students with learning disabilities: From theory to practice* (pp. 325–354). Austin, TX: Pro-Ed.

Renick, M. J., & Harter, S. (1988). Manual for the self-perception profile for learning disabled students. Unpublished manuscript, University of Denver.

Renick, M. J., & Harter, S. (1989). Impact of social comparisons on the developing self-perceptions of learning disabled students. *Journal of Educational Psychology, 81,* 631–638.

Roditi, B. (1993). Mathematics assessment and strategy instruction: An applied developmental approach. In L. J. Meltzer (Ed.), *Strategy assessment and instruction for students with learning disabilities: From theory to practice* (pp. 293–324). Austin, TX: Pro-Ed.

Rogers, H., & Saklofske, D. H. (1985). Self-concepts, locus control and performance expectations of learning disabled children. *Journal of Learning Disabilities, 18,* 273–278.

Sawyer, V., Nelson, J. S., Jayanthi, M., Bursuck, W. D., & Epstein, M. H. (1996). Views of students with learning disabilities of their homework in general education classes: Student interviews. *Learning Disabilities Quarterly, 19,* 70–85.

Schunk, D. H. (1985). Self-efficacy and classroom learning. *Psychology in the Schools, 22,* 208–223.

Schunk, D. H. (1989a). Self-efficacy and achievement behaviors. *Educational Psychology Review, 1*(3), 173–205.

Schunk, D. H. (1989b). Self efficacy and cognitive achievement: Implications for students with learning problems. *Journal of Learning Disabilities, 22*(1), 14–22.

Scruggs, T. E., Bennion, K. E., & Lifson, S. A. (1985). An analysis of children's strategy use on reading achievement tests. *Elementary School Journal, 85,* 479–484.

Scruggs, T. E., & Mastropieri, M. (1988). Are learning-disabled students test-wise? A review of recent research. *Learning Disabilities Focus, 3,* 87–97.

Scruggs, T. E., & Mastropieri, M. (1992). Classroom applications of Mnemonic instruction: Acquisition, maintenance and generalization. *Exceptional Children, 58,* 219–229.

Scruggs, T. E., & Mastropieri, M. (Eds.). (1995). *Teaching test-taking skills: Helping students show what they know.* Cambridge, MA: Brookline Books.

Scruggs, T. E., & Tolfa, D. (1985). Improving the test-taking skills of learning disabled students. *Perceptual and Motor Skills, 60,* 847–850.

Short, E. J., & Ryan, E. B. (1984). Metacognitive differences between skilled and less skilled readers: Remediating deficits through story grammar and attribution training. *Journal of Educational Psychology, 76,* 225–235.

Sternberg, R. J. (1985). *Beyond IQ: A triarchic theory of human intelligence.* Cambridge, MA: Cambridge University Press.

Stone, C. A., & Conca, L. (1993). The origin of strategy deficits in children with learning disabilities: A social constructivist perspective. In L. J. Meltzer (Ed.), *Strategy assessment and instruction for students with learning disabilities: From theory to practice* (pp. 23–59). Austin, TX: Pro-Ed.

Stone, C. A., & Michals, D. (1986). Problem solving skills in learning disabled children. In S. J. Ceci (Ed.), *Handbook of cognitive, social, and neuropsychological aspects of learning disabilities,* Vol. 1. (pp. 291–315). Hillsdale, NJ: Erlbaum.

Swanson, H. L. (1985). Assessing learning disabled children's intellectual performance: An information processing perspective. In K. Gadow (Ed.), *Advances in learning and behavior disabilities* (pp. 225–272). Greenwich, CT: JAI Press.

Swanson, H. L. (1987). The influence of verbal ability and metamemory on future recall. *British Journal of Educational Psychology, 53,* 179–190.

Swanson, H. L. (1989). Strategy instruction: Overview of principles and procedures for effective use. *Learning Disabilities Quarterly, 12,* 3–15.

Swanson, H. L. (1991). Learning disabilities and memory. In B. Y. L. Wong (Ed.), *Learning about learning disabilities* (pp. 103–127). San Diego: Academic Press.

Swanson, H. L., Hoskyn, M., & Lee, C. (1999). *Interventions for students with learning disabilities: A meta-analysis of treatment outcomes.* New York: Guilford Press.

Vaughn, S., Hogan, A., Kouzekanani, K. B., & Shapiro, S. (1990). Peer acceptance, self-perceptions and social skills of learning disabled students prior to indentification. *Journal of Educational Psychology, 82,* 101–106.

Winne, P. J., Woodlands, M. J., & Wong, B. Y. L. (1982). Comparability of self-concept among learning disabled, normal, and gifted students. *Journal of Learning Disabilities, 15,* 470–475.

Wong, B. Y. (1986). Metacognition and special education: A review of a view. *The Journal of Special Education, 20,* 9–29.

Wong, B. Y. L. (1987). How do the results of metacognitive research impact on the learning disabled individual? *Learning Disability Quarterly, 10,* 189–195.

Wong, B. Y. L. (1991). Assessment of metacognitive research in learning disabilities: Theory, research, and practice. In H. L Swanson (Ed.), *Handbook on the assessment of learning disabilities: Theory, research, and practice* (pp. 265–283). Austin, TX: Pro-Ed.

Chapter 8

Structure and Effective Teaching

Margaret P. Weiss
University of North Carolina-Chapel Hill

John Wills Lloyd
University of Virginia

It is no accident that the words *structure* and *instruction* share the Latin root *struere*, meaning "to heap together" or "to arrange." Structure is apparent in instruction in many ways. Ordering classroom environments to promote appropriate behavior and transfer of learning, teaching students to use step-by-step strategies, and systematically arranging teaching presentations each reflects the influence of structure in instruction. Each of these aspects of instruction is important not only for students with disabilities but also for teaching in general.

One does not have to look deeply into the works of William Cruickshank to find emphasis on these fundamental building blocks of teaching. They are evident, for example, in the title of the first chapter in *A Teaching Method for Brain-injured and Hyperactive Children* (Cruickshank, Bentzen, Ratzeburg, & Tannhauser, 1961): "The Educational Problem and Design." Furthermore, Cruickshank and colleagues considered four elements to be essential in teaching these students: reducing environmental stimuli, reducing space, structuring classrooms, and increasing the salience of materials. Though his ideas were developed and published in the 1950s and 1960s, components of Cruickshank's theories are apparent in effective instructional practices used with students with learning, attention, and emotional or behavioral disabilities in the twenty-first century. In this chapter we take up each of these elements, providing a combination of retrospective review and illustrations of how vestiges of them are still present in contemporary special education.

MODIFICATIONS TO THE PHYSICAL ENVIRONMENT

In *A Teaching Method,* Cruickshank and colleagues (1961) noted that "the children herein under consideration are frequently characterized by marked and abnormal distractibility, and they are unable to refrain from reacting to unessential stimuli" (p. 15). To teach these children successfully, the authors recommended reducing a child's exposure to environmental stimuli and reducing the child's space within a classroom. Together, these two elements were used to promote students' attention to the instructional task exclusively.

Reduced Environmental Stimuli

Reducing environmental stimuli meant that:

> The color of the walls, woodwork, and furniture should match the floor; windows should be made opaque; bulletin boards and pictures should be removed; intercommunication systems should be disconnected and pencil sharpeners removed; ceilings and walls near halls should be sound-treated . . . , all furniture should be removed except that which is absolutely essential to the teaching program; and the number of children in the group should be significantly reduced below normal registration for an elementary classroom. (Cruickshank et al., 1961, p. 16)

Within the experimental classrooms set up by Cruickshank and colleagues to test their theory, researchers used blackboards with only white or yellow chalk and did not post daily schedules. Teachers covered the bulletin boards and did not display student work until the end of the year. In addition, cabinets were enclosed and other storage spaces eliminated or covered. Eliminating unneeded stimulation was not meant to impoverish the learning environment, rather Cruickshank hypothesized that "if the learning environment can be stripped of unessential stimuli, other things being equal, . . . the hyperactive child has an increased opportunity to attend for necessary periods of time to those stimuli which are essential to his learning and achievement" (Cruickshank et al., 1961, p. 16).

Reduced Working Space

Cruickshank and colleagues also recommended that students work in reduced amounts of space. This included using a classroom that was just large enough to contain the desks and chairs of students so that "busy hands and feet cannot reach out to touch anyone" (p. 148). Reduced space also meant students would work in individual cubicles that did not contain any posted work or papers that were not in use. Cruickshank et al. described the cubicles as follows.

> [T]he walls...should be painted the same color as other structures in the room; they should be solid to the floor and approximately seven feet high. Each cubicle will be open on the fourth side. Each child's desk will be facing away from the open side toward the back wall. The two side walls will be constructed so as to terminate about six to eight inches beyond the child's back when he is seated at this desk to obviate distraction which may otherwise come peripherally to the child from the adjoining cubicles. The desk will be permanently fixed to the cubicle walls to minimize motor disinhibition. (1961, p. 17)

As with other adaptations, the reason for using cubicles within the classroom was to control the environmental stimuli and to condition students to attend to instructional materials.

Research on These Components

Cruickshank and colleagues developed a demonstration project to test their theory. They included 40 students ranging from 6 years 11 months to 10 years 11 months in age and who were identified as having significant attention problems. After a year in this program, the experimental group made gains in perceptual–motor skills and degree of distractibility but not on measures of intelligence or achievement. In addition, at a one-year follow-up, the gains had disappeared.

Some of the components of Cruickshank's theory were tested individually with equivocal results. In a pretest–posttest design using the Wechsler Intelligence Scale for Children and the Wide-Range Achievement Test, Rost and Charles (1967) found no significant differences between students using cubicles and those who did not. In contrast, Shores and Haubrich (1969) measured the reading rates, arithmetic rates, and attending behavior of students who were of average intelligence but who were hyperactive and distractible. They placed the students in cubicles for short periods of time and found that students showed increased attending in cubicles but no increase in reading or arithmetic rates. Scott (1970) compared the mathematics productivity of four students with hyperactivity in cubicles versus in normal classroom conditions and found a significant difference in number of correctly completed problems favoring the cubicles (average 27.3 problems completed) over the normal conditions (average 18.4 problems completed). Though the results of these studies varied and did not unambiguously support reduced environmental stimuli, the theory of stimuli reduction influenced other aspects of special education programs.

Influence on Special Classes

Ideas about modifying the learning environment contributed to the development of special classrooms in the 1960s and 1970s. Special classrooms carried assumptions about the effectiveness of reduced class size, and thus reduced stimuli. Glass and Smith (1979) analyzed 725 effect sizes across 77 studies conducted from 1900–1979 and found that "class size differences at the low end of the scale have quite important effects on achievement; differences at the high end have little effect" (p. 11). Substantial differences in achievement came from comparisons of teacher:pupil ratios of 1:1 to ratios of 1:40 and 1:25, and from comparisons of ratios of 1:5 to 5:25. Although they vary in size, special education classrooms have been predicated on reduced class sizes and other instructional changes, features that should affect the achievement of students with disabilities. In general, it appears that the benefits of reductions in class size become clearer as the size goes below 1:15 and begins to approximate the size of many traditional special education arrangements.

Following analysis of class sizes, Carlberg and Kavale (1980) used meta-analysis to examine the effects of special class placement. They reported negative effects on students with disabilities placed in special education classrooms when studies of all disability groups were considered together, with an overall effect size of −.12 for placement and specific effects of −.15 for achievement, and −.11 for social outcomes. When broken down by disability category, however, special classes for students with learning disabilities or behavior disorders produced an overall effect size of .29. That there were unique outcomes according to the characteristics of the students served in the special classes indicates the importance of not focusing solely on overall means; perhaps there is something specific about children with learning and behavior problems that makes a special class setting beneficial for them where it is not for other children. Though we do not know the particulars of reduced stimuli in these classrooms, we can assume that they contained fewer stimuli than general education classrooms. Could this be the difference? Could it be that the special class setting allowed teachers to serve individual differences? The studies included in the Carlberg and Kavale review are old now, and it would serve education well to have another analysis incorporating results from newer studies.

In summary, studies indicate equivocal evidence for the reduction of extraneous stimuli and reduced work space for children with hyperactivity, distractibility, or learning disabilities. To date, it is not clear what environmental modifications really are needed that are separate from instruction. With the current trend away from special classes and increasing participation in general education classrooms, the focus of research is away from control of environmental conditions. Unfortunately, this leaves educators with more questions than answers about whether or to what extent reducing extraneous stimuli is necessary in classrooms for students with learning, attention, or emotional or behavioral disabilities.

STRUCTURE IN THE CLASSROOM ROUTINE

In addition to reduction in environmental stimuli and work space, Cruickshank and colleagues (1961) recommended a structured classroom and life plan. This structure was to begin as entirely teacher-directed with no choice available to the child. According to the theory, many of the failure experiences children with hyperactivity had gone through were due to random stimuli in the environment and an inability to respond appropriately. Cruickshank and colleagues described structure in this way:

> For example, upon coming into the classroom the child will hang his hat and coat on a given hook—not on any hook of his choice, but on the same hook every day. He will place his lunch box, if he brings one, on a specific shelf each day. He will then go to his cubicle, take his seat, and from that point on follow the teacher's instructions concerning learning tasks, use of toilet, luncheon activities, and all other experiences until the close of the school day. The day's program will be so completely simplified and so devoid of choice (or conflict) situations that the possibility of failure experience will be almost completely minimized. (1961, p. 18)

This structure included clear, consistent teacher expectations and directly teaching these expectations from the beginning of the school year. The purpose was to develop control from within by beginning with control from without. Teachers controlled all aspects of the school program and only slowly, after much instruction, practice, and success, would control be turned over to students.

Structure and Behavioral Approaches to Intervention

Cruickshank's version of structure corresponds with many of the concepts underlying applied behavior analysis, particularly the control of behavioral antecedents. Haring (a doctoral student of Cruickshank's) and Phillips (1962) designed a program for students with emotional and behavioral disorders in which they compared a regular classroom with consultation, a special class with unstructured instruction, and a special class with a high level of structure. According to Kauffman, structure, as evidenced in Cruickshank et al.'s and Haring and Phillips, classrooms, "consisted of three primary elements: clear directions, firm expectations that the child would perform as directed, and consistent follow through in applying consequences for behavior" (1981, p. 54). In the Haring and Phillips project, the highly structured classroom was the most effective with these students. Hewett (1968) completed a study of 8 through 12 year olds with emotional and behavior disorders in an engineered classroom. In this situation, the teacher considered three components of the environment: the task, the reward, and the structure. This structure was defined as "the degree of teacher control present in the learning situation" (p. 67). The students in the experimental group who had previously been in normal classroom situations showed improvement in math fundamentals and exceeded their peers in attention to task in the final three of four observation intervals. The idea of an engineered classroom began the drive in theory and research to emphasize controlling the environment or antecedents in order to teach behaviors in much the same way as teaching academics.

Versions of structure founded on behavior modification have also produced beneficial outcomes. According to a meta-analysis by Skiba and Casey (1985), the average effect size for students with emotional or behavioral behavioral disorders in experimental classrooms was .93. Stage and Quiroz (1997) reported similar results about methods for decreasing disruptive behavior. They found that methods predicated on behavior modification techniques produced effect sizes of .65, .86, and .97 in general education classrooms, resource rooms, and self-contained classrooms, respectively. Similarly, DuPaul and Eckert (1997) found that contingency management interventions yielded beneficial effects on learning and behavior, especially when used in special education settings. Perhaps it is possible to use these sorts of powerful methods more effectively in some settings. Perhaps students with more severe problems are more amenable to behavior modification methods and are the very students who are placed into more restrictive classrooms because of the severity of their problems.

Structure and Instructional Management of Behavior

Although such results imply that managing behavior is a critical aspect of teaching, others have been concerned about working on the instructional side of teaching. This has led to the concept of using stimulus control and structure in instruction, as well as behavior management. For example, Ayllon and Roberts (1974) studied five fifth-grade boys with discipline problems. Their average academic accuracy at baseline (measured in terms of reading performance) was 40% and the average amount of time of disruptive behavior was 50%. When teachers structured the reading task and provided systematic reinforcement of reading performance, the students' accuracy increased to 85% and disruption decreased to 4%. Alberto and Troutman (1982) describe stimulus control and classroom structure as providing the discriminative stimuli to teach students when, where, and how to use certain behaviors. The components of structure include (a) verbal structure (classroom rules), (b) physical structure (teacher observation, physical separation, clear delineation of work areas, and study carrels), (c) time structure (predictable time schedule and timing of assignments), and (d) materials structure (using materials that are different from those students have failed with). In the same meta-analysis in which they found contingency management procedures to be effective, DuPaul and Eckert (1997) found that academic interventions yielded beneficial effects on learning and behavior; the effects were especially pronounced when the interventions were used in special education settings. These descriptions illustrate the extension of Cruickshank's ideas to alternative yet productive views that emphasize another important feature: structuring the environment via academic instruction.

Though we discuss them in further detail later in this chapter, it is important to point out the major components of this shift in focus. The Direct Instruction (DI) model (Engelmann, 1969) that developed concurrently with the behavior modification methods "uses the various techniques available to the contingency-management approach but it adds a new dimension to contingency-management by controlling the communication the learner receives" (Engelmann & Colvin, 1983, p. 9). In a more recent version, Kameenui and Darch describe the DI approach to classroom management as proactive: "the teacher teaches carefully and strategically all that is required so that students will have the information necessary to behave appropriately.... The basic assumption of the instructional classroom management approach... is that teachers must first teach students how to behave in every circumstance for which the teacher expects appropriate behavior" (1995, p. 3). The authors also argue that teachers must send "clear, unambiguous messages" to students about academics and about appropriate behavior. Corresponding concepts are stressed in the proactive management of student behavior, as exemplified in the work of Walker, Colvin, and Ramsey (1995). These ideas can be readily interpreted as sophisticated extensions of Cruickshank's ideas in that they emphasize the same components: structure in the classroom environment, predictable routines, and success in academics. The concepts have laid the foundation for a variety of research-proven instructional strategies for students with disabilities.

STRUCTURE IN TEACHING CONTENT AND OPERATIONS

Cruickshank and colleagues (Cruickshank, 1967; Cruickshank et al., 1961) recommended adopting instructional materials that were characterized by increased stimulus value, hoping that visually or tactually stimulating materials would draw children's attention to the materials in contrast to the relatively plain environment surrounding the students.

> The goal is to provide a learning situation so stimulating that the child's attention will be drawn to the task for a sufficient period of time to permit a positive condition to be effected. Hence, in preparing reading materials the teacher will utilize different colors in each word or in the numbers comprising a problem to be solved. The word "dog," for example, can be increased threefold in stimulus value if different sizes, shapes, and colors are used in the three letters comprising the word. (Cruickshank et al., 1961, p. 20)

In addition to increasing the salience of materials, however, they provided detailed recommendations for instructional materials and practices for teaching sensory and motor competence (e.g., eye–hand coordination), writing, arithmetic, reading, and even art (see chapter five in *A Teaching Method for Brain-injured and Hyperactive Children*, Cruickshank et al., 1961).

Methods and Materials

Many of these additional recommendations reflect an eclectic approach to instruction, but some presage contemporary consensus about effective practices. For example, recommendations for reading instruction included a strong emphasis on teaching competencies similar to what current researchers refer to as phonemic or phonological awareness and an approach to decoding based on word families (Adams, 1990; Simmons & Kameenui, 1998). More important, however, is an underlying emphasis on providing systematic, step-by-step, scaffolded instruction. This emphasis is reflected in the contemporary work on structuring academic materials and teaching practices.

Most learning of academic material—and arguably, most learning of other material as well—requires acquisition of concepts or operations or both. That is, academic competence is composed of knowing things and knowing how to do things. There are structures inherent in both the conceptual and operational sides of academic performance, and these structures are worthy of consideration in teaching students with disabilities. Developing cognitive structures, teaching students strategies for approaching tasks, and presenting lessons in systematic ways illustrate this contemporary emphasis on structure in instruction.

Strategies as Structure

Cognitive strategies serve to structure students' approaches to tasks. The strategies provide a repeatable set of steps through which students can progress systematically and that will lead to solution of the problem presented by the task.

Teaching students to follow strategies in handling academic tasks was one of the hallmarks of instructional research during the last 20 years of the twentieth century. Reviews of literature routinely emphasize the central importance of teaching students with learning disabilities strategic approaches to tasks (e.g., Lloyd, 1988; Miller, Butler, & Lee, 1998; Swanson, 2000). Strategies are an integral part of entire curricula (e.g., the *Mastering Fractions* program studied by Kelly, Carnine, Gersten, & Grossen, 1986) as well as the foundation of a curriculum designed expressly for students with learning disabilities (the Kansas strategies model; see Tralli, Colombo, Deshler, & Schumaker, 1996). Furthermore, strategies have been developed, studied, and refined across diverse academic areas by independent research groups, including

- Written expression: C. S. Englert (e.g., Englert, 1990) and S. Graham, K. Harris, and colleagues (Graham & Harris, 1989; De La Paz, 1997);
- Reading comprehension: D. Carnine and colleagues (Carnine & Kinder, 1985; Gurney, Gersten, Dimino, & Carnine, 1990), J. Borkowski and colleagues (Groteluschen, Borkowski, & Hale, 1990), S. Vaughn and colleagues (e.g., Vaughn & Klingner, 1999), J. Williams and colleagues (e.g., Williams, 1998);
- Verbal math problem solving: E. Jones and colleagues (Jones, Krouse, Fereone, & Saferstein, 1985), A. Jitendra and colleagues (Jitendra, Hoff, & Beck, 1999).

Ideally, learning strategies or cognitive operations should lead to the acquisition of a more strategic approach to thinking in general. Whether this is the case has yet to be demonstrated. As currently implemented, though, there are sufficient specific strategies to show that we can make operational most areas of academic endeavor and teach them.

Cognitive Structures

Research on cognitive processing demonstrates the importance of helping students develop cognitive structures (Rosenshine, 1997). Knowledge structures are relationships among pieces of knowledge. The structures permit learners to make connections among related bits of knowledge, and the more well organized the structures, the more rapidly and easily students can retrieve information and use related bits of knowledge.

Simply having an adequate store of facts is one critical component of developing knowledge structures, and curricula, such as proposed by Hirsch (1995), will go a long way toward providing those critical building blocks. However, it is important for students to learn the relationships among these facts, too. They must learn to organize the bits of information and use the connections among them. For such learning, mnemonic strategies are one valuable method of teaching. It is plain that mnemonic methods are highly structured, and they also produce substantial learning effects in children with disabilities (Mastropieri & Scruggs, 1989). Similarly, Butler's (1998) Strategic Content Learning Approach promotes integration of content.

Consistent with the theme of this chapter, methods of teaching mnemonic strategies are highly organized and systematic, involve extensive practice, and make salient the critical aspects of the content to be learned. Another means of developing such relationships is to create visual-spatial displays of the facts and the relationships among them, a method described by Engelmann and Carnine (1981), which is incorporated into instructional programs by Engelmann and his colleagues (e.g., *Your World of Facts,* Engelmann, Davis, & Davis, 1983). Visual-spatial displays have also produced beneficial effects on the acquisition of content knowledge in students with learning disabilities (see Crank & Bulgren, 1993, for further discussion).

Structure in Presentations

Strategies provide structured ways for students to approach tasks or problems. However, structure is also apparent in the instructional presentations used in teaching students with learning and behavior problems. Aspects of cognitive-behavioral methods and of DI illustrate how structure is used in teaching presentations.

Work using cognitive-behavioral methods with students with learning and behavior problems has often incorporated a sequence of teaching steps in which teacher support was systematically reduced until it was eliminated. One sequence was based on work by Meichenbaum and

Goodman (1971) and involved having a teacher move from modeling an completion of a task to having a student complete it independently. First, the teacher models completion of the task while asking her- or himself self-guiding questions; second, the student completes the task while the teacher asks the self-guiding questions; third, the student completes the task while asking her- or himself self-guiding questions; fourth, the student completes the task while whispering the self-guiding questions to her- or himself; and fifth, the student completes the task while asking her- or himself self-guiding questions subvocally. This procedure has been applied to both academic (e.g., Case, Harris, & Graham, 1992) and attention problems (e.g., Hallahan, Lloyd, Kosiewicz, Kauffman, & Graves, 1979).

The DI model that has received both empirical (e.g., White, 1982, for a meta-analysis) and increasing public support (American Association of School Administrators, 1999; American Federation of Teachers, 1999) provides another example of structure in teaching presentations. One of the most readily identifiable features of DI is the scripts from which teachers present lessons. A teacher presents segments of lessons by reading a prescribed series of statements that direct the children to respond in a specific way. Those segments that share features have a common format, with only the specific item to which the children respond varying. Thus, the children's attention is focused on the specific information that they are to learn. Distracting or irrelevant aspects of the lesson are, therefore, reduced.

DISCUSSION

The emphasis on structure in this chapter did not require great inference on our part. Cruickshank presented the case bluntly:

> In the classroom for brain-injured children nothing should be left to chance. Structure must be employed at all times. Proper structuring of the child's environment should always be uppermost in the mind of teacher. Some elementary educators protest against this emphasis on structure; structuring reduces opportunities for choice, we are reminded. Children must have opportunities to be creative, to plan, to decide, to learn by self-directed experience, they say. Children must be given an opportunity to structure their lives in their own daily activities under the guidance of permissive teacher. This may be the correct approach for normal children, as this writer prefers to believe. It is not correct for brain-injured children, however. Self-direction for them results in confusion, and in additional fracturing of the ego. (Cruickshank, 1967, p. 127)

These are sentiments that we share. That we are favorably disposed to structured instruction has several sources. Of course, one is our reading of the literature. We think it is clear that the best available evidence about interventions for students with learning and behavior problems shows the importance of structure in teaching. Although there are notable exceptions (e.g., Bay, Staver, Bryan, & Hale, 1992), an extensive review of the evidence indicates that direct and systematic teaching methods predict better outcomes for students with learning disabilities (Swanson, 1999).

Our views of appropriate educational practice are also strongly influenced by the work of those who preceded us. The first teaching experience of one of us (JWL) came in the mid-1960s when many of these issues were largely unstudied. The teachers with whom he worked maintained highly structured classrooms and sought ways of systematically teaching academic skills. At first, such practices were accepted on their face and from authority. However, the developing areas of behavior modification and (a few years later) DI rapidly lent support to continued use of structured teaching practices.

Clearly, the work of Cruickshank and his colleagues pioneered many important aspects of contemporary special education. To be sure, Cruickshank was not alone in his emphasis on many of the factors discussed here; recommendations of Cruickshank's contemporary, S. A. Kirk, include similar concepts about explicit, systematic instruction (Bos & Vaughn, 1998). Furthermore, the effective practices we have discussed here probably would have evolved anyway, regardless of whether Cruickshank recommended them. The relevant consideration is not whether there is a linear progression from his recommendations to current practice, but that he made so many recommendations that so clearly presaged what we have come to know as the state of the art in special education.

There are issues remaining to be addressed in instruction for students with learning, attention, and behavior problems. Although special educators have learned a lot, problems remain. For example:

- The extent to which effective practices apply at different grade levels and across different subject areas needs investigation; for example, in secondary classrooms there is far greater emphasis on self-direction, learning from material, and producing projects that require extended periods of time.
- The issue of whether systematic instruction engenders a generally more highly organized style of approaching tasks is still pending.
- The means to get effective instructional practices into the day-to-day instruction delivered to students with learning, attention, and behavior problems continues to plague us.

These calls for research—and the catalog could be much longer—raise one final point about the influence of Cruickshank's work on special education. However right or wrong he may have been about specific practices (e.g., using cubicles), he and his colleagues were willing to put their ideas to the test. They did not simply recommend the practices, they examined them empirically. If only one contribution is passed along to succeeding generations of special educators, we hope that this is the one.

REFERENCES

Adams, M. J. (1990). *Beginning to read: thinking and learning about print.* Cambridge, MA: MIT Press.

Adams, M. J., Foorman, B. R., Lundberg, I., & Beeler, T. (1998). The elusive phoneme: Why phonemic awareness is so important and how to help children develop it. *American Educator, 22*(1 & 2), 18–29.

Alberto, P. A., & Troutman, A. C. (1982). *Applied behavior analysis for teachers.* Columbus, OH: Merrill.

American Association of School Administrators. (1999). *An educators' guide to schoolwide reform.* Washington, DC: Author. Retrieved 18 April 2000 from the World Wide Web: http://www.aasa.org/reform/

American Federation of Teachers. (1999). *What works: Five promising remedial reading interventions programs.* Washington, DC: Author. Retrieved 18 April 2000 from the World Wide Web: http://www.aft.org/edissues/whatworks/wwreading.htm

Ayllon, T., & Roberts, M. D. (1974). Eliminating discipline problems by strengthening academic performance. *Journal of Applied Behavior Analysis, 7,* 71–76.

Bay, M., Staver, J. R., Bryan, T., & Hale, J. B. (1992). Science instruction for the mildly handicapped: Direct instruction versus discovery teaching. *Journal of Research in Science Teaching, 29,* 555–570.

Bos, C. S., & Vaughn, S. (1998). Samuel Kirk's legacy to teaching reading: The past speaks to the present. *Learning Disabilities Research & Practice, 13,* 22–28.

Butler, D. L. (1998). The Strategic Content Learning Approach to promoting self-regulated learning: A report of three studies. *Journal of Educational Psychology, 90,* 682–697.

Carlberg, C., & Kavale, K. A. (1980). The efficacy of special versus regular class placement for exceptional children: A meta-analysis. *Journal of Special Education, 14,* 296-309.

Carnine, D., & Kinder, D. (1985). Teaching low-performing students to apply generative and schema strategies to narrative and expository material. *Remedial and Special Education, 6*(1), 20–30.

Case, L. P., Harris, K. R., & Graham, S. (1991). Improving the mathematical problem-solving skills of students the learning disabilities: Self-regulated strategy training. *Journal of Special Education, 26,* 1–19.

Crank, J. N., & Bulgren, J. A. (1993). Visual depictions as information organizers for enhancing achievement of students with learning disabilities. *Learning Disabilities Research & Practice, 8,* 140–147.

Cruickshank, W. M. (1967). *The brain-injured child in home, school, and community.* Syracuse, NY: Syracuse University Press.

Cruickshank, W. M., Bentzen, F. A., Ratzeburg, F. H., & Tannhauser, M. T. (1961). *A teaching method for brain-injured and hyperactive children: A demonstration-pilot study.* Syracuse, NY: Syracuse University Press.

De La Paz, S. (1997). Strategy instruction in planning: Teaching students with learning and writing disabilities to compose persuasive and expository essays. *Learning Disability Quarterly, 20,* 227–248.

DuPaul, G. J., & Eckert, T. L. (1997). The effects of school-based interventions for attention Deficit hyperactivity Disorder: A meta-analysis. *School Psychology Review, 26,* 5–27.

Engelmann, S. (1969). *Preventing failure in the primary grades.* Chicago: Science Research Associates.

Engelmann, S., & Carnine, D. (1981). *Theory of instruction: Principles and applications.* New York: Irvington.

Engelmann, S., & Colvin, G. (1983). *Generalized compliance training: A Direct Instruction program for managing severe behavior problems.* Austin, TX: Pro-ed.

Engelmann, S., Davis, K., & Davis, G. (1983). *Your world of facts: A memory development program.* Chicago: Science Research Associates.

Englert, C. S. (1990). Unraveling the mysteries of writing through strategy instruction. In T. E. Scruggs & B. Y. L. Wong (Eds.), *Intervention research in learning disabilities* (pp. 186–223). Hillsdale, NJ: Erlbaum.

Glass, G. V., & Smith, M. L. (1979). Meta-analysis of research on class size and achievement. *Educational Evaluation and Policy Analysis, 1,* 2–16.

Graham, S., & Harris, K. R. (1989). Components analysis of cognitive strategy instruction: Effects on learning disabled students' compositions and self-efficacy. *Journal of Educational Psychology, 81,* 353–361.

Groteluschen, A. K., Borkowski, J. G., & Hale, C. (1990). Strategy instruction is often insufficient: Addressing the interdependency of executive and attributional processes. In T. E. Scruggs & B. Y. L. Wong (Eds.), *Intervention research in learning disabilities* (pp. 87–101). Hillsdale, NJ: Erlbaum.

Gurney, D., Gersten, R., Dimino, J., & Carnine, D. (1990). Story grammar: Effective literature instruction for high school students with learning disabilities. *Journal of Learning Disabilities, 23,* 12–22.

Hallahan, D. P., Lloyd, J., Kosiewicz, M. M., Kauffman, J. M., & Graves, A. W. (1979). Self-monitoring of attention as a treatment for a learning disabled boy's off-task behavior. *Learning Disability Quarterly, 2*(3), 24–32.

Haring, N. G., & Phillips, E. L. (1962). *Educating emotionally disturbed children.* New York: McGraw-Hill.

Hewett, F. (1968). *The emotionally disturbed child in the classroom: The orchestration of success.* Boston: Allyn & Bacon.

Hirch, E. D. (1987). *Cultural literacy: What every American needs to know.* Boston: Houghton-Mifflin.

Jitendra, A. K., Hoff, K., & Beck, M. (1999). Teaching middle school students with learning disabilities to solve multistep word problems using a scheme-based approach. *Remedial and Special Education, 20,* 50–64.

Jones, E. D., Krouse, J., Feorene, D., & Saferstein, D. A. (1985). A comparison of concurrent and sequential instruction of four types of verbal math problems. *Remedial and Special Education, 6*(5), 25–31.

Juel, C. (1988). Learning to read and write: A longitudinal study of 54 children from first through fourth grades. *Journal of Educational Psychology, 80,* 437–447.

Kameenui, E. J., & Darch, C. B. (1995). *Instructional classroom management: A proactive approach to behavior management.* White Plains, NY: Longman.

Kauffman, J. M. (1981). *Characteristics of children's behavior disorders* (2nd ed.). Columbus, OH: Bell & Howell.

Kelly, B., Carnine, D., Gersten, R., & Grossen, B. (1986). The effectiveness of videodisc instruction in teaching fractions to learning-disabled and remedial high school students. *Journal of Special Education Technology, 8*(2), 5–17.

Lloyd, J. W. (1988). Direct academic interventions in learning disabilities. In M. C. Wang, M. C. Reynolds, & H. J. Walberg (Eds.), *The handbook of special education: Research and practice* (Vol. 2; pp. 345–366). Oxford, England: Pergamon press.

Mastropieri, M. A., & Scruggs, T. E. (1989). Constructing more meaningful relations: Mnemonic instruction for special populations. *Educational Psychology Review, 1*(2), 83–111.

Meichenbaum, D., & Goodman, J. (1971). Training impulsive children to talk to themselves: A means of developing self-control. *Journal of Abnormal Psychology, 77,* 115–126.

Miller, S. P., Butler, F. M., & Lee, K. (1988). Validated practices for teaching mathematics to students with learning disabilities: a review of literature. *Focus on Exceptional Children, 31*(1), 1–24.

Rosenshine, B. (1997). Advances in research on instruction. In J. W. Lloyd, E. J. Kameenui, & D. Chard (Eds.), *Issues in educating students with disabilities* (pp. 197–220). Mahwah, NJ: Erlbaum.

Rost, K. J., & Charles, D. C. (1967). Academic achievement of brain injured and hyperactive children in isolation. *Exceptional Children, 34,* 125–126.

Scott, T. J. (1970). The use of music to reduce hyperactivity in children. *American Journal of Orthopsychiatry, 40,* 677–688.

Shores, R. E., & Haubrich, P. A. (1969). Effect of cubicles in educating emotionally disturbed children. *Exceptional Children, 36,* 21–26.

Simmons, D. C., & Kameenui, E. J. (1998). *What reading research tells us about children with diverse learning needs: Bases and basics.* Mahwah, NJ: Erlbaum.

Skiba, R., & Casey, A. (1985). Interventions for behavior disordered students: A quantitative review and methodological critique. *Behavioral Disorders, 10,* 239–252.

Stage, S. A., & Quiroz, D. R. (1997). A meta-analysis of interventions to decrease disruptive classroom behavior in public education settings. *School Psychology Review, 26,* 333–368.

Swanson, H. L. (1999). Instructional components that predict treatment outcomes for students with learning disabilities: Support for a combined strategy and direct instruction model. *Learning Disabilities Research & Practice, 14,* 129–140.

Swanson, H. L. (2000). What instruction works for students with learning disabilities? Summarizing the results from a meta-analysis of intervention studies. In R. Gersten, E. P. Schiller, & S. Vaughn (Eds.), *Contemporary special education research: Syntheses of the knowledge base on critical instructional issues* (pp. 1–30). Mahwah, NJ: Erlbaum.

Tralli, R., Colombo, B., Deshler, D. D., & Schumaker, J. B. (1996). The Strategies Intervention Model: A model for supported inclusion at the secondary level. *Remedial & Special Education, 17*(4), 204–216.

Vaughn, S., & Klingner, J. K. (1999). Teaching reading comprehension through collaborative strategic reading. *Intervention in School & Clinic, 34,* 284–292.

Walker, H. M., Colvin, G., & Ramsey, E. (1995). *Antisocial behavior in school: Strategies and best practices.* Pacific Grove, CA: Brooks/Cole.

White, W. A. T. (1988), A meta-analysis of the effects of direct instruction in special education. *Education and Treatment of Children, 11,* 364–374.

Williams, J. P. (1998). Improving the comprehension of disabled readers. *Annals of Dyslexia, 48,* 213–238.

Chapter 9

The Concept of the Least Restrictive Environment and Learning Disabilities: Least Restrictive of What? Reflections on Cruickshank's 1977 Guest Editorial for the *Journal of Learning Disabilities*

Jean B. Crockett
Virginia Polytechnic Institute and State University

James M. Kauffman
University of Virginia

> *A child placed in a so-called least-restrictive situation who is unable to achieve, who lacks an understanding teacher, who does not have appropriate learning materials, who is faced with tasks he cannot manage, whose failure results in negative comments by his classmates, and whose parents reflect frustration to him when he is at home, is indeed being restricted on all sides.*
>
> (Cruickshank, 1977, p. 193)

In a 1977 editorial for the *Journal of Learning Disabilities*, Bill Cruickshank suggested that policies defining the regular classroom as the least restrictive placement for all students reflect administrative wishful thinking. With his ironic portrayal of the hapless child whose opportunities for learning and acceptance are "restricted on all sides," Cruickshank made his educational position clear: Nothing restricts a child more than lost opportunities to learn.

Challenging state and local policies across the United States for ranking various instructional settings from "most restrictive" to "least restrictive," Cruickshank (1977) raised the question, "Least restrictive of what?" Inquiring how regular class placement came to be considered less restrictive than any other placement, he asked: "Was this an administrative decision based on thought? Based on theory? Based on research? Based on opportunism? Based on fears of parental pressures of legal threats?" (p. 193). Noting that no administrative remedy can compensate for inadequate instruction, he remarked, "The fact of the matter is that there is no research to demonstrate that one type of educational placement is less restrictive than others. All types are needed, but all must be high quality" (p. 193).

Concerned with educational consequences, Cruickshank asked, Who will be held accountable when the least restrictive placement fails to provide the magic cure? Will the focus of blame rightfully fall back on educational leaders who sought redemption through untested structural changes instead of appropriate pedagogy? Or will blame fall to the alleged inadequacies of the child, or his parents, or the supposed incompetencies of the educators who tried to teach him? Said Cruickshank, "The child with learning disabilities deserves more than this. If the concept of least-restrictive placement is to prevail and not result in a new generation of tragedy for learning disabled children, then school leadership must attack its deficiencies with unrelenting vigor" (p. 194).

CONTINUING CONTROVERSIES IN SERVICE DELIVERY

Twenty-five years after the publication of Cruickshank's (1977) editorial, controversy still surrounds service delivery to students with learning disabilities (LD) regarding which students should be served, which curricula and instructional methodology should be used, and where instruction should take place. Teachers and administrators, frequently coping with their own inadequate preparation for educating exceptional learners, continue to face professional challenges in accommodating increasing numbers of students with disabilities into general education classrooms (Crockett & Kauffman, 1998; Scruggs & Mastropieri, 1996). However, these challenges to professional knowledge and skills have not been exclusively an American experience. As Pijl and Meijer (1994) point out, "the integration of students with special needs into regular education and—and a wider context—the integration into society of all kinds of segregated groups have been debated in the last decades throughout practically the whole western world" (p. xi).

The field of special education has a long tradition of advocating for the educational rights and the social acceptance of children and youth with disabilities in both schools and the larger society. This advocacy has been important and significant in advancing the universal acceptance of persons with disabilities and increasing society's accountability for the well-being of each of its members. Now that access to an equitable education for all students has been established by legislation in many countries and total exclusion from schooling is less of a threat for students with disabilities, a more subtle but no less threatening challenge remains. For some students with learning disabilities, the *functional* exclusion Cruickshank (1977) described is still a reality in contemporary classrooms: "Many students do not have the ability to keep pace with the curriculum the way it is structured within the general education classroom and thus may experience a different kind of segregation—the exclusion from the basic right to learn" (Schumm et al., 1995, p. 335).

Cruickshank's Guiding Perspective

Cruickshank's (1977) editorial perspective is that of a special educator informed from scholarship and practice about educating students with learning difficulties—an educator armed not merely with hope and good intentions but also with knowledge of both students *and* schools. With his references to student failure and concern for those "unable to achieve," Cruickshank situates productive learning through specific instruction as the educational sine qua non for students with extreme individual differences. In characterizing the plight of the ill-served child "restricted on all sides," he realistically implies that schools and classrooms have ecological features that facilitate achievement for students with learning disabilities such as interactions with understanding teachers and peers, instructional interventions, and appropriate curricular organization and management.

Cruickshank troubles over the purpose of educational access for students with learning disabilities, the availability of opportunities to enhance their performance, and valid accountability to prevent their academic and social failure. He proceeds from the presumption that harm can befall individual students when appealing but theoretical, untested social policies are given priority over proven instructional approaches. Cruickshank's concerns are similar to our own.

The Framework for Our Discussion

In discussing the concept of least restrictive environment (LRE) for students with learning disabilities, we are mindful of contemporary special education's dual roots in the contexts of effective pedagogy and public policy. We organize our thoughts about the conceptual issues and practical realities affecting students with learning disabilities by addressing the following questions: (a) What is involved in providing students with *access to the general curriculum,* and ensuring that *the general education curriculum is accessible to* students with learning disabilities who might require extraordinary approaches to derive its benefits? (b) How can inclusive policies be balanced with imperatives for individually appropriate learning? (c) How can practitioners best respond to presumptive positivism when instruction in the general education class or curriculum is determined to be a flawed preference for individual students with learning disabilities?

Our intention is to examine the purpose of the LRE requirement in American public policy and to probe its character as a rebuttable presumption of inclusive placement. Legal reasoning frequently proceeds from presumptions of truth or benefit understood from a positivist perspective. Justice relies on the presentation of convincing evidence of ensuing harm to rebut presumptions about placement in individual cases. The most classic example in American law is the presumption of innocence until guilt is proven. In special education, "rebuttable presumptions are universal prescriptions for programming that are assumed innocent until proven guilty of not addressing the educational benefit of vulnerable students" (Crockett, 1999, p. 4). We believe it is critical for special educators to be knowledgeable about the characteristics of students with learning disabilities and to develop prowess in specialized instruction to address their needs. Teachers who know what to look for, what to do, and what data to collect to best guide and portray their students' progress have the best chance of blending the intents of pedagogy and public policy. They will have the skills of argument and the stores of evidence that allow them, when necessary, to rebut placement presumptions on behalf of students who often require different resources to achieve different results. In probing the legal presumptions surrounding the concept of LRE, we rely on data we gathered in the positivist tradition from the multiple perspectives of parents, legislative developers, and educational professionals in our comprehensive study of the origins and interpretations of LRE (Crockett & Kauffman, 1999).

Our intent in this discussion is to focus on the educational needs of students with learning disabilities and to consider how parents and professionals in the United States and elsewhere attempt to balance social policies with learning imperatives. We begin each major section of our discussion with Cruickshank's words.

PROCEEDING FROM THE PRINCIPLES OF SPECIAL EDUCATION

> *There are few, if any, who would argue with the spirit of the concept of least restrictive placement. The fact of the matter is that in terms of current educational practices, the* "least" *may more often be the most restrictive place for learning disabled children to receive their education.*

(Cruickshank, 1977, p. 5, italics in original)

The concept of LRE weaves together the educational elements of place and practice and raises questions of what schools are for and how they are to be judged. Cruickshank's (1977) characterization of the child most restricted by placement in what is supposed to be a least restrictive learning environment draws attention to a basic question of educational access: What is the purpose of providing access to the regular class for students with learning disabilities if appropriate learning is not made individually accessible to them there?

According to Cruickshank (1977), the context of American schools prevents the individual consideration required to provide appropriate instruction to students with learning disabilities. Among the factors that conspired to make the "least" the most restrictive placement, in his view, were thoughtlessness and haste in developing appropriate mainstreaming programs, lack of instructional preparation for regular teachers, an abundance of administrators unprepared to support mainstreamed instruction, and an overreliance on evaluation rather than instruction as the means to prevent school failure. Contemporary reviews of inclusive practice continue to identify the same factors, despite sincere efforts to restructure schools (Burdette & Crockett, 1999; Cook, Semmel, & Gerber, 1999).

In what he describes as the underresearched and rampant spread of public school programs that misconstrued mainstreaming to mean placements that are "unselectively appropriate" (p. 194), Cruickshank's concerns were prescient. Although early interpretations of LRE did not begin with the presumption of regular class placement in every case, recent changes in federal law have endorsed such placement as a rebuttable preference, despite the continuing absence of a defensible research base. If there were ready access to systematic knowledge from intervention research about the outcomes of inclusive schooling, Swanson (2000) suggests that the unfortunate controversy surrounding LRE might be avoided. Although he acknowledges that policy in special education is rarely inspired by research, Swanson takes the position that the full continuum of placements should be available unless it can be shown that all children with learning disabilities do not benefit from pullout programs. To do otherwise would jeopardize their educational opportunity.

Cruickshank (1977) and Swanson (2000) both grapple with the dual discourses endemic to the field of special education. Speaking from his years of experience at the intersection of pedagogy and public policy, Gallagher (1984) refers to a critical aspect of social policy: "It is necessary to have a clear sense of your goals and a determined persistence in pursuing them if you want a change to succeed" (p. 214). The primary goal and centerpiece of the Individuals with Disabilities Education Act

(IDEA) is its requirement that students with disabilities are to be assured the right to a free appropriate education. Also under IDEA, students with disabilities, to the maximum extent appropriate to their learning, are to be educated with children who are not disabled (20 U.S.C. Sec. 1412 (a)(5)(A)).

Setting Clear Goals

Because the IDEA guides individualized decisions about educational programming and placement, LRE problems occur when there is confusion about what a learning environment is supposedly restricting for a particular child—educational opportunity or social integration. Our concern is that the social goals of inclusion have been articulated but not clearly aligned with goals for enhanced student outcomes. For example, although the recent amendments to the 1997 IDEA target educational results, they advocate the inclusion of all students in the general education curriculum and in wide-scale accountability systems, which are often of questionable relevance to meaningful individualized instruction. Although this policy strategy might be described as presumptive positivism (Sunstein, 1996), it can sometimes obfuscate and distort the individualized intentions of the federal law.

In calling for agreement on common goals for educating students with learning disabilities, Swanson (2000) advocates for a guiding policy less obsessed with placement and more concerned with *minimizing errors* (weak gains in achievement) in instruction. Although admitting that nothing is foolproof and that some of his suggestions are tongue-in-cheek, Swanson offers ways of handling errors with multiple options to prevent a poor fit between environment and child needs. His suggestions address early identification and evaluation of students with learning disabilities, selective hiring of teachers and school psychologists, and teacher preparation and practice. If the instructional environment is still at risk, says Swanson, "change the environment in which policy is developed" (p. 48). Swanson remarks: "The specific aim of meeting the needs of learning disabilities children is to prepare them for citizenship in general society. Providing an effective array of options does this. Sometimes, in the debate on full inclusion we find that our aim is not well focused" (p. 48).

Brooding Creatively about Purpose

Norman Cousins (1974), long-time editor of the *Saturday Review World*, remarked on the need for leaders "to brood creatively about purpose"

(p. 4) without becoming overwhelmed by discontinuity and unremitting arbitration—two pitfalls familiar to decision-makers coping with issues of student placement. Worrying over the purpose of education in general, Sarason and Doris (1979) advocated for both academic and social development, proposing that education addresses coequal goals for American students: "Productive learning and mutuality of living" (p. 407). Expanding on this definition, Sarason (1996) characterized productive learning as the product of "the social contexts that are necessary to arouse and sustain a combination of intellectual curiosity and striving, a sense of personal worth and growth, and a commitment to the educational enterprise" (p. 261).

With regard to educating exceptional learners, Cruickshank (1967) noted that "democracy... accepts the responsibility for the education of all children" (p. 21) but provides individual consideration when its responsibilities cannot be ordinarily met. "Thus, special methods and provisions must be developed for children who... are termed exceptional and who often cannot be educated with the typical frame of reference deemed appropriate for the so-called normal child" (p. 21). Gallagher (1994) points out that educational equity "does not consist of educating all children in the same place at the same time (and with the same curriculum?) but in ensuring that the student has basic needs met and is traveling a well thought-out road to a career and a satisfying life style" (p. 528). Schooling is not a place, says Gallagher; it is a continuing educational responsibility.

Principled Leadership in Special Education

Noting the administrative tendency to lead from rules of policy rather than principles of instruction, Sarason and Doris (1979) remarked that when the purposes of the LRE concept are considered, discussions quickly become "mired in the controversies centering around law, procedures, administration, and funding" (p. 392). Consequently, decisions seem to spring more from compliance concerns than conceptual understanding. We suggest that this occurs because the goals of special education for students with learning disabilities are assumed to be understood by teachers and administrators rather than explained as part of a foundational set of principles that ensure the following: (a) universal educational access and accountability; (b) individual consideration; (c) educational benefit; (d) effective programming; and (e) productive partnerships among students, parents, professionals, and communities that foster high expectations, support research-based strategies, and target positive results for exceptional learners (Crockett, 1999).

LEGAL REASONING AND THE PRESUMPTION
OF POSITIVISM IN REBUTTAL

> *Special education involves meeting the needs of children. This is not a hollow*
> *cliché, but a mandatory concept.*
>
> (Cruickshank, 1967, p. 47)

From the legal perspective of the IDEA, the purpose of schooling exceptional learners is very clear: "to ensure that all children with disabilities
have available to them a free appropriate public education that emphasizes special education and related services designed to meet their
unique needs, and prepare them for employment and independent living" (20 U.S.C. Sec. 1400, (1)(A)). The requirement to provide students
with farsighted, appropriate programming raises a basic question: How
can inclusive policies be balanced with imperatives for individually appropriate learning? What kind of evidence will be taken as rebuttal of
general education placement?

The Continuum of Alternative Placements

As an American scholar of education and human exceptionality, Bill
Cruickshank's pedagogical views became an integral part of the foundation upon which the IDEA was based. Cruickshank's (1967) advice to
teachers about educating exceptional children and youth reads like a
primer to the IDEA; so much of what he describes as intensive and individualized practice for students with disabilities was incorporated into
the statute. The main difference between the texts is that Cruickshank's
prescriptions are couched in the educational context of pedagogy, and
those of the IDEA are set in the legal context of students' rights. For
example, this difference is particularly evident in the language Cruickshank chose to describe student placement; *selective placement* is his term.
The process he describes, however, is the close, careful scrutiny from
multiple perspectives that is required by what would become, in the legal discourse, "factor-guided placement in the LRE"—a more complex
analysis than mere placement in classrooms ranked more or less restrictive regardless of students' needs.

From 1975 to the present, in approximately 15,000 school districts, the
provision of an appropriate education has relied on the cascade of services model (see Deno, 1970) to operationalize the requirement of providing the LRE under American law. The cascade model offers students
with disabilities instruction across a continuum of alternative placements
extending from regular classrooms, separate classes, day schools, residential settings, to hospital and homebound services. The educational

intent of the continuum of alternative placements is to provide a variety of settings in which appropriate individual programming might be offered to a student with disabilities. The legal intent of the continuum is to ensure that a free appropriate public education (FAPE) can still be provided to students who are not making satisfactory progress in the regular class, despite the assistance of supplementary aids and services.

Presumptive Positivism

Within the legal discourse, the least restrictive appropriate placement for any student is presumed to be the regular class. Pedagogy can rebut this presumption, however, if decision-making teams find a mismatched relationship between a student's unique learning characteristics and the ecological elements in the regular setting necessary to provide the student with appropriate educational access or benefit. Distinguishing legal presumptions from hard and fast rules is as critical to educational decision-makers as it is to legal advocates for the defense. Rebutting presumptions in special education placements requires an understanding of FAPE. It also requires that those who seek an alternative to the placement presumption possess both the drive to rebut it and the data (i.e., evidence in the positivist tradition) to succeed.

In allowing for presumptions about placements and their rebuttal, the law gives privilege to evidence and prevents discrimination. Presumptions about access to general education classrooms and curricula are considered to be preferences unless evidence suggests that such preferences would cause harm in particular cases. The term *presumptive positivism* (cf. Sunstein, 1996) describes a data-based alternative to the application of rules when rules might produce "weird or palpably unjust outcomes in particular cases" (p. 127). Sunstein suggests that this strategy, which allows for escape from rules in extraordinary circumstances, may be the best that we can do: "If exceptions will be made in cases of absurdity, then it is possible to ask, in every case, whether the particular application is absurd" (p. 127).

The Concept of LRE as a Rebuttable Presumption

In U.S. policy, the LRE concept has been variously interpreted as a legal principle enhancing integration and an educational strategy linking integration to appropriate programming. LRE was never intended to be an unyielding rule for the integrated placement of students with disabilities in the regular classroom. Rather, it is best described as a rebuttable presumption that favors the inclusion of disabled and nondisabled students in regular classes, but allows separation in certain instances (Turnbull, 1990; Yell, 1998).

In researching its legal roots, we found that the term *LRE* is derived from the concept of the least restrictive alternative (LRA), which has its legal basis in the U.S. Constitution and serves to accommodate both individual and state interests. "As long ago as 1819, Chief Justice Marshall of the United States Supreme Court . . . indicated that regulation affecting citizens of a state should be both 'appropriate' and 'plainly adapted' to the end sought to be achieved" (Burgdorf, 1980, p. 278). This principle has been applied widely from cases of inter-state commerce to education, and it has been couched in various judicial forms, including the phrase "less drastic means for achieving the same basic purpose."

Edwin Martin, who served as Chief of the U.S. Bureau of Education for the Handicapped when the concept became part of the federal regulations, told us that the term LRE was not in the original statute, but that the reference to a continuum of placements was built into the law from the start:

> LRE was an important element of the law, but it was down the list of elements. The most important element was a "free appropriate public education." The assumption was not that all children would be educated in the regular classroom with non-handicapped children . . . just where "appropriate." Appropriate placement is based not on the philosophy of the school but on the individual IEP under the law. (In Crockett & Kauffman, 1999, p. 75)

The LRE concept has been described as a means by which to balance the values surrounding the provision of an "appropriate education (the student's right to and need for an appropriate education) with the values of individual rights of association" (Turnbull, 1990, p. 148). "Presumptively . . . [a] segregating placement is more harmful than regular school placement. Only when it is shown that such a placement is necessary for appropriate education purposes in order to satisfy the individual's interests or valid state purposes is the presumption overcome" (p. 163).

Turnbull views rebuttable presumptions as positive policy tools that offer affected parties greater "*freedom of choice*" (p. 163, italics in original), and protection from having no alternative to what they perceive as harmful. In the case of LRE, determining what constitutes a suitable rebuttal can be complex and relies on a fact-specific (positivist) inquiry. The concept of LRE "is inextricably tied to the notion of appropriateness, which makes it all the more complex because appropriate education itself is difficult to define" (Turnbull, 1990, p. 161). While the constitutional basis of LRE requires the government, when it has a legitimate interest, to take actions that least drastically restrict a citizen's liberty, "it is another thing altogether to answer the question: What is an unwarranted or unnecessary restriction of a handicapped child when the state is required to educate him or her appropriately?" (p. 162).

As Cruickshank (1977) suggested, *the concept of LRE was never intended to mean that the student could or should be situated solely in the regular classroom.* Congress, in developing the original Education for All Handicapped Children Act in 1975, viewed the regular class as the optimal setting but acknowledged the views of special educators like Bill Cruickshank that instruction should be offered in multiple environments if individual needs are to be appropriately met. However, when amending the statute in 1997, Congress shifted its presumptive stance. Acknowledging that decisions for students with disabilities are to be based on individual need, Congress, nevertheless, called for justification in the student's Individual Education Program (IEP) when decisions require an alternative placement to regular classes. Huefner (2000) remarked that "although the content of the statutory provisions governing the least restrictive environment and requiring a continuum of placement options did not change, Congress, in effect, introduced a shift via the side door" (p. 198).

Problems with Presumptions of FAPE

Although only minor changes have been made to the LRE provisions in the federal regulations, extensive alterations addressing each student's participation and progress in the general education curriculum are now prescribed under the heading of FAPE. The general school reform agenda has been grafted to each IEP in an effort to ensure that each special education student receives at least a comparable education to his or her classmates. However, the intent of the IDEA has long been to offer a more personalized standard of educational opportunity to students with learning disabilities through individualized, not comparable, educational programming. The pervasive emphasis on participation and progress in the general curriculum for each student with a disability, if not understood as a presumed preference of the law, could subtly shift the focus of accountability from the child's appropriate progress to the adequacy of the school district's service provision.

These policies endorsing curricular inclusion and accountability rely on a presumption that more children will be successful than we think if they are included in and tested on their competence in the general education curriculum. However, further presumptions are also implied: (a) the presumption that the general education curriculum is challenging, (b) the presumption that low expectations for their success will continue without a mandate to report on the progress of exceptional learners in that curriculum, and (c) the presumption that curricular and instructional alternatives are de facto less challenging without considering for whom they are less challenging and under what circumstances they are less challenging.

American parents and professionals welcome efforts to measure the educational progress of students with disabilities, but they do so with concerns about confusing the principles of ensuring universal access and accountability with providing effective programming that is reasonably calculated to provide individual students with educational benefit. In other words they are suspicious that presumptions of FAPE serve the political agenda of equalizing access for *all* students to the *same* high standards and the *same* curricular offerings without stopping to consider that access to these standards and this presumably rich curriculum might not help *some* students to achieve meaningful outcomes at all (Crockett, 1999).

Employing a System of Factors

It is one thing to apply presumptive positivism to the concept of LRE; placement concerns are only one factor in providing FAPE. But irony surrounds the application of presumptive generalities to the inherently individualized nature of FAPE. Presumptions are blunt instruments, ill-fitting and heedless of individual specifications. They neither respect what is individually considered to be true nor clarify what is not understood. They make a point that begs a counterpoint when the fortunes of the few are threatened by generalities. Presumptive rules are by nature confrontational; they are indigenous to the argument culture (cf. Tannen, 1998). Unlike the more refined legal tool of factors, presumptions provoke a challenge rather than provide procedures for thoughtful deliberation. Factors guide decision-making by setting out the elements to be considered in responding to rules or presumptions; for example, the presumptions of LRE are rebutted with (positivist) evidence guided by a set of mandatory and qualified factors set out in the federal regulations to the IDEA (cf. Bateman & Chard, 1995). Factors provide the counterpoint by looking at a range of particulars and allowing decisions to emerge from multiple criteria. A system based on factors requires appreciation for diversity, ambiguity, multiple perspectives, attention to much of the broad situation, attention to particulars, attention to how others in similar circumstances have been treated, allowance for different values placed on assumed benefits, and agreements based not on theory but on the particular circumstances and positivist data under review: "Tests of this sort imply a wide and close look at individual circumstances. On this view, justice is far from blind. It tries to see a great deal" (Sunstein, 1996, p. 144).

REALITIES OF PROFESSIONAL PRACTICE

> *If the concept of least-restrictive placement is to prevail and not result in a new generation of tragedy for learning disabled children, then school leadership must attack its deficiencies with unrelenting vigor. Time is not on the side of leadership any longer.*
>
> (Cruickshank, 1977, p. 194).

Students with learning disabilities will need double indemnity if administrators fail to balance social policies with learning imperatives and fail to ensure systematic and explicit instruction by teachers highly skilled in delivering it. *If* LRE, as a legal concept, is to be considered as a rebuttable presumption of inclusive placement, *and if* requirements for FAPE are linked with general school reform, *then* practitioners need to know when and how to make legitimate exceptions. These concerns raise the following question: How can practitioners best respond to *presumptive positivism* when instruction in the general education class or curriculum is determined to be a flawed preference for individual students with learning disabilities? As Cruickshank suggests, the task requires more than hope and good intentions. Reliable data are critical.

Cruickshank's Remedies: Addressing Conceptual and Practical Deficiencies

Among the remedies Cruickshank (1977) suggests is the establishment of universal in-service training through which all teachers can be brought to a basic understanding about the complex problems of students with learning disabilities. For master teachers, however, he recommends "in-depth preparation under competent professors" (p. 6). He offers two final prescriptions: the subordination of diagnosis to instruction, and the provision of a variety of educational programs to serve a variety of student needs. In addressing the realities of professional practice, we consider his prescriptions in reverse order, addressing first his conceptual concerns with variety, and tackling second his practical concerns with what teachers and administrators need to know and be able to do.

Offering a Variety of Educational Programs

Cruickshank's (1977) vision of corresponding varieties of students and programs is similar to the positions taken by several groups advocating for the educational benefits of students with disabilities. Although many students with learning disabilities benefit from inclusion in regular classes, The Learning Disabilities Association of America (LDA) posits that "the regular education classroom is not the appropriate placement for a number of students with learning disabilities who may need alternative instructional environments, teaching strategies, and/or materials that cannot or will not be provided within the context of a regular classroom placement" (LDA, 1993).

Cruickshank's calls for variety are also reminiscent of Hornby's (1999) appeals for responding to inclusion with diversity in England. Hornby targets inclusion in the community after students have left school "as the actual end that educators are seeking. Inclusion in mainstream school may be a means to that end but is not the end itself" (p. 125). Hornby suggests that accessing high-quality instruction that leads to a successful postschool life relies less on an obsession with curricular or classroom inclusion for special education students and more on providing a diversity of settings, strategies, and curricular options responsive to their diverse needs and strengths.

Special educator Karen Silver's observations reflect an appreciation for the variety and diversity of programs that are hard-won through parental advocacy and professional support. Speaking from her perspective as the parent of a special education student, she cautions that not all parents of children with disabilities view the regular classrooms in their neighborhoods as having the capacity to provide meaningful opportunities to learn.

> Not all children who require special education are the same. The diversity of programs which exist today came about because parents and educators fought for them, recognizing that there was no single setting which could possibly meet the wide-ranging needs of the disabled school-age population. (Silver in Crockett & Kauffman, 1999, p. 184)

As Cruickshank (1977) suggests, a variety of program options requires teacher development and instructional expertise. Time is definitely not on the side of unprepared practitioners any longer.

Specific Requests for Specific Instruction

Some parents of students with learning disabilities have given up on unresponsive schools and are removing their children from public programming at increasing rates, attributing learning gains to instructional methods used in private schools (e.g., Kingsley, 2000). In recent instances, challenges to placement have been associated with parental requests for alternative curricula and specialized methodology in reading instruction. After reviewing 27 legal decisions involving students with learning disabilities and parental requests for specific reading methods, Bhat, Rapport, and Griffin (in press) observed that when making their decisions, hearing officers and justices relied most frequently on the twin criteria of appropriateness of district programming and the academic progress of the student with learning disabilities.

Student performance was at the center of each case, with hearing officers and judges sympathetic to parental complaints when student achievement in reading and spelling fell below three or more years of grade level. In the 16 decisions that found district programming appropriate to the needs of the particular students with learning disabilities, the school districts each offered a variety of language-based programs targeting decoding and spelling skills. Of particular interest is the fact that a majority of these cases involved students with learning disabilities in the secondary grades whose parents were alarmed at their lack of academic achievement. Parental optimism with standard reading instruction in the early grades faded from exposure to the obvious disparities between classmates and their child as academic demands increased. "As parents became acutely aware of the skill deficits their children experienced, they also realized how essential it was for them to have highly effective instructional interventions that would provide immediate benefits" (Bhat, Rapport, & Griffin, in press). Perhaps these cases best illustrate courts' presumptive positivism—their tendency to presume that data, not theory alone, will be the basis for judgment.

What Do Practitioners Need to Know about Students with Learning Disabilities?

Judicial demands for data rather than assumptions about the performance of students with learning disabilities continue to rely on pedagogical decision-making by teachers highly skilled in assessment and specialized instruction. In asserting that there is something special, indeed, about special education, Cruickshank (1967) remarked, "special education exists because some children present problems which cannot be readily solved by general education" (p. 21). Cruickshank (1977) expressed concern that educators had little understanding about the complex problems faced by students with learning disabilities and called for both universal teacher in-service and in-depth special education preparation for master teachers to understand both the characteristics of students with learning disabilities and programming demonstrably effective in helping such students to learn.

Special Education Means Specialized Instruction

After researching issues of mainstreaming and inclusion for 30 years, Naomi Zigmond (2000) notes from her observations that what the IDEA describes as special education is not being provided to students with learning disabilities. Her conclusion is that special education needs to be reinvented according to its initial design.

> As others have said before me, special education is, first and foremost, instruction focused on individual need. It is carefully planned. It is intensive, urgent, relentless, and goal directed. It is empirically supported practice, drawn from research. To provide special education means to set priorities and select carefully what needs to be taught. It means teaching something special and teaching it in a special way.... To provide special education means monitoring each student's progress... and taking responsibility for changing instruction when the monitoring data indicate that sufficient progress is not being made. (Zigmond, 1997, pp. 384–385)

According to Zigmond, none of these elements was visible in the multiple classrooms she studied in a comprehensive report of what inclusion looks like in American elementary schools (cf. Baker & Zigmond, 1995). She advocates reinventing special education as an effective medium of instruction for students with learning disabilities by redefining the responsibilities of general educators to address the individual differences of students who require less than the specialized, intensive attention demanded by the IDEA. For students with learning disabilities who require more than an education comparable to that received by the majority, Zigmond calls for a return to "special education that is temporary, intensive, and delivered in a pull-out setting ... because the general education classroom learning environment is not conducive to intensive instruction" (pp. 386–387). She also advocates for preserving a unique and specialized preparation for special educators so that "special education [can be] provided by a highly trained professional capable of assessing the child, of planning a teaching program based on this assessment, and implementing the teaching plan" (p. 386). Zigmond's essential message for practitioners, policy makers, advocates, and researchers in special education is to focus "on defining the nature of special education and the competencies of the teachers who will deliver it" (p. 389).

In reflecting on the links between research and service delivery, Keogh (1999) remarks that parents and professionals continue to rely on availability and advocacy, not appropriateness or effectiveness in making programming decisions. Bryan (1999) also notes that effective programming in both general and special education is often undermined by circular and recurrent changes rather than progressive reforms based on scientific data. "How can 40 years of research, some of it quite elegant, be swept aside by fads?" she asks. "Does the adoption of fads or nonscientifically supported methods of instruction mean the field of education is fundamentally antiscience? The field of education should be the bastion of scientific endeavor" (p. 445).

What Do Practitioners Need to Do to Demonstrate Instructional Results?

Considering that legal reasoning relies on fact-specific, positivist evidence to rebut placement presumptions, we would expect teachers and administrators to be cognizant of the characteristics of students with learning disabilities and knowledgeable about research-validated practices for their instruction. We would also expect special educators to be skillful in prescribing and applying these practices appropriately for a particular student in a particular set of circumstances. In addition, we suggest that practitioners come to recognize when elements of educational law constitute presumptions so that rebuttals can be made when appropriate, and, in the case of placement presumptions, evidence can demonstrate when a learning environment might restrict rather than facilitate a child's learning.

CONCLUDING THOUGHTS

Three decades after the publication of Cruickshank's (1977) editorial, Swanson (2000), restated Cruickshank's theme: "The major premise guiding policy for children with learning disabilities should be concerned with minimizing errors in terms of instruction" (p. 47). This statement encapsulates the view of positivist science, which has as its foundation stone "the admission that one can simply reach a wrong conclusion due to various forms of error" (Kauffman & Brigham, 2000, p. 168). As we have noted, the courts rely upon concepts of science and positivism to judge whether the presumption of appropriate placement of students with learning disabilities (and other disabilities) in general education is tenable. Yet antiscientific, antipositivist, "dubiously coherent relativistic views about the concepts of truth and evidence really have gained wide acceptance in the contemporary academy...," and "this onset of relativism has had precisely the sorts of pernicious consequences for standards of scholarship and intellectual responsibility that one would expect it to have" (Boghossian, 1998, p. 23). Special education and general education reformers today seem particularly likely to abandon the positivist view for the notion that the key to improvement is structural change. However, others contend that structure is not the heart of the problem of improving special education (e.g., Kauffman & Hallahan, 1993).

Experts in the field of educational administration would seem to agree that structure is not the central problem, suggesting that issues of instruction are ill-served by structural solutions. Murphy (1995) takes the position that inclusion is primarily an organizational, not an educational intervention. Agreeing that results of inclusive programming should not be assumed and assessment of student outcomes should be pursued, Murphy acknowledges a theoretical dilemma: "Organizational changes—whether of the macro-level variety, such as the centralization or decentralization of governance and management, or of the more micro-level variety, such as student grouping—have not, do not now, and never will, predict organizational effectiveness" (p. 210). Elmore, Peterson, and McCarthey (1996) point out that reforms, such as inclusion, are based on the shaky premise that changing structure changes practice: "Stripped to its essentials, school restructuring rests on a fundamental belief in the power of organizational structure over human behavior. In this belief, traditional school structures are the enemy of good teaching practice, and fundamental structural changes are the stimulus for new practices" (p. 4). A more realistic approach to the issue of instructional placement—an approach less reliant on "administrative wishful thinking"—might suggest that norms and behaviors of schools and teachers need to change before structures are eliminated and redesigned. Such an approach "would require reformers to treat structural change as a more contingent and uncertain result of change in practice, rather than as a means of reaching new practice" (Elmore, 1995, p. 26). As Conquest (2000) puts it, "certainty on matters in which our knowledge is inevitably imperfect is the enemy of good understanding and good policy" (p. 14).

In his closing remarks, Cruickshank (1977) suggested that "there is nothing magical about an administrator's decision to foster less-restrictive placement of children" unless, at a minimum, the elements he identified as needing remedy were addressed. Several generations later, yet still without thoroughly trained teachers, informed administrators, intensive instruction, and a variety of educational programs, students with learning disabilities risk "failure to thrive" in supposedly least restrictive placements. We wonder if their low achievement despite their inclusive participation in general education settings might turn the optimism of some advocates into cultural critique and despair if they perceive, erroneously, that there is little else that educators can do to improve the performance of students with learning disabilities. We suspect that Bill Cruickshank would say in response: "The child with learning disabilities deserves more than this."

REFERENCES

Baker, J. M., & Zigmond, N. (1995). The meaning and practice of inclusion for students with learning disabilities: Themes and implications from the five cases. *The Journal of Special Education, 29,* 163–180.

Bateman, B., & Chard, D. J. (1995). Legal demands and constraints on placement decisions. In J. M. Kauffman, J. W. Lloyd, D. P. Hallahan, & T. A. Astuto (Eds.), *Issues in educational placement: Students with emotional and behavioral disorders* (pp. 285–316). Hillsdale, NJ: Lawrence Erlbaum Associates.

Bhat, P., Rapport, M. J., & Griffin, C. (In press). A legal perspective on the use of specific reading methods for students with learning disabilities. *Learning Disabilities Quarterly.*

Boghossian, P. A. (1998). What the Sokal hoax ought to teach us. In N. Koertge (Ed.), *A house built on sand: Exposing postmodernist myths about science* (pp. 23–31). New York: Oxford University Press.

Bryan, T. (1999). Reflections on a research career: It ain't over till it's over. *Exceptional Children, 65,* 438–447.

Burdette, P. J., & Crockett, J. B. (1999). An exploration of consultation approaches and their implementation in heterogeneous classrooms. *Journal of Education and Training in Mental Retardation and Developmental Disabilities, 34*(4), 2–22.

Burgdorf, Jr., R. L. (1980). *The legal rights of handicapped persons: Cases, materials, and text.* Baltimore, MD: Paul H. Brookes.

Conquest, R. (2000). *Reflections on a ravaged century.* New York: Norton.

Cook, B. G., Semmel, M. I., & Gerber, M. M. (1999). Attitudes of principals and special education teachers toward the inclusion of students with mild disabilities. *Remedial and Special Education, 20,* 199–207, 243.

Cousins, N. (1974, November 16). Thinking through leadership. *Saturday Review World, 4.*

Crockett, J. B. (1999). *Preventing disabilities from handicapping the futures of our children.* Keynote address presented at the annual conference of the Association of Special Education Administrators in Queensland, Australia, September 20, 1999.

Crockett, J. B., & Kauffman, J. M. (1998). Classrooms for students with learning disabilities: Realities, dilemmas, and recommendations for service delivery. In B. Y. L. Wong (Ed.), *Learning about learning disabilities* (2nd ed.) (pp. 489–525). San Diego, CA: Academic Press.

Crockett, J. B., & Kauffman, J. M. (1999). *The least restrictive environment: Its origins and interpretations in special education.* Mahwah, NJ: Lawrence Erlbaum Associates.

Cruickshank, W. M. (1967). *Education of exceptional children and youth.* Englewood Cliffs, NJ: Prentice-Hall.

Cruickshank, W. M. (1977). Least-restrictive placement: Administrative wishful thinking. *Journal of Learning Disabilities, 10,* 193–194.

Deno, E. (1970). Special education as developmental capital. *Exceptional Children, 37,* 229–237.

Elmore, R. F. (1995). Structural reform and educational practice. *Educational Researcher, 24,* (9), 57–64.

Elmore, R. F., Peterson, P. L., & McCarthey, S. J. (1996). *Restructuring in the classroom: Teaching, learning, and school organization.* San Francisco: Jossey Bass.

Gallagher, J. J. (1984). The evolution of special education concepts. In B. Blatt & R. J. Morris (Eds.), *Perspectives in special education: Personal orientations* (pp. 101–124). Glenview, IL: Scott, Foresman.

Gallagher, J. J. (1994). The pull of societal forces on special education. *The Journal of Special Education, 27,* 521–530.

Hornby, G. (1999). Inclusion, exclusion, and confusion. *Liberty, 46,* 121–125.

Huefner, D. S. (2000). The risks and opportunities of the IEP requirements under IDEA '97. *The Journal of Special Education, 33,* 195–204.

Individuals with Disabilities Education Act of 1997. 20 U. S. C. §1400 *et seq.*

Kauffman, J. M., & Brigham, F. J. (2000). Editorial. *Behavioral Disorders, 25,* 168–169.

Kauffman, J. M., & Hallahan, D. P. (1993). Toward a comprehensive service delivery system. In J. I. Goodlad & T. C. Lovitt (Eds.), *Integrating general and special education* (pp. 73–102). Columbus, OH: Merrill/Macmillan.

Keogh, B. (1999). Reflections on a research career: One thing leads to another. *Exceptional Children, 65,* 295–300.

Kingsley, E. (2000, March 14). Rescued from the mainstream: One mom learns that special treatment is best for her son with ADHD. *The Washington Post/Health,* 9.

Learning Disabilities Association of America. (1993). Position paper on full inclusion of all students with learning disabilities in the regular education classroom. *LDA Newsbrief, 28* (2).

Murphy, J. (1995). Insights on "the context of full inclusion" from a non-special educator. *The Journal of Special Education, 29,* 209–211.

Pijl, S. J. & Meijer, C. J. W. (1994). Introduction. In C. J. W. Meijer, S. J. Pijl, & S. Hegarty (Eds.), *New perspectives in special education: A six-country study of integeration* (pp. xi–xiv). London: Routledge.

Sarason, S. B. (1996). *Barometers of change: Individual, educational, and social transformation.* San Francisco, CA: Jossey-Bass.

Sarason, S. B., & Doris, J. (1979). *Educational handicap, public policy, and social history.* New York: Free Press.

Schumm et al. (1995). General education teacher planning: what can students with learning disabilities expect? *Exceptional Children, 61,* 335–352.

Scruggs, T. E., & Mastropieri, M. A. (1996). Teacher perceptions of mainstreaming/inclusion, 1958–1995: A research synthesis. *Exceptional Children, 63,* 59–74.

Sunstein, C. R. (1996). *Legal reasoning and political conflict.* New York: Oxford University Press.

Swanson, H. L. (2000). Issues facing the field of learning disabilities. *Learning Disabilities Quarterly, 23,* 37–50.

Tannen, D. (1998). *The argument culture.* New York, NY: Random House.

Turnbull, H. R. (1990). *Free appropriate public education: The law and children with disabilities* Denver, CO: Love.

Yell, M. L. (1998). *The law and special education.* Upper Saddle River, NJ: Prentice-Hall.

Zigmond, N. (1997). Educating students with disabilities: The future of special education. In J. W. Lloyd, E. J. Kameenui, & D. Chard (Eds.), *Issues in educating students with disabilities* (pp. 377–390). Mahwah, NJ: Lawrence Erlbaum.

Zigmond, N. (2000). Reflections on a research career: Research as detective work. *Exceptional Children, 66,* 295–304.

Chapter 10

Learning Disabilities:
A Life Span Approach

Paul J. Gerber, Ph.D.
Professor of Education Virginia Commonwealth University

Oftentimes, there are a few words or a phrase that describe the prevailing wisdom of a field or a movement, and those words shape conventional wisdom and practices. In the field of learning disabilities not quite a half-century ago the phase was, "Don't worry he (or she) will outgrow it." Thus, the promises of pediatricians and specialists created a mind-set in professionals, individuals with learning disabilities, and their parents that their learning disability was only temporary, a bump in the road of development. In the formative years of the learning disabilities movement, the focus was school-age children, and primarily those who were in the elementary grades. It was almost as if learning disabilities in adolescence and adulthood did not exist.

Nowhere in the learning disabilities literature is it ever stated or inferred that there are discreet developmental boundaries in learning disabilities. Yet there are distinct markers of learning disabilities according to stage and phase of development, level of school programming, and delivery of services. Why the field departed from a holistic view of learning disabilities is curious, and why the entire continuum of development was not acknowledged until the last two decades of the twentieth century is somewhat of a mystery as well.

HISTORICAL CONTEXT OF LIFE SPAN ISSUES

One not so commonly known fact about learning disabilities is that it was borne via the clinical and scientific investigations of physicians who treated adults. It was adults with brain injury who piqued the curiosities of physicians studying the relationship of brain and behavior. There was Gall and Hinshelwood, Broca and Werneike, and Goldstein (Wiederholt, 1974). All of these European doctors had intense interest in adults who had experienced normal development but had evidenced intellectual and psychological difficulties as a result of an acquired injury to their brain. Each physician noticed pronounced difficulties, particularly in the area of speech and language function as well as adaptive behavior.

It was not until the work of the European physicians reached American shores that brain injury took a decided turn to the childhood years. Dr. Samuel Orton, who was influenced greatly by the work of Dr. James Hinshelwood, initially worked with the same kind of adults as the European physicians, but then he turned his attention to children who showed a similar constellation of symptoms. Moreover, two German scientists, Dr. Alfred Strauss and Dr. Heinz Werner, who were strongly influenced by the pioneering work of Dr. Kurt Goldstein, began their new lives in the United States by investigating children with brain injury at the Wayne County Training School just outside of Detroit, Michigan. Orton and Strauss' and Werner's work with children changed the focus of investigation and squarely brought the "professional conversation" to the school-age years, particularly the elementary grades. Most important, they shifted the focus of brain injury from adults to children and from acquired to developmental brain pathology. With this shift the die was cast for decades in what later would be called the field of learning disabilities. Front and center were children, and adolescent and adult issues seemed to all but vanish from the scene.

Subsequent pioneers in the field of learning disabilities followed suit. The work of Cruickshank, Kirk, Kephart, Frostig, Lehtinen, Wepman, deHirsch, and Johnson and Myklebust focused on children of elementary grades. The agenda of adolescents and adults was, in effect, put on hold while basic research and subsequent writing weaved together the issues of child development, learning disabilities, and intervention. In addition, the concern and efforts of parents reinforced the emphasis of children with learning disabilities in the earlier grades. In the last analysis, implicitly the field had chosen to stake out childhood as the building block for the field of learning disabilities. In time the full developmental continuum would be addressed. It was just a matter of when.

The words that "he (or she) will outgrow it" were, of course, wishful thinking. Students would pass through the elementary years and enter junior high and senior high school programs as adolescents with learning disabilities. The lack of research and writing about secondary programming and adolescence is apparent as late as the mid-1970s. What little literature existed focused on juvenile delinquency and learning disabilities. Very few had embraced the areas of adolescence, transition, or adulthood as areas of interest. Textbooks on learning disabilities did not address these issues at all. Adolescents with learning disabilities became an important agenda item for the field with the advent of Public Law 94-142, the Education of All Handicapped Children's Act. The law mandated a free and appropriate education for students with disabilities, including learning disabilities, from ages 5 to 21. By way of public policy, adolescents with learning disabilities joined a very crowded learning disabilities agenda. This law necessitated thought about adolescents with learning disabilities. How were they different from children with learning disabilities, and how could they be taught consistent with their unique developmental needs? What was missing at that point was an acknowledgment that there needed to be an exit strategy from school, and that at the age of 18 (when adolescents typically left school) they were on the cusp of adulthood, albeit young adulthood.

The concept of beyond school entered into the thinking of the field. With the advent of transition, the field of learning disabilities needed to conceptualize something that it had never formally addressed—the years after school, in essence, the adult years. For so long the field had set its sights on school-age programming, and there was little to draw from in terms of research, writing, established programs, or conceptual models. Even the work of the European physicians was not useful. Their clinical investigations seemed to have little practicality for a field that was struggling to catch up.

There were pockets of activity, however; they stemmed from legislation and public policy initiatives. Even prior to the passage of the first mandatory special education law (P.L. 94-142 in 1975), the Rehabilitation Act of 1973 was passed by the U.S. Congress. Included in that legislation was Section 504, which was given the moniker *the civil rights law for people with disabilities*. In spirit and intent, it sought to ensure that individuals with disabilities would not be discriminated against on the basis of their disability. Thus physical and programmatic access was mandated for all entities that received funding from the U.S. government. Arguably, the effects of this law were nascent for some time. Without question, the impact for individuals with learning disabilities was minimal despite growing activity in colleges and universities around the United States that tried to provide programmatic access to its students with learning disabilities. It was not until the passage of the Americans with Disabilities Act (P.L. 100-336) in 1990 that the rest of the loop was closed. The legislation mandated access for all individuals with disabilities, including learning disabilities, in nonpublic venues.

In a relatively short period of time the field of learning disabilities was thrust into addressing the needs of individuals whom it had traditionally thought of as learning disabled through the lens of childhood. Not only were adolescents added to the learning disabilities agenda, but they were added to the mission of the nation's schools. In addition, the field of learning disabilities needed to grapple with the complex issues of life beyond school, the adult years, which was seemingly a formidable task. Essentially, they needed to think about the other 70 years (Gerber & Reiff, 1994), the adult span of development.

The field of learning disabilities had gone full circle. Beginning with the work of physicians whose curiosities focused on adults with acquired brain injury, the focus shifted to children with developmental challenges. Interest evolved from children to adolescents and then to adults. The field of learning disabilities began to address the full continuum of development—a life span approach. Although much of the agenda was fostered by legislation and public policy, the underpinning to the movement consisted of thinking that incorporated lifespan issues from a developmental and learning disabilities perspective.

DEVELOPMENTAL CONTEXT OF LIFE SPAN ISSUES

The field of learning disabilities, not surprisingly, follows a developmental framework in addressing the life span challenges of individuals with learning disabilities. This approach can be seen in the curricular goals and educational provisions implemented during the school-age years. Hence, it is common for school programs at the elementary school level to focus on the development of basic skills (including reading) and acquisition and application of skills in a variety of content areas. However, as students with learning disabilities move along the educational continuum the program focus changes. In adolescence the educational programs of students with learning disabilities change according to the unique profiles of the students themselves. Serious consideration is given to life beyond the school-age years, and mandated transition plans are designed for students with learning disabilities beginning at age 14.

Beginning with transition plans, the realities of educational outcomes are projected beyond the schoolhouse doors. Professionals consider plans for vocational or postsecondary training, and ultimately employment. Taken into consideration for the first time are the kinds of skills and accommodations students with learning disabilities will need in their behavioral repertoires to succeed in all the societal systems they must interact within during their adult years. Moreover, there is a general acknowledgment that there is a culture of school and a culture of beyond school and that they are vastly different in a wide variety of ways. Paramount in the thinking of adjustment to the culture of beyond school is what we generally know from outcome studies of adults with learning disabilities. They are destined to a life of independent living, competitive employment, and active participation in familial and community systems (Gerber & Reiff, 1994).

If we acknowledge the validity of the observation that there is a culture of school and a culture of beyond school, then there are stiff challenges to prepare students with learning disabilities for when they leave school. Adolescent and adult development literature specifies the benchmarks that need to be achieved in the world beyond the school-age years. Included are emotional and economic independence from parents, the capability to live independently, completion of high school and possible postsecondary training, commitment to a personal set of values and goals, participating as a citizen in a community, and thinking of life partners with the possibility of parenthood (Rice, 1995). All of the developmental benchmarks are to be reached via a diversity of contexts including school, community, family, peer group, and work group. Accomplishing these benchmarks is a lifespan endeavor.

IN SEARCH OF A CONCEPTUAL MODEL

The field of learning disabilities has struggled to develop a conceptual model for the development of adolescents and adults with learning disabilities largely because of the paucity of basic research. As the field extended beyond the elementary-age years, it became standard practice to extrapolate what was known about childhood learning disabilities and superimpose the knowledge onto adolescents and adults with learning disabilities. This strategy did not fit the dire need for knowledge about these two rather "undiscovered" populations. A developing literature and research base emerged through the early efforts of Kronick (1976) and Siegel (1974), who wrote about adolescents, and intensive follow-up studies by Cruickshank, Morse, and Johns (1980) and Rogan and Hartman (1976) about adults. Their work departed from the follow-up studies that were typically narrow in focus, studying very specific academic, social, or vocational outcomes. They told the stories of the struggles and triumphs that embodied the adolescent and adult learning disabled experience.

What did emerge as a blueprint for the field was postulated by a group of individuals who gathered at the Learning Disabled Adult State-of-the

Art meeting held in Georgetown, a section of Washington, DC. The meeting was convened for a number of reasons. As a result of Assistant Secretary of Education Madeline Will's efforts, the field was dealing with a new concept called transition that had an impact on the secondary school years as well as the adult years. P.L. 94-142, which mandated free and appropriate education for all students with disabilities from ages 5 to 21 years, was relatively new. That law drew the attention of the learning disabilities community to address the multiplicity of educational needs and services for adolescents and young adults. Moreover, as a result of the reauthorization of the Rehabilitation Act in 1981, some adults with learning disabilities were made eligible for services within the vocational rehabilitation system for the first time (Gerber, 1981).

What emerged from the Georgetown meeting was an initial consensus of the group that there was no state and very little art. But what resulted was full acknowledgment that an agenda needed to be set for adults with learning disabilities that encompassed the full range of issues consistent with the lifespan issues for individuals with learning disabilities (Gerber & Mellard, 1985). This agenda had an impact on not only adulthood but also on preparation for adulthood (both secondary programming and transition). It incorporated the wide array of issues that fully addressed the greater part of the life span for persons with learning disabilities.

The agenda that was proffered to the field reflected the diversity of contexts and tasks that needed to be addressed in adulthood and gave direction to the curriculum of students with learning disabilities in middle and high school programs. Among the listed items were:

1. Determine what social skills are at issue for adults with learning disabilities.
2. Identify the vocational skills that are at issue for adults with learning disabilities.
3. Establish definitions of community adjustment. Determine which ones apply to adults with learning disabilities.
4. Identify and investigate the setting demands in post secondary training. (Gerber & Mellard, 1985, p. 63)

What became increasingly obvious in the collective thinking of professionals was that life span issues were a challenge that needed more thinking and ultimately more refinement. Cronin, Patton, and Polloway (1994) provided a "top down" conceptual framework of life span issues that addressed the multidimensional elements of lifelong adjustment. They suggested that the "major life demands" for individuals with learning disabilities be classified into six domains: employment-education, home and family, leisure pursuits, community involvement, emotional and physical health, and personal responsibility and relationships. They added important commentary to their conceptualization.

> Clearly adjustment problems in any of the six areas can have a significant impact both on the choices one makes in life and how successful one is within one's chosen path. Within the life span perspective, the relative importance of selective domains will change throughout an individual's life, whereas absolute importance of all domains remains constant. (Bassett, Polloway, & Patton, 1994, p. 17)

Their thinking was influenced greatly by the work of Baltes, Reese, and Lipsett (1980), who proposed an integrative model of lifespan development. Their theory provided the counterpoint to the traditional stage theories of adult development. It was predicated on four assumptions:

1. Developmental processes may begin at any time during a lifetime and may evidence varying degrees of intensity and duration.
2. The processes may not be linear in nature but may take on an erratic course.
3. Development can begin any time along the age continuum with acceleration, deceleration and possibly no movement at all.
4. Because of the complexity of development a wide array of variation between individuals increases with age.

Bassett, Polloway, and Patton (1994) commented on the utility of using this approach when considering the life span issues of individuals with learning disabilities. Writing specifically about adults with learning disabilities, they stated:

> The pluralistic model offers a unique perspective for considering the development of adults with learning disabilities. Because this population is acknowledged to be widely heterogeneous, individuals may vary greatly in the ages and stages at which they develop. Further, it is obvious that other influences have already altered their lives in ways that may set them apart from their nondisabled counterparts. By viewing adult development as pluralistic, one can begin to recognize the extreme variation and impact of life experiences at all ages and design interventions accordingly. (p. 16)

Although there is no conceptual model that emerges from best practices in the field of learning disabilities, there is a conceptual model that fits the life span on a generic basis. This promising model was developed from work sponsored by the U.S. Department of Labor called the Secretary's Commission on Achieving Necessary Skills (SCANS). The

TABLE 10.1
SCANS: Eight Areas of preparation for the Workplace of the Future

Skill Areas	Selected List of Skills
Basic Skills	Able to read and write
	Can perform basic arithmetic
	Can listen effectively
	Able to make self understood through speaking
Thinking	Can think creatively
	Has effective decision-making skills
	Can reason well
	Knows how to learn
Personal Qualities	Can take on responsibility
	Is honest and has integrity
	Has healthy self-esteem
	Can manage self in a variety of social settings
Resources	Has effective time management skills
	Can manage money
	Can allocate material and facility resources
Information	Able to gather and analyze information
	Can organize and maintain information
	Can interpret and communicate information
	Able to utilize computers for information purposes
Interpersonal	Can participate effectively on a team
	Can serve customers/clients successfully
	Can work in culturally diverse settings
	Able to or can explain how to teach others
Systems	Able to understand the workings of systems
	Can monitor own performance and make adjustments
	Able to improve system and give suggestions
Technology	Able to select appropriate technology
	Can apply technology to a task
	Able to maintain and "troubleshoot" applications

SCANS report outlines the requisite skills that all exiting high school students should have in order to be successful in long-term employment and for preparation in business environments of the twentyfirst century. Table 10.1 shows the eight areas of preparation laid out by the SCANS report.

THE OTHER 70 YEARS

As was noted earlier in this chapter, the adult stage of development can last for 70 years or longer. All that is done from a curricular perspective during the school-age years is predicated on what knowledge and skills will be needed after formal schooling is complete. If one is to look at selected learning disabilities follow-up studies in the adult years, the research is instructive about what lifespan issues are being dealt with on an ongoing basis.

The follow-up studies of former students from the famous Cove School by Rogan and Hartman (1976, 1990) suggest that there are myriad life span issues that evidence themselves in adulthood. There are issues pertaining to inadequate basic skills, such as reading, as well as cognitive processes including attention, memory, and organization. The dominant concern of most of the participants in the study was a lack of adequate social and personal relationships. Moreover, these issues crept into the settings and activities of daily life functioning. For instance, vocational problems seemed related more to social inadequacies than to vocational competence. Rogan and Hartman found that individuals with learning disabilities had adult outcomes across a continuum, from highly successful to marginally successful to very dependent.

Blalock (1981), in an analysis of adults with learning disabilities, saw issues of functioning in a wide variety of areas. They included education, employment, social and emotional functioning, and daily living skills. Her clinical work portrayed a population of adults with learning disabilities whose intraindividual differences made adaptation to adulthood very challenging. It underscored the complexity of planning for, and navigating through, the adult years.

The work of Gerber Ginsberg and Reiff (1991) corroborated the findings of the Rogan and Hartman study and the Blalock report. They found that there were a variety of outcomes in adults with learning disabilities related to severity, academic capabilities, and social ecologies. Moreover, they observed that persistence of learning disabilities into adulthood was undeniable. Gerber and Reiff (1991) chronicled the lives of three groups of adults with learning disabilities according to two broad criteria—achievement and adjustment. They identified three subgroups: highly adjusted, moderately adjusted, and marginally adjusted. The dimensions of their adjustment were analyzed through domains such as education, vocation, social/emotional, and daily living. Concluding their study, Gerber and Reiff wrote,

> One must understand that this problem may not be mitigated with age and may, in fact, continue to evolve within the various phases of adult development. The implications of learning disabilities for the entire lifespan still remain to be studied. (p. 136)

An extension of the Gerber and Reiff (1991) work continued with the focus on highly successful adults with learning disabilities (Gerber, Ginsberg, & Reiff, 1992; Reiff, Gerber, & Ginsberg, 1997). These studies concentrated on the dynamic processes of adaptation to employment. What the researchers found was a set of "alterable patterns" for success whose main variable was control. Furthermore, control could be divided into internal processes (desire, goal orientation reframing) and external manifestations or adaptability (persistence, goodness of fit, learned creativity and social ecologies). Their findings provided a possible explanation for success in the experiences that adults with learning disabilities encounter every day in a variety of contexts—the underpinnings to successful adjustment. More important, they began the link of school programming to life beyond school and gave more insight into the dichotomous culture of each.

EMPOWERMENT, REFRAMING, AND SELF-ADVOCACY

There are a number of important lifespan issues that are embedded in school-age programming but take on increased importance in the adolescent and adult years. All of them lead to the overriding issue of empowerment. Empowerment is a major goal of the disabilities community and the cornerstone of the Americans with Disabilities Act (ADA). At the signing of the ADA in 1990, President George H. W. Bush called for an end to paternalism toward individuals with disabilities and a movement toward empowerment. His clarion call had important implications for those students with learning disabilities who after leaving school are destined to a life of competitive employment, independent living, and maintenance of familial and community roles. Therefore, if individuals with learning disabilities are going to be successful in their lifelong adjustment (including transition from school to beyond school), then reframing and self-advocacy are very important to empower them.

Reframing has been identified as an important element of success in adulthood and throughout the lifespan for individuals with learning disabilities (Gerber, 1996; Reiff, Gerber, & Ginsberg, 1997). In essence, reframing is the ability of a person to be introspective about his or her learning disability. Most individuals with learning disabilities who are successful reframers think of their disability as positive and associate it with productive behavior and accomplishment. It is akin to the process of demystification (Levine, 1987), which should be incorporated into the school-age experience as early as possible.

Reframing is an internal process that can be broken down into four stages that are sequential but not always mutually exclusive. They are recognition, understanding, acceptance, and setting a plan of action (Gerber, Ginsberg, & Reiff, 1992; Reiff, Gerber, & Ginsberg, 1997).

If a person with learning disabilities is to adjust successfully during school or beyond the school-age years, then reframing is imperative. Lack of reframing ability has been associated with unsuccessful adult outcomes and marginal adjustment to adulthood. Thus it is the lynch-pin for adaptation in the wide variety of settings found in the adult years.

Reframing the learning disabled experience allows one to take an inventory of strengths and weaknesses and envision areas in which success is possible. It facilitates the process of finding the best "fit" or niche when adapting to real-world situations. An excellent example of reframing by an adult with learning disabilities was captured in an interview by the writer in the north of Holland. The Dutchman proudly stated that his learning disability had vanished when he graduated high school. How could he think differently? He was the successful owner of a bike store and a master bicycle mechanic. Everyone in his region sought his advice about the latest trends in the cycling world. Moreover, he proudly pointed out, "I am only learning disabled on rare occasions since leaving high school."

The importance of reframing cannot be overstated because it is also the key to self-advocacy. In turn, self-advocacy is central to successful adjustment in the culture of beyond school for a wide variety of reasons. Recently, a Roper Poll sponsored by the Tremaine Foundation found that the majority of individuals in the general public confused learning disabilities with mental retardation, often thinking that the two were synonymous. This finding alone underscores the necessity of self-advocacy. Moreover, there are implications for the workplace. Without the ability to advocate for oneself, there is little doubt that individuals with learning disabilities would be stymied by the following questions from a potential employer (Gerber, 1996).

1. What exactly is your disability?
2. What does learning disability or dyslexia mean?
3. What kinds of modifications do you need in your work environment?
4. What reasonable accommodations do you need? Why/how do you view them as reasonable?
5. How can you best be efficient?
6. Will your learning disability interfere with your productivity?
7. If we need to train you, how do you learn best?
8. Can you work well on a team?
9. Can you be given the lead role in a work group?
10. Am I taking a risk hiring a person with a learning disability? (p. 99)

Chances are that without the ability to reframe successfully it would also be perplexing to respond to questions in other adult settings. Moreover, self-disclosing, articulating needs, seeking accommodations, and expressing feelings emanating from being learning disabled could be difficult as well. Self-advocacy is important because of its portability. It is also challenging because of the solitary nature of the task. It has implications for every juncture of the lifespan and is the foundation of lifelong adaptation

CONCLUSION

The complexity of life span adjustment for individuals with learning disabilities is as individual as learning disabilities itself. Each person with learning disabilities has his or her own unique profile in terms of severity, cognitive strengths, intellectual ability, and adaptive behavior. The childhood and adolescent years contain more structure with the influences of schooling and parenting. The independence of the adult years contains myriad challenges over a protracted length of time.

Without question, each stage of development has its own trials, tribulations, and triumphs. None is greater than those in the adult years. In theory, planning for the transition from the culture of school to the culture of beyond school can be most challenging. There are simply so many "wild cards" in the course of a lifetime. An illustration of this point is the case of TJ (Gerber, 1992, 1998), now an adult who has had an extraordinary 36 years. Upon completing high school in the post–P.L. 94-142 years, he went straight to work in his community like the majority of persons with learning disabilities (school to work). After failing in several jobs, he was encouraged to pursue a university education by a counselor at his local vocational rehabilitation office. He attended a state university with the intention of teaching as a career (school to work to school). He completed his bachelor's degree requirements and obtained employment teaching students with learning disabilities (school to work to school to work). His first two years were characterized as successful. The end of his third year of teaching was also the abrupt end of his teaching career. After that, there was a period of unemployment, frustration, and loneliness. Currently, however, he is employed servicing ATM machines, is making two and half times his teaching salary, and has a steady female companion. His situation probably could be analyzed via the literature of resilience, but in TJ's case it is more fitting to view it as a life of unintended situations as well as serendipity. After his first year of teaching this writer observed,

His accomplishments in year one portend the beginnings of a productive and successful career, but year two may not be any easier. This may be the fate of one who has a learning disability. It does not, even in the smallest way diminish the competence, talent and qualifications TJ has shown in his first year of teaching. (p. 231)

The fate, so to speak, of individuals with learning disabilities has not yet been fully investigated. Ultimately, the question emerges, What will be the destiny of persons with learning disabilities through the entire lifespan? It is possible that individuals with learning disabilities will have approximately the same outcomes as those who are not disabled when the "other 70 years" are examined. In that case, those outcomes will look alike, but the path probably will appear to be markedly different. In the event that the outcomes are different from adults who are nondisabled, we can assuredly link that finding to the learning disabled experience and its unique impact over the entire life span.

REFERENCES

Americans with Disabilities Act of 1990, (PL 101-336). 42 U.S.C. 12101 *et seq.*

Baltes, P. B., Reese, H. W., & Lipsett, L. D. (1980). Lifespan developmental psychology. *Annual Review of Psychology, 31,* 65–110.

Bassett, D. S., Polloway, E. A., & Patton, J. R. (1994). Learning disabilities: Perspectives on adult development. In P. Gerber & H. Reiff (Eds.), *Learning disabilities in adulthood* (pp. 10–19). Austin, TX: Pro-Ed.

Blalock, J. (1981). Persistent problems and concerns of young adults with learning disabilities. In W. M. Cruickshank & A. Silver (Eds.), *Bridges to tomorrow* (pp. 3–56). Syracuse: Syracuse University Press.

Cronin, M. E., Patton, J. R., & Polloway, E. A. (1994). Preparing for adult outcomes: A model for a life skills curriculum. *Remedial and Special Education, 4,* 23–31.

Cruickshank, W. M., Morse, W., & Johns, J. (1980). *Learning disabilities: The struggle from adolescence toward adulthood.* Syracuse: Syracuse University Press.

Education for All Handicapped Children Act. (1975). (PL 94-142). 20 U.S.C. 1401–1420.

Gerber, P. J. (1981). Learning disabilities and eligibility for vocational rehabilitation services: A chronology of events. *Journal of Learning Disabilities 14,* 422–425.

Gerber, P. J. (1992). Being learning disabled and a beginning teacher and teaching a class of students with learning disabilities. *Exceptionality, 3,* 213–231.

Gerber, P. J. (1996). Reframing the learning disabled experience. *Journal of Learning Disabilities, 29*(1), 98–101.

Gerber, P. J. (1998). Trials and tribulations of a teacher with learning disabilities through his first two years of Employment. In R. J. Anderson, C. E. Keller, & J. M. Karp (Eds.), *Enhancing diversity: Educators with disabilities* (pp. 41–59). Washington, DC: Galludet University Press.

Gerber, P. J., Ginsberg, R., & Reiff, H. B. (1992). Identifying alterable patterns of success in employment in highly successful adults with learning disabilities. *Journal of Learning Disabilities, 25,* 475–487.

Gerber, P. J., & Mellard, D. (1985). Rehabilitation of learning disabled adults: recommended research priorities. *Journal of Rehabilitation, 51,* 62–64.

Gerber, P. J., & Reiff, H. B. (1991). *Speaking for themselves: Ethnographic interviews with adults with learning disabilities.* Ann Arbor, MI: The University of Michigan Press.

Gerber, P. J., & Reiff, H. B. (1994). *Learning disabilities in adulthood.* Austin, TX: Pro-Ed.

Kronick, D. (1976). *Three families.* San Rafael, CA: Academic Therapy Publications.

Levine, M. D. (1987). *Developmental variations and learning disorders.* Cambridge, MA: Educator's Publishing Service.

Rehabilitation Act of 1973, (PL 93-112). 29 U.S.C. 701 *et seq.*

Reiff, H. B., Gerber, P. J., & Ginsberg, R. (1997). *Exceeding expectations: Highly successful adults with learning disabilities.* Austin, TX: Pro-Ed.

Rice, F. P. (1995). *Human development.* Saddle River, NJ: Prentice Hall, Inc.

Rogan, L. L., & Hartman, L. (1976). *A follow-up study of learning disabled children as adults.* Final report (Project No. 443CH600100, grant No. OEG-0-7453), Washington, DC: Bureau of the Education of the Handicapped, U.S. Department of Health, Education and Welfare.

Rogan, L. L., & Hartman, L. (1990). Adult outcomes of learning disabled students ten years after follow-up. *Learning Disabilities Focus, 5,* 91–102.

Schiamberg, L. B., & Smith, K. U. (1982). *Human development.* New York: Macmillan Publishing Co.

Secretary's Commission on Achieving Necessary Skills. (1991). *What work requires of schools: A SCANS report for america 2000.* Washington, DC: U.S. Department of Labor.

Siegel, E. (1974). *The exceptional child grows up.* New York: Dutton.

Wiederholt, J. L. (1974). Historical perspectives on the education of the learning disabled. In L. Mann & D. A. Sabatino (Eds.), *The second review of special education* (pp. 103–152). Philadelphia, PA: JSE Press.

Chapter 11

Learning Disabilities in Australia

John Elkins
Fred and Eleanor Schonell Special Education Research Centre, Graduate School of Education, The University of Queensland, Brisbane, AUSTRALIA

This chapter falls into two parts. The first is a description and analysis of the field of learning disabilities in Australia. Because the Australian approach to learning problems does not use the exclusionary factors in the standard definition of learning disabilities, the second part is a commentary on learning and the circumstances in which students may find learning unexpectedly difficult.

LEARNING DISABILITIES AND LEARNING DIFFICULTIES IN AUSTRALIA

Australia is a commonwealth of six states and two territories formed from a number of colonies in 1901. Its constitution blends a British parliamentary system with the American Federal structure of a House of Representatives and Senate. Originally, education was a responsibility of the states and territories. By the end of the twentieth century, however, the national government had intervened substantially through targeted funding, particularly in literacy and numeracy and for certain targeted groups such as students with disabilities. There are three broad groups of schools in all states and territories: government schools, which are fully funded at state or territory level; Catholic systemic schools, which serve more than one-quarter of all students; and independent schools, which may have religious or nondenominational status. Nongovernment schools receive some means-tested state and federal funding, but all charge tuition fees. Unlike in the United States, schools are not supported by local taxes.

Because the executive and legislative arms of government are combined, it is unusual for Australian governments, federal or state, to pass legislation that binds themselves. Education laws are designed to permit the expenditure of public funds, and to ensure that parents enroll their children during the compulsory school years. State governments establish policy and regulations for the activities of schools. Thus, no legislation comparable to Individual with Disabilities Education Act has been passed, though the services provided for students with special needs are similar to those in the United States. Instead of special education law, antidiscrimination legislation offers a remedy to persons with disabilities who believe that they have been discriminated against in education, as well as other areas such as age, sex, and race. Furthermore it is unclear whether students with learning disabilities fall under its ambit, because in few cases can we demonstrate that the student has an underlying impairment, which is surely the sine qua non of a disability.

It is generally agreed that the American learning disabilities movement has been very influential in Australia, particularly with the parent advocacy groups and academic researchers, though, as will be shown later, education authorities have preferred to use the label *learning difficulties.* Parent groups, notably AUSPELD (Australian Specific Learning Difficulties), had their greatest success in the mid-1970s, when they created considerable public awareness about the needs of students who were failing to acquire basic skills. AUSPELD convinced the Australian House of Representatives to hold an inquiry into all aspects of learning disabilities. The report of the Select Committee of the House of Representatives took a strong stand on the matter of terminology, its members being politicians who were unconvinced that the difficulties experienced by students were usually of constitutional origin. Thus the committee recommended the use of the term *learning difficulties.* I have argued elsewhere (Elkins, 1983) that learning difficulties are best understood to be experiences of students, and that the term learning disabilities should be restricted to limitations in learning arising from a constitutional impairment. A comparison between special education textbooks in Australia and the United States would reveal a pronounced difference in two areas—the lack of special education law such as IDEA and the approach to high-incidence educational problems, which are understood broadly with little reference to the notion of disability as it applies in the United States. The impact of the U.S. definitions of learning disabilities on academic researchers has been to force them to choose either to adopt the U.S. definition in order to link their work to that published in the dominant international journals, or instead to research low academic achievement in the Australian context.

Australian interest in learning disabilities can be traced back at least to the appointment of Fred Schonell to the Chair of Education at the University of Queensland in 1950. An Australian who had gained a PhD at the University of London, Schonell had conducted extensive research in the UK on "backwardness in the basic subjects." On returning to Australia he established a remedial clinic, commenced a research program, founded a journal (now named the *International Journal of Disability, Development and Education*), and instituted a Certificate in Diagnostic Testing and Remedial Teaching, which provided a growing supply of remedial teachers. Andrews (1982, 1983) has documented the extensive contributions of Fred Schonell and his wife, Eleanor, whose research in cerebral palsy was well known to Bill Cruickshank.

Elkins (1975, 1983, 2000) has described the ways in which Australian views of the field of learning disabilities differ from those pertaining in North America. Indeed, had this term been used strictly, and had prevalence data remained below 2%, Australian researchers and administrators might have accepted the construct. However, it is my opinion that many students who are identified and served under the label learning disabilities in the United States today are a heterogeneous group of low-achieving students. Indeed, this was evident 25 years ago, as the students in the early services for students with learning disabilities were below average in IQ and had severe reading problems (Kirk & Elkins, 1975).

Louden et al. (2000) have completed a major study to map the current Australian situation concerning elementary school students with learning difficulties, with particular reference to literacy and numeracy. These latter terms have special significance in Australian government education policy. Literacy signifies the use of spoken and written language to enable students to function in school and society appropriate to their age. Numeracy has a similar meaning with respect to those aspects of mathematics that are functionally important, and includes not only number, but space, measurement, estimation, data, and chance.

Benchmark testing aims to identify children who do not meet agreed-upon standards at a particular grade level. Thus, the results can be used to establish the prevalence of low-achieving students irrespective of cause. The passing rates on the benchmark tests in reading at grade three are 87%, with a range from 72% in the Northern Territory to 91% in New South Wales (Kemp, 2000). The low results in the Northern Territory are thought to reflect the higher proportion of indigenous students. Some of the students who fail the benchmark tests will be recent migrants from non–English-speaking backgrounds, but most will be what some have referred to as garden-variety poor readers. It is likely that benchmark testing will be introduced in numeracy.

As part of the Louden et al. study, Rivalland and House (2000) have reviewed the provision of services for students with learning difficulties in Australia. At the national level there has been a strong commitment to improved outcomes in literacy for several years, and more recently numeracy has been included. The Commonwealth Government provides supplementary funding to all schools to promote the attainment of its literacy and numeracy goals and has encouraged collaboration among the states and territories, as well as among government, Catholic, and independent schools. No specific Commonwealth funding is provided for students with learning difficulties, but in accordance with principles of equity, schools are required to give special attention to any students experiencing disadvantage. These students would include those experiencing undue difficulty in learning, along with those experiencing poverty, those of non–English- speaking background, isolated students, and indigenous students.

States and territories do not generally distinguish between learning difficulties and learning disabilities, using the former term to cover all students with high-incidence educational problems. Increasingly, the term learning disabilities is reserved for those who have not responded to remedial intervention. Most government and independent schools generally provide support for all students with low academic attainment in basic curriculum areas (e.g., literacy and numeracy) whose problems cannot be attributed to intellectual, emotional, physical, or sensory disability. A study has recently been completed that maps the provision of services to such students with identified low-incidence disabilities who are included in regular schools (van Kraayenoord, Elkins, Palmer, Rickards, & Colbert, 2000). These students usually have specific support as indicated on their Individual Education Program, such as an aide, consultant support for the teacher, special equipment, or a modified curriculum.

Thus, the Australian approach to service provision includes students who fit the North American definition of learning disabilities, but is broader and includes more than 10% of students, sometimes up to 30% in particular schools, depending on their context (Andrews, Elkins, Berry, & Burge, 1979; Rohl, Milton, & Brady, 2000). Indeed, it is generally accepted that the decision whether to provide support for a student is not context-free. For example, a low-achieving student in a school with high test scores might not be given help if he or she were to transfer to a school with low test scores, because many more students in that school would be regarded as in greater need.

In the National Survey of Special Education (Andrews, Elkins, Berry, & Burge, 1979), the average prevalence across schools was around 11%, a figure not causing any surprise. However, great variability between schools was noted. It is tempting to speculate about why such variation exists and what the implications are for Australian responses to the challenge of children with learning difficulties in our schools.

In the UK, Thomas and Davis (1996) examined the consistency of need in reading across schools. They found that "where mean reading levels are higher, a child is more likely to be considered to have a reading difficulty than an equivalent child in a school where mean levels are lower" (unpaginated). These authors suggest that some assessment that establishes levels across the school system is important to distribute resources equitably. Thomas and Davis also noted that the percent of students with reading difficulties was relatively high ranging from 16% in high-achievement schools to 24% in schools with below average reading levels. In another analysis, they found that the average reading level of students with learning difficulties was lower in schools with lower average achievement.

Most Australian schools have some systematic early identification and intervention at the classroom level. For example in the state of Queensland, a Year 2 Diagnostic Net operates in which class teachers monitor all students over the first two years of formal schooling to "catch" those who are making slow progress in literacy or numeracy. The emphasis in early identification is upon class-wide teacher checklists, with subsequent individual assessment of those students whose progress is of concern. In some schools, Reading Recovery (Clay, 1987a) is used as a first level of intervention with those students who do not make satisfactory progress other than with the help they receive from support teachers. Some schools have intervention services in numeracy, but this area of the curriculum is less well-served than literacy.

For older students, identification may result from teachers or parents requesting assessment of the student by a support teacher or psychologist. Government and Catholic systemic schools usually have a consistent approach to assessment in each state, with independent schools determining their own approaches. Some educational and psychological tests are developed in Australia, but the costs involved in standardization mean that the range is limited. Sometimes tests developed in the United States or UK are used with an occasional adjustment because of cultural differences in systems of currency or vocabulary. In such cases it is assumed that the norms are appropriate for Australian students. Although this is hardly ideal, when tests are used clinically, few problems appear to result.

Consistent with seeing learning difficulties as a mainstream issue, schools usually rely on mainstream curriculum approaches to guide intervention. Because most classroom teachers use eclectic teaching methods and a wide variety of teacher-made as well as commercial materials, support teachers may choose to emphasize aspects in which students appear to have experienced particular difficulty, such as in phonemic awareness or automaticity in number facts. Overall, support teachers try to ensure that their efforts are coordinated with those of the class teacher, and they rarely adopt teaching methods likely to conflict with what the class teacher uses and cause students to be come confused. However, teachers have professional discretion in their work. Thus, hundreds of programs and strategies are used by schools (Rivalland & House, 2000). In addition to Reading Recovery (Clay, 1987a), mention should be made of the First Steps professional development program in literacy; in addition, programs for intervention in numeracy have been developed in several states.

Some special approaches are also used, such as School Wide Early Language & Literacy (Center & Freeman, 1997; Center, Freeman, & Robertson, 1998), which is an Australian adaptation of Success for All (Wasik & Slavin, 1993), and Making Up Lost Time in Literacy (Wheldall & Beaman, 2000), which is an intensive skill-development small-group program. Spalding's multisensory methods have a small but enthusiastic following in independent schools (Moore, 1998), and the Teaching Handwriting Reading and Spelling Skills system, which emphasises phoneme/grapheme correspondences, is popular in a few states. Special mention should be made of the contribution in the area of phonemic awareness of Australian researchers such as Bowey (1996) and Byrne and Fielding-Barnsley (1995). Also, Farrell (1996) found that most grade one teachers whose approach was labelled as whole language actually incorporated a substantial amount of phonics in their programs. Although classroom approaches to mathematics teaching have a constructivist emphasis, many teachers are ensuring that students also engage in regular practice to ensure rapid recall of basic addition and multiplication facts. Thus, there seems to be an eclectic approach to teaching that avoids the excesses of the periodic fads that affect education.

States expend substantial sums to support the identification and intervention approaches described by Rivalland and House (2000), but it is very difficult to obtain reliable information on the costs of either identification or intervention. One reason is that there is a dynamic relationship among classroom literacy and numeracy teaching, early intervention such as Reading Recovery, and remedial intervention. Presumably (because there is little empirical evidence), if increased expenditure on mainstream teaching reduces the number of "failing" students, then the costs of remediation should lessen. Intensive individual intervention programs, such as Reading Recovery, are costly and are not available in all schools. Most intervention staff (usually termed *support teachers*) operate a mixture of small-group tutoring with in-class support and consultation. Extensive use is made of volunteers and teacher aides, often using structured systems such as Support-a-Reader, Support-a-Writer, and Support-a-Maths Learner, which were developed by the state education department in Queensland. It is somewhat disconcerting that those students who need most help may be being assigned to those least qualified, and we need research on the effectiveness of tutoring by paraprofessionals and volunteers. It is also evident that private providers of diagnostic and intervention services play an important role, particularly in independent schools (Greaves, 2000). Of concern is that private providers use many unproven methods, and parents and schools often lack the information needed to enable them to make valid decisions among programs.

There are few full-time programs for students with severe or long-term problems. A recent case study of a learning disability class in a primary school indicated that it provided intensive teaching for up to 10 students drawn from a district with 28 schools (Elkins & Dole, 2000). All students had failed to profit from some years of intervention provided in their home schools. Reintegration of the students into regular classes was an important goal of the special class program, though it might take as much as two years before the students acquired the assurance and self-management skills to enable them to progress in a regular class. There is no real debate in Australia about inclusion of students with learning difficulties as this is the dominant approach. A very small proportion of those referred for assessment will be placed in full- or part-time special classes. However, there is general acceptance that limited withdrawal support programs may be appropriate without this being against the spirit of inclusion, which schools generally espouse.

In all states, there are university courses and in-service programs to train teachers in assessing and teaching students with learning difficulties. In general, support teaching is a second career step undertaken by experienced teachers. Thus, we train few if any teachers for support teaching as their initial teaching assignment. There are no enforceable standards for certification as a support teacher, though from one to two years' study beyond the initial teaching qualification is accepted as desirable. Most teachers acquire these additional qualifications through part-time or distance study. It seems that incentives for teachers to obtain specialist skills may be insufficient to ensure adequate numbers of trained support teachers, especially in rural and remote areas of the nation, where schools have appointed many teachers who have undertaken little relevant graduate study to support roles.

Overall, Rivalland and House (2000) characterize the Australian scene as complex and diverse, with "some commonalities in how systems and sectors define learning difficulties, identify children with difficulties, access services from private providers and implement programs and strategies to support children with learning difficulties. . . . There is considerable diversity in the way in which systems or sectors report prevalence, provide funding and supply professional development." (p. 158)

It appears as if future developments in the field Australians term learning difficulties will come from the national priority to have all students gain functional literacy and numeracy, rather than as part of national special education initiatives. Professionals will reserve the term learning disabilities for a small group of students with severe problems who have not benefited from typical support services.

AN AUSTRALIAN PERSPECTIVE ON THE FIELD

In this section I seek to explore some underlying issues that may partly account for the way in which education systems in Australia have developed their responses to students whose lack of progress in learning basic skills causes concern to their teachers, parents, and the students themselves. As society has changed, the activities with which students fill their time have changed. Children play computer games rather than catching crayfish, resulting in a different repertoire of skills had by children of a generation ago. With the advent of new forms of literacy (Luke & Elkins, 1998), influenced by the rise of information technology and globalization, what a learning difficulty refers to may have been enlarged beyond code breaking and comprehension of narrative to understanding exposition and argument, to following procedural texts and critical appreciation of the way in which authors position the reader (Freebody & Luke, 1997; Luke & Freebody, 1997).

Students may differ for reasons that include innate preferences and socialization practices, so that each demonstrates strong interests or dislikes in his or her learning. Whatever we may think of the implications of gender differences in young children, few can have failed to notice some young boys apparently obsessed by earthmoving machinery, able to discriminate among excavators, backhoes, and cranes, and others obsessed with rescue services, whereas girls may have quite different interests. The point is not to approve or disapprove (though there are important issues here), but to recognize that there are very many pathways of learning that children follow. Neither parents nor teachers are particularly effective in guiding this learning, much of which appears to be influenced by the unique appeal of certain knowledge and skills to individual learners and by broad social pressures.

This leads to a consideration of how culture affects what is learned. Some of these differences relate to opportunity. As a child I could not have developed computer skills, but few students today are aware of the intricacies of sharpening slate pencils on a brick, which I mastered at the age of six (Elkins, 1998). Skills of identifying "bush tucker" can be developed by Aboriginal children living in traditional communities, without the need to read or write. However as Elley's (1991) research amply demonstrated, most Pacific island children can learn to read if villages are well-stocked with interesting, culturally relevant books.

Thus learning happens whether we like it or not, and the task of schools, families, and society generally is to maximize the value and extent of what is learned. This leads me to adopt the perspective of Vygotskian (or sociohistorical) psychology and to state an assumption about teaching—that its purpose is to support and influence learning. Note that this view of teaching is not directly about instruction (though instruction has its place in helping motivated learners to learn efficiently).

Theories of Learning and Learning Disabilities

One major challenge facing support services is to ensure at least minimally useful levels of literacy for virtually all students. That is, we should be concerned both with students with learning difficulties/disabilities and those who have been labeled slow learners/mildly intellectually impaired/educationally handicapped. Thus, a theoretical framework is needed that can encompass a wide range of student difficulties, while allowing more specialized explanations that might apply for particular groups of students or individuals.

None of the dominant models in learning disabilities is adequate to fit the definition of teaching as "supporting learning," nor is there strong empirical evidence of their utility. Yet, it would be unwise to discard them, since each has a partial view of truth. These models (medical, psychological process, behavioral, and cognitive strategy) are each too narrow to be useful for all students (Poplin, 1988). Each needs to be contextualized in the way that Tharp and Gallimore (1988) did in their challenging book *Rousing Minds to Life.* They show how different teaching techniques need not be in competition, and how they fit within a broader theoretical framework derived from Vygotsky.

What encourages students to learn useful and potentially interesting things? Certainly there are social conditions that mediate and support learning. There may be peers or adults who help sustain the conditions for learning. As expertise increases, the individual learner is able to mimic these supports and teach him- or herself. This is not the same thing as discovery learning. So some students who experience learning difficulties may have lacked the motivation or the support for learning. Others, as Clay (1987b) expressed it, may "learn to be learning disabled" (p 154), and thus represent the casualties of classrooms unable to meet individual needs.

Depending on the implicit theories shared by members of a family or cultural group, various things are latched on to as worthy of supportive intervention—modeling a grammatical structure or pronouncing a difficult word, counting aloud while pushing on a swing, and "pairing" while a child reads aloud are obvious examples. Whether support is well-received may depend on whether the learner has formed the opinion that the thing being taught is worth learning. A child living in a small town with few hills will probably have observed bicycles being ridden for pleasure or to some material end and will need no encouragement to learn to ride, though he or she will need support in the beginning stages. This leads to a consideration of motivation, for society provides not only the support for learning, but also by its social practices, the reason why something is worth learning.

In many cases children pursuing personally relevant (and often socially desired) learning will do so as a social activity, rather than as a lone learner. In these circumstances, there is a valid sense in which learning is "a social process of knowledge construction" (Salomon & Perkins, 1998, p. 4). This view recognizes that all participants can support the learning of others, and all take something away. Even those ostensibly doing the teaching may learn.

Reading, writing, calculating, and other mathematical skills are examples of culturally created tools that can themselves scaffold further learning. Thus, those students who experience learning difficulties are doubly disadvantaged because they find it difficult to use these tools and are unusually reliant on individual assistance. In most cases, students with learning difficulties will need to be supported in an apprenticeship mode, often requiring individual attention till they can perform independently. However, practice is needed to consolidate newly learned skills. Lack of automaticity limits the ability to apply high-level thinking in literacy or mathematics (Cumming, & Elkins, 1999; Johnson & Layng, 1992).

Students' Learning Problems and Teachers

It is important to recognize inadequacies in teaching as a factor that contributes to students' learning difficulties. The profession of teaching includes the role of assuring that students learn, whether they wish to or not. This is evident in the public demand for teachers to be more accountable. Teachers have to show that their students have learned what others, particularly employers, deemed essential.

Over many years I have observed different responses to learning problems. One extreme is the exceptional teacher who cannot accept that any student in her classroom should fail. She takes every possible measure to ensure that all students are successful, and it is both a challenge and a responsibility to ensure that no student fails. At the other extreme is the staff-room talk among teachers that legitimizes failure by branding certain students as hopeless, as typical of their family or race (Freebody, Ludwig, & Gunn, 1995). Among students, failure may be a constant fear, which inhibits risk-taking and constrains learning to a narrow domain near to what is already known. And always looming is the possibility of failure being punished by some stigmatizing form of assistance. As Stone (1998) points out, the language of failure today is often sanitized, and we avoid dunce, idiot, nincompoop, and similar terms. School failure is, however, real, and may signal failure in life in western societies where so few opportunities exist for students who do not possess the necessary graduation certificates.

It is revealing that we speak of student failure much more than of teacher failure; sometimes of parent failure, but rarely of societal failure. And this in turn derives from a consideration of which groups have power. There is a need both to behave ethically with respect to the language of failure and to work to establish schooling without failure for both students and teachers (Elkins, 1987).

Data are needed also on other factors that might influence the likelihood that students will be regarded as having learning difficulties. These include the socioeconomic status of the school, the experience of the teachers, and whether there is a whole school approach to learning difficulties. Volume 3 of the recent study by Louden et al. (2000) contains 20 case studies of schools considered to have high-quality approaches to serving students with learning difficulties. These case studies suggest that it may be very important to have a coherent plan to which all parts of the school community contribute. Thus, classroom teachers have key responsibilities for the long-term education of students, and support teachers contribute specialist instruction, detailed assessment, and advice to class teachers and parents. Parents are encouraged to contribute their emotional support and, if they wish, are taught how to help at home with regular homework and extra practice. Classmates can also contribute through formal peer tutoring and offering informal support in cooperative classrooms. The wider school community can also contribute as volunteer tutors and by moderating the extremes of political pressures on schools that arise through the standards movement and excessive use of high-stakes achievement testing.

It is important also not to neglect learning difficulties in areas other than literacy. A British intervention, *Numeracy Recovery* was developed by Askew, Bibby and Brown (1996). It has three main elements: (a) centrality of mental processes, (b) the difficulty of abstracting mathematical ideas from experience, and (c) the importance of assessment. These authors argue that "deducing number facts helps pupils commit more facts to memory" (not paginated), and that "recalled facts help expand the range of strategies for deriving facts" (not paginated). They also note a problem observed in Australian research by Cumming and Elkins (1999)—that students who gained success in calculating simple addition facts using an inefficient strategy (such as counting on) rarely progressed to more efficient approaches, such as ready recall. Askew, Bibby, and Brown (1996) also noted that careful teacher explanation was needed to support the development of mathematical abstractions from concrete experience. Furthermore, assessment must be a fine grained, insightful analysis of what students do, because "what a pupil learnt was often different from what had been taught" (unpaginated). This may be an example of "learning to be learning disabled" in mathematics.

CONCLUSION

Australian educators appear to be moving toward the acceptance of a three-phase model to understand learning difficulties and learning disabilities. The first phase is the regular classroom program. Professionals are placing an increased emphasis on ensuring that the regular classroom program is of high quality, and there is an increasing emphasis on accountability. Many schools have restructured the curriculum to devote more time to literacy and numeracy, especially in the primary grades. If improvements can be achieved, then there should be a reduced need for more expensive support services. The second phase is early identification of those students who are making limited progress, and the provision of intensive support for up to half a year in the hope of achieving accelerated learning such that the students can be successful in the regular classroom. While Reading Recovery is a prime example of this second phase, in many schools the support teacher provides small group intervention within or outside the regular classroom. It is not known how effective second-phase programs are in the longer term, though research by Center, Wheldall, Freeman, and McNaught (1995) suggests that schools may need to give more attention to ongoing in-class support after students have completed the intensive intervention phase. The third phase is typified by providing ongoing part-time or full-time small-group instruction. Here, depending on the availability of resources, students are likely to be supported for several years, but always with the goal of giving them the skills to profit from regular class placement. Few would quarrel with the labeling of these students as learning disabled on the basis of the severity of their problems.

I have mentioned nothing in this chapter about such topics as ADD/ADHD, language delay and disorders, or Asperger's syndrome, which certainly are present in Australian students and may affect school learning. However, these labels are applied only after relevant professionals have undertaken some diagnostic assessment and an IEP has been developed. Little is known about the prevalence of these disorders, though concern is sometimes expressed at the number of students who are being prescribed medication for attention deficits.

Australian educational administrators and policy makers are striving to develop an affordable collection of supports for all students who experience difficulties in learning. They are seeking evidence that programs are effective to guide them in apportioning resources among regular class instruction, early identification/intervention, and longer-term intensive support. Most Australian educators would find the ecological model presented recently by Wolery (1999) a suitable viewpoint for understanding learning difficulties.

REFERENCES

Andrews, R. J. (1982). A happy venture: The contributions of Fred and Eleanor Schonell to special education. Part 1 – Fred and Eleanor Schonell's contribution to special education in the United Kingdom: 1929-1949. *The Exceptional Child, 29,* 155–190.

Andrews, R. J. (1983). A happy venture: The contributions of Fred and Eleanor Schonell to special education. Part 2 – The Fred and Eleanor Schonell Educational Research Centre: 1952-1982. *The Exceptional Child, 30,* 3–56.

Andrews, R. J., Elkins, J., Berry, P. B., & Burge, J. (1979). *A survey of special education in Australia: Provisions, needs and priorities in the education of children with handicaps and learning difficulties.* St. Lucia, Qld: Fred and Eleanor Schonell Educational Research Centre, The University of Queensland.

Askew, M., Bibby, T., & Brown, M. (1996, September). *Numeracy recovery. Exploring practices through group observation.* Paper presented at British Educational Research Association Annual Conference, Lancaster. http://www.leeds.ac.uk/educol/

Bowey, J. A. (1996). Phonological sensitivity as a proximal contributor to phonological recoding skills in children's reading. *Australian Journal of Psychology, 48,* 113–118.

Byrne, B., & Fielding-Barnsley, R. (1995). Evaluation of a program to teach phonemic awareness to young children: A 2- and 3year followup and a new preschool trial. *Journal of Educational Psychology, 87,* 488–503.

Center, Y., & Freeman, L. (1997). A trial evaluation of SWELL (Schoolwide Early Language and Literacy): A whole class early literacy program for at-risk and disadvantaged children. *International Journal of Disability, Development and Education, 44,* 21–39.

Center, Y., Freeman, L., & Robertson, G. (1998). An evaluation of Schoolwide Early Language and Literacy (SWELL) in six disadvantaged schools. *International Journal of Disability, Development and Education, 45,* 143–172.

Center, Y., Wheldall, K., Freeman, L., & McNaught, M. (1995). An evaluation of Reading Recovery. *Reading Research Quarterly, 30,* 240–263.

Clay, M. M. (1987a). Implementing Reading Recovery: Systematic adaptations to an educational innovation. *New Zealand Journal of Educational Studies, 22,* 35–58.

Clay, M. M. (1987b). Learning to be learning disabled. *New Zealand Journal of Educational Studies, 22,* 155–173.

Cumming, J. J., & Elkins, J. (1999). Lack of automaticity in the basic addition facts as a characteristic of arithmetic learning problems and instructional needs. *Mathematical Cognition, 5,* 149–180.

Elkins, J. (1975). Reading disability research in Australia. *The Slow Learning Child, 22,* 109–119.

Elkins, J. (1983). The concept of learning difficulties: An Australian perspective. In J. D. McKinney & L. Feagans (Eds.), *Current topics in learning disabilities* (Vol 1, pp. 179–203). Norwood, NJ: Ablex.

Elkins, J. (1987). Education without failure? Education for all? *The Exceptional Child, 34,* 5–20.

Elkins, J. (1998). "Slates away!": Penmanship in Queensland, Australia. *History of Reading News, XXI*(2), 1–2.

Elkins, J. (2000). The Australian context. In W. Louden et al. (Eds.), *Mapping the Territory. Primary students with learning difficulties: Literacy and numeracy.* (Vol 1, pp. 29–39). Canberra, ACT: Department of Education, Training and Youth Affairs.

Elkins, J., & Dole, S. (2000). Thornburn primary school: The learning disability class. In W. Louden et al. (Eds.), *Mapping the Territory. Primary students with learning difficulties: Literacy and numeracy.* (Vol 3, pp. 399–411). Canberra, ACT: Department of Education, Training and Youth Affairs.

Elley, W. B. (1991). Acquiring literacy in a second language: The effects of book-based programs. *Language Learning, 41,* 375–411.

Farrell, M. E. (1996). The relationship between teacher beliefs and practices, and literacy acquisition. Unpublished doctoral thesis, University of Queensland.

Freebody, P., Ludwig, C., & Gunn, S. (1995). Everyday literacy practices in and out of school in low socio-economic urban communities. Canberra, ACT: Department of Employment, Education and Training.

Freebody, P., & Luke, A. (1997, August). The four roles of a reader. Paper presented at Meeting the Challenge: NSW State Literacy Strategy Conference, Sydney.

Greaves, D. (2000). Private provider services for students with learning difficulties. In W. Louden et al. (Eds.), *Mapping the Territory. Primary students with learning difficulties: Literacy and numeracy.* (Vol 1, pp. 135–155). Canberra, ACT: Department of Education, Training and Youth Affairs.

Johnson, K. R., & Layng, T. V. J. (1992). Breaking the structuralist barrier: Literacy and numeracy with fluency. *American Psychologist, 47,* 1475–1490.

Kemp, D. M. (2000). Media release: Percentage of Year 3 students achieving the reading benchmark. *http://www.deetya.gov.au.* (Accessed 3 April).

Kirk, S. A., & Elkins, J. (1975). Characteristics of children enrolled in Child Service Demonstration Centers. *Journal of Learning Disabilities, 10,* 630–637.

Louden, W., Chan, L. K. S., Elkins, J., Greaves, D., House, H., Milton, M., Nichols, S., Rivalland, J., Rohl, M., & van Kraayenoord, C. (2000). *Mapping the territory. Primary students with learning difficulties: Literacy and numeracy.* Vols 1, 2 & 3. Canberra, ACT: Department of Education, Training and Youth Affairs.

Luke, A., & Elkins, J. (1998). Editorial, Reinventing literacy in "new times." *Journal of Adolescent and Adult Literacy, 42,* 4–7.

Luke, A., & Freebody, P. (1997). Shaping the social practices of reading. In S. Muspratt, A. Luke, & P. Freebody. (Eds.), *Constructing critical literacies: Teaching and learning textual practice.* Creskill, NJ: Hampton Press.

Moore, S. (1998). Spalding in Australia: A pilot research study. Canberra, ACT: Department of Employment, Education, Training and Youth Affairs.

Poplin, M. S. (1988). Holistic/constructivist principles of the teaching/learning process: Implications for the field of learning disabilities. *Journal of Learning Disabilities, 21,* 401–416.

Rivalland, J., & House, H. (2000). Mapping system provision for learning difficulties. In W. Louden et al. (Eds.), *Mapping the territory. Primary students with learning difficulties: Literacy and numeracy.* (Vol 2, pp. 125–159). Canberia, ACT: Department of Education, Training and Youth Affairs.

Rohl, M., Milton, M., & Brady, D. (2000). Survey of schools. In W. Louden et al. (Eds.), *Mapping the territory. Primary students with learning difficulties: Literacy and numeracy.* (Vol 2, pp. 7–45). Canberra, ACT: Department of Education, Training and Youth Affairs.

Salomon, G., & Perkins, D. (1998). Individual and social aspects of learning. *Review of Research in Education, 23,* 1–24.

Stone, L. (1998). Language of failure. In B. Franklin (Ed.), *When children don't learn: Student failure and the culture of teaching* (pp. 1–27). New York, NY: Teachers College Press.

Tharp, R., & Gallimore, R. (1988). *Rousing minds to life: Teaching, learning and schooling in social context.* New York: Cambridge University Press.

Thomas, G., & Davis, P. (1996, September). *The identification of 'need' in reading.* Paper presented at the British Educational Research Association Annual Conference, Lancaster. http://www.leeds.ac.uk/educol/

van Kraayenoord, C., Elkins, J., Palmer, C., Rickards, F., & Colbert, P. (2000). Literacy, numeracy, and students with disabilities. Canberra, ACT: Department of Education, Training and Youth Affairs.

Wasik, B. A., & Slavin, R. E. (1993). Preventing early reading failure with one-to-one tutoring: A review of five programs. *Reading Research Quarterly, 28,* 179–201.

Wheldall, K., & Beaman, R. (2000). An evaluation of MULTILIT: Making up lost time in literacy. Canberra, ACT: Department of Education, Training and Youth Affairs.

Wolery, R. A. (1999). Preventing reading difficulties in young children: A mix of responsibility. *Journal of Behavioral Education, 9,* 55–64.

Chapter 12

Learning Disabilities in Canada

Bernice Y. L. Wong
Simon Fraser University

Nancy Hutchinson
Queen's University

In understanding and studying learning disabilities in Canada, two important facts come to the fore and must be registered. First, there is the unique autonomy of provinces in matters concerning health and education. Specifically, after the federal government transfers funds to the provinces, the latter have absolute power in the use of those funds for health and education. Second, there is no federal or provincial legislation that requires mandatory access to special education services for every elementary or secondary student diagnosed with learning disabilities (LD). In British Columbia for example, the ministry of education provides each school district two sets of funds: one for core programs in regular education, the other is supplementary funding targeting funding within special education. Together with students with behaviour disorders (BD) and those who are educable mentally retarded (EMR), students with severe learning disabilities (SLD) are included in the supplementary funding of high-incidence special needs students. However, the British Columbia government can impose a cap on the funding of these students, as it does at present, at 4.5%. Thus, regardless of the actual number of students with SLD in any school district, only a certain percentage gets served with special education services. How does such government capping translate into distribution of service delivery? To answer this question, we give the following example. In the suburban school district of Coquitlam in British Columbia, this 4.5% cap translates to 2% SLD, 2% BD and .5% EMR students, with an allocation of $3,200 per student. Although the cap applies to all school districts in special needs service delivery in British Columbia, variations may occur in what high-incidence special needs student categories are subsumed under it.

As mentioned earlier, there is no Canadian legislation to mandate access to special education services for a student with LD in the school district where she or he attends school. There is the Canadian Charter of Rights, but it is not specifically tied to a student's right of access to special education services. Should there be law suits in the future filed by students with LD against particular school districts, then this linkage may be more explicitly and legally defined.

The above two facts highlight the vulnerability of children and adolescents with LD, and the need for advocates regarding their educational welfare. None serve them better than their own parents who formed/join local municipal chapters and provincial LD associations (LDAs). Provincial LDAs across Canada fulfill a vital role in advocating for children, adolescents, and adults with LD. However, provincial LDAs lack consistency of leadership and galvanizing energy. Such inconsistency seriously erodes their ability to impact on educational funding policies in provincial governments. To redress this problem, maintain a high profile with federal and provincial governments on behalf of individuals with LD, we need a strong and central LDA. This explains the emergence of the national LDA of Canada (LDAC).

Essentially in Canada, because of its achievements in serving individuals with LD, mention of the term *learning disabilities* is closely interwined with LDAC. In turn, LDAC needs the support and collaboration of the provincial LDAs. Consequently, in writing about learning disabilities in Canada, we are really describing the respective roles and contributions of the provincial LDAs and LDAC, and the complementary contributions of researchers.

In this chapter we trace the original development of the first LDA and subsequent mushrooming of the other provincial LDAs. As well, we introduce the emergence of the national LDAC. We then delineate the contributions of the provincial LDAs, followed by a full depiction of those of the national LDAC. After that, we summarize the contributions of researchers to LD in Canada. We conclude with an epilogue.

THE HISTORY OF LEARNING DISABILITIES ASSOCIATIONS OF CANADA

The history of learning disabilities in Canada shows that since its inception in 1963, the Learning Disabilities Association of Canada (LDAC) and the provincial associations have been concerned with meeting needs, forming partnerships, and influencing policy. Both consumers and professionals have played roles in this history. In its early days in Canada, LDAC was called the Association for Children with Learning Disabilities of Canada. This organization was started in 1963 by three parents of children with learning disabilities (LD)—Doreen Kronick, Harry Wineberg, and Bob Shannon, who all resided in Toronto, Ontario. Circumstances fortuitously drew them together. The three families were driven by the need to obtain services for their own children with LD, and were cognizant that other parents of children with LD would welcome support and information about the phenomenon and about treatment. Kronick, Wineberg, and Shannon boldly took charge to fulfill their shared vision, namely, establishing an association for children with LD. Thus was born the Association for Children with Learning Disabilities including the Brain Injured Child in Toronto, Ontario, Canada in 1963. It was incorporated in 1964. Simultaneously, Kronick, Wineberg, and Shannon engaged media publicity to draw attention to the need for diagnostic facilities in Ontario and to reach other parents whose children needed services (personal communication with Doreen Kronick, January 2000).

The initial focus of the Ontario Association for Children with Learning Disabilities (ACLD) was meetings for parents to share information and to network. The organization also negotiated with local school boards and provincial governments to introduce services for children with LD. Kronick wrote information booklets and, together with other founding members of the Ontario organization, she answered mail from parents across Canada. Kronick worked tirelessly encouraging parents to start local chapters of ACLD in their respective home provinces.

In the United States, Sam Kirk began the learning disabilities movement in 1963 in a spontaneous way when he suggested the term to a group of parents (Wong, 1996). Hence, it is interesting that learning disabilities organizations began independently in the same year in Canada and the United States. From 1964 to 1967, the Ontario ACLD was an affiliate of the American ACLD. The affiliation status meant that for every membership in the Ontario ACLD, one dollar went to the American ACLD (personal communication with Doreen Kronick, January 2000). Doreen Kronick even served as a vice president of the American ACLD organization at one point. However, in 1967 the American ACLD moved to incorporate federally and found the Canadian affiliate a hindrance in their actions. According to the records, the two organizations broke off relatively amicably. The American influence also occurred on the educational front. William Cruickshank taught credit courses in Toronto during the 1960s, at the invitation of the Ontario ACLD. He trained many special education teachers in his methods of teaching brain-injured children and children with LD. Doreen Kronick was among his students.

By 1968, 33 affiliate Canadian groups were operating in provinces outside of Ontario, thanks to the zeal of Kronick and her associates. At this time, the Directorate of the Ontario ACLD invited Kronick and the other founding members to initiate the development of a national ACLD. The status of the national ACLD was shaky at first. Local and provincial associations questioned the need for and expense of a national organization when they perceived themselves to be doing an effective job of raising public awareness about LD and of increasing services and support to individuals with LD. However, successive Canadian ACLD presidents have provided strong leadership. Strong presidential leadership, committed advisory board members, competent executive directors (June Bourgeau, formerly, and Pauline Mantha, at present), and hard work have enabled the national organization to rise to prominence and undisputed leadership across the country.

In 1985, the national association changed its name to Learning Disabilities Association of Canada (LDAC) and the provincial associations were renamed accordingly. By this time, the associations had begun to focus on adolescents and adults with learning disabilities as much as on children. Through its newsletter and biennial national conference, LDAC provides leadership and current information from the national office. Its representatives sit on federal committees that concern the welfare of individuals with LD and it provides tacit guidance to provincial LDAs.

ACHIEVEMENTS AND SERVICES: FOCUS ON THE PROVINCES

To families and individuals with LD, it is very important that there is a Learning Disabilities Association (LDA) in all ten provinces and in two of the three territories in northern Canada (Yukon and Northwest Territories). Nunavut Territory, created in 1999, has yet to establish an LDA. There is also a network of chapters in more than 140 communities across the country. This network is critical because Canada is a large country with a relatively sparse population for its size. Over 30 million people are spread over almost 10 million square kilometers. About half the population lives in metropolitan areas and the rest access services in small communities and rural areas (*Canadian Global Almanac 2000*, 1999, p. 55). These provincial and local LDAs provide support and information at every stage of a family's experience with LD—from early identification concerns through securing services in schools to providing support during difficult transitions. The support given by LDAs explains, at least in part, why consumers of services, for example, individuals with LD and their families, form close ties to these associations.

The achievements of provincial LDAs across the country have been many. We spotlight five: (a) increasing public awareness of LD; (b) obtaining accommodations for students with LD in schools, colleges, and universities; (c) providing in-service and resources to teachers; (d) providing support and training to parents; and (e) advocacy.

Increasing Public Awareness of LD

Learning disabilities are now formally and publicly acknowledged as a legitimate disability and March has been designated Learning Disabilities Awareness month across Canada. Each provincial LDA develops public awareness events for its members and communities. For example, LDA Manitoba presents an annual public lecture funded through a trust held by the Jewish Foundation of Winnipeg [http.//www.mbnet. mb.ca/enable/ldamb/services.html].

Accommodation of Students with LD in High School, College, and University

Students with LD in high school, college, and university manifest substantial reading comprehension and writing problems (Alexander, Garner, Sperl, & Hare, 1998; Graham, Harris, MacArthur, & Schwartz, 1998; Wong, in press). Because written assignments and examinations figure prominently in the grading systems in high school, college, and university, it is important that students with LD receive accommodations commensurate with their writing needs. The provinces have developed guidelines for accommodations to written examinations for students with LD and other disabilities in high school. For illustration purposes, we describe the "Interim Policy Accommodations for Students with Special Diploma Examination Writing Needs" in Alberta (information provided by the Alberta LDA, January 2000). This policy provides guidelines indicating that to qualify, students need documentation of identification as a special needs student, including results of assessment by qualified professionals. It also details the procedures that are to be followed by school principals, teachers, and counselors to secure appropriate examination accommodations for students with LD or other special needs. The range of recommended accommodations to examination writing for students with all disabilities include "audiotape version, additional time, word processor, scribe, large print version, Braille version, sign language interpreter, taped response, and miscellaneous accommodations as approved by the Special Cases Committee" (information provided by the Alberta LDA, January 2000).

Accommodations in postsecondary education for students with LD and other disabilities are ubiquitous. In 1999 LDAC published a *Resource Directory* with listings of resources for each province under a number of headings including Post Secondary Education with separate listings for community colleges and universities, contact people, and services available. Most publicly funded postsecondary institutions in Canada are listed. This *Resource Directory* is also available on the website of LDAC [http://educ.queensu.ca/-lda]. Most colleges and universities provide Disability Services that usually include a coordinator whose multifaceted job involves negotiating accommodations for adults with LD such as taping lectures and extended time for writing examinations. Both Queen's University and Simon Fraser University have such coordinators.

In-service and Resources for Teachers

All provincial and local LDA associations are active in in-service. Many hold annual conferences or workshops that focus on state-of-the-art instructional strategies for students with LD. Invited speakers from Canada and the United States are featured and theme-based workshops that respond to local needs are presented. For example, in 1998, LDA Yukon sponsored 21 workshops designed to help service providers to be more effective when working with people with disabilities. About 300 participated in these workshops; participants in the workshops included consumers, teachers, staff of correctional institutions, Yukon College students, tutors, volunteers, staff of community organizations, parents, caregivers, and staff of government departments. In August 1998, LDA Yukon reported that the association had received funding from the Community Development Fund to conduct a workshop on LD in every Yukon community [http://www.nald.ca/PROVINCE/YUKON/lday/ecw/edconwrk.htm].

Provincial LDAs also provide resource materials, including assessment guides, curriculum guides, and teaching materials for students with LD. They have collections of books, videotapes, and information pamphlets on many topics for use by teachers and other professionals working with individuals with LD. Other initiatives involve teaming up with the provincial education ministry to produce resource materials. For example, in partnership with the provincial department, Learning Alberta, Alberta LDA has published numerous resource materials.

Parent Support and Training

Provincial LDAs provide support to parents of children, adolescents, and adults with LD in numerous ways. First, they provide current research information on LD, and on related disabilities such as attention deficits, and comorbidity of LD and attention deficit-hyperactive disorder (ADHD). Second, some LDAs offer special courses in parent advocacy, transition planning, and social skills training to parents (see SVI-LDA). Third, some LDAs have trained counselors on staff to help parents of LD individuals to cope (e.g., South Vancouver Island LDA [SVI-LDA] in British Columbia). Support may also be provided to individuals or to small groups by well-trained volunteers. Regular meetings ease parents' anxieties and frustrations arising from struggles to obtain better educational services for their children.

Advocacy

Both advocating on behalf of people with LD and enhancing self-advocacy are at the heart of the provincial and local mandates. In recent years, LDA Ontario has increased its focus on adults with LD. One feature of its website is a page titled "For Adults Only" on which it posts *Reflections* submitted by adults with LD. The invitation reads, "Got something you'd like to see reflected here? If you're an adult with LD and you've got experience to share, we'd like to hear about it." The submission guidelines suggest "Submissions should be generally positive and shed light on some aspect of your experience with learning disabilities: coping strategies you've developed, useful tools or accommodations, or just general effects of LD on your daily life" [http:/www.ldao.on.ca/articles/adrefl.html]. All the reflections, read by these authors, have included practical strategies for self-advocacy that individuals recommend to others. This innovative method of promoting self-advocacy complements the opportunities provided by counseling and workshops by LDAs.

In March of every year, LDAs blitz the respective provinces with an awareness campaign by designating that month as one for LD. Additionally, LDAs keep a close eye on provincial educational funding to ensure that budgets for special needs escape the finance minister's blade. They also work ceaselessly to have the ear of the government. They contribute to educational reviews conducted by provincial ministries of education. Recently, both LDA of Nova Scotia and British Columbia participated in province-wide reviews of special education ordered by their respective ministries of education.

Clearly, provincial LDAs maintain close contact with their ministries of education, and watch vigilantly the trends in government policy and funding. LDAs seize every opportunity to be involved in government committees charged with overseeing provincial programs and funding for educating students with LD.

ACHIEVEMENTS AND SERVICES: FOCUS ON
THE NATIONAL LDAC

The Learning Disabilities Association of Canada (LDAC) is a national, nonprofit, volunteer-led charitable organization with a membership of about 10,000. Its mission is "To advance the education, employment, social development, legal rights and general well-being of people with learning disabilities." LDAC collaborates with professionals and service consumers in many ways. The Professional Advisory Committee consists of 15 professionals in related disciplines who are appointed by the Board of Directors. These professionals, from pediatrics, psychology, neuropsychology, educational psychology, learning disabilities, speech and language pathology, and justice, afford LDAC ready access to differential expertise. A parallel group, the Consumer Advocacy Committee, helps the organization to respond to regional issues and makes recommendations about the programs and publications of LDAC. This group of adults with LD represents all provinces and territories. Thus it can be seen that LDAC works closely with professionals and with its members.

It is important that LDAC's mission receives strong support from provincial LDAs, because much decision-making is decentralized in the Canadian system of government. As mentioned at the start of our chapter, education is solely a provincial responsibility in Canada. Each provincial ministry of education sets its own policies and procedures for the education, placement, assessment, and accommodations that must be provided to children, adolescents, and adults with LD in educational settings. This means that provincial LDAs must lobby local government representatives, educational bureaucrats, and organizations like teachers' federations in each province, and maintain a presence to lobby at the federal level where the ministry of health funds projects that support individuals with disabilities. Thus provincial associations play a large role as partners with LDAC in the field of LD in Canada.

LDAC also collaborates with researchers who seek partnerships with it to facilitate their projects. Researchers also participate in national, provincial, and community conferences organized by LDAC. While LDAC is involved in many initiatives at any one time, we have chosen to describe seven projects currently under way that demonstrate the commitment and leadership that characterize LDAC. These seven initiatives are: (1) National Children's Alliance; (2) Think Tank; (3) the book, *Advocating for Your Child with Learning Disabilities* (1998); (4) the *Resource Directory*, published in 1999; (5) Learning Disabilities and the Disability Tax Credit; (6) Project Success; and (7) Destination Employment.

The National Children's Alliance

The National Children's Alliance is a coalition of about 30 national organizations formed as a result of an initiative from LDAC. In the past, LDAC has been invited to present several briefs to Federal Parliamentary Standing Committees (e.g., Finance, Justice, Environment, Health) on issues concerning the impact of federal policy changes and programs on Canadians with LD. Participating in the National Children's Alliance raises the profile and the capacity of LDAC to steer public policy at the federal level as it relates to early childhood development programs and services for children with LD. Through its vast network of provincial and territorial affiliates, the National Children's Alliance has the potential to mobilize communities across Canada and to influence public policy at all levels of government.

The Think Tank

The Think Tank refers to a position paper under development by LDAC. In 1997, LDAC received a mandate from its members to establish a Think Tank on Learning Disabilities. The primary purpose of the Think Tank was to investigate the most current research that shows a neurological basis for LD, and to publish its findings in a position paper. LDAC and its membership felt that a well-researched paper on the neurobiological basis of learning disabilities written by Canadian experts would serve as a building block to a comprehensive approach to the identification and treatment of young Canadians with learning disabilities. Once published, a summary of the scientific paper will be widely promoted and distributed to departments of education, Human Rights Commissions, departments of justice, and other officials.

The Book Advocating for Your Child with Learning Disabilities

The book *Advocating for Your Child with Learning Disabilities* was published by LDAC in 1998 with funding from Health Canada (Health Promotion and Programs Branch). Written in an encouraging and supportive tone by educators, parents, psychologists, and other practitioners, this book offers parents critical information and guidelines on how to become informed and advocate for their children with LD.

The Resource Directory

Funded by Health Canada (Childhood and Youth Division), the *Resource Directory*, published in 1999, provides comprehensive up-to-date listings of services throughout Canada for children, youth, and adults with LD. Each provincial and territorial LDA contributed to researching the information that appears in the final product. Listings are provided for each province about camps, schools, postsecondary education, remedial services, adult literacy programs, vocational/employment services, assessment services, scholarships, LDA chapter listings, Ministry of Education Special Education Department, and French services. An additional information section contains five reference articles with guidelines for obtaining services for children and adults with LD. There is also a referral section with information on national organizations and agencies in Canada and the United States that work with individuals with LD. The book format is available from LDAC while the full resource is available online at the LDAC website [http://educ. queensu.ca/-lda]. Linked to provincial and territorial LDAs as well as other organizations, the LDAC website serves as a hub for those seeking resources in their own communities and those seeking international contacts.

Disability Tax Credit

Learning Disabilities and the Disability Tax Credit is a project of which the LDAC is especially proud. It means that those who seek an assessment of their child or themselves by a psychologist will obtain some tax relief if the person assessed is identified as having a learning disability. Psychologists will now be able to sign the Disability Tax Credit Certificates to support individuals with LD who apply for tax credits on their income tax returns. Previously, only medical doctors and optometrists were authorized to complete this documentation. Eligibility criteria for the Disability Tax Credit are based on the effects rather than the presence of the impairment. One may qualify for the Disability Tax Credit if one has a severe and prolonged disability that markedly restricts the ability to perform a basic activity of daily living. In completing the relevant section of the form, the applicant needs to provide information on the effects that LD have on the applicant or the applicant's child. The applicant also must report how the learning disability markedly restricts the ability to perform basic activities of daily living in the areas of perceiving, thinking, and remembering. LDAC lobbied effectively to bring about this tax relief for parents of children identified with LD and for individuals with LD. It represents not only a financial gain for the LD community but also demonstrates the growing acceptance, by our lawmakers, of the effects of LD on the daily lives of Canadians (Gudbranson, 1999).

Project Success

Project Success is a national tutoring program designed to help children and youth and those with LD who are experiencing difficulties reading and writing within the school system, and who wish to and need to improve their literacy skills. Two Project Success sites were inaugurated in winter 1999, one in Kingston, Ontario, and one in Saskatoon, Saskatchewan. The site in Saskatoon focuses on enhancing literacy for youth over 12 years of age who want to improve their employment opportunities, while the site in Kingston focuses on elementary and secondary students. Project Success is continuing in these sites and additional sites are under development. Project Success has been and will continue to develop through partnerships between LDAC, local chapters of LDA, local agencies, and corporate partners. LDAC hopes to gradually develop self-sustaining sites for Project Success in communities across Canada. Through this project, LDAC has demonstrated that as well as supporting families and individuals, it can have a direct, measurable impact on children and youth with LD [http://educ.queensu.ca/~lda/ldindepth/projectsuccess.htm].

Destination Employment

Destination Employment is the first Canadian national employment program designed to meet the specific needs of adults with LD. Funded by the Opportunities Fund, Human Resources Development Canada, Destination Employment sites have been established by LDAC in collaboration with provincial LDAs in 13 sites across Canada. Participants are recruited through local social service agencies and screened by the LDA. Those whom screening shows are at risk of LD receive a formal assessment by a local psychologist. The 12-week program provides the adult with LD on social assistance with employment preparation skills, realistic career objectives, and a plan of action. The Destination Employment program includes small-group discussions, individual counseling, and on-the-job training. It offers participants experiences to enable them to seek, obtain, and maintain appropriate employment.

At many of the Destination Employment sites, an employability program called Learning and Employment Assessment Profile (LEAP) is being used. LDA Ontario developed LEAP to help individuals with LD to become more effective at finding and keeping employment [http://www.ldao.on.ca.leap.html].

It is apparent that in concert with provincial and local associations, LDAC is a vibrant and accomplished organization. It advocates and provides leadership for services, research, and policy to meet the needs of children, adolescents, and adults with LD, as well as supports educators, employers, and researchers. In the next section, we turn our attention to some of the Canadian researchers who have contributed to the growth of basic and applied knowledge in the field of LD.

RESEARCH

Canadian researchers who engage in research with students with LD deserve a special tribute for their concerted efforts and matter-of-fact persistence in composing and assembling grant applications, because of the fierce competition they must face to obtain research funds. There is no special federal funding agency that is earmarked for their grant applications. They must compete along with researchers in other domains of education and in psychology, and apply to the same funding agency for research money, the Social Sciences and Humanity Research Council.

Many Canadian researchers have contributed to research in the field of LD. We have chosen a few to highlight: from eastern Canada, Nancy Heath (McGill University, Montreal, Quebec), Nancy Hutchinson (Queen's University, Kingston, Ontario), Judith Wiener and Dale Willows (both at the University of Toronto), the team of Anne Jordan and Paula Stanovich, and Keith Stanovich (Ontario Institute for Studies in Education at the University of Toronto). From western Canada, we describe the research of C. K. Leong (University of Saskatchewan), Marilyn Samuels and Jac Andrews (both at the University of Calgary), Linda Siegel and Deborah Butler (both at the University of British Columbia), Dan Bachor (University of Victoria), and Bernice Wong (Simon Fraser University).

At McGill, Nancy Heath researches self-perceptions of competence of children with LD, and the role these self-perceptions play in their depression. Heath found that depressed children with LD had more accurate self-perceptions of academic and social competence than their nondepressed counterparts (Heath, 1995; Heath & Wiener, 1996). Heath and Ross (in press) also found that girls with LD reported higher mean levels of depressive symptoms and higher prevalence of depression than girls without LD. Heath is currently investigating the role of student perceptions of feedback in self-perception and mood in children with LD.

At Queen's, much of Nancy Hutchinson's research has comprised instructional studies in schools, for example, her studies in teaching algebra problem solving to individual adolescents with LD (1993), and to small groups and entire classes (1997). With John Freeman, she developed and evaluated Pathways, a five-volume instructional program in career education for adolescents with LD for use in resource rooms as well as in inclusive classrooms (Hutchinson & Freeman, 1994; Hutchinson, Freeman, & Quick, 1996). Her current research involves co-operative education including analyses of current policies that will culminate in an instructional program for cooperative education and work experience for adolescents with disabilities (Hutchinson, Munby, & Chin, 1997; Hutchinson et al., 1998).

Judith Wiener at the University of Toronto studies the social status of children with LD. Her findings in the early 1990s converged with prior research by Tanis Bryan and associates on the unpopularity and rejection of children with LD (Wiener, Harris, & Duval, 1993; Wiener, Harris, & Shirer, 1990). In a recent study, Kuhne and Wiener (in press) found that children with LD with rejection social status early in the school year maintained such status at the end of the school year. Those who began the school year with average social status tended to become rejected or neglected by the end of the school year. Thus, Wiener's research suggests that children with LD may need interventions to maintain as well as to enhance their social status among peers.

In the past five years, Dale Willows (University of Toronto) has focused on researching the use of a balanced approach to literacy learning and teacher in-service. She found that teachers maintained the approach over two years following in-service and that their students had higher scores on word recognition, reading comprehension, spelling, and composition (Collins-Williams & Willows, 1998; Haas & Willows, 1998; Jackett & Willows, 1998). Moreover, whether English was a child's first language did not affect the scores on reading achievement measures. Clearly, Willows' research suggests that school literacy can be changed through in-service teacher education.

Anne Jordan and Paula Stanovich have focused their joint program of research on teaching students with LD in inclusive classrooms. They have found that strong predictors of effective teaching behavior in classrooms include the school principal's attitudes and beliefs about heterogeneous classrooms and the beliefs of individual teachers about their effectiveness in teaching exceptional children (Stanovich & Jordan, 1998). Their recent work extends these findings to suggest that the self-concepts of exceptional and at-risk students are closely related to teacher beliefs and teacher–student interactions (Jordan & Stanovich, in press).

Keith Stanovich's extensive body of research has focused primarily on the cognitive processing of children with reading disabilities. He has contributed significantly to the converging evidence for phonological and surface subtypes of reading disability (Stanovich, Siegel, & Gottardo, 1997). He has argued for more inclusive definitions of reading disability that do not rely on the reading-IQ discrepancy (Stanovich, 1996). Recently he has called for a halt to what have been called the "Reading Wars," passionately asking all parties to find commonalty in their basic research base and to put aside political agendas and hasty generalizations from basic research findings to practice (Stanovich, 1998).

At the University of Saskatchewan, C. K. Leong has been actively researching reading and reading disabilities and has extended his research interests into the cross-language domain (English and Chinese).

He developed a theoretical framework that considers the analysis and synthesis of phonological and morphological components of words to be building blocks of reading acquisition and early literacy. In his cross-language domain research, Leong investigates the commonalties and differences in reading an alphabetic writing system such as English and the morphosyllabic writing system of Chinese. On the basis of his empirical findings, Leong suggests that in learning to read Chinese, phonological processing is important and necessary, but not sufficient (Leong, 1997; Leong & Joshi, 1997). He is extending this research to Japanese.

There are three major strands discernible in Linda Siegel's research at the University of British Columbia: (1) definitional issues in learning disabilities that pertain to diagnosis, (2) phonological processing deficits and reading disability, and (3) subtype research. She also has interests in the adult with LD, and the contribution of the LD status to adolescent suicide (McBride & Siegel, 1997). Siegel has long been involved in the debate on the role of intelligence (IQ) in the definition of LD. She has consistently argued that IQ has no place in defining LD because it measures an individual's learned skills, not potential to learn (Siegel, 1999), and because children of various IQ levels did not show differential performances on a wide range of reading, spelling, language, memory, and arithmetic tests (Siegel, 1989). Siegel's second area of research interest has led to a large-scale early intervention study involving classroom teachers as trainers.

Using the Strategic Content Learning (SCL) model that she has developed, Deborah Butler at the University of British Columbia conducts programmatic research on its efficacy in increasing strategic learning and problem solving in postsecondary students with LD and/or head injury (Butler, 1995). Central to the SCL model is the principle of guiding students to develop more effective strategies that build on their extant strategic repertoires. In this way, the new strategy results from negotiations between teacher and student, and is personalized. The efficacy of the SCL has been shown in numerous studies that involve one-on-one tutoring, peer tutoring, and small groups of students working on similar tasks such as reading comprehension or writing (Butler, Elaschuk, & Poole, in press). Butler is presently extending her research population to high school students with and without LD.

The research interests of Dan Bachor at the University of Victoria cover four areas: questioning research, mathematics (assessment, word problems, thinking skills/strategies), assessment involving low achievers and special needs students, and personnel preparation for learning assistance teachers.

Marilyn Samuels at the University of Calgary in 1974 started the Learning Centre, now known as the Calgary Learning Centre. The Centre was a joint effort of the Learning Disability Association of Calgary, the Alberta Children's Hospital, two local school boards, the University of Calgary, and several other groups. The Centre accomplished multitasks including providing services to individuals with LD, training service providers, researching "best practices," and conducting research. Of theoretical and practical import is Samuels' application of dynamic assessment and cognitive education approaches with children with LD and ADHD (Samuels & Conte, 1987). In recent years, she has extended her research and practice to include adults with LD, and focuses on developing assessment, learning strategies, adaptive (computer) technology, and transition issues (Samuels & Todd, 1996; Samuels & Scholten, 1993).

Jac Andrews, also at the University of Calgary, has done work in social skills interventions of children with LD. One example is his participation in a successful social skills intervention study with children with LD from a special school for LD. The training consisted of coaching, role-playing, and information sharing (Conte, Andrews, Loomer, & Hutton, 1995). Another is his study on increasing social cognitive processing of children with LD in which he used a social cognitive intervention model (Andrews & Conte, 1993). Of importance is that these interventions occurred in the classrooms. Andrews also conducts research on cognitive strategy-based instruction.

At Simon Fraser University, Bernice Wong is extending her intervention research interests in writing to a content area, English literature. She is designing guided journal response prompts to promote deeper cognitive and affective engagement with literature among students with and without LD in inclusive high school English classes. Such engagement may then be reflected in superior test performance of treatment groups. Wong is also exploring means of enabling more effective ways of inclusion of students with LD. Specifically, she is researching complementary instructional roles for both classroom and Learning Assistance teachers in promoting successful inclusion of adolescents with LD.

EPILOGUE

Essentially in Canada, the structural relations between federal and provinical governments differ vastly from those between federal and state governments in United States. Specifically, Canadian provinces have sole jurisdiction in the use of educational funds once they are transferred from the federal government. This autonomy explains the absence of national (federal) policies on the education of students with LD. Within provinces, educational funding trends for students with LD are tied to the economic vicissitudes of provinces and to the particular political leanings of provincial governments. Such government contexts explain the importance of provincial LDAs and the national LDAC in championing the cause of individuals with LD and serving as their advocates. While no discernable educational funding trends regarding students with LD exist in the provinces, there appears to be an emergent trend for parents of children with LD to turn to the courts for redress in the lack of educational services and the dire consequences on the literacy skills of their children (private communication with Pauline Mantha, executive director of LDAC, May 1, 2000). The outcome of such lawsuits clearly holds important implications for service delivery in schools for children and adolescents with LD.

Learning disabilities associations in Canada had a similar origin as those in the United States. Driven by needs for service and shared interests in the welfare of their children with LD, three individual parents spearheaded the development of the first LDA in Ontario. Through their dogged efforts and singlemindedness in purpose, the development of LDAs spread across the country, and culminated in the need for a national LDA. The emergence of the LDAC transformed the original provincial LDAs and local chapters in several ways. (1) LDAC brought into the national limelight the phenomenon of LD. (2) It increased significantly the clout with federal government and through representations on particular committees, directly influences federal policy, programs, and funding concerning those with LD (e.g., Destination Employment program for adults with LD, public policy on early childhood programs, the national tutoring program of Project Success). The most recent example of LDAC's successful lobbying is the announcement by the federal financial minister, Mr. Paul Martin, that the federal government would guarantee students with SLD would have access to the Canada Study Grant (CGS). The CGS covers 75% of the expenses of one diagnostic assessment for LD to a maximum of $1,200. (3) It provides leadership to provincial LDAs and harnesses them to achieve: unity of purpose regarding LDAC's mission statement (given earlier), consensus on the position on LD, collaboration and facilitation in obtaining federal research funds for specific projects, for example, Project Success. (4) Through liaison with various funding agencies in the federal government, LDAC accesses research funds to support Canadian researchers' research (e.g., Project Success). (5) LDAC disseminates research and service information through sophisticated means, for instance, websites. In sum, the national LDAC, together with its network of provincial LDAs and local chapters ensures that individuals with LD in Canada are well-served. We are proud to state that these associations, notably LDAC in its leadership role, have done and continue to do an efficacious job in meeting the multidimensional needs of children, adolescents, and adults with LD in Canada. At the same time, Canadian researchers steadily advance knowledge and intervention efficacy in learning disabilities. They are perhaps the unsung heroes and heroines in their persistent efforts at grant applications, for there is no specially carved out funding programs for special education research in Canadian federal research funding. Researchers in LD must compete with researchers from other domains in education, special education, and psychology for funding from the same federal research funding agency (Social Science and Humanities Research Council, SSHRC). Nevertheless, they soldier on and to good effect!

ACKNOWLEDGMENTS

We thank the following people and organizations for their generous cooperation and help: Doreen Kronick, Pauline Mantha (Executive Director), LDA Canada, Joan Schiff, LDA Ontario, Gail Desmoyers, LDA Quebec, Annie Baert, LDA Nova Scotia, Dr. Harvey Finnestad and Sylvia McKeeman, LDA Alberta, Maryse Neilson, LDA Victoria, South Vancouver Island, and Sandra Gephart, B.C., Vancouver chapter, Gary Morgan, District Principal, Personnel and Employee Relations, Coquitlam School District, and Dr. Peter Kosonen, Director of Instruction, Burnaby School District. Last but not least, we thank Devi Pabla, Eileen Mallory, and Surjeet Siddoo for keying in drafts of this chapter.

REFERENCES

Alexander, P. A., Garner, R., Sperl, C. T., & Hare, V. C. (1998). Fostering reading competence in students with learning disabilities. In B. Y. L. Wong (Ed.), *Learning about learning disabilities* (2nd ed.) (pp. 343–366). San Diego: Academic Press.

Andrews, J., & Conte. (1993). Enhancing the social cognitive processing of learning disabled children within the classroom: A social cognitive intervention model. *Exceptionality Education Canada, 3*(1 & 2), 157–176.

Butler, D. L. (1995). Promoting strategic learning by postsecondary students with learning disabilities. *Journal of Learning Disabilities, 28,* 170–190.

Butler, D. L., Elaschuk, C. L., & Poole, S. (In press). Promoting strategic writing by postsecondary students with learning disabilities: A report of three case studies. *Learning Disability Quarterly.*

Canadian Global Almanac 2000. (1999). Toronto, ON: Macmillan Canada.

Collins-Williams, M. A., & Willows, D. (1998, December). *A longitudinal study of the effects of in-service teacher education on primary students' literacy success.* Paper presented at the annual meeting of the National Reading Conference, Austin, TX.

Conte, R., Andrews, J., Loomer, M., & Hutton, G. (1995). A classroom-based social skills intervention for children with learning disabilities. *The Alberta Journal of Educational Research, XLI*(1), 84–102.

Cunninghan, A. E., & Stanovich, K. E. (1997). Early reading acquisition and its relation to reading experience and ability 10 years later. *Developmental Psychology, 33,* 934–945.

Gottardo, A., Chiappe, P., Siegel, L., & Stanovich, K. E. (1999). Patterns of word and nonword processing in skilled and less-skilled readers. *Reading and Writing: An Interdisciplinary Journal, 11,* 465–487.

Graham, S., Harris, K. R., MacArthur, C., & Schwartz, S. (1998). Writing Instruction. In B. Y. L. Wong (Ed.), *Learning about Learning Disabilities* (2nd ed.) (pp. 391–423). San Diego, CA: Academic Press.

Gudbranson, C. (1999, Winter). Learning disabilities and the disability tax credit. *The National: Newsletter of the Learning Disabilities Association of Canada, 36*(3), 10–12.

Haas, E., & Willows, D. (1998, December). *The development of spelling in a balanced literacy program: Assessing growth of phonological and orthographic knowledge.* Paper presented at the annual meeting of the National Reading Conference, Austin, TX.

Heath, N. L. (1995). Distortion and deficit: Self-perceived versus actual academic competence in depressed and non depressed children with and without learning disabilities. *Learning Disabilities Research and Practice, 10,* 2–10.

Heath, N. L., & Ross, S. (In press). The prevalence and expression of depressive symptomatology in children with and without learning disabilities. *Learning Disability Quarterly.*

Heath, N. L., & Wiener, J. (1996). Depression and nonacademic self-perceptions in children with and without learning disabilities. *Learning Disability Quarterly, 19,* 34–44.

Hutchinson, N. L. (1993). Effects of cognitive strategy instruction on algebra problem solving of adolescents with learning disabilities. *Learning Disability Quarterly, 16,* 34–63.

Hutchinson, N. L. (1997). Creating an inclusive classroom with young adolescents in an urban school. *Exceptionality Education Canada, 6*(3&4), 51–67.

Hutchinson, N. L., Chin, P., Munby, H., Mills De Espana, W., Young, J., Edwards, K. L. (1998). How inclusive is co-operative education? Getting the story and the numbers. *Exceptionality Education Canada, 8*(3).

Hutchinson, N. L., & Freeman, J. G. (1994). *Pathways.* Scarborough, ON: ITP Nelson Canada.

Hutchinson, N. L., Freeman, J. G., & Quick, V. E. (1996). Group counseling intervention for solving problems on the job. *Journal of Employment Counseling, 33*(1), 2–19.

Hutchinson, N. L., Munby, H. A., & Chin, P. (1997). *Guidance and career education: Secondary curriculum background research.* Commissioned by the Ontario Ministry of Education and Training.

Jackett, E., & Willows, D. (1998, December). *Development of story schemata in the written compositions of primary students: A longitudinal case study of The Balanced and Flexible Literacy Diet.* Paper presented at the annual meeting of the National Reading Conference, Austin, TX.

Jordan, A., Lindsay, L., & Stanovich, P. (1997). Classroom teachers' instructional interactions with students who are exceptional, at risk, and typically achieving. *Remedial and Special Education, 18,* 82–93.

Jordan, A., & Stanovich, P. (In press). Student academic self-concept and patterns of teacher student interaction in inclusive elementary classrooms. *International Journal of Development, Disability and Education.*

Kuhne, M., & Wiener, J. (In press). Stability of social status of children with and without learning disabilities. *Learning Disability Quarterly.*

Learning Disabilities Association of Canada. (1998). *Advocating for your child with learning disabilities.* Ottawa, ON: Author.

Learning Disabilities Association of Canada. (1999). *Resource directory.* Ottawa, ON: Author <http://educ.queensu.ca/~lda > (2000, March 5).

Learning Disabilities Association of Canada. (n.d.). *Project Success.* <http://educ.queensu.ca/lda/ldindepth/projectsuccess.htm> (2000, March 5).

Learning Disabilities Association of Manitoba. (n.d.). *Annual lectureship.* <http://www.mbnet. mb.ca/enable/ldamb/services.html> (2000, March 5).

Learning Disabilities Association of Ontario. (n.d.). *Reflections.* <http:/www.ldao.on.ca/ articles/adrefl.html> (2000, March 5).

Learning Disabilities Association of Ontario. (n.d.). *Learning and employment assessment profile.* <http://www.ldao.on.ca.leap,html> (2000, March 5).

Learning Disabilities Association of Yukon. (n.d.). *Education/Conferences/Workshops.* <http://www.nald.ca/PROVINCE/YUKON/lday/ecw/edconwrk.htm> (2000, March 5).

Leong, C. K. (1997). Paradigmatic analysis of Chinese word reading: Research findings and classroom practices. In C. K. Leong & R. M. Joshi (Eds.), *Cross-language studies of learning to read and spell: Phonologic and orthographic processing* (pp. 379–417). Dordrecht: Kluwer Academic Publishers.

Leong, C. K., & Joshi, R. M. (1997). The role of phonological and orthographic processing in learning to read and spell. In C. K. Leong & R. M. Joshi (Eds.), *Cross-language studies of learning to read and spell: Phonologic and orthographic processing* (pp. 1–29). Dordrecht: Kluwer Academic Publishers.

McBride, H., & Siegel, L. S. (1997). Learning disabilities and adolescent suicide. *Journal of Learning Disabilities, 30*(6), 652–659.

Samuels, M., & Conte, R. (1987). Instrumental enrichment with learning disabled adolescents: Is it effective? *Journal of Practical Approaches to Developmental Handicap, 11*(2), 4–6.

Samuels, M., & Scholten, T. (1993). A Model for the assessment of adults encountering learning difficulties. *International Journal of Cognitive Education Learning 3*(3), 135–151.

Samuels, M., & Todd, A. K. (1996). *Assessment of Adults in the Workplace—CD-ROM Calgary.* University of Calgary Communications Media.

Siegel, L. S. (1989). J. Q. is irrelevant to the definition of learning disabilities. *Journal of Learning Disabilities, 22*(8), 469–479.

Siegel, L. S. (1999). Issues in the definition and diagnosis of learning disabilities: A perspective on Guckenberger v. Boston University. *Journal of Learning Disabilities, 32*(4), 304–319.

Stanovich, K. E. (1996). Toward a more inclusive definition of dyslexia. *Dyslexia, 2,* 154–166.

Stanovich, K. E. (1998). Twenty-five years of research on the reading process: The grand synthesis and what it means for our field. *National Reading Conference Yearbook, 47,* 44–58.

Stanovich, K. E., Siegel, L., & Gottardo, A. (1997). Converging evidence for phonological and surface subtypes of reading disability. *Journal of Educational Psychology, 89,* 114–127.

Stanovich, P., & Jordan, A. (1998). Canadian teachers' and principals' beliefs about inclusive education as predictors of effective teaching in heterogeneous classrooms. *The Elementary School Journal, 98,* 221–223 8.

Wiener, J., Harris, P. J., & Duval, L. (1993). Placement, identification and subtype correlates of peer status and social behaviour of children with learning disabilities. *Exceptionality Education Canada, 3*(1&2), 129–153.

Wiener, J., Harris, P. J., & Shirer, C. (1990). Achievement and social-behavioral correlates of peer status in LD children. *Learning Disability Quarterly, 13,* 114–127.

Wong, B. Y. L. (1996). *The ABC's of Learning Disabilities.* San Diego: Academic Press.

Wong, B. Y. L. (In press). Writing strategies instruction for expository essays for adolescents with and without learning disabilities. *Journal of Language Disorders.*

Chapter 13

Learning Disabilities in Germany: A Retrospective Analysis, Current Status, and Future Trends

Günther Opp
Martin-Luther-Universitat, Halle-Wittenberg

RETROSPECTIVE ANALYSIS

The Expansion of Education

The age of Enlightenment of the late eighteenth century fostered the notion that the perfection of man was dependent on education. Educational inclusion at that time was conceived as the provision of public education services and as participation in public education efforts. The purpose of education was to strive for human perfection, the formation of man (*Bildung*) and the development of learning competencies. Educators focused on the young generation and, as such, the direction of a future-enlightened society. For example, early efforts in educating deaf children were still based on theology rather than science. The prevailing notion was that, through the acquisition of verbal language, deaf children should be able to communicate with God and, therefore, rescue their souls (Lane, 1988). The success with deaf children in the first residential educational institution for deaf children in Paris, along with schools for blind, crippled, and mentally retarded children and Itard's famous education experiments with the wild boy of Aveyron (Lane, 1988), produced evidence for the educability of children with disabilities. Theologians, physicians, and later on specialized educators (*Heilpädagogen*) searched for the educational *remedium* (Comenius) to help children with disturbed educability (*gestörte Bildsamkeit*, Herbart).

217

Differentiated educational methods for disabled children and specified educational institutions were established and demonstrated success.

The inclusion of children with disabilities in public education services was the banner of the early special education efforts. Yet, within the educational system, the prevailing practice was separate educational settings. Social selection based on educational achievement distinguished from social selection through birth was the great promise of the bourgeois society. Thus, achievement-oriented selection became the fundamental mode of operation of the newly founded school systems. Unity and difference was an educational problem in the form of an increased heterogeneity of students. At the same time, there was little time for critical reflection concerning the attainability of educational goals for all students.

In the nineteenth century, there were tremendous organizational differentiation and expansion of the educational system. Between 1816 and 1871, school attendance in Germany rose from 60% to 92% (Drewek, 1997, p. 195). But the inclusionary success of the compulsory education movement was counterbalanced by insufficient staffing and resources for the schools in the second half of the nineteenth century. Classrooms were crowded and the heterogeneity of the larger student population was dramatically increased.

Social selection was reintroduced into German schools by differentiating three types of schools with specified task descriptions. Students remaining in the basic educational track went on after four years of a unitary elementary school to attend the *Volksschule* (grades 1–9). The *Realschule* represented a kind of middle track of education for grades 7–10. The upper educational track for students grades 5–13 was the *Gymnasium*. This is still the basic organizational pattern of the German school system. Historically, the school system reflected a three-class model of society (working class, middle class, upper class), and the schools had to prepare their student population for their future functions within these social classes. The most dramatic developmental feature of the educational system in the last two centuries was growth and differentiation. Whereas in Prussia in the late eighteenth century only 16,000 male students attended the Gymnasium, close to 2.2 million, that is more than a third of all students in German secondary schools, attended the Gymnasium in 1995 (Statistische Veröffentlichungen der Kultusministerkonferenz, 1997, II.2). In the context of equal educational opportunities espoused in the 1960s and 1970s, a side effect of the growth of student population in the German Gymnasium was increased awareness of the critical selective functions of the school system. Although upward selective decisions are usually consensual, downward selection is a sensitive matter in education.

The *Hilfsschule* or Remedial School

The three tracks of German schools relieved the school systems of making teaching accommodations for more gifted students. However, there remained the challenge to instruct students of lesser talents and students failing in school who were not disabled according to the then existing traditional categories of disabilities. Again, the school systems reacted with a differentiated organizational structure. Starting in 1820, more and more resource rooms or remedial classrooms for children with special learning needs (*Nachhilfeklassen*) were established. In 1867 Heinrich Ernst Stötzner founded the first *school for children with deficits in learning* (*Schule für schwachbefähigte Kinder,* Stötzner, 1864), later called *Hilfsschule* (remedial school). One or more *Hilfsschulen* were soon established in all major German cities by 1920 (Ellger-Rüttgardt, 1997).

The history of the Hilfsschule in Germany is a success story. Apart from educational intentions for remediation, the Hilfsschulen fulfilled at least three functions: (1) They relieved the regular education system from students with problems in learning and behavior. (2) By identifying a high-prevalence category of disabilities, an independent school form for educationally disadvantaged children was established. (3) The existence of a specialized school system for students with disabilities supported special educators in pursuing professional autonomy. The promise was to guarantee successful learning processes and positive vocational integration for a problematic student population through the use of specified teaching methods, the use of a modified curriculum, and the creation of homogeneous groups of learners in special schools. In view of the chance to establish an independent school form and the desire to establish professional autonomy, education was bound to optimistic self-descriptions and sometimes self-deluding promises concerning its effects.

Waving the banner of the Hilfsschule, teachers of special schools fought for professional autonomy. In 1898 a small number of educators founded the Association of Remedial Schools in Germany (*Verband der Hilfsschulen in Deutschland*) now the *Verband Deutscher Sonderschulen,* *VDS* (Association of German Special Schools) and the largest special education organization in Germany (Möckel, 1998). The "noble goal" to expand the number of Hilfsschulen in Germany was the overriding motivation expressed in the foundation call for the establishment of such an association (Aufruf, 1898). The authors called for "restless research" in order to understand the nature of the disability and find ways to stimulate and form the minds of these children. The students of the Hilfsschule were described as poor in mind, poor in their living conditions, poor in their body due to organic deficits and physically weak.

It is interesting to see that *Lernbehinderung* (learning disabilities) from the beginning was understood as a complex interplay among psychological, physical, and organic deficits strongly influenced by the socioeconomically deprived environments these children grew up in. The early special educators were aware of the devastating effects of poverty on children. They also knew about the stigmatizing effects of labels and of the separate schooling for the children. In order to circumvent the stigmatizing effects of the commonly used notion of feeble mindedness (*Schwachsinn*), Stötzner (1864) already had focused on educational remediation, calling his school for children with deficits in learning remedial school (*Nachhilfeschule*). This later became the *Hilfsschule*. From the beginning of specialized schooling, special educators expressed discomfort with the separation of disabled students from their peers (Weise, 1820). Alternative and integrative school systems, for instance in Mannheim (Sickinger, 1920) and Berlin (Fuchs, 1927), were put into practice after the First World War and ended with Nazi terror.

Following the foundation of a professional organization, another cornerstone of progress was the opening of a one-year special education training course at the University of Munich in 1922 (*Heilpädagogischer Lehrerausbildungsgang*; Speck, 1997). For the first time, this credited special education academically. The intended setting up of a professorial chair for Heilpädagogik at this university only failed because of a disagreement between the philosophical and medical faculties about where it should be located. In 1924 the internationalization of the Heilpädagogik was advanced with the founding of the *Internationale Gesellschaft für Heilpädagogik* and the organization of a first *Internationalem Heilpädagogischen Congress* in Munich.

The Years of World War II

The German Heilpädagogik as a profession at that time was internationally a forerunner of progress until the Nazis came to power. During the Nazi regime in Germany, individuals with disabilities were branded as social ballast for the society. It is estimated that about 200,000 individuals with disabilities were victims of euthanasia and another 300,000 to 400,000 were sterilized in order *to prevent them from having genetically deformed offspring* (Ellger-Rüttgardt, 1997, 254 ff.)

Invoking the argument of economic usefulness of their student population, the Hilfsschule managed to survive the Nazi regime and, possibly, working under the scarcest of conditions, saved the lives of many. It is fair to say, however, that many educators and teachers in special institutions adopted the Nazi ideology. A full account of the role of special educators and special education institutions during that time is still not available. However, many leading scientists like Bruno Bettelheim, Marianne Frostig, Kurt Goldstein, Fritz Redl, Alfred Strauss, and Heinz Werner had fled their country. Together with their prominent students, they developed special education as a discipline and as a practical field in the United States. This left a tremendous scientific gap in Germany. Due to the interruption of progressive developments during the period of the Nazi terror, with their focus on race, path-breaking findings in the psychoneurologic field did not make their way into Germany during that time.

Postwar Development

After the war, not only the shortage of qualified special education teachers but also a lack of scientific support for the educational practice with special needs students were hurdles in building up a new special education system. German special education was at first restored in its traditional context. In 1960 an Expert Opinion of the Secretaries of Education of All Federal States (*Gutachten der Kultusministerkonferenz, KMK*) suggested the build up of a special education system including twelve different kinds of special schools organized along categories of disabilities, including the Hilfsschule as the type of special school with the highest number of students. Parallel with the German *Wirtschaftswunder,* an immense growth in the number of special schools and student population occurred in the 1960s and 1970s when Germany became an affluent nation again (*Sonderschulwunder,* Speck, 1991, p. 603). The number of students attending special schools in Germany grew between 1950 and 1976 from 105,000 to 400,000 (Herrlitz, Hopf, & Titze, 1986; Klemm et al., 1990). In the midst of institutional expansion, special education, after a 40-year developmental break, was established as a scientific discipline in German universities in the 1970s. There was a professionally enforced academization of special education teacher training resulting in a higher status of the profession. As a consequence of the dominance of teacher training in the universities, special education as a discipline developed an identity as supporting special schools. This was one of the basic reasons why the field of special education experienced a heated integration debate in the 1980s.

Teacher Training

The training of special education teachers currently comprises five years in a university (phase I) and culminates with a two-year seminar experience in schools (phase II). Under the supervision of a master teacher, the young teachers learn to plan lessons and teach in a classroom. In the second year of seminar, the young teachers take charge of a class, which they teach for a limited number of hours. Teacher training in Germany is categorically structured. In most universities, two categories of disabilities are studied. Special education teachers are decently paid and enjoy a number of social benefits, including tenure. Very few teachers leave the teaching profession. However, due to fiscal problems, there is less payment and fewer social benefits for teachers in East Germany.

Sonderschule für Lernbehinderte (Learning Disabilities)

Following the suggestion of The German Advisory Council For Education (*Deutscher Bildungsrat 1973* Kanter, 1974) the label *Lernbehinderung* (learning disabilities) was introduced and the *Hilfsschule* was renamed, "*Lernbehindertenschulerr*", although a straight translation of *learning disabilities* it is not equivalent with the Anglo-American notion. It is defined by intellectual deficits ranging in IQ between 55/60–70/75. Although the term Hilfsschüler was strictly a school organizational term, the notion of learning disabilities implied an educational program aimed at remediation. The change in terminology also reflected the growing scientific finding of the covariance of Lernbehinderung with socially deprived living arrangements (Begemann, 1970; Klein, 1996; Weiss, 1996) and the assumption that Lernbehinderungen and poverty are causally related. In trying to structure a rather twisted definitional discussion, it could be said that Lernbehinderung is evidenced by school failure due to intellectual deficits, which are possibly but not necessarily reflected in an organic finding. Along with cognitive deficits, perceptual, psycho-motoric and socioemotional problems are observed in this student population. But contrary to an Anglo-American understanding, the focus of attention is not learner characteristics in the sense of basic psychic functions but school failure. Lernbehinderung in the German sense, therefore is a school-related term.

According to Kanter (1974, p. 213) Lernbehinderung could hardly be diagnosed in early childhood, because one of the essential criteria of diagnosis is school failure. In fact, the term *Lernbehinderung* is only used in the context of schools. Within the sector of vocational education and the legal provisions of rehabilitation laws in Germany, the notion of Lernbehinderung is not applied. Looking at the student population attending the *Sonderschule für Lernbehinderte*, it was obvious that the diagnostic criteria vary dramatically, that there are large regional variations in the number of students classified, and notwithstanding the German definition of Lernbehinderung, a significant number of students with average and above average IQ are being taught in these schools. More than 80% of the classified student population came from families with low socioeconomic backgrounds (Begemann, 1970; Bleidick, 1973; Klein, 1973), and lately a significant overrepresentation of children from minority families in Lernbehindertenschulen has been documented (Kornmann & Klingele, 1996, Kornmann, Klingele, & Iriogbe-Ganninger, 1997). Bleidick in this context sarcastically stated that lernbehindert is a student who attends a Sonderschule für Lernbehinderte (Bleidick, 1980, p. 130).

The German Advisory Council For Education (1973; "Deutscher Bildungsrat") estimated a 2.5% prevalence of learning disabled children. The IQ cutoff points were raised from 55 to 85 and connected with the assumption that about 10% of all students at least temporarily demonstrate problems in learning. In practice, this implies that the high number of children at risk for school failure, of which 3–4% according to the Council are at risk to develop a disability, are neither classified as disabled nor should they attend special schools. In newer publications, the overall school population being at risk for a variety of problems in learning is estimated at around 15%, including 2.5% children with manifest and differentially caused impairments of learning disabilities (Opp, 1996; Schröder, 1999, 188 ff.). This argument, of course, is politically relevant. The intent is not to classify any higher number of students disabled. It also does not argue for the expansion of special schools. Rather, in this perspective, regular education is challenged to offer quality education services to support the learning processes of this large group of students at risk. This is viewed as part of an integrative responsibility of regular schools and should be supported through special education services in regular schools.

Due to a lack of an international perspective, the German development of terminology about Lernbehinderungen paralleled but was little influenced by Anglo-American discussions on learning disabilities. The scientific description of hyperactivity, minimal brain dysfunction, deficits in perceptual processing, and other related symptoms, in children reached German shores in the late 1960s and was picked up first by pediatricians, child psychologists and psychiatrists. Compared with the American situation, these newly identified conditions in Germany met an existing special school system with deep historical rules. The description of neurologically based symptom pictures of deficits in perception processes was not strong enough to establish a new category of handicaps because there was considerable overlap between newer descriptions of specific learning disabilities and the population of students attending the Sonderschule für Lernbehinderte.

CURRENT STATUS

Childhood and Youth in Modern Societies

As a consequence of the increasing social modernization processes in Germany a growing number of children are at-risk. Socioeconomic trends for families are currently not favorable. The economic conditions for children and youth, the quality of living arrangements, and the compatibility of labor and family have decreased (Internationales Jahr der Familie, 1994). In Germany, poverty was fought successfully by active social policies for a long period of time. Now, poverty is high on the agenda again. Children and youth are particularly affected. Twelve percent of the children and youth in West Germany and 22% in East Germany grow up in poverty (Zehnter Kinder,- & Jugendbericht, 1998, p. 88 ff.). Poverty reduces the quality of the social environment and the health status of children. In addition, it is associated with significant restrictions of educational chances (Lauterbach, Lange, & Wüest-Rudin, 1999). All too often, child and youth poverty go hand in hand with violent neighborhoods, abuse, neglect, uncontrolled exposure to modern media, and poor nutritional habits.

We look at a contradictory picture. A large number of children would profit from increasingly child-oriented families and from extensive educational opportunities in the schools. However, there is a growing number of socially deprived children and youth. In elementary schools a more and more dramatic "*developmental scissors' effect*" between educationally advantaged and disadvantaged children is noticed (Fölling-Albers, 1995, p. 48). Parallel with the expansion of educational systems and the time individuals spend in educational settings over the lifespan, we observe the contrary rise in students dropping out of educational institutions (*Bildungskeller*; Hiller, 1994; Klemm, 1996).

Inclusion (*Integrationspädagogik*)

The integration of students with disabilities in German schools is not a common practice on the federal level. There are, however, many schools all over the country with more than 20 years of integrative experiences. Many of these schools are projects with some kind of a scientific support. Forerunners of integrative practices in German schools typically started in big cities like Berlin (Preuss-Lausitz, 1981), Bremen (Feuser & Meyer, 1987), Frankfurt (Deppe-Wolfinger, Prengel, & Reiser, 1990), Hamburg (Wocken & Antor, 1987), Munich (Hellbrügge, 1977; Speck et al., 1978). Overall, the project schools have demonstrated that integrative education with different disabled student populations is possible.

From the beginning, the professional interest in integration was aimed at the abolishment of the special schools for students with learning disabilities and/or behavior disorders. It was the assumed similarities of that student population with the students in regular schools that suggested that their integration could be effective. Similar to other countries, integrative practices in most cases were initiated and often heavily supported by engaged parents of children with disabilities.

Research findings from studies of integration are colored by the ecological framing of the particular schools and integration projects and with sampling difficulties, for example, the impossibility of forming identical student groups for comparison. However, findings from some studies yield generalizations. Learning effects of students with Lernbehinderungen in integrative settings are superior to learning effects on special schools. Students in integrative settings seem to profit from the increased learning expectations in regular classes and the higher competitive standards among their nondisabled peers. At the same time, the gains of integrative practices seem to be contrasted by unfavorable socioemotional effects and lower self-esteem, fewer social contacts, and more rejection of the disabled students by peers (Bless, 1995; Haeberlin et al., 1990; Tenth et al., 1991; Willand, 1999). The finding of higher learning gains of learning disabled students in integrative settings, however, was not confirmed, when the average achievement levels of integrative classes of schools in socially disadvantaged living areas were compared with other regular elementary classes (Hinz et al., 1998, p. 131).

Wocken (1987, p. 302), one of the prominent representatives of the *Integrationspädagogik* in Germany, stated that there is a "*deadlock situation*" concerning the effects of the competing school models. Hinz et al. (1998), summarizing the experiences of an integrative school project in Hamburg lately, confirmed Wocken's position. These authors speak of the central importance of the situational "dynamic of pedagogical creation" in order to shape the educational quality of integrative classes (p. 112). Despite the apparent similarity of students with learning disabilities to their nondisabled peers, students with learning disabilities are characterized by a certain resistance concerning instructional intentions. The acceptance of heterogeneity by teachers and the amount of participation (*Teilhabe*) of the learning disabled students in integrative settings, the *community of learners,* is critical for integrative successes. It is an ideal notion of the Integrationspädagogik, however, to base achievement norms on individual learning progress alone and to detach it from group comparisons. Yet an integrative perspective on school functions, by itself, does not leave out the norms of reference groups nor does it create independence from society-based norms (Reiser, 1997, p. 270).

On the positive side is a tendency of schools to open up and to refor-mulate school concepts. However, because integrative practices are not used universally in Germany, the schools that participate could be posi-tively biased toward school reform in the first place. Concerning teacher attitudes toward integrative practices, Hinz (1999, p. 295) reported a *"dramatic transformation"* of teacher attitudes working in the Hamburg project of integrative elementary school classes. The project schools were situated in socially deprived neighborhoods. Although teachers were ex-tremely positive about their experiences in the integrative classes at the end of first grade, teacher judgments after fourth grade were between "positive" and "mixed." I would offer some additional possible explana-tions for a change in teacher attitudes concerning integrative practices in higher grades: (1) In fourth grade a realistic turn in terms of the assessment of student achievement takes place. After four years of ele-mentary school, successful students step over into the Gymnasium. (2) The continuation of integrative classes into secondary schools is still in an initial state in German schools. (3) The heterogeneity of student groups increases dramatically over the four years of schooling. Teachers feel that, with the increasing heterogeneity of learners, "the risk to fail" is augmented (Hinz, Katzenbach, Rauer, Schuck, Wocken & Wuttke, 1998, p. 131). Although the call for an education of plurality (*Pädagogik der Vielfalt,* Prengel, 1993) is indispensable in modern societies, the ques-tion is unsolved regarding how much heterogeneity individual teachers, and even educational teams, are able to handle and how many additional resources they would need in a specific situation.

Teachers basically agree with the theoretical principles of inclusive schools but demonstrate a remarkable hesitance when they are asked for their readiness to teach children with disabilities in their own classrooms (Dumke, Krieger, & Schäfer, 1989; Dumke & Krieger, 1990; Reiser et al., 1995). Studying the attitudes of principals and elementary school teach-ers in the state of Hessen, Reiser et al. (1995) found that only one-third of the principals favored the concept of an integrative elementary school. In many cases these principals did not find support among their staff. The majority of teachers were, under certain conditions, willing to accept children with disabilities in their classroom. However, a majority of teach-ers agreed with the prevailing achievement orientation and selective task description of German elementary schools. It was a puzzling finding of the study that the same teachers supported school reform approaches that are favored in school concepts of the Integrationspädagogik. The professional conflict that teachers expressed is the reflective blind spot of the educational profession being twisted between the selective oper-ation of the school system on one side and the inclusionary educational goals of professionals and their educational propaganda on the other side. Special educators cannot abolish selection in schools by advocating integration (Reiser, 1997, p. 268). And it should be added that the abolishment of selection in the public school systems in an achievement-oriented and competitive modern society is a distant pedagogical vision. In this frame of reflection, elementary teachers emphasized the need for additional resources in order to complement their own educational mission but not for the purpose of the inclusion of students with disabilities (Reiser, Loeken, & Dlugosch, 1995, p. 103). In essence, elementary school teachers did not view school failure as a problem of the school but as an individual problem of the student. The individualization of school failure marked an operational borderline by which special education was given a predominant position in working with failing students. For Reiser, Loeken, & Dlugosch (1995) this reflects an underdeveloped school structure and immature profession (p. 110).

Integrationspädagogik leaves the pedagogical problem of disability categories unsolved. The call for integrative schooling to some extent evolved from the critique of the stigmatizing effects of labels. Eloquent advocates of inclusive schools, in a wholesale disregard of the value of special education, denied the existence of mental retardation (Feuser, 1996). Wocken (1996, p. 36) provocatively stated that "*since learning, speech and behavior problems are the most normal thing in the world,*" we have to accept differences of children without using stigmatizing labels. Eberwein (1997) put in question whether Lernbehinderungen is a *fact* or a constructed disability category. Indeed, Lernbehinderung in the sense of disability category is a theoretical construct. But the persistent learning and social problems of the children for whom we use the term *lernbehindert* are fact (Schröder, 1999, p. 191). Fact, too, is their need for additional remedial support. There continues to be an unsolved dilemma between labels and resources (*Ettiketierungs–Ressourcen–Dilemma;* Füssel & Kretschmann, 1993, p. 43 ff.) in inclusive schools. Politically and administratively, labels provide and protect funds. Even integrative school projects usually used the problematic per-child model to channel additional funds and resources. Instead of traditional disability categories, inventive terms were created to fulfill these administrative needs.

Notwithstanding the argument of possible devastating effects of labels, the hidden decategorization trend in inclusive schooling (Benkmann, 1994) is combined with three antagonistically constituted consequential problems.

- It results in an administrative problem of how to ensure that decategorized funds reach the target group of students with disabilities. Should the schools have the autonomy to decide about increased resources?

- Block funding models introduce a problem of educational rights. Does the individual student with a disability have a right for individualized special education services from the school system or is that right already determined by whatever the schools offer? In the latter case, the special educational needs of the child could easily be a victim of fiscal savings because needs could be defined by the availability of special education services. The question is whether individual special education rights survive without labels.

- On the one hand, decategorization trends reflect the real complexities of individual disabilities and their particular ecological context. On the other hand, labels are a means to reduce complexity for organizational purposes and for professional communication (terminology). The current trends towards decategorization dissolve the terminologic basis of special education.

The promise of decategorization and block funding models is that they allow schools to develop better inclusive qualities for all children and provide hope that better school quality will result from including students with disabilities. The readiness of schools for inclusive practices could be related to the visibility of disabilities. Discriminating effects of inclusion might be stronger for discrete forms of disabilities. Stoellger (1995, p. 572) noticed for Berlin that children with learning disabilities are significantly underrepresented in integrative classes. Concerning the learning disabled student population being integrated in regular schools, Stoellger questioned whether they fit the diagnostic criteria. As long as integration is not a total system approach, the schools favor selective inclusionary practices.

Statistical Data

Due to the different kind and tracks of schools, the different periods of school attendance and the nonuniform data flow in different Federal States in Germany, statistical data on school systems are difficult to interpret. In 1996–97, 398,566 students attended special schools. Of the 220,753 students classified lernbehindert, 146,676 were taught in West German and 74,077 in East German Schools. This is 2.23% of the total student population in regular schools. There are not statistical data on the number of students with Lernbehinderungen in some kind of an integrative setting. Special schools in Germany are significantly higher financed than regular schools. In 1995, the per-pupil expenditure in elementary schools was 6000 DM, in *Gymnasium* 10,100 DM, and 19,900 DM in special schools (Lünnemann, 1998, p. 148 f.). Compared with the cross-national product, the new eastern Federal States spend a larger share for education than the Federal States in the west (Hetmeier, 1998, p. 308). But due to the depressed economy in these states, this is just about equal educational spending on a federal level.

Schröder (1993) demonstrated differences in special education practices in different Federal States. Schleswig-Holstein schools classified 3.1% of the students as lernbehindert compared to 2.5% in Berlin where integrative practices play a more important role. Trends in the new Federal States in East Germany are important. With restructuring the school systems in East Germany, the criteria of classifications were changed and new categories of disabilities were introduced. With the exception of Brandenburg, all eastern states started to build up a special school system patterned after the western Federal States. Although representing only a fifth of the total German population, more than half of all students with Lernbehinderungen are currently attending special schools in East Germany (Langfeldt & Kurth, 1994). There are a number of reasons to explain the adoption of the West German special education system. (1) There were strong desires for rapid changes, and it was easiest to adopt an existing model. (2) The educational challenges in East German school systems, resulting from the social/political antagonism after the German Reunification, were difficult to master for teachers who had lived all their professional lives in the GDR. (3) Through an increase in the number of students, the teachers in East Germany hoped to secure their threatened jobs.

A number of innovative educational practices have become part of East German schools. A tremendous pedagogic development has taken place. However, there are four major challenges that confront the system of education and special schools in East Germany. First, the expansion of the system of special schools is not backed by qualified personnel; and there is still, more than 10 years after the German Reunification, an immense need for teacher training and in-service training. Second, integrative practices and models of interdisciplinary cooperation in schools are still limited in number. Third, the student numbers, following a 50% birthrate decline for some years after the German Reunification, are a multifaceted problem that has already reached the school systems and will be felt most dramatically in the next few years. Fourth, because there is no turnover of teachers in Germany, there is a fiscal question of how many newly trained teachers espousing new pedagogical ideas will be hired despite declining student numbers.

Vocational Integration

In 1999, an estimated 22,000 students left or graduated from special schools (Statistische Veröffentlichungen der Kultusministerkonferenz,

1997, 1.2). Many of these young adults moved to the differentiated and nationwide system of promotional vocational courses. Educational rights for individuals with disabilities over the lifespan are financed through assistance of integration (*Eingliederungshilfe*), comprising funding for early intervention services, day care, vocational training, and support of daily living. In 1998, about one-third of the income support budget of 49.8 billion DM was spent for individuals with disabilities (Seewald, 1998, p. 514 ff.).

Vocational training for young adults is usually a three-year long apprenticeship and has a long-standing tradition in Germany. Vocational training in the regular form of an apprenticeship is financed in a dual mode by the state (vocational school) and the employers providing in-house training and a limited salary. Having a formal vocational qualification plays an important role in the German labor market and improves job opportunities. Young adults with learning disabilities are at relatively high risk on the labor market. It is often difficult for these students to find an apprenticeship position. Often, young adults with Lernbehinderungen cannot keep their jobs due to high work demands. For these reasons, vocational promotion of individuals with disabilities is highly needed in Germany.

Schwerbehindert (in the legal sense *Schwerbehindertengesetz*) is everybody who due to his or her condition (and not only temporarily) is impaired in daily living for more than 50% of the time. It is estimated that 8% of the total population are *severely disabled* in the sense of the law. Out of this population, 924,290 severely disabled persons had an occupation, 195,433 were unemployed (Vierter Bericht der Bundesregierung, 1998). Employers with at least 18 employees are legally obliged to employ at least one severely disabled person. Employers who do not comply with the provisions of the law have to pay a monthly fine of 200 DM (*Ausgleichsgabe*), which added up to 1.15 billion Mark in 1996. The money is used to promote vocational chances for individuals with disabilities, for instance, to finance work assistants. Because Lernbehinderung is a school-based notion, it is not used in German social laws. Young adults who attended the Sonderschule für Lernbehinderte receive services under the broader category of psychic and social impairments.

Job counseling in German special schools starts two years before compulsory education is over. A specialized job counselor from the regional Federal Office of Employment contacts the schools and offers an array of information services. There are ample chances for students with disabilities to extend their time of school attendance if this is promising for their development. There are also particular classes combining basic vocational education with academic advancement beyond compulsory school attendance (*Berufsgrundschuljahr, Berufsvorbereitungsjahr*). Each regional branch of the Federal Office of Employment has a vocational information center (*Berufsinformationszentrum,* BIZ) where information about all kinds of professions is provided via different media. Between 1994 and 1996, the number of young adults with Lernbehinderungen looking for advice rose from 50,847 to 60,194 and in programs of vocational promotion from 116,128 to 149,011 (Vierter Bericht der Bundesregierung, 1998, p. 64). Altogether, the Federal Office of Employment in 1996 spent 4.82 billion Mark for vocational rehabilitation programs. The total sum has doubled since 1987 (p. 59).

A significant number of young adults who could not find or hold an apprenticeship position, where a limited salary is usually paid, attended state-financed vocational preparation and training courses (*Förderlehrgänge*). About 50% of the young adults with disabilities in vocational promotion programs attended Förderlehrgänge. There are three particularly relevant courses: (1) *Förderlehrgang* 1 (up to 12 months) for young adults who are considered able to succeed in a regular apprenticeship after the training course. (2) *Förderlehrgang* 2 (up to 24 months) for young adults who are expected not to succeed in a regular apprenticeship due to the degree of their disability. (3) *Förderlehrgang* 3 (up to 36 months) for young adults who would not be challenged in sheltered workshops.

The Federal Office of Employment also finances a basic vocational training course that lasts (*Grundausbildungslehrgang*) two months or 12 months if an apprenticeship position was not found or if a vocational decision could not be made. There also exists a 12-month training course to improve the vocational chances of socially deprived youth (*Lehrgang zur Verbesserung beruflicher Bildungs-und Eingliederungschancen,* BBE) and a three-month vocational training for delinquent, socially deprived and otherwise disadvantaged youth (*TIP-Lehrgang*). Additionally, there are 27,500 places for individuals with disabilities where in-house training and vocational schools are combined in one facility (*Berufsförderungswerke, Berufsbildungswerke*). The percentage of young adults transferring into jobs on the free labor market after finishing their vocational education in this institution is between 60% and 80%. Educational support, accompanying vocational training, consisted of remedial support in professional knowledge and skills, the advancement of learning strategies, language lessons for youth of ethnic minorities and immigrants, help in dealing with administrative bodies and support in pastime arrangements and activities for 72,198 trainees in 1997.

The broad spectrum of services and training opportunities to support the vocational integration of disabled persons does not obscure the fact that 29% of all young adults who started an apprenticeship did not finish their vocational education. Storz (1997, p. 398 f.) estimated that over 50% of the former students of the special schools for *Lernbehinderte* have not finished any vocational training and that about 30% do not find a job in the labor market. There is a tremendous need for jobs in a second state subsidized labor market and different kinds of subsidized project firms where individuals with disabilities and/or otherwise disadvantaged persons find a somewhat protected employment, providing them with an opportunity for self-subsidized living instead of dependence on social welfare.

FUTURE PERSPECTIVES

Terminology

Educational and developmental risks of children and youth in modern societies are individually shaped, calling for individually designed social support. Along with the individualization of developmental risks, the number of children at risk seems to increase. In the face of "the pluralization of life conditions and the individualization of life styles" (Achter Jugendbericht, 1990), the standardization of educational problems in the form of categories of disabilities is losing its appeal. In Germany, definitional criteria, particularly in overlapping problem areas like school failure, behavior disorders, and speech disorders, have not proved to have good selectivity. Thus the claim of specificity has been put into question. The dominance of the notion of an impairment was substituted by the notion of special educational needs (*sonderpädagogischer Förderbedarf*). A conceptual figure-ground reversal took place. Central in the current discussion is the pedagogical idea of *Förderung*, which has no direct translation in English but can mean advancement, remediation, promotion, assistance, or support. The idea of categories in the high-prevalence disabilities has moved into the background. Because of the openness and positive connotation of the term *Förderung*, the Association of German Special Schools (VDS) proposed a renaming of the *Schule für Lernbehinderte* to *Förderschule* (Verband Deutscher Sonderschulen, 1987). Currently, the names *Förderschule* or *Förderzentrum* are used in all German Federal States. The Förderzentrum often is a school attended by a mixed population of students with Lernbehinderungen and/or behavioral and emotional disorders, and/or speech disorders. The advantage of the centers is the acceptance of overlapping comorbid conditions. The result is the giving up of special education terminology as well as the educational idea of classification-driven special education efforts.

Organizational Flexibility

The concept of *Förderung*, which also carries forth the idea that children with disabilities could be educated in different organizational settings, comprises prevention and professional and institutional cooperation. The special educational Förderzentrum, in practice, is characterized by three different organizational features of service provision. The Förderzentrum could be: (1) a special school for children diagnosed as lernbehindert or for children with different disabilities. The students are taught in the center. Eventually, and if the center is big enough, there could be different tracks of achievements, providing the students of the higher tracks with better chances for reintegration into the regular school, (2) a special education center without students, with the staff traveling to the schools and providing services in the regular schools, and (3) a special education center, with special classes, but also providing support to regular schools.

The idea of the Förderzentrum broke with standard procedures of diagnosing a disability and then referring the child to a special school focused on that disability. It implies a common responsibility of the regular school and special educators for children with disabilities and children at risk based on a partnership (KHK, 1994, p. 17). The special educational needs of children could find their pedagogical answer in specialized settings as well as in integrative settings.

Professionalism

What do these developments imply for a modern understanding of professionalism? The breakup of a rigid special educational model of service delivery provides more flexibility. At the same time, it implies the need for interdisciplinary cooperation and enforced responsibility for the professionals in shaping educational quality. Due to the at least partial detachment from the traditional teacher role, the trend to free professionals from rigid organizational structures is also endangered by deprofessionalization trends. On its positive side, it is a challenge to develop a new and reflective form of professional identity (Opp, 1998). Reflective professionalism would mean the acceptance of the uncertainties and antagonisms of educational practices.

School Quality

Over the past few decades, we have witnessed many school reforms and have seen that most reforms, despite the best of intentions, have failed. But there is wide agreement that the inclusion of children with disabilities and children at risk is highly correlated with school quality. Obviously, there are significant differences in the quality of schools. A *reflective professionalism* in the sense of a permanent collegial discussion and evaluation of educational practices is an indicator of the quality of schools. Schools need resources and support in their struggle for quality. They also need in-service training and organization counseling to improve their education for children with disabilities and children at risk.

Learning Disabilities in Germany: Challenges for the Future

There is a growing awareness that the educational challenge of learning disabilities has two different but overlapping facets. (1) There is a specific syndrome picture of learning disabilities in the sense of circumscribed problems of learning, attention deficit disorders, hyperactivity, and impulsivity with an assumed neuropsychological background across different IQ ranges. (2) At the same time, we see a larger population of children with a less specific but similar condition combined with sociocultural disadvantages. Framing the problem of learning disabilities in this way, school failure and IQ are important but not sufficient diagnostic criteria.

The future challenge for the field of learning disabilities in Germany is, foremost, the need for a much more systematic consideration of the educational needs of children and youth with specific learning disabilities. Service delivery for this population in Germany is lacking in four dimensions: (1) Early diagnosis of specific learning disabilities, despite an extensive medical screening system for children 0–6 years in Germany, is still randomly provided. (2) The accompanying psychosocial conditions of specific learning disabilities (comorbidity) are widely underestimated. (3) Because the syndrome of specific learning disabilities is not given the status of a disability, the financial bases for educational and therapeutic services for this population are frail. (4) The challenge of inclusionary school practices is still unsolved.

Although the German language is phonologically much more transparent than English, the problem of dyslexia, particularly among students with average and beyond average intelligence, is not given adequate attention in educational institutions. Well-developed abilities to read and to write are fairly unquestioned prerequisites of educational success in Germany. Within the selectively structured German school systems, there is still little appreciation for the human potential of dyslexic children. It is close to impossible for a dyslexic student to succeed and make his or her way through university. It is necessary to strengthen the awareness and the educational responsibility for these students in the teaching profession. At the same time, individuals with specific learning disabilities need more individually designed support in their vocational integration as they strive to attend the higher tracks of education by entering colleges and universities.

Parents of children with specific learning disabilities, due to the lack of adequate services and the ignorance of many schools concerning the educational needs of their children, are often in great despair. It is an important professional task in the future to promote the foundation of initiatives and organizations of families with specifically learning disabled to advocate for the educational rights of their children.

REFERENCES

Achter Jugendbericht. (1990). Der Bundesminister für Jugend, Familie, Frauen und Gesundheit (Hrsg.), Bonn.

Aufruf zur Gründung eines Verbandes der Hülfsschulen Deutschlands. (1898). Zeitschrift für Heilpädagogik 1998, 49, Nachdruck 1998.

Begemann, E. (1970). Die Erziehung der sozio-kulturell benachteiligten Schüler. Hannover: Schroedel.

Benkmann, R. (1994). Dekategorisierung und Heterogenität-aktuelle Probleme schulischer Integration von Kindern mit Lernschwierigkeiten in den Vereinigten Staaten und der Bundesrepublik. In Sonderpädagogik, 24, 4–13.

Bleidick, U. (1973). Die Struktur der Gesamtschule im Hinblick auf Unterricht und Erziehung von Behinderten. In H. Beyer & G. Klein (Eds.), Aspekte der Lernbehindertenpädagogik (pp. 21–45). Berlin: Marhold.

Bleidick, U. (1980). Lernbehinderte gibt es eigentlich gar nicht. Oder: Wie man das Kind mit dem Bacle ausschüttet. In: Zeitschrift für Heilpadagogik, 21, 127–143.

Bless, G. (1995). Zur Wirksamkeit der Integration. Bern: Haupt.

Deppe-Wolfinger, H., Prengel, A. & Reiser, H. (1990). Integrative Pädagogik in der Grundschule. Weinheim: Juventa.

Deutscher Bildungsrat. (1973). (Hrsg.), Empfehlungen der Bildungskommission: Zur pädagogischen Förderung Behinderter und von Behinderung bedrohter Kinder und Jugendlicher. Bonn.

Drewek, P. (1997). Geschichte der Schule. In K. Harney & H. H. Krüger (Eds.), Einführung in die Geschichte von Erziehungswissenschaft und Erziehungswirklichkeit. Opladen: Leske + Budrich, 183–208.

Dumke, D., & Krieger, G. (1990). Einstellungen und Bereitschaft von Sonderschullehrern zum integrativen Unterricht. In Zeitschrift für Heilpädagogik, 41, 235–245

Dumke, D., Krieger, G., & Schäfer, G. (1989). Schulische Integration in der Beurteilung von Eltern und Lehrern. Weinheim: Beltz.

Eberwein, H. (1997). Lernbehinderung–Faktum oder Konstrukt? In: Zeitschrift für Heilpädagogik, 48, 14–22.

Ellger-Rüttgardt, S. (1997). Geschichte der sonderpädagogischen Institutionen. In K. Harney & H. H. Krüger (Eds.), Einführung in die Geschichte von Erziehungswissenschaft und Erziehungswirklichkeit. Opladen: Leske + Budrich, 247–271.

Feuser, G. (1996). "Geistigbehinderte" gibt es nicht! Projektionen und Artefakte in der Geistigbehindertenpädagogik. In Geistige Behinderung, 35, 18–25.

Feuser, G., & Meyer, H. (1987). Integrativer Unterricht in der Grundschule-Ein Zwischen-
bericht. Solms-Oberbiel: Jarrick.

Fölling-Albers, M. (1995). Schulkinder heute. Weinheim: Beltz (2. Auflage).

Fuchs, A. (1927). Das Sonderschulwesen in Berlin. Berlin.

Füssel, H.-P. & Kretschmann, R. (1993). Gemeinsamer Unterricht für behinderte und nicht-
behinderte Kinder. Pädagogische und juristische Voraussetzungen. Bonn: Witterschlick.

Haeberlin, U., Bless, G., Moser, U., & Klaghofer, G. (1990). Die Integration von Lernbehinderten. Bern: Haupt.

Hellbrügge, Th. (1977). Unser Montessori-Modell. München: Kösel.

Herrlitz, H.-G., Hopf, W., & Titze, H. (1986). Deutsche Schulgeschichte von 1800 bis zur
Gegenwart. Atheneum: Königstein (2. Aufl.).

Hetmeier, H.-W. (1998). Öffentliche Finanzen für Bildung Wissenschaft. In: StBA Wirtschaft
und Statistik, 4, 307–308.

Hiller, G. G. (1994). Ausbruch aus dem Bildungskeller. Ulm: Vaas (3. Aufl.).

Hinz, A., Katzenbach, T., Rauer, W., Schuck, K.-D., Wocken, H., & Wuttke, H. (1998). Die integrative Grundschule im sozialen Brennpunkt. Ergebnisse eines Hamburger Schulversuchs.
Hamburg: Feldhaus Verlag.

Hinz, A. (1999). Sonderpädagogische Arbeit in Integrativen Regelklassen. Eine Studie zur
Praxisentwicklung im ersten und vierten Schuljahr. In: Katzenbach, D. & Hinz, A. (Hrsg.):
Weginarken und Stolpersteine in der Weiterentwicklung der Integrativen Grundschule.
Hamburg: Hamburger Buchwerkstatt, 201–301 (überarbeitete Fassung).

Internationales Jahr der Familie. (1994). Bericht der Deutschen Nationalkommission für das
Internationale Jahr der Familie 1994. Bonn.

Kanter, G. (1974). Lernbehinderungen, Lernbehinderte, deren Erziehung und Rehabilitation.
In Sonderpädagogik 3 (Deutscher Bildungsrat Gutachten und Studien der Bildungskommission. Bd. 34) Stuttgart: Klett, 117–234.

Klein, G. (1973). Die soziale Benachteiligung der Lernbehinderten im Vergleich zu den
Hauptschülern. In G. Heese & A. Reinhartz (Eds.), Aktuelle Probleme der Lernbehindertenpädagogik (pp. 7–22), Berlin: Marhold.

Klein, G. (1996). Soziale Benachteiligung: Zur Aktualität eines verdrängten Begriffs. In G. Opp
& F. Peterander (Hrsg.), Focus Heilpädagogik. München: Reinhardt, 140–149.

Klemm, K. (1996). Bildungsexpansion und keine Ende? In: Helsper. W., Kruger, H. -H., Wenzel,
H. (Hrsg.): Schule und Gesellschaft im Umbruch. Band 1: Theoretische und internationale
Perspektiven. Weinheim, 427–442.

Klemm, K. et al. (1990). Bildungsgesamtplan 1990. München: Juventa.

KMK (Hrsg). (1994). Empfehlungen zur sonderpädagogischen Förderung in Schulen in der
Bundesrepublik Deutschland. Bonn-Bad Godesberg.

Kornmann, R., & Klingele, Ch. (1996). Ausländische Kinder und Jugendliche an Schulen für
Lernbehinderte in den alten Bundesländern. In Zeitschrift für Heilpädagogik, 47, 2–9.

Kornmann, R., Klingele, Ch., & Iriogbe-Ganninger, J. (1997). Zur Überrepräsentation
ausländischer Kinder und Jugendlicher in Schulen für Lernbehinderte: Der alarmierende
Trend hält an. In: Zeitschrift für Heilpädagogik, 48, 203–207.

Lane, H. (1985). Das wilde Kind von Aveyron. Frankfurt/M.: Ullstein. (Original work published
in 1976 in English.)

Langfeldt, H.-P., & Kurth, E. (1994). Sonderpädagogische Förderung in den neuen Bundesländern und Berlin (Ost). Bundesministerium für Bildung und Wissenschaft. Bonn.

Lauterbach, W., Lange, A. & Wüest-Rudin. (1999). Familien in prekären Einkommenslagen.
Konsequenzen für die Bildungschancen von Kindern in den 80iger und 90iger Jahren? In
Zeitschrift für Erziehungswissenschaft, 2, 361–384.

Liberman, L., & Liberman, M. (1985). Special education and regular education: A merger
made in heaven? In Exceptional Children, 51, 513–516.

Lünnemann, P. (1998). Methodik zur Darstellung der öffentlichen Ausgaben für schulische Bildung nach Bildungsstufen sowie zur Berechnung finanzstatistischer Kennzahlen für den Schulbereich. In: StBA Wirtschaft und Statistik, 2, 141–152.

Möckel, A. (Hrsg.). (1998). Erfolg-Niedergang-Neuanfang. 100 Jahre Verband Deutscher Sonderschulen-Fachverband für Behindertenpädagogik. München: Reinhardt.

Opp, G. (1996). Schulische Integration: Impulse für eine Neubestimmung der Diskussion. In Zeitschrift für Heilpädagogik, 47, 354–359.

Opp, G. (1998). Reflexive Professionalität-Neue Professionalisierungstendenzen im Arbeitsfeld der Kinder- und Jugendhilfe. Zeitschrift für Heilpädagogik, 49, 148–158.

P.L. 105–17, Individuals with Disabilities Education Act (IDEA) of 1997.

Prengel, A. (1993). Pädagogik der Vielfalt. Verschiedenheit und Gleichberechtigung Interkultureller, Feministischer und Integrativer Pädagogik. Opladen: Leske + Budrich.

Preuss-Lausitz, U. (1981). Fördern ohne Sonderschule. Konzept und Erfahrungen zur integrativen Förderung in der Regelschule. Weinheim: Beltz.

Preuss-Laussitz, U. (2000). Sonderpädagogik der Zukunft? Vom Ghetto zur sozialen Kohäsion. In F. Albrecht, A. Hinz, & V. Moser (Hrsg.), Perspektiven der Sonderpädagogik. Disziplin- und professionsbezogene Standortbestimmungen. Neuwied: Luchterhandt.

Reiser, H. (1997). Lern- und Verhaltensstörungen als gemeinsame Aufgabe von Grundschul- und Sonderpädagogik unter dem Aspekt der pädagogischen Selektion. In Zeitschrift für Heilpädagogik, 48, 266–275.

Reiser, H., Loeken, H., & Dlugosch, A. (1995). Bedingungen der Problemwahrnehmung von Leistungsversagen in der Grundschule am Beispiel zweier hessischer Landkreise. Forschungsstelle Integration, Institut für Sonder- und Heilpädagogik am Fachbereich Erziehungswissenschaften der Johann-Wolfgang-Goethe-Universität, Frankfurt.

Schröder, U. (1993). Alle reden von Integration - und die Zahl der Sonderschüler steigt!? In Sonderpädagogik, 23, 130–141.

Schröder, U. (1999). Integrative Pädagogik bei Kindern und Jugendlichen mit Lernbehinderung. In: Ortmann, M., Myschker, N., Integrative Schulpedagogik. Stuttgart: Kohlhamme, 182–215.

Seewald, K. (1998). Ergebnisse der Sozialhilfe- und Asylbewerberleistungen 1996. In: Wirtschaft und Statistik, 6, 509–519.

Sickinger, A. (1920). Arbeitsunterricht, Einheitsschule, Mannheimer Schulsystem. Leipzig: Quelle & Meier.

Speck, O. (1991). Das Selbstverständnis des heilpädagogischen Schulsystems im Wandel. Zeitschrift für Heilpädagogik, 42, 599–607.

Speck, O. (1997). 75 Jahre Sonderschullehrerbildung-Universitäre Heilpädagogik am Scheideweg? In Behindertenpädagogik in Bayern, 40, 244–258.

Speck, O., Gottwald, P., Havers, N., & Innerhofer, P. (Hrsg.) (1978). Schulische Integration lern- und verhaltensgestörter Kinder. München: Reinhardt.

Statistische Veröffentlichungen der Kultusministerkonferenz. (1997, August). Vorausberechnung der Schüler- und Absolventenzahlen 1995–2015. NR 141–.

Stoellger, N. (1995). Die aktuelle Situation der Beschulung Lernbehinderter. In Zeitschrift für Heilpädagogik, 46, 568–575.

Storz, M. (1997). Schöne neue Arbeitswelt. Anmerkungen zur beruflichen (Teil-) Integration von marktbeteiligten Jugendlichen und jungen Erwachsenen in postindustrieller Zeit. In Zeitschrift für Heilpädagogik, 48, 398–405.

Stötzner, H. E. (1864). Schulen für schwachbefähigte Kinder. Berlin: Marhold.

Tent, L., Witt, M., Schoche-Lieberung, Ch., & Bürger, W. (1991). Über die pädagogische Wirksamkeit der Schule für Lernbehinderte. In Zeitschrift für Heilpädagogik, 42, 289–320.

Verband Deutscher Sonderschulen e.V. (1987). "Förderschule" statt "Schule für Lernbehinderte." In Zeitschrift für Heilpädagogik, 38, 907.

Vierter Bericht der Bundesregierung über die Lage der Behinderten und die Entwicklung der Rehabilitation. Bundesministerium für Arbeit und Sozialordnung (1998). Bonn.

Weise, T. (1820). Betrachtung über geistesschwache Kinder in Hinsicht der Verschiedenheit, Grundursachen, Kennzeichen und der Mittel, ihnen auf leichte Art durch Unterricht beizukommen. Zeitz.

Weiß, H. (1996). Armut als gesellschaftliche Normalität. Implikationen für die kindliche Entwicklung. In G. Opp & F. Peterander (Hrsg.), Focus Heilpädagogik. München: Reinhardt Verlag, 150–162.

Willand, H. (1999). »Wie geht es Dir so in Deiner Schule?" Oder noch einmal über die emotional Befindlichkeit von Schülern mit Förderbedarf in Schulen für Lernbehinderte und in integrierten Sekundarstufe I-Schulen. In: Zeitschrift für Heilpädagogik, 50, 546–554.

Wittmann, B. (1997). Die Zahl der Sonderschüler wächst. Eine Auswertung neuester Statistiken. In Die neue Sonderschule, 42, 443–450.

Wocken, H. (1987). Schulleistungen in Integrationsklassen. In H. Wocken & G. Antor (Hrsg.), Integrationsklassen in Hamburg. Solms-Oberbiel: Jarrick Oberbiel, 276–306.

Wocken, H. (1996), Sonderpädagogischer Förderbedarf als systemischer Begriff. Sonderpädagogik, 26, 34–38.

Wocken, H., & Antor, G. (Hrsg.) (1987). Integrationsklassen in Hamburg. Solms-Oberbiel: Jarrick.

Zehnter Kinder und Jugendbericht. (1998). Bundesministerium für Familie, Senioren, Frauen und- Jugend. Bonn, 48 ff.

Chapter 14

British Orientations to Specific Learning Difficulties

K. Wedell
Emeritus professor of special needs education, Institute of Education, University of London.

In Britain, the word *difficulty* rather than *disability* is now used in relation to specific learning difficulties. The origin of this preference reflects a significant switch in orientation toward children's special educational needs in Britain. The 1944 Education Act had referred to those requiring special education as having "disabilities of body or mind". This implied that the needs originated in factors "within" the child, and at that time children's needs were defined in terms of eleven categories of handicap. The word *disability* was associated with this "within-child" view. During the subsequent years, in Britain as well as in other countries, there was a growing awareness that children's needs were the outcome both of factors within a child and of factors within the environment. It was the interaction between these two groups of factors—both at one time and in the course of the child's development—which was crucial. The relative importance of each group of factors might of course vary greatly in individual instances and at particular times.

By 1974 opinions had moved toward the interactive view. This and other developments were the impulse for a reconsideration of the way in which children's special educational needs and the provision for them should be conceived. As a result, a national committee of inquiry was set up by the government at the time—the Warnock Committee (named after its chairperson). The Committee reported its findings in 1978 (Department for Education and Science, 1978). One of the main proposals in the Report was that the 1944 definitions of handicap should be abandoned, and that the general term *special educational needs* should be adopted to reflect the interactive view of "handicap". In discussing the implications of its orientation, the Committee referred to children with specific learning difficulties rather than disabilities. At that time, the term *specific learning difficulties* was used primarily in connection with literacy attainment, and with more severe and long-term difficulties in its acquisition. The Committee referred to difficulties in the plural, because another report, which had been commissioned to look into the problem of "dyslexia", had concluded that the term *dyslexia* tended to be used for a variety of difficulties affecting literacy acquisition (Advisory Committee on Handicapped Children, 1972). The Warnock Committee's use of the term also included the criterion that pupils' attainment in literacy was disproportionately low in comparison with their at least average level of general achievement (the discrepancy criterion).

In the 1970s, special education in Britain was also influenced by the focus in the United States on the proposed dysfunctions underlying specific learning difficulties. There was great interest in the work of American special educators such as Frostig (on visual perceptual difficulties), Kephart (on perceptuo-motor difficulties), and Kirk and Kirk (on language difficulties) (Wedell, 1973). Similar to the situation in the United States, these authors' work had led to the promotion of specific training in these areas of function in children on the assumption that remediation of these dysfunctions would help to overcome difficulties in literacy acquisition. However, in Britain, as in the United States, evaluation studies began to indicate that the impact which these training approaches might have on literacy was not as direct as had been assumed (Wedell, 1973). Nonetheless, the view that particular cognitive dysfunction underlies specific learning difficulties has continued to be held. For example, the Code of Practice for the Identification and Assessment of Special Educational Needs introduced by the government in 1994 (Department for Education, 1994), in referring to specific learning difficulties, mentions the discrepancy criterion and also

> evidence of clumsiness, significant difficulties of sequencing or visual perception, deficiencies in working memory or significant delays in language development. (p. 61)

However, in the Code's reference to appropriate teaching methods, there is no specific mention of the kind of "ability training' which was proposed in the 1970s.

Another strand in the application of the concept of learning difficulties in Britain has been the link between dysfunction and neuropathology. This strand, which is also common in other countries, links the specific forms of dysfunction causally to various forms of neuropathology usually associated with findings in the clinical neurology of adults. So the difficulties were given names derived from clinical neurology, such as *dyspraxia*, *dysphasia*, and *dyslexia*. The use of these terms often reflects the kind of professional who is asked to assess a child or young person's difficulties. Not surprisingly, the terms are particularly often used within the medical profession.

This strand of thinking has a long history in special needs education, and with the distinction between general learning difficulties and those disabilities which are presumed to be caused by particular forms of neuropathology (Wedell, 1975). Often, the link is inferred from the manifest link which has been established in adults who have lost specific functions as the result of various forms of brain injury. In children, the specific difficulties are usually developmental, and consequently the causal origins are hard to disentangle. The question which this strand of thinking about specific learning difficulties has raised is whether attributing them to neuropathology offers any implications for the practicalities of intervention and education. In general, the answer to this question has to be no. This is not to deny that the concept of "specific" implies that the children's difficulties are not attributable solely to the generally recognized environmental and experiential factors, and therefore are assumed to have an organic basis. Another important consideration is that giving the difficulties labels associated with organic dysfunction makes teachers feel that they cannot be expected to cope with them.

PARENTS' VIEWS

In Britain as elsewhere, the development of more focussed provision for children and young people with specific learning difficulties has been the result of research which increased the differentiation among learning needs. Parents also became concerned that their children's particular learning needs were not being accurately recognized and met within the educational provision which was available, both in special and in mainstream schools. As research into the differentiation of learning needs progressed, parents were able to identify the corresponding specific features of learning difficulty experienced by their children, and they started to lobby for more appropriate provisions to be made. As in other countries, for the purpose of lobbying, it was important to use a label which could identify the particular aspect of learning difficulty which characterized the children who were not being adequately served. Similarly, the discrepancy criterion represented by the term *specific* became important, since parents felt that it distinguished their particular children's difficulties from the general run of learning difficulties. This helped to make the argument that if only correspondingly specific educational measures were taken to overcome these particular difficulties, their children could go on to realize their true potential. Consequently, the use of the more "medical-sounding" labels also had the implication that, like other medical conditions, there might be a specific cure for the difficulties.

Another perceived benefit of the use of the terms was the implication that the difficulties were neither the fault of the parents' neglect nor faulty upbringing, nor due to genetic imperfections. These attributions in the use of the terms by parents were therefore very understandable. The utility of the terms was also very strategic. It helped parents to rally groups to lobby for provision for the particular difficulties their children experienced. As a result, there are parent groups for children with difficulties labelled as Attention Deficit Hyperactivity Disorder (ADHD), dyspraxia, dysphasia, and dyslexia. Concern with dyslexia has been the most long-standing, and the main parent group has now become a very powerful lobby with the national government. The parent groups are usually not only concerned with lobbying, but also with fund-raising for services such as information dissemination and sometimes also for research in the areas of their particular concern. Most parent organizations have local groups which provide support for and advice to their members.

AREAS OF GENERALLY RECOGNIZED SPECIFIC DIFFICULTIES

Areas of generally recognized specific difficulties in Britain at present can be divided into two groups—those directly affecting particular areas of curricular achievement, and those having a more general impact on achievement and behaviour. The latter consist of difficulties associated with descriptors such as ADHD, dysphasia, and dyspraxia, and the former are the difficulties associated with descriptors such as dyslexia and dyscalculia. In this chapter I will not go into detail about the controversies concerning whether or not such descriptors can be regarded as defining a universally accepted symptomatology. These controversies are current in most countries, and the general finding is that in practice, none of the difficulties occur in such "pure" forms as the use of these labels would imply. What is noteworthy is that each of these areas of difficulty has long been recognized, but is recurrently given new recognition and referred to with new labels. In the following, I indicate some of the currently prevailing views about these difficulties in this country.

Dyslexia

Dyslexia is the term commonly used to cover the main area of difficulty with the curricular area of literacy. Some have also used it with respect to difficulties in numeracy. Because of the degree of controversy in the use of the term in Britain, the Division of Educational and Child Psychology of the British Psychological Society (British Psychological Society, 1999) set up a working party to make recommendations. The working party's report probably provides one of the most extensive examinations of the issues involved. It distinguishes between aspects of definition which offer descriptions and causal explanations. The working party finally came up with what it called a "working definition' as follows:

> Dyslexia is evident when accurate and fluent word reading and/or spelling develops very incompletely or with great difficulty. This focuses on literacy learning at the "word level" and implies that the problem is very severe and persistent despite appropriate learning opportunities. It provides the basis for a staged process of assessment through teaching. (p. 8)

This definition thus focuses on the particular curricular area of difficulty—word level—which relates to a section of the National Curriculum (NC) which I discuss in a later section. It refers to the finding that the generally applied teaching approaches are not proving successful. Consequently the definition asserts that the understanding of the difficulties emerges through evaluated outcomes of teaching, and so links assessment with teaching. The report fully recognizes the significance of the children's difficulties, and goes on to state:

> The report gives full recognition to the plight of learners with difficulties of a dyslexic nature. These difficulties can act as barriers to educational, social and vocational opportunities. (p. 8)

Another important point made by the working party is that its working definition does not necessarily exclude other concurrent difficulties. For example, the difficulties defined do not exclude moderate learning difficulty, or indeed sensory impairment such as hearing loss. To this extent, the definition does not put such an emphasis on the "specificity" criterion, although it obviously does not preclude it. The report does, however, cast doubt on the validity of the discrepancy criteria in defining dyslexia. Quoting the contributions to a special issue of the journal *Dyslexia*, it states:

> the current balance of opinion in the research literature [is] strongly weighted against the validity of discrepancy definitions. (p. 58)

Some, while recognizing the various specific difficulties which children and young people may experience in acquiring literacy, prefer not to use the term *dyslexia* because of the uncertain associations of the term. They tend instead to speak of "specific literacy difficulties" to emphasize the variety of forms in which these may be manifested. It is interesting therefore, that even with its very carefully considered position, the British Psychological Society working party report's conclusions continue to use the term. Even so, the defining constraints proposed would not necessarily be acceptable to some of the lobbying groups. The main parents' group is called the British Dyslexia Association, which became a national organization in 1972 (Contact a Family Website, 2000).

Dyspraxia

The term *dyspraxia* has relatively recently come into wider use in relation to children to refer to the specific perceptuo-motor difficulties which have long been recognized as Henderson (1995) has noted. These difficulties have also been referred to as the "clumsy child syndrome". These difficulties belong to the group which has a more indirect impact on educational achievement as Wedell (1973) indicated. Both he and Henderson mention that these difficulties may manifest themselves in children's difficulties in fine or gross motor competence or both. They may affect children's achievement in drawing and writing, and in dressing. They may also make it difficult for children to succeed in various kinds of sport, particularly where hand-eye coordination is concerned. Henderson points out that poor achievement in these areas is likely to impact on children and young people's self-esteem, since for example, they will often be the last to be picked by their peers in team games.

These specific difficulties have often not been acknowledged as such, and many professionals have tried to reassure parents that their children "will grow out of them'. However, Henderson reports studies which show that the difficulties do persist into later development if remedial measures are not taken. A parents' group, the Dyspraxia Foundation was formed in 1987 (Contact a Family Website, 2000).

Attention Deficit Hyperactivity Disorder (ADHD)

The difficulties referred to by this term have also been long recognised as having a pervasive—rather than focussed—impact on educational achievement. The difficulties and their remediation, were of course a major part of Bill Cruickshank's own research (Cruickshank, 1961). It is significant that Cruickshank associated these difficulties with neuropathology, and this still represents one of the main controversies regarding these difficulties. In Britain there is considerable disagreement about whether it is appropriate to use drugs as a method of treatment. Cruickshank stressed that the children with these difficulties needed carefully planned educational intervention and developed methods for achieving this.

There is also considerable disagreement about whether ADHD refers to a single set of difficulties, since the children labelled in this way often manifest a variety of problems. For example, some descriptions overlap with the difficulties included under the term dyspraxia. While there is a body of opinion that these children "grow out" of these difficulties. it is also recognised that the difficulties have significant emotional and behavioural consequences, which impact on teachers' and schools' capacity to cope with the children. Furthermore, the difficulties are liable to interfere with children's capacity to benefit from the teaching offered. The general consensus appears to recognise that a proportion of children who manifest these difficulties respond to medication, but that this treatment is inadequate unless it is backed up—and subsequently superceded—by appropriate emotional and behavioural support (Cooper, 1997). There seems at present to be little agreement about which children respond to medication and which do not, with the result that medication is often given on an experimental basis. Unfortunately, there is frequently inadequate communication between the medical personnel responsible for prescribing and the teachers responsible for the children's education (Wedell, 1999) so that the drug intervention is not effectively monitored. An active parents' group (ADHD Family Support Group) has been formed to promote the better understanding of these children's difficulties and effective intervention for them (Contact a Family Website, 2000).

Dysphasia

This term is used to refer to specific difficulties of a developmental nature in expressive and/or receptive language. These are specific difficulties which have long been recognized. It is generally accepted that they have secondary consequences for children's educational progress and may occur in very severe forms where children's capacity to communicate becomes the main concern. However, in milder forms, where children acquire reasonable communicative competence in the course of development, there may well be residual consequences, particularly for the acquisition of literacy. Indeed, these difficulties are included in some users' definition of dyslexia.

The Code of Practice, mentioned above, includes these difficulties within its list of special educational needs. This is largely because of the very effective lobbying by the parents' group while the Code was being drafted. The Code's description of the difficulties emphasizes the criterion of discrepancy with other areas of the children's functioning. However, recent research (Dockrell and Lindsay, 2000) shows that there is still a good deal of disagreement within and among the various groups of professionals about the exact criteria for defining the specificity of these difficulties. The main parents' group is called Afasic (Contact a Family Website, 2000).

CONTEXT—THE BRITISH EDUCATION SYSTEM

Although the education systems in the various parts of the United Kingdom have overall similarity, the systems in Scotland and Northern Ireland differ from those in England and Wales to some degree. In addition, there are minor differences between the systems of England and Wales. For the purposes of this chapter, I will focus on the education system as it applies in England. The last Conservative government made major changes in the education system during the late 1980s and early 1990s, and these changes have in many respects been continued under the present Labor government.

The National Curriculum

In the late 1980s, a National Curriculum (NC) was established which applied to all except private schools. Compulsory schooling extends from the age of five to sixteen, and the NC covers this period. Primary education is generally provided by schools for children aged five to eleven, and secondary education is provided for children aged eleven to sixteen. The majority of secondary schools continue to provide education up to age eighteen, but in some areas these later years of education may be offered in so-called Sixth Form Colleges and in other further education colleges. Schooling for children aged five to eighteen is free. Education for children below age five is not compulsory and is available in a variety of forms, both free and fee-paying. The participation rate in preschool education varies in different parts of the country, as does the proportion of full- and part-time provision.

The NC was designed to specify the content to which all pupils were entitled thus ensuring a degree of uniformity across schools in all parts of the country. Another important aspect of the imposition of the NC was the process by which pupils' attainment was assessed. The end of compulsory schooling has for a long time been assessed for the majority of pupils by a semipublic system of examination, which, however, did not cover pupils at the lower end of achievement. The NC introduced national assessment procedures for pupils at ages seven, eleven, and fourteen as well. Originally, the NC and its assessment were detailed to a degree which proved impracticable. Inevitably, this level of prescription has been considerably modified over subsequent years, involving both teacher assessment and nationally determined procedures. In addition, there is now a move to introduce a "baseline" assessment for pupils following their entry in the first year of schooling.

The aggregate pupil attainment levels in the NC assessments are published annually for all schools, and currently efforts are being made to find ways of relating these to the actual added value provided by each school. In addition, Local Education Authorities (LEAs) are now required to set each school aggregate targets for improving their pupils' levels of attainment, and schools will be judged on their capacity to reach these targets.

The Organization of Schooling

Until the late 1980s, the provision of schooling was primarily the responsibility of LEAs in the various counties and urban authorities. These provided the funding for schools, derived partly from local taxes, but mainly through allocation from central government. The LEAs were responsible for allocating funding to schools and for providing support services. In the late 1980s, the previous government began a policy to increase the autonomy of individual schools, and at the same time to relate their funding increasingly to the number of pupils they could attract. These policies were also directed at reducing the role of LEAs. Previously the LEAs were responsible for advising and inspecting schools, but then a centrally controlled system of inspection was set up, which now also extends to inspecting the LEAs in their residual roles. LEAs are now required to delegate the majority of their funding to schools, which can then decide whether or not to avail themselves of the LEA services on a buy-back basis—including the special needs support services.

These policy changes raised considerable anxiety among those responsible for meeting children's special educational needs. The imposition of competition for pupils between schools and the running down of LEA services were seen to jeopardize the attention and support, which schools could give to pupils with learning difficulties. As a result of lobbying, the previous government was induced to draw up the Code of Practice for the identification and assessment of special educational needs (DFEE, 1994) as mentioned earlier. This prescribed a staged process of support, requiring all schools to respond to children's learning difficulties and to call in outside specialist support if the schools' intervention proved insufficient. All schools were required to appoint a teacher as a Special Needs Coordinator, whose responsibilities included drawing up a special needs policy for the school; supporting teachers in meeting individual pupils' needs; in direct support of pupils where necessary, and calling in outside specialist help (Wedell, 1995).

The final two stages of the Code allowed the school—or parents—to require the LEA to arrange for a multiprofessional assessment of a pupil's learning needs in order to come to a decision whether the LEA would provide resources over and above those generally available to schools. Such a decision involved the school in formulating a Statement of the pupil's needs and how the needs were to be met—whether through support in the mainstream school or in a special school or unit. A tribunal service was set up to decide on cases where parents disagreed with the provision chosen by the LEA. The legislation required provision to be made in mainstream schools, unless parents did not wish it and unless various practicality conditions could not be met. The present government responded to further lobbying by strengthening the inclusion requirement (Department of Education and Employment, 1998). In practice, these policies present some difficulties in implementation, because of other concurrent policies. These include reducing the funding which LEAs have available for central support services, and putting pressure on schools to increase the aggregate achievement levels of their pupils.

PROVISION FOR PUPILS WITH SPECIFIC LEARNING DIFFICULTIES

Various aspects of the requirements of the NC and its assessment have a direct relevance to provision for pupils with specific learning difficulties. At the pre-school level, the government agency responsible has drawn up a set of curricular "early learning goals" for children covering social and more "pre-academic" areas. There is also a move to support those working in preschool provision to observe and identify children who are showing signs of particular difficulties. The baseline assessments following entry to school provide a similar opportunity.

An important aspect of the National Curriculum is its prescription about literacy and numeracy mentioned above, including the literacy and numeracy "hours". The concern has been to enable the majority of children to achieve requisite levels by the age of eleven. The teaching methods for both the literacy and the numeracy hours encourages whole class and small group work to facilitate support for pupils at differing attainment levels. Additional funding is being provided centrally to offer some further professional development and advice for teachers in carrying out the literacy and numeracy strategies. The government is currently planning to introduce similar curricular work in the lower levels of secondary education.

The present government has introduced measures to limit the number of pupils in the lower forms in primary schools to a maximum of thirty, in the hope that teachers will have less difficulty in responding to the individual needs of children. In addition, central funding is being directed at providing Learning Support Assistants for teachers. These are also used in applying a scheme to offer additional learning support to pupils who are not making expected progress. The central government is encouraging schools to make optimal use of information and communications technology, and is backing this with additional funding. In principle, these various aspects of provision should contribute a range of early support for pupils with specific learning difficulties.

Where the individual children's needs are not responding to these approaches by the teacher and the learning support assistant, the school's Special Educational Needs Coordinator (SENCO) should be available to provide additional ideas to the teacher about teaching approaches. The SENCO is also required to formulate an Individual Education Plan (IEP), which sets targets and timelines for the pupil's expected progress, and methods for the teacher to adopt in meeting the pupil's learning needs. Schools are also required to institute Behavior Support Plans for pupils with behavior problems. Unfortunately in primary schools, the constraints on funding often result in the teacher with the SENCO role having little or no noncontact time away from their main responsibility for class teaching, and so the actual advice and support they are able to offer may be very limited (Lewis, Neill, & Campbell, 1996). An electronic mailing list (the SENCO Forum) has been set up to enable SENCOs to share their questions and solutions, and this now has around 800 members (Wedell et al., 1997). In addition, the government has contracted with one of its agencies to set up an "inclusion website" offering information on good practice in teaching and learning.

The next level of support is provided by LEAs through their learning support services and their educational psychology services. As mentioned above, these services may or may not operate on a "buy-back" basis for schools. The services also vary as to how far they are able to allocate time to preventive work, such as supporting schools to implement a whole-school policy for early indentification and intervention and providing in-service training for school staff, in order to enhance their capacity to respond to pupils' individual needs. Often, the learning support services may find themselves limited to responding to referrals for help with individual pupils, which may take the form of weekly tuition sessions for a given period of time.

Schools are in principle also able to access help from the National Health Service speech and language therapists, occupational therapists, and clinical psychologists through their school doctor's referral. However, these services differ in their practice of providing school-based rather than clinic or hospital services, and in general tend to be too pressured to respond except to severe needs. Parents are also able to access these National Health services through their family doctors. This health provision is free at the point of delivery, but funded through taxation.

If these various approaches to meeting a child or young person's learning needs are not proving sufficient, as mentioned above, the Code of Practice enables schools—and parents—to ask the LEA to arrange to assess a child, and to consider provision through the Statement procedure. Such provision may be made in mainstream schools, or in special units in mainstream schools, or in special schools run by the LEA. Approximately 2%–3% of pupils nationally have their needs met in this way. Since the funds for this level of provision have to be met by the LEA, the thresholds for provision may be set to give priority to those with the most severe and persistent learning needs (OFSTED, 1999).

The assessment for a Statement is carried out by an educational psychologist from the LEA's service and by a school doctor allocated for the purpose from the National Health Service. The school is required to provide a report, which is usually drawn up by the SENCO. The parents are also encouraged to make their comments. The decision as to whether the LEA will provide support within the Statement procedure is then commonly made by a panel of LEA service officers and the LEA administrator responsible for making provision. The Statement procedure requires that pupils' progress is reviewed annually, to check whether the provision made is meeting the prescribed outcomes.

Provision to meet children and young people's specific learning difficulties through a Statement is normally made within mainstream schools. The present government is committed to promoting inclusive education for all pupils (Department for Education and Employment, 1998). This policy has, in principle, been promoted for many years, but is always subject to the conditions of practicality mentioned earlier. Clearly, it is easy to apply these conditions in a way which frustrates inclusion as well as promotes it. The most common provision offered is a number of hours of learning support assistant (LSA) time per week, under the general supervision of the LEA's learning support service and the SENCO in the school. LSAs may be appointed by the school or may be provided from a pool built up within the LEA. A recent study of the employment of LSAs (Department for Education and Employment, 2000) has found that much more attention needs to be paid to ensure that LSAs are able to provide the support required. One of the main problems has been that the pressure of work on teachers has made it difficult for them to provide specific briefing for LSAs about how they are intended to support the pupils. As a result, the LSAs sometimes are not able to work in a sufficiently focused way with pupils, and consequently are not in a position to help the teacher by monitoring the pupils' progress effectively.

Some LEAs have set up resource bases in primary and secondary schools where more intensive help may be offered. Such provision may be made for pupils with specific literacy difficulties or with other forms of specific difficulties. Needless to say, a decision about where a particular pupil may be placed often depends on the perception of the individual assessing specialist recommending provision, and on the perceptions of the Statement panel. Pupils with more severe behavioral difficulties associated with ADHD may be placed in special resource bases, either attached to schools or in separate locations, along with other pupils with emotional and behavior difficulties. A proportion of pupils may be attending these latter units because they were excluded from school on account of their behavior. In a study of pupils in behavior support units in an inner-city area, it was found that nearly half the pupils in the primary unit could be regarded as having ADHD (Arcelus et al., 2000). The corresponding proportion in the secondary age unit was smaller, and the researchers thought that by this age the pupils' difficulties might already have accumulated and become more complex so that it was more difficult to identify the element of ADHD. Pupils with specific learning difficulties are generally unlikely to be placed in LEA special schools, although there are also some privately run schools which have been set up to cater to particular forms of difficulties. LEA Statement panels may occasionally place individual pupils with more severe difficulties in such schools.

As mentioned earlier, if parents feel that the provision specified in a Statement does not match the nature and degree of their child's needs, they may appeal to a Tribunal (they may also appeal against an LEA decision not to assess a child for a Statement). These Tribunals operate under the aegis of the central government and have the power to require an LEA to alter its proposed provision. Both the parents and the LEA can be formally represented at a hearing. Approximately 35% of appeals are about decisions made for meeting pupils' needs regarding literacy (Evans, 2000).

Tribunals may make decisions regardless of the cost of alternative provisions which may fall on LEAs. For example, if a Tribunal agrees with a claim by parents that none of the provision made by an LEA is suitable, it may decide to order that a child be placed in a private school, even though such a placement will involve the LEA in great expense. Needless to say, this aspect of the Tribunal procedure has raised considerable concern about the equity of allocating resources within an LEA area. It is not only the cost of Tribunal procedures, but more particularly the cost of additional provision resulting from the Tribunals' decisions, that may well cut into the total funds available to an LEA for meeting the remaining children's special needs. Appeals are inevitably more likely to be made by parents who are articulate and willing to fight for their particular children.

TEACHER TRAINING FOR SPECIFIC LEARNING DIFFICULTIES

A government agency—the Teacher Training Agency (TTA)—is at present responsible for specifying the content of the initial teacher training which is provided in colleges and universities. These specifications also include a requirement that teachers should be able to identify pupils who have specific learning difficulties, and to know about the available sources of additional support. The present government has also reinstated an "induction year" for newly qualified teachers, during which the SENCOs in their schools should provide further guidance as part of their further training.

Most LEAs provide a range of short courses for teachers interested in furthering their understanding and skills in teaching children with specific learning difficulties. These courses are normally taken out of school hours and are usually funded out of a combination of LEA and central government sources. Specialist training leading to academic qualifications is provided by colleges and universities, sometimes in collaboration with LEAs. Qualifications in the teaching of children with special educational needs have recently been the subject of extensive debate at a national level. Following an initiative by those involved in further professional development for special educational needs, a report was produced which encouraged the government to set up standards of qualifications, including those for teachers of children with specific learning difficulties. This led the TTA to consult about standards, and the Agency issued guidance on this at the end of 1999 (Teacher Training Agency, 1999). The TTA proposals covered "Core" standards, which apply across the range of teaching in special educational needs, and "Extension" standards, which apply to the education of pupils with particular needs. The Extension Standards cover four dimensions of need—communication and interaction; cognition and learning; behavioral, emotional, and social development; and sensory and physical development. This approach to special needs education is intended to ensure an approach which avoids a simplistic focus on particular disability labels. It is evident that specialist teaching for specific learning difficulties will require a coverage of all these four dimensions, with varying emphasis for individual pupils. Those responsible for College and University Specialist qualifications in special needs education will now be required to take into consideration these standards in planning the content and methods of their courses. At the time of writing, the government department responsible for education has just taken over responsibility for further professional development in special educational needs from the TTA.

CONCLUSION

The topic of specific learning difficulties has raised dilemmas in Britain as in other countries. The dilemmas relate both to conceptual and to provision issues. Conceptually, there are dilemmas about reconciling the various causal explanations, and particularly how these apply to the needs of those who are engaged in providing practical support for children. The dilemmas relating to provision derive from the often conflicting aims of inclusion and of matching provision to need—quite apart from the constraints of funding. In addition, the dilemmas in provision relate to the problems of achieving equity for the individual and for the wider population of those with special educational needs. In Britain, as is evident from the above, there is currently a policy to increase schools' capacity generally to respond to individual pupils' needs. A degree of progress has definitely been achieved, but even this progress is sometimes hampered by the consequences of countervailing policies.

REFERENCES

Advisory Committee on Handicapped Children. (1972). *Children with specific reading difficulties.* London: Her Majesty's Stationary Office.

Arcelus, J., Munden, A. C., McLaughlin, A., Vickery, L., & Vostanis, P. (2000). Attention deficit hyperactivity disorder, behavioural and emotional problems in children excluded from mainstream education: A preliminary study of teachers' ratings. *European Journal of Special Needs Education, 15*(1), 79–87.

British Psychological Society. (1999). *Dyslexia, literacy and psychological assessment.* Leicester: British Psychological Society.

Contact a Family Website. (2000). www.cafamily.org.uk.

Cooper, P. (1997). Biology, behaviour and education: ADHD and the bio-psycho-social perspective. *Educational and Child Psychology, 14*(1), 31–38.

Cruickshank, W. M. (1961). *A teaching method for brain-injured and hyperactive children.* Syracuse

University special education and rehabilitation monograph series 6. Syracuse: Syracuse University Press.

Department for Education. (1994). *The code of practice on the identification and assessment of special educational needs.* London: Department for Education.

Department for Education and Employment (DFEE). (1998). *Meeting special educational needs: A programme of action.* London: DFEE.

Department for Education and Employment (DFEE). (2000). *The management, role and training of learning support assistants.* London: DFEE.

Department of Education and Science. (1978). *Special educational needs (the Warnock Report).* London: Her Majesty's Stationary Office.

Dockrell, J., & Lindsay, G. (2000). Meeting the needs of children with specific speech and language difficulties. *European Journal of Special Needs Education, 15*(1), 24–41.

Evans, J. (2000). Personal communication.

Henderson, S. (1995). Children with specific perceptuo-motor difficulties: where do we stand now? In I. Lunt & B. Norwich (Eds.), *Psychology and education for special needs* (pp. 25–44). Aldershot: Arena, Ashgate Publishing Co.

Lewis, A., Neill, R. S. S., & Campbell, R. J. (1996). *The implementation of the Code of Practice in primary and secondary schools.* Warwick: University of Warwick.

OFSTED (Office for Standards in Education). (1999). *Pupils with specific learning difficulties in mainstream schools.* London: OFSTED.

Teacher Training Agency. (1999). *National special educational needs specialist standards.* London: The Teacher Training Agency.

Wedell, K. (1973). *Learning and perceptuo-motor disabilities in children.* London: John Wiley.

Wedell, K. (1975). Specific learning difficulties. In K. Wedell (Ed.), *Orientations in special education* (pp. 59–70). London: Wiley.

Wedell, K. (1995). *Putting the Code of Practice into practice: Meeting special educational needs in the school and classroom.* London: Institute of Education, University of London.

Wedell, K., Stevens, C., Waller, T., & Matheson, L. (1997). SENCOs sharing questions and solutions, *British Journal of Special Education, 24*(4), 167–170.

Wedell, K. (1999). Points from the SENCO Forum: Ritalin, *British Journal of Special Education, 26*(3), 170.

Chapter 15

Learning Disabilities in Japan

Masayoshi Tsuge
The National Institute of Special Education

PREFACE

The Ministry of Education Science, Sports and Culture's (hereinafter referred to as the Ministry of Education) Conference of Cooperators in the Study of Children with Learning Disabilities and Similar Difficulties in Learning presented its final report in 1999 (Ministry of Education, 1999d). According to this report, the establishment of a system in Japan for educating children with learning disabilities has entered the stage of concrete work. At present, children receiving special education in Japan represent slightly over 1% of all school children. This figure represents children who are taught at special schools for children with visual impairments, speech and hearing handicaps, and intellectual and physical disabilities and health impairments, in special classes set up in elementary and middle schools and in some resource rooms. Children with learning disabilities are not covered by special education. However, in recent years, concurrent with the heightening interest in education for children with learning disabilities, there has been the introduction of the idea of inclusion. Consequently, people have begun to demand special education services for children in regular classes, something that had not been discussed expressly in Japan heretofore.

The Ministry of Education, academic institutions (The National Institute of Special Education [NISE], universities, etc.), the Japanese Academy of Learning Disabilities, the National Association of Parents of Children with Learning Disabilities, and schools (prefectural and municipal boards of education, educational centers, special education centers, schools) began efforts concerning learning disabilities around 1990. Fortunately, respective districts had already begun progressive trial efforts in educating children with learning disabilities at each educational level, without waiting for the aforementioned 1999 report of the Ministry of Education. In particular, along with looking for ways to provide support in regular classes, education at the elementary and middle school levels also began trial efforts, such as the use of resource rooms and special classes. On the other hand, there are no similar support systems at the senior high school level, where only the upper divisions of special schools accept children with learning disabilities in the public school system. However, several private free schools that are not authorized and operated by parents and other related persons, correspondence courses, and so on, provide education for older children with learning disabilities. In addition, at the university and junior college level, a public support system has not yet been established for students with any type of disability, and support for students with learning disabilities is being provided on a trial basis as a part of research projects.

Regular education has begun to change greatly as the twenty first century has approached. Now, it is difficult to imagine that the discussion of education for children with learning disabilities will be carried out only from the perspective of special education. Rather, it will probably not be possible to avoid cooperation between or a blending of regular education and special education. In addition, when this is done hereafter, it will probably be necessary to link basic research, educational administration, and educational practice, which seem to have been advanced independently, keeping a degree of distance from each other to date.

INTRODUCTION

In July 1999, the Conference of Cooperators in the Study of Children with Learning Disabilities and Similar Difficulties in Learning, set up by the Ministry of Education, issued a report on "Instruction for Children with Learning Disabilities." Heretofore, Japan had not provided special education for children with learning disabilities and similar children who were mainly enrolled in regular classes. However, the report clearly indicated the way education for learning disabilities should be hereafter in Japan. Therefore, it is hope that the establishment and practical application of education for children with learning disabilities in Japan will progress in the future.

The History of Learning Disabilities in Japan

The Brain-Injured Child in Home, School, and Community, a book by William M. Cruickshank (Cruickshank, 1967), was translated into Japanese and published in Japan in 1974. A later edition, entitled *Learning Disabilities in Home, School, and Community,* was translated and published in 1980. It should be noted that from the 1970s to the early 1980s, the term *learning disabilities* almost never arose as a topic of concern in Japan, even in schools or educational administration, not to mention research. Therefore, there was great significance to the fact that Cruickshank's books were translated and introduced during such times. However, this is not to say that efforts in relevant fields began quickly as a result. It was not until the latter half of the 1980s that we were able to perceive definite action. It is safe to say that Japan began to take full-fledged action concerning learning disabilities with the establishment of the National Association of Parents of Children with Learning Disabilities in 1990. In addition, from about this time newspapers and other media increased their introduction of this topic, and there was rapidly heightened interest in learning disabilities from people concerned from various standpoints. Therefore, educational administration, academic research, and educational practice regarding learning disabilities eventually commenced. In other words, the Ministry of Education issued the aforementioned report in about the tenth year since the various relevant fields concretely began to take action.

Heightened Interest in Learning Disabilities

Interest in learning disabilities heightened rapidly during the 1990s, as seen by such things as advancing research; publication of books for teachers, parents and guardians; and introductions through television and other media. At the same time, people in Japan began to learn of research and educational practice concerning support for children with learning disabilities and similar developments in the United States and other countries, including legislation and litigation, supporting these efforts.

The International Standard of Inclusion

One extremely important event during the 1990s was the introduction into Japan of the idea of inclusion. Related academic societies and periodicals promptly introduced the contents of the 1993 United Nations resolution concerning inclusion ("48/95, Positive and full inclusion of persons with disabilities in all aspects of society and the leadership role of the United Nations therein") and the 1994 Salamanca Statement. Therefore, the concept of inclusion quickly became common knowledge among researchers, educators, people in charge of educational administration, and other concerned parties. Furthermore, people in Japan also began to learn that, as a result of this ideology, basic research, educational practice, and educational administration in western and Asian countries had already begun to advance in the direction of inclusion. Therefore, it is predicted that the international standard of inclusion will have substantial impact on the state of special education in Japan in the future. I believe that Japan has arrived at the point at which it needs to examine how it will incorporate the concept of inclusion in the special education and regular education systems.

The Past and Coming 10 Years

As described above, along with the unexpectedly great advances made, a variety of new problems have also become evident in the various relevant fields over the past 10 years. In particular, it has become clear that the framework of Japan's conventional special education program cannot adequately accommodate education for children with learning disabilities because there is not partnership between regular education and special education in Japan. We know that it will also be important to promote the blending of special education and regular education hereafter, and we have come to sense that inclusion is in fact an important keyword in Japan's overall educational reform. In this way, if the 10 years from 1990 to 1999 constituted the period from the start to the search for the way to carry out learning disabilities education in Japan, then the 10 years from 2000 to 2009 probably can be considered the period of its substantial preparation and enrichment (Tsuge, 1999).

The Objective and Methodology of This Paper

Based on the above, my objective is to examine the future direction of learning disabilities education in Japan in the various related fields, along with surveying its progress to date and its current state. In order to gain a grasp of not only learning disabilities education, but also the state of education in other countries, it will be important to conduct a comprehensive analysis from three standpoints: basic research, educational administration, and educational practice (Tsuge, 1998). Therefore, I proceed with a comprehensive analysis from those three perspectives.

EDUCATIONAL SYSTEM

Regular Educational System

Japan implements the 6-3-3 system—six years of elementary school, three years of middle school, and three years of senior high school—and the nine years in elementary and middle school are compulsory education. Senior high school is not compulsory. However, according to a Ministry of Education survey, as of 1999 the ratio of students who go on to senior high school was 97% and the ratio of students who go on to a four-year university or two-year junior college was 49%. Also, most children spend several years in a kindergarten or nursery school prior to entering elementary school. The Ministry of Education stipulates the curriculum at each level, from kindergarten to senior high school, and textbooks for each subject taught are provided based on the respective curricula. Prefectures form their own curricula on the basis of the Ministry of Education's curriculum, and this is used as the standard for the curriculum of each school (Ministry of Education, 1999e).

Special Education System

Children receiving special education represent slightly over 1% of all school children. Special education is provided in three settings: special schools (for children with visual impairments, speech and hearing handicaps, and intellectual and physical disabilities and health impairments), special classes, and resource rooms. There are no special education services provided in regular classes. Although special schools are available at the elementary, middle, and senior high school levels, there are none at the senior high school level. There is one national junior college for students with visual impairments and speech and hearing handicaps, but there is no public system established for special education services in institutions of higher learning, such as regular universities and junior colleges. In addition, the educational cost per pupil enrolled at a special school is over 9.5 million yen a year, over ten times the approximately 900,000 yen per pupil receiving regular education at an elementary or a middle school (Ministry of Education, 1999c).

Relationship Between Regular and Special Education

A variety of efforts is being put into practice to coordinate regular and special education. There is a program of joint activities in which children in special classes in elementary and middle schools learn in regular classes. There are joint activities that students in special schools and regular kindergartens and elementary, middle, and senior high schools participate in. There is education to promote understanding, which aims to help children in regular classes understand children and adults with disabilities. There is also a program of personnel exchange between regular class teachers and teachers of special classes at elementary and middle schools and special schools. Although most teachers return to teaching regular classes in a few years, some teachers remain engaged in the field of special education for a long time, obtaining special education certificates or undergoing specialized training. In addition, in accordance with the revision of the Teachers' Certificate Law, students who began studying at universities in April 1999 will be required to study subjects related to special education regardless of the educational level—kindergarten, or elementary, middle, or senior high school—or the subject in which they major.

HISTORY AND CURRENT STATE OF LD EDUCATION

Table 15.1 indicates the history of educational administration, academic research, and educational practice for learning disabilities in Japan.

Ministry of Education

In 1992, the final report of the Conference of Cooperators in the Study of Resource Rooms recognized learning disabilities, and in the same year the Ministry of Education established the Conference of Cooperators in the Study of Instructional Methods for Children with Learning Disabilities and Similar Learning Difficulties. As a result of this, several schools nationwide began experimental learning disabilities programs. The interim report in 1995 defined learning disabilities (Ministry of Education, 1995). Thereafter, the Ministry of Education prepared public information leaflets (Ministry of Education, 1996) and instruction books for teachers (Ministry of Education, 1997). Furthermore, several districts experimentally began circulating guidance offered by specialists. In 1999, the aforementioned conference submitted its final report, which included items such as a revision of the definition of learning disabilities, a plan to diagnose and evaluate students, an examination of instructional methods, an examination of the support system (placement), and the establishment of learning disabilities committees within schools and professional committees outside of schools.

TABLE 15.1
History of Education Policy, Academic Research, and Educational
Practice for Learning Disabilities (LD) in Japan

Year	Field	Contents
1989	R	Japanese Association of Special Education sets up a learning disabilities division at its annual conference.
1990	P	The National Association of Parents of Children with Learning Disabilities is founded.
	G	The Ministry of Education inaugurates the Conference of Cooperators in the Study of Regular Classes, and studies measures to support children with learning disabilities or related difficulties in this Conference.
	E	Miharashidai Gakuen, a free school for LD children, is founded in Aichi Prefecture.
1991	E	Hisho, a free school for LD children, is founded in Kanagawa Prefecture.
	R	The National Institute of Special Education begins the Special Research Project: Subtype and Intervention Research on Pupils and Students with Learning Difficulties in Specific Academic Skills (1991–1994) (nationwide survey conducted).
1992	R	The Japanese Academy of Learning Disabilities is founded and holds its first annual conference.
	G	The Ministry of Education inaugurates the Conference of Cooperators in the Study of Children with Learning Disabilities and Similar Difficulties in Learning.
	E	Schools cooperating with the study are established in several prefectures and educational practice trials begin.
1995	R	The National Institute of Special Education begins its Special Research Project: Intervention Research on Children with Learning Difficulties (1995–1998).
	G	The National Institute of Special Education holds workshops for instructors in learning disabilities. The workshops is open to instructional directors and others, of boards of education and Special Education Centers nationwide. The workshops is held every year thereafter.
1996	G	The Ministry of Education prepares and distributes a leaflet introducing the definition, and more, of learning disabilities.
1997	G	The Ministry of Education prepares and distributes a pamphlet on instructional methods for children with learning disabilities or related difficulties.
1998	G	The Ministry of Education's Council on Curriculum discusses learning disabilities in its report and points out the necessity of enlightenment and individual instructional plans.
	G	The Course of Study is revised (for kindergartens and elementary and middle schools).

(Continued)

TABLE 15.1

(*Continued*)

Year	Field	Contents
1999	G	The Course of Study is revised (for senior high schools and special schools).
	R	The National Institute of Special Education begins its Special Research Project: Intervention Research on Actual Conditions, Instructional Methods, and Support Systems for Children with Learning Disabilities (1999–2002).
	E	A private senior high school using the correspondence course system is opened for students with learning disabilities.
	G	The Ministry of Education's Conference of Cooperators in the Study of Children with Learning Disabilities and Similar Difficulties in Learning submits its final report.
2000	G	The Ministry of Education publicizes in its public information bulletin the proposal that the existing Special Education Division will become the Special Supportive Education Division as a result of the organizational reform of the Ministry.
	E	As a result of the Ministry of Education's report on learning disabilities, model projects are instituted in several prefectures nationwide.

Note: G: educational administration, R: academic research, E: educational practice, P: parents' association

The National Institute of Special Education (NISE)

Special Research Phase 1 (1991–1994), "Subtype and Intervention Research on Pupils and Students with Learning Difficulties in Specific Academic Skills," revealed that close to 10% of children at the fifth- and sixth-grade level in elementary school lagged behind by two or more years in Japanese language and arithmetic (NISE, 1995). The following Special Research Phase 2 (1995–1998), "Intervention Research on Children with Learning Difficulties," suggested that along with direct instruction for children with learning disabilities or related difficulties, it is important to take an ecological approach that includes support for teachers, classes, schools, families, districts, and so forth (NISE, 1999). Furthermore, NISE has commenced with Special Research Phase 3 (1999–2002), "Intervention Research on Actual Conditions, Instructional Methods and Support Systems for Children with Learning Disabilities." In addition, NISE conducts five-day workshops for those teachers who are in charge of education for children with learning disabilities or related difficulties, every year for about 100 participants. This course is open to instructional directors of boards of education, special education centers, and educational centers nationwide, and teachers fulfilling a leadership role in school education.

Academic Research

Beginning about 1990, research concerning education for students with learning disabilities by individuals and project teams increased. This was strongly related to the setting up of a learning disabilities division at the 1989 conference of the Japanese Association of Special Education and the establishment of the Japanese Academy of Learning Disabilities in 1992. In addition, important studies in various fields have been amassed; for example, both of these Japanese academic societies have issued reports on research concerning assessment, instructional methods, support systems, regional resources, and so forth at their annual conferences (Tsuge, 1997, 2000).

Japanese Academy of Learning Disabilities

The Academy held its first conference in 1992. Since then, in addition to holding a conference every year, it publishes its journal twice a year and a newsletter regularly. Following its two-day annual conference, it conducts a one-day study program that deals with timely topics such as assessment techniques and employment for teachers and concerned parties.

National Association of Parents of Children with Learning Disabilities

The Liaison Conference of the National Association of Parents of Children with Learning Disabilities (later renamed the National Association of Parents of Children with Learning Disabilities) was established in 1990. It was initially composed of nine organizations and had about 300 members. At present, the membership is close to 3,000. The annual conference of the Japanese Academy of Learning Disabilities has publicized this parents' association and holds symposiums and other meetings and events from the standpoint of guardians. In addition, representatives of the parents' association participate in the special research projects by NISE, which were mentioned earlier, as research cooperators.

Regional Educational Administration

Special education centers and educational centers in the prefectures have begun to increase their educational consultations concerning learning disabilities. Coupled with this, they have begun surveys to ascertain the actual state of learning disabilities and studies to determine the way instruction should be provided. Moreover, in many districts the fruits of these efforts have led to the preparation of leaflets and instruction books and the distribution of these materials to schools. Furthermore, a variety of training courses have been established that mainly target teachers of regular classes. However, regions differ greatly in the state of their progress in tackling learning disabilities.

CURRENT STATE OF LD EDUCATION

At present, Japan does not have a special public support system for students with learning disabilities. Fortunately, districts nationwide have already made various preparations in the public education system, and there is a valuable accumulation of endeavors.

Kindergartens and Nursery Schools

In kindergarten and nursery school, there are no special classrooms, such as resource rooms or special classes; instead, education for students with learning disabilities is integrated into regular classes. There is not always a special support system available, and the differences between districts and schools are great. Depending on the municipality or school, special considerations may be made, such as stationing additional teachers or providing training.

Elementary Schools

At the elementary level, several schools have set up resource rooms or special classes. And special classes have incorporated programs of joint activities with regular classes. Only 0.32% of children are served in resource rooms, and 46% of schools have special classes (Ministry of Education, 1999f, 1999g). In addition, there are schools that provide support in the form of team teaching in regular classes. However, this is not always support that specializes in learning disabilities. Some municipalities have begun to allocate their own funds to post assistant teachers in regular classes that include children with learning disabilities or who require related special support.

Middle Schools

Special education in middle school for students with learning disabilities is basically the same as for elementary schools. However, only 0.02% of the pupils use resource rooms, a much lower percent when compared with elementary schools. Forty-eight percent of middle schools have special classes, about the same percent as elementary schools (Ministry of Education, 1999f, 1999g). In addition, because middle schools employ a system of teachers by subjects, in which each teacher teaches one subject, there are difficulties in providing support that are not encountered by elementary schools.

Senior High Schools

In addition to regular high schools, there are vocational high schools, such as industrial, commercial, and agricultural high schools. Moveover, besides completely day high schools, which conduct classes during the day, there are part-time high schools, which conduct classes at night. Unlike elementary and middle schools, high schools do not have resource rooms or special classes. Although we think students with learning disabilities or related difficulties are enrolled in high schools as well, surveys of the actual conditions concerning such students have only been conducted partially. In addition, it is conceivable that these students are also enrolled in the upper divisions of special schools or special senior high schools.

Universities, Junior Colleges

There is no public support system for students with learning disabilities at the postsecondary level. In addition, there has been no survey of actual conditions concerning such students conducted at the higher education level.

Private Schools

Although they are not certified as private or public schools, several free schools for children with learning disabilities at the middle and senior high school division levels have been established since 1990. In addition, a correspondence system high school was established in 1999.

EDUCATIONAL REFORM AND LD

Education in the Future

In the latter half of the 1990s, organizations such as the Central Council on Education, the Teacher Development Council, and the Council on Curriculum have issued reports. In 1998 and 1999, the Ministry of Education issued a new Course of Study for kindergartens; elementary, middle, and senior high schools; and special schools (Ministry of Education, 1998a, 1998b, 1998c, 1999a, 1999b). In the field of special education, the new Course of Study discusses enrichment of education for children with relatively mild disabilities by means of such things as education through resource rooms and special classes, and support for children with learning disabilities. Furthermore, it promotes for the first time programs of joint activities with children with disabilities even in regular education. It establishes time for general learning, whereby topics such as social welfare activities can be dealt with. In addition, it has begun to require that all university students wishing to become teachers, not only those wishing to become special education teachers, take courses that cover special education, and to introduce practical training at special schools or welfare institutions. These are all changes that are related to both regular and special education or to their blending. At present, there is an attempt to make substantial changes in education in Japan.

Furthermore, several of the aforementioned topics appear to be related to problems in regular education that have rapidly begun to be addressed as major social problems. These include the decline in the scholastic abilities of elementary, middle, and senior high school and university students; the collapse of classrooms in elementary and middle schools; and long-term student absences at elementary, middle, and senior high schools (more than 30 days per year). These problems are espacially acute with regard to learning disabilities. Some prefectures have begun to discuss and actually look for solutions to the problems of class size and school choice and the improvement of teaching quality. In addition, there is heightening interest in schools similar to the charter schools in the United States, which, although being public schools, have a high degree of freedom in many areas, such as curriculum, personnel matters, and financial affairs. These developments are in line with the direction of the aforementioned report by the Central Council on Education, which pointed out the necessity of expanding the degree of freedom of regional boards of education from the national government and of schools from regional boards of education.

Ministry of Education Report

In July 1999, the Ministry of Education's Conference of Cooperators in the Study of Children with Learning Disabilities and Similar Difficulties in Learning issued its final report (Ministry of Education, 1999d). This report revised the definition of learning disabilities presented in its interim report and discussed the assessment of learning disabilities; tentative standards for diagnosing learning disabilities; and instructional methods, forms, and venues of instruction for children with learning disabilities. The definition of learning disabilities presented was: "learning disabilities are a variety of conditions that indicate marked difficulty in acquiring or using a specific ability from among the following: listening, speaking, reading, writing, calculating or reasoning, although there is basically no delay in general intellectual development" (p. 3). The report did not cover the problems related to movements and gestures. Regarding the assessment and diagnosis of learning disabilities, the report presented a concrete tentative plan composed of a two-step process in which actual conditions are ascertained in the school and a team of outside experts makes an assessment. Regarding instructional methods for children with learning disabilities, along with presenting concrete examples, the report called for ongoing research by institutions such as NISE. Lastly, regarding forms and venues of instruction for children with learning disabilities, it deemed instruction in regular classes as the basic venue of instruction. However, it also recommended ongoing research on the use of team teaching and the establishment of venues of instruction that would be similar to "instruction through regular classes." Furthermore, the report asks NISE to study the ideal way to provide training to educate specialists, as well as to study the program of providing circulating guidance by specialists.

This report tentatively presented the direction for education of students with learning disabilities in Japan and its requirements. However, there is not universal agreement on who should be identified as learning disabled, as seen by the fact that the preface states that "we noticed that when discussing learning disabilities, there were situations where even learned people did not necessarily have the same targets in mind." This will produce difficulties in studying instructional methods and support systems and in educational administration and financing.

Necessary Conditions of LD Education Sought Hereafter

Sought from Educational Administration

Regular education and special education should be blended further in the future. Therefore, some specific concerns of the very near future are the further enrichment of education to promote conceptual and programmatic integration of regular and special education, the enrichment of lectures and practical training in related fields at the teacher education level, and on-the-job training for teachers of regular classes. When carrying out these enrichments, there should be a shift to considering what special educational needs exist, rather than being bound by the conventional framework of children with and without learning disabilities. Within that framework, it is necessary to begin studying problems such as the assessment of persons who qualify as having learning disabilities and the state of actual support provided. In addition, regarding the current plan for the organizational reform of the Ministry of Education, which is related to the reorganization of central government ministries and agencies planned to be instituted in January 2001, the proposal presented would have the existing Special Education Division become the Special Supportive Education Division (Ministry of Education, 2000). It is inevitable that this will have a major impact on measures concerning learning disabilities.

Sought from Academic Research

Along with basic and experimental research concerning effective instructional methods, we need research concerning the effectiveness of diverse instructional systems from an ecological point of view (Speece & Keogh, 1996). In order to ascertain the direction of research within the country and look toward its future direction, we need to survey domestic research trends and promote meta-analysis (Swanson, 1999; Tsuge, 1997, 2000). Next, although international comparative research is already gradually beginning, covering fields such as administration, research, and educational practice (Tsuge & Keogh, 1999, 2000; Tsuge, 2000), more will be demanded in the future. Furthermore, introducing the results of Japanese research on learning disabilities (Abe, 1998; Simahara & Sasaki, 1995; Takizawa, 1998; Tsuge, Kiyonaga, & Nakamura, 1998) broadly to the world and receiving a variety of comments on them will suggest to Japan its direction for the future. In addition, the research will be part of the basic data that countries that will be starting special education and learning disabilities programs hereafter can use.

Sought from Educational Practice

First, it is important that schools further promote the accumulation of curricula and instructional methods that meet the needs of students with learning disabilities. At the same time, it is important to look for a variety of support programs within schools. Furthermore, regional educational administration organizations need to set up and facilitate the function of committees of experts outside schools, and promote collaboration with nearby universities, special institutions, and, in certain cases, hospitals. Along with this, regional educational administration organizations should plan periodic surveys to monitor the current state and problems of support programs in schools under their jurisdiction. This will lead to the establishment of a support system for learning disabilities that corresponds to actual regional circumstances. When doing this, special attention should be paid to promoting cooperation between regular education teachers and special education teachers, and between teachers and other specialists. In addition, it is important that there be common recognition that it is important to endeavor to determine what special educational needs an individual has, rather than spend a lot of time determining whether or not the individual has a learning disability, and to assess what kind of support to provide for that disability.

Blending of Regular and Special Education and Cooperation among Concerned Institutions

Special education and regular education have independently dealt with education for children exhibiting learning difficulties. Hereafter, not only should the two approach the same problem from their separate perspectives, but they should also combine their knowledge and, to begin with, blend their approaches (Tsuge, 1999). Furthermore, a strengthening of the relationships among administration, research, and educational practice will be sought even more strongly in the future (Carnine, 1997; Keogh, 1999).

CONCLUSION

Moa-in, a school for people with visual, speech, and hearing impairments, opened in Kyoto in 1878, during the Meiji era. Ever since then, Japan has been quick to establish special education programs and has established and enriched its special education system. In particular, various forms of support, such as through special schools and special classes at elementary and middle schools, form the core of this system. As a result, at present, children receiving special education represent slightly over 1% of all school children. Furthermore, parallel to these programs, the Ministry of Education has established departments and universities to train special education teachers in prefectures nationwide. It has also set up prefectural and municipal Special Education Centers and carried out training for teachers, research, and educational consultation. However, in recent years there have been strong calls to establish an educational system for children with mild disabilities who are mainly enrolled in regular classes. This would include children with learning disabilities, mild intellectual disabilities, advanced functional autism, and mild behavioral problems who are mainly enrolled in regular classes.

In 1963, Dr. Kirk gave a speech that is considered to be the start of interest in the learning disabilities field in the United States. Close to

40 years have elapsed since then. Meanwhile, it has been only 10 years since learning disabilities education began in Japan. Nevertheless, its development over these 10 years is extremely similar to development in the field in the United States since 1963 (Tsuge & Keogh, 1999). Therefore, when considering future learning disabilities education in Japan, it will be very useful to study the current state and process of establishing and enriching learning disabilities programs in other countries, including the United States, which has enjoyed early success in this field. In addition, it is hoped that Japan will take into consideration its geography, culture, and natural features as a country, and the position of learning disabilities programs in its overall educational system as it builds and nurtures its own learning disabilities education system.

REFERENCES

Abe, Y. (1998). Special education reform in Japan. *European Journal of Special Educational Needs Education, 13,* 86–97.

Carnine, D. (1997). Bridging the research-to-practice gap. *Exceptional Children, 63,* 513–521.

Cruickshank, W. M. (1967). *The brain-injuted child in home, school, and community.* Syracuse, NY: Syracuse University Press.

Keogh, B. K. (1999). Reflections on a research career: One thing leads to another. *Exceptional Children, 65,* 295–300.

Ministry of Education. (1995). Gakusyushogai oyobi koreni ruijisuru gakusyujyou no konnan wo yuusuru jidouseito no sidouhouhou ni kansuru tyousakyouryokusya Kaigi: tyukan houkoku [Interim report of the Conference of Cooperators in the Study of Children with Learning Disabilities and Similar Difficulties in Learning].

Ministry of Education. (1996). Gakusyushougai(LD) ji tou no rikai ni mukete: Mistumeyou hitorihitori wo -Gakusyuujyou tokubestuna hairyga hituyouna kodomotati [Toward understanding children with learning disabilities (LD): Looking at each child-Children requiring special learning considerations].

Ministry of Education. (1997). Gakusyushougai(LD) ji tou no rikai ni mukete: Mistumeyou hitorihitori wo -Gakusyuujyou tokubestuna hairyga hituyouna kodomotati [Understanding and teaching children with learning disabilities (LD): Looking at each child-Children requiring special learning considerations].

Ministry of Education. (1998a). Youchien kyouiku Youryou [Kindergarten course of study].

Ministry of Education. (1998b). Shougakkou gakusyu sidou youryou [Elementary school course of study].

Ministry of Education. (1998c). Chugakkou gakusyu sidou youryou [Middle school course of study].

Ministry of Education. (1999a). Koutougakkou gakusyu sidou youryou [Senior high school course of study].

Ministry of Education. (1999b). Mougakkou, rougakkou oyobi yougogakkou youchibu kyouiku youryou, syougakubu & chugakubu gakusyuu sidou youryou, & koutoubu gakusyu sidou youryou [Kindergarten course of study, elementary and middle division course of study, and senior high division course of study for special schools for children with visual impairments, special schools for children with speech and hearing handicaps, and special schools for children with intellectual disabilities, physical disabilities, and health impairments].

Ministry of Education. (1999c). Ikiruchikara wo hagukumu tameni [To encourage zest for living—Special education in Japan].

Ministry of Education. (1999d). Gakusyu shogaiji ni taisuru sidou nituite: Gakusyushogai oyobi koreni ruijisuru gakusyuujyou no konnan wo yuusuru jidouseito no sidouhouhou ni kansuru tyousakyouryokusya kaigi saisyuuhoukoku [Instruction for children with learning disabilities: Final report of the Conference of Cooperators in the Study of Children with Learning Disabilities and Similar Difficulties in Learning].

Ministry of Education. (1999e). Education in Japan 2000 -Graphic Presentation -Gyosei.

Ministry of Education. (1999f). Gakkou kihon chousa houkokusyo (Heisei 11 nendo) [Basic survey report on schools (1999)].

Ministry of Education. (1999g). Tokusyu kyouiku siryou (Heisei 10 nendo) [Special education information (1998)].

Ministry of Education. (2000). Monbu kouhou, Heisei 12 nen 1 gatsu 25 nichi gou (No.1016) [Ministry of Education public information, January 25, 2000 edition (No.1016)].

National Institute of Special Education. (1995). Tokubestu kenkyu: kyoukagakusyu ni tokuina konnan wo shimesu jidouseito no ruikeika to sidouhouhou ni kannsuru kenkyu [Special research report: Subtype and intervention research on pupils and students with learning difficulties in specific academic skills].

National Institute of Special Education. (1999). Tokubestu kenkyu: Gakusyu konnanji no shidouhouhou ni kansuru jisshouteki kenkyu [Special research report: Intervention research on children with learning difficulties].

Simahara, N., & Sasaki, A. (1995) *Learning to teach in two cultures: Japan and the United States.* NY & London: Garland Publishing.

Speece, D. L., & Keogh, B. K. (1996). *Research on classroom ecologies: Implications for inclusion of children with learning disabilities.* Mahwah, NJ: Lawrence Erlbaum Associates.

Swanson, H. L. (1999). *Interventions for students with learning disabilities: A meta-analysis of treatment outcomes.* New York: Guilford Press.

Takizawa, S. (1998). Current status of learning disabilities and teacher training problems in Japan. *Annual Report, Faculty of Education, Hokkaido University, Japan, 21,* 43–45.

Tsuge, M. (1997). "Journal of Learning Disabilities" ni Mirareru Kenkyu Doukou ni Kansuru Chousa Kenkyu -1968(Soukan), 1978, 1988, 1995 nen no 4 ki wo Tooshite- [Analysis of Research Trends in the *Journal of Learning Disabilities: 1968* (1st issue), 1978, 1988, and 1995]. *The National Institute of Special Education Research Bulletin, 24,* 117–126.

Tsuge, M. (1998). *Research on educational support system for adolescents with learning difficulties in California, U.S.A.* Unpublished visiting report, University of California, Los Angeles.

Tsuge, M. (1999) Nihon ni okeru gakkou kyouiku to LD: Koremadeno 10 nen, korekarano 10 nen [School education and learning disabilities: Toward next ten years in Japan]. *Japanese Academy of Learning Disabilities Journal; Learning Disabilities Research and Practical Application, 8*(1), 2–8.

Tsuge, M. (2000). *Research Trends in Major Journals for Learning Disabilities in Japan and USA.* CEC Special Education World Congress 2000, Vancouver, Canada.

Tsuge, M., & Keogh, B. K. (1999). *Special education services for students with learning disabilities in Japan and the U.S.A.: A Comparison.* YAI/National Institute for People with Disabilities, 20th annual international conference, New York.

Tsuge, M. & Keogh, B. K. (2000). Minami California no chugakkou to koutougakkou niokeru sapooto nikansuru chousa kenkyu: Tujyou gakkyu, risousu ruumu, oyobi tokusyu gakkyu no kyoushi to gakkouchou heno chousa [Study concerning support in middle and senior high schools in southern California: Questionnaire survey of teachers in regular classes, resource rooms and special classes and school principals]. *The National Institute of Special Education Research Bulletin, 27,* 101–112.

Tsuge, M., Kiyonaga, N., & Nakamura, N. (1998). *Social skill training for a child with learning difficulties under cooperation with parents and professionals.* American Association on Mental Retardation, 122nd annual conference, San Diego, CA.

ABOUT THE AUTHOR

Masayoshi Tsuge, Ph.D., is a chief of section, Section of Education for Children with Mild Intellectual Disabilities in the National Institute of Special Education, Japan. The institute is under the direct control of the Ministry of Education, Japan. Tsuge was a visiting research fellow at the University of California, Los Angeles (UCLA), under Professor B. K. Keogh, from 1997 to 1998. Professor Keogh provided tremendous support to Tsuge in the compilation of this paper.

Chapter 16

Learning Disabilities in the Netherlands

Luc M. Stevens, Ph.D.
Wim van Werkhoven, Ph.D.
Utrecht University, The Netherlands

INTRODUCTION

It was around 1970 that the concept of learning disabilities (LD) became established in the Netherlands. To a large extent influenced by the work of William Cruickshank and his pupils, there rapidly arose high expectations for the new psychoneurological orientation toward learning and behavioral problems in the classroom. These expectations were reinforced by the trust that was growing at the time in the potential of the task-analysis paradigm. In the 30 years since then, the concept has undergone major developments. This is to a large extent related to the local context. The concept of LD as such has never been included in legislation. Rather, since 1949, special schools have existed for children with learning and behavioral problems, problems that were not related to mental retardation or sensorimotor disorders. Hence, the interest in the Netherlands for the LD concept was more for the implication it had for diagnostics and treatment than for the potential offered for the social and educational emancipation of an as yet "undiscovered" group of pupils with problems in school. A differentiated system of provisions already existed for the pupils who could not satisfy the expectations of general education. However, the expectation that development of the LD concept based on scientific research would lead to differential diagnostics and treatment for the group or part of the group concerned was never fully realized. This has contributed to the gradual inclusion of the

LD concept in the Netherlands into the more general concept of "learning and behavioral problems", and to the growing preference to refer to aspects of it with terms such as *dyslexia* and *ADHD*. Such developments are, of course, related to the success of interest groups and other social forces but also to the problem priorities as formulated by schools. For instance, the term dyslexia has in the Netherlands become of topical interest through the influence of the network of parents and professionals operating under the same name. The current popularity of the diagnosis of ADHD seems for a great part attributable to the tension that schools experience between the willingness and competency of pupils to adapt and the behavioral standards that schools demand of them. These developments reflect a shift from focusing on the characteristics of a group, that can be identified according to the discrepancy criterion and described as such in more detail, to focusing on disturbances in the learning process. With this shift, the LD concept, both with respect to research and in educational practice, came to be seen in a more general context in the Netherlands.

Partly in connection with the finding that the LD concept was not of particular differential importance for treatment, a radical change in the educational policy of the Dutch government has enhanced the existing ambivalence toward the LD concept as a valid, comprehensive concept. The reason for this was the linear growth in the last two decades in the number of pupils in the elementary special schools for children with learning and behavioral problems, the majority associated with LD, and an acceleration of growth at the secondary level. This growth proved not so much an expression of the "success" of the LD concept but rather a system failure. If there is an established system of schools for special education in place and no limits are imposed on the size of a school for general or special education, the assumption can be made that such a provision will stimulate demand, especially in those cases where the diagnosis is unclear. In 1990, the Dutch government broke through this mechanism using legislation and alternative financing for special education. At the same time it removed the distinction between schools for Mild Mentally Retarded (MMR) and LD, bringing the two populations together in one setting: schools for special elementary education. The schools concerned have been integrated into networks of general schools. At the secondary level, the schools for MMR and LD have been disestablished and integrated into schools for general education.

The policy that these measures are founded on is that the care for children with learning or behavioral problems is an aspect of the quality of general education, and that it is a responsibility that is shared between special and general education. Both types of school are obligated to provide every child with the possibility of "uninterrupted" development.

This policy, defined as the striving for adaptive education, is flanked by policy with respect to the quality of education, put into practice through standards. These developments can, in summary, best be described as part of the striving toward social and curricular integration and toward more effective education. It can also be said to be an unmistakable shift of the problem focus, from the child to the educational environment.

These trends are not bound exclusively to the context as it exists in the Netherlands. They can be found in the international literature, to which Dutch researchers expressly orient themselves.

In the remainder of this article, we describe in more detail the picture given here. In doing so we roughly follow two orientations: the progress of the development of the LD concept over time and the researchers who have played an important role in that development. In this, we neither attempt to be complete, nor can we abstain from making choices. Because of the specific character of this contribution, namely the developments in the Netherlands, we mainly rely on articles that have been published in the Netherlands.

THE ESTABLISHMENT OF THE LD CONCEPT IN THE NETHERLANDS

The Netherlands is a small, open country with a highly developed governmental infrastructure and a closely knit network of professionals. Moreover, it is a country in which the resources are relatively easily accessible. These conditions promote the adaptation of new ideas and practices and the exchange of critical information, including in education. The introduction of the LD concept has demonstratively profited from this situation. The concept, as traditionally understood in North America and introduced in the Netherlands about 1970, had, however, a homegrown predecessor, developed and described in terms of a partial defect (Bladergroen, 1952). Bladergroen, who was knowledgeable of the work of Piaget, proposed a functional disorder in the development of intelligence as the possible explanation for severe problems at school. This disorder expressed itself in striking problems in sensorimotor coordination and in the ordering of space and time. These problems pointed to the dysfunctional development of the thinking and acting schemes, rooted in locomotor development, that serve as the foundation for the development of higher functions. Furthermore, Bladergroen hypothesized a link between the availability of an adequately functioning observational and locomotor apparatus and the origins of "basic security" in early development. She interpreted the neurotic fear that she observed in children with severe learning problems in this way. Although the theories regarding learning disabilities as sensorimotor or perceptuo-motor dis-orders subsequently received little support (Wedell, 1973), the (mainly clinical) work of Bladergroen broke through the idea of "lagging be-hind" in school as a homogenous phenomenon and made the way clear for a more differentiated approach. In 1970 and 1971, three influential publications on learning disabilities appeared in the Netherlands. The first (The School Readiness Curriculum, Dumont & Kok, 1970) con-cerned an extensive educational program for young children who had been identified as being not yet ready for school, but were suspected of having learning disabilities. The second is a translation of Cruickshank's *The Brain-injured Child in Home, School and Community* by the neurologist Jaap Valk under the Dutch title *Buitenbeentjes* (1970). The third con-cerned the monograph *Leerstoornissen* (Learning Disabilities) written by Dumont (1971). The three publications are in close harmony with each other with respect to the interpretation of severe and persistent learning problems as expressions of psychoneurological dysfunctions. It is true that the curriculum and the monograph have a European character due to Dumont being an expert on Piaget, but both were relatively consistent with the North American tradition of the time, referring to the work of Strauss and Lethinen, Kephart, Bateman, Cruickshank, and Myklebust. Incidentally, the references to Myklebust are interesting in the sense that with the introduction of his work (Myklebust, 1968, 1971) the focus in definition, diagnostics, and treatment of persistent learning problems in terms of the dissociation concept shifted to an interpretation in terms of auditory information processing (see also Rispens, 1974).

The translation of Cruickshank's book was a great success and would remain so for several years. It offered parents and teachers a definition of learning and behavioral problems that attributed the cause internally, Minimal Brain Dysfunction, and at the same time offered a perspective to the practice of education, the principle of stimulus reduction. William Cruickshank was a very welcome guest in the Netherlands. The first "cubicles" appeared in the special schools for children with learning and behavioral problems. The principle of stimulus reduction, translated into the prescriptive term *offering structure*, proved to be very influential for a long time in the practice of special education in the Netherlands. This influence was strengthened by the growing trust at the time in the principles of behavior modification.

The importance of the first publication mentioned, the School Readi-ness Curriculum, was mainly because it offered a model for theory-based program development that was characterized by functional observation in the classroom, and led to subsequent suggestions for treatment. In this case the observations concerned the development of the functional conditions for learning to read, to spell, and to do arithmetic in the visual and auditive domains, but also the development of a wide range of practical and social skills. The importance of the first monograph about learning disabilities from Dumont lay mainly in the definition and meaning for diagnostics and treatment. The definition of what was called by him a specific or primary learning disability was very close to the one from the American National Advisory Committee on Handicapped Children from 1967 and excluded learning disabilities as a result of mental, sensory, locomotor, emotional, and social environmental factors. The latter were referred to as "secondary learning disabilities." Dumont, who was seen as the father of the LD concept in the Netherlands, would in the years following continue to defend the specific character of learning disabilities and by doing so support the important discrepancy criterion, especially with respect to dyslexia. In 1976, Dumont formulated a definition of Learning Disabilities as primary disabilities:

> Primary learning disabilities are dysfunctions in the development processes of the sensorimotor system, perception, language, thought, memory and concentration, leading to discrepancies between actual educational results and potential educational results in reading, writing and arithmetic, in otherwise normal intelligent children without sensory disabilities, severe physical disabilities, emotional disturbance, or resulting from a severely neglected upbringing or poor education, while the cause may be assumed to be a psychoneurological dysfunction of biological, hereditary or developmental psychological nature. (p. 210, Trans. LMS)

More confidently than his fellow researchers in Dutch universities, Dumont remained attached to the most important characteristics of the original LD concept.

Characteristic of the situation described here is the amalgamation of experimental, clinical, and empirical research. The first studies were representative of this "mixed" tradition, such as the following: a study into the temporal order perception of children who learn to read slowly (Bakker, 1971); a study into the developmental conditions for learning to read, to spell, and to do arithmetic (Van der Laan, 1973); an evaluation study of the School Readiness Curriculum (Stevens, 1975); a review of studies into the effect of sensorimotor training programs (Franken, 1977); an experimental psychological study into the differential importance of neurological risk factors in young children (Kalverboer, 1975); and a study into problems with arithmetic (Borghouts-van Erp, 1978). Separately from these studies should be mentioned the publication of a comprehensive and influential task-analytical program for the training of auditory prerequisites for learning to read from In den Kleef (1975).

The development of diagnostic tests and programs, especially for young children with learning difficulties, was continued forcefully. It is striking how the Minimal Brain Dysfunction (MBD) issue faded into the background as the allied issues of language, reading, and spelling development came to the fore. Arithmetic problems also got more attention, but research into them was and still is less directed at the problem itself than at arithmetic education.

CHANGING INTEREST

One of the most important developments in the 1980s and 1990s was the reduction in interest in the behavioral characteristics of children with learning difficulties in favor of a growing interest in teaching and instruction processes and in the strategies used while learning to read, to spell, and to do arithmetic. The influence of cognitive psychology was felt. Although the need to label learning difficulties remained, the definition of LD through exclusion and the discrepancy criterion were abandoned and a more general perspective was chosen in which the development of a functional, "positive" definition was searched for. An example of this is a definition of reading difficulties as a problem "in the flexible application of reading strategies that determine the technical ability to read" (Van der Leij, 1983, p. 251, Trans. LMS). Or a definition of dyslexia as "a difficulty that arises, despite appropriate reading tuition, in the identification (the ability to decode and recognize) of written or printed words, so that it is not possible to correctly and quickly read *what is written*" (Van den Bos, 1995, p. 26, Trans. LMS). The work of the two researchers mentioned here, and also the work of Van Bon (1993) and Ruijssenaars (1995), has played an important role in the shift from a problem-group oriented approach to a functional approach.

There was a need to link the analyses of task and process, to anticipate the instructional needs of the pupils (Van der Leij, 1983), and to link up with the tradition of reading research. An example is the acceptance of the importance of results from psycholinguistic research concerning the approach to reading problems, which has found expression in the so-called bottom-up, top-down discussion. In this context, Van der Leij (1982) developed the "Look and Listen" approach to children with reading problems. This approach distanced itself from the common direct and explicit exercises of partial skills (the so-called prerequisites) and tried to use the aspects of the reading process that were relatively strongly developed in the pupil. It works not so much in a remedial, but in a compensatory way. This means that the emphasis is not on achieving partial skills, but on the end result of being able to read fluently. Because the compensatory possibilities of individual pupils differ, the term *differential instruction susceptibility* was introduced (Van der Leij, 1983; see also Van Bon, 1996). The principle of (conscious) compensation in training was for Van der Leij connected to the, from his point of view, most important problems in reading difficulties: making symbol–sound associations automatic. For him the first formed the action complement to the latter.

Another example of the interest in process research in the Netherlands in the last two decades is the work of Van den Bos (1995). He also argued for a more plain definition of learning disabilities, especially for dyslexia. "What we have in mind with a more plain definition is the creation of opportunities to efficiently give as much as possible *attention focused on reading components* to *all* pupils with reading difficulties" (p. 25, Trans. LMS). The most important components in his opinion were word identification and language comprehension. In his research Van den Bos concentrated mainly on the first component and developed a test for reading pseudo words based on the "dual route" theory: Words can be recognized via the direct or orthographic route (there is direct access to the internal lexicon), or via the indirect route of phonological decoding. The test is developed for both testing theoretical propositions and for clinical purposes. A third focus of research concerns phonemic awareness and phonemic segmentation. In this respect, we mention the work of Van Bon (1994), who mainly operates in the spelling domain. His publications concern both differential diagnostic issues and the training of segmentation skills.

In summary, one can say that in the growing tradition of the cognitive process orientation of research into reading and spelling difficulties in the Netherlands, there are three central concepts: word identification, automatization of sound and symbol association, and phonemic awareness. However, this orientation, when concerned with the demand for instruction, cannot be seen separately from a task-analysis approach. The complexity of this relationship forms the subject of recent discussions (Van den Broeck, 1997; Struiksma, 1998).

A somewhat separate place in research in the Netherlands is occupied by the experimental work of the neuropsychologist Bakker (1986), not unknown in North America. It follows in the long line of LD research based on hemisphere dominance theories. Bakker's thesis is that the processing of information in the right hemisphere is most facilitating for the initial reading process, because the perceptual aspect is more dominant in this first phase and the right hemisphere is specialized in visual–spatial processes. When reading has started then mediation by the left hemisphere is the most facilitating, because this hemisphere is better equipped for processing linguistic information. The second assumption is that the reader has a preference for processing written information in one of the two hemispheres. In 60% of the cases, Bakker thinks that he has established this in his research population of children with reading difficulties. Based on his thesis (described here in very simple terms), Bakker distinguishes two types of dyslexia: the P-type and the L-type. When reading, children with P-type dyslexia concentrate on perceptual information and move too slowly to processing the same information in the left hemisphere. Their reading remains slow but accurate. Children with L-type dyslexia have the reverse problem: when they read they mainly guess, paying little attention to the perceptual characteristics of the text, thus minimizing processing in the right hemisphere. The principle of the treatment proposed by Bakker is that for a P-dyslexic the left hemisphere is stimulated by exercises and for an L-dyslexic the right hemisphere. For those children for whom it is unclear to which type they belong, the exercises are based on the supposed development of processing from the right to the left hemisphere in learning reading. Incidentally, the exercises are for a large part based on results from task and process analysis. Bakker understandably calls his model the balance model (see also: Kappers, 1995). Although the balance model has much appeal and is generally known in the Netherlands, it is not widely practiced because of its experimental nature and the uncertainties that still exist.

The rapid developments in neurological sciences have given rise to new hypotheses about the origin of reading disabilities. In the Netherlands, relatively unique research was started in this area by Been (1994). His proposition is that there are not only surprisingly frequent disorders in the auditory system of poor readers, but that in dyslectics disorders are often also found in that part of the visual system that is responsible for pattern recognition. These disorders could be the result of so-called reductions in the system (fewer cells, fewer connections). This results in the system having a lower frequency. Problems can occur when the potential values of a continuous series of stimuli (such as text) touch the frequency of the system itself with so-called jump resonance as a result. This could explain the relative unpredictability of reading errors in dyslectics (Van den Bos, 1995). Incidentally, Been points out that the part of the visual system concerned, the magnocellular part, develops very early and therefore its integrity can be evaluated at an early stage (Been & Zwarts, 1996).

A completely different aspect of LD research concerns the attention and the motivation of pupils during instruction and when working independently. In LD research in the Netherlands, the importance of the quality of the meta-cognitive activities of the pupils during the teaching–learning process is regularly pointed out, as are the problems in this respect in children with learning difficulties. However, few researchers are explicitly engaged in this area. In this respect we mention the work of Stevens and Van Werkhoven (Stevens, 1994) that has as its subject the cognitive inactive character of learning of children with problems. Based on a cognitive motivational model, they propose that pupils who "fall behind" in the classroom, through the lack of prospect of experiencing success or the experience of competence, through low expectations of themselves (possibly mediated by low expectations of their teacher), and through unproductive attributions, can "decide" to not actively participate. It is also proposed that, in the event of problems, the increased activity of teachers to control the instruction processes and the behavior of the pupil may threaten pupils' authonomy. The help of teachers can in this manner be counterproductive.

In this context, researchers seek to understand the quality of the teacher–pupil interaction in terms of the demand for agreement in the motivational significance of a task situation for teacher and pupil. In the pedagogical sense the question should be raised as to what extent the teacher understands the motivational status of the pupil. This question appears all the more important, in view of the relationship that is assumed in the basic model between the quality of the meta-cognitive functioning and the quality of the current motivation of the pupil. For the benefit of the teacher, a strategy was developed that could support him or her in aligning his or her perspective to that of the pupil: the so-called attunement strategy (Stevens, Van Werkhoven, & Castelijns, 1997, p. 63). The importance of this is in the challenge made by the teacher to his or her pupil to put the perception of the problem into words and to make a proposal of how to tackle it. This has to do with the teacher posing the correct questions and dispensing fewer prescriptions. Experimental implementation of the concept and the strategy has received considerable appreciation from the teachers (they recognize for instance their low expectations and their need for exercising control), but an alternative approach to pupils requires considerable counseling.

We will now pay some attention to the research into arithmetic disorders in the Netherlands. The study of arithmetic disorders is not typically within the tradition of LD research. Although the chance that arithmetic disorders will occur in the group of children with LD is presumably significantly higher than in the normal population, they are rarely investigated in the Netherlands as a (possible) characteristic for the group. Arithmetic research is mainly context linked, this means that it is linked to arithmetic education (Van Luit & Ruijssenaars, 1996). Nevertheless, in the Netherlands two monographs appeared (Borghouts-van Erp, 1978; Ruijssenaars, 1992). Both are mainly concerned with arithmetic problems of young children, the developmental conditions, and intervention possibilities. An important question associated with this is to what degree partial skills and strategies can be and must be explicitly taught. The various programs that have been developed for young children, especially by Van Luit (1994), give varying results. It seems possible to speed up the development of the conditions, but the gains are not always maintained.

Finally, we draw the attention to the learning potential research that was until recently carried out in the Netherlands (Hamers, Sijtsma, & Ruijssenaars, 1993; Hamers, 1994). Although this type of research does not typically belong in the LD research tradition, the Netherlands initiative maintains a direct link to it. Learning potential research points to the problem that the discrepancy definition raises, namely the inability of intelligence tests to represent success in school tasks and the assumptions about underlying processes. Initially, the research was mainly concerned with the construction of learning tests and the question of prediction. In this phase the intelligence test tasks were still used (Hamers & Ruijssenaars, 1984). Surprising differences were found in learning curves and instructional needs. Steps were taken to make the tasks more similar to the tasks that are specific for the learning process in school: curriculum-bound tasks. Examples of these are the ability to be sufficiently task oriented, to manipulate auditive material, to learn grapheme–phoneme correspondences, to discover and learn to apply rules and learning to solve problems that demand simultaneous and successive information processing (Ruijssenaars, 1994). The propositions were addressed further in two detailed partial studies (Tissink, 1993; Hessels, 1993). The most successful result of this was the so-called learning test for ethnic minorities (LEM). A program for inductive thinking came about as a consequence of the work concerning the construction of the learning test (Hamers & Overtoom, 1997).

TWO MILESTONES IN THE HISTORY OF LD IN THE NETHERLANDS AND THE CONTINUATION OF THE DEBATE

Professor Joep Dumont died in January 1994. We see this event as a milestone in the sense of a break in the continuity of the discussion about the nature, the definition, and the practice of diagnostics and treatment of learning disabilities. Neither the discrepancy criterion nor the exclusivity criterion will be defended by anyone so strongly as he defended them. The break is felt especially where Dumont showed himself to be a protagonist of a living and lively relationship between researchers themselves and between scientific research and the practice of caring for children with learning disabilities. He was also the person who in 1985 took the initiative for the, renowned in the Netherlands, annual congress on dyslexia. It was his intention "with regard to both the description and determination of what dyslexia is and to the suitability and effectiveness of dyslexia treatment to achieve more consensus" (Van der Leij, 1996, p. 11, Trans. LMS). For educational practice, the death of Dumont marked the end of a period in which learning problems were a high priority for teachers. The emotional and behavioral problems in the classroom now have become his or her most important concern.

A second milestone concerns the advice from the Dutch National Health Council with respect to diagnostics and treatment of dyslexia (Ruijssenaars & Gersons-Wolfensberger, 1995; Gersons-Wolfensberger & Ruijssenaars, 1997). This council decides on a descriptive working definition of dyslexia. "The council recognizes dyslexia to be when the automatic word identification (reading) and/or written representation does not, or only very incompletely or extremely laboriously, develops" (Ruijssenaars & Gersons-Wolfensberger, 1995, p. 47, Trans. LMS). With this definition, the council does not make any judgment regarding cause and does not make any exclusion criteria, although it determines that there must be a certain degree of mental maturity and undamaged senses. Furthermore, the council proposes three characteristics to make this operational. The first concerns the seriousness of the reading and spelling shortcomings. The score of the pupil in standardized tests for reading and spelling must be within the lowest decile when measured repeatedly. The second characteristic, related to the first, concerns the persistence of the problems: the extra, planned, and intensive efforts of the school (such as individualization of instruction in class and remedial teaching) have not had the desired effect. This effect (expressed in speed of development) should have been reached within half a year after identification of the problem. The third characteristic concerns incomplete and laborious automatic word recognition and spelling. For practical assistance to the pupils concerned, the council makes concrete proposals and it formulates quality requirements. The aim of treatment is to achieve as quickly as possible the highest possible level of automatization, or to get at a point where the problem of gaining automaticity can be coped with by the child. This advice of the Dutch National Health Council is not only important for its content, but also psychologically, because an agreement could be made in a committee in which the diverse voices within the dyslexia debate in the Netherlands were represented.

The LD debate in the Netherlands appears, in the context given here, to have become more open and at the same time to have gained more real value. This does not make the debate less complex, but the symptoms that the LD concept refers to are also not less complex. It is even possible to argue that the LD concept itself, as a referrer, has not succeeded in making this complexity understandable. In other words: the concept has, in any event at the empirical level, not been able to offer the integrating or binding potential that was expected.

In the Netherlands, two research directions are being followed at the moment. The first direction is characterized by a continuing of the research described here at the level of task and process analysis and the growing attention for the neurobiological background of dyslexia. The second direction concerns research into the prevention and treatment of language, reading, and spelling problems. Because the latter has influenced the current discussion most strongly, we will address it in more detail.

Generally speaking, attention is shifting from diagnostic questions to questions concerning the validity and effectiveness of treatment, both at the level of individual help and at the level of education in school. In the first case, the fundamental work of Ruijssenaars is important (Ruijssenaars, 1995). He calls into question the validity of scientific knowledge in the practice of treatment, and with it the significance of the training experiment. In his opinion the latter cannot be compared with treatment in practice. Good practice is not necessarily good practice through the use of tested knowledge, but through the use of clear and well-founded decision rules. Because of the complexity of the context of the treatment, the (direct) use of knowledge cannot be a valid activity. It is much more likely that the available knowledge is represented in the decisions of the professional. "Treatment is a continuous process of assessment, decision, choice and evaluation. In addition to scientifically based knowledge, the experience and skill of the practitioner play an important role, but the client also brings knowledge, experience and skills into the equation. And both think and act based on their own standards and values in, and are influenced by, a wider social context. Within the treatment process the practitioner and client temporarily *share* their choices" (Ruijssenaars, 1995, p. 17, Trans. LMS). It is therefore important that there is a good fit between the cognitive motivational status of the client and the significance that the practitioner (and his or her behavior) has for the client. However, the systematic and objective character of the treatment remains just as important. In Ruijssenaars opinion, this is found in the reflective nature of the treatment process that can be reinforced by formulating (heuristic) decision rules that can guide the process.

Recent developments also include the rapidly growing importance given to the literacy concept in the Netherlands. We close this chapter with an impression of the research and development efforts that are being made at the junction between the LD tradition and the literacy tradition in the Netherlands. In a 1995 general survey into the value of written language and the problems that arise in acquiring the skills for it,

Reitsma, a dyslexia researcher, introduced the notion of "functional literacy" among his fellow researchers. In his writing, he refers this notion to the practice of reading and the context-related meaning of what is being read. As such, the notion contains the suggestion that, in the practice of reading and spelling education, in the event of problems, not too much notice should be taken of the common prescriptions in the curriculum.

Active exploration of the significance of the literacy concept can be found in the work of the researchers Bus (1995) and Verhoeven (1996). Although both have different research backgrounds, a striking similarity exists in their understanding of the development of reading and writing skills. It is supposed that the basic knowledge for reading and writing arises prior to formal instruction. Both skills are rooted in the development of language and in the early use of language, initially strongly context linked, and later less so, when notice is taken of the form aspects of the language that marks the origin of meta-linguistic awareness. In this respect, very early forms of reading and writing already make a contribution to written language development, according to Bus. She is a protagonist of very early writing, because this promotes the relationship between text and meaning, as well as phonemic awareness. "From research into early literacy, it appears that the whole process of becoming literate can stem from worthwhile and functional experience with written language, as long as children are guided by more literate people" (Bus & Van Oostendorp, 1996, p. 40, Trans. LMS).

The work of Verhoeven expressly focuses on the prevention of reading and spelling problems in the school. Verhoeven's assumption is that learning problems can, to a considerable extent, be prevented by paying early, systematic, goal-oriented, and intense attention to the process, however, on condition that an appeal is made to the initiative of the children and that there is mutual interaction and mutual instruction (Verhoeven & van de Ven, 1997). It is especially these conditions that we consider to be of importance, because with them, formal reading education changes in character, for instance, the pupil gets the opportunity to experience him- or herself as an autonomous learner, an essential condition for meta-cognitive activity. The approach of Verhoeven is supported in practice by a system of tutors, who are important for monitoring the process and for the affective support of the pupils concerned.

THE CONTEXT OF EDUCATIONAL POLICY

To be able to understand better the developments sketched above, it is important to describe the developments in the political context of the last two decades. As already mentioned in the introduction, the

Netherlands has a highly developed system of schools for special education that is used by a relatively high percentage of the total population of pupils. One in 10 pupils will attend at any one moment a school for special education (Pijl, 1997). Special classes and resource rooms are not common. The majority of the pupils in special education (70%) attend schools for LD and MMR.

In the first half of the 1980s, two reasons arose for the Dutch government to decide on sweeping changes at the end of the decade. It became obvious that attendance in schools for LD was growing linearly. Furthermore, the initiated policy of identifying and supporting at-risk pupils in general schools at an earlier stage failed. The schools that were facilitated for doing so were not being seen as examples in the way that had been expected. Nevertheless, in 1986 all schools for elementary education were given the statutory obligation to offer all pupils the chance of uninterrupted development. The intention of this was especially to avoid pupils having to repeat school years. During the same period, research was started into the reasons behind the continuous growth of special education (Doornbos & Stevens, 1987). The not unexpected conclusions of this research pointed to two key factors: the selective operation of the system, which persisted with expectations that could not be satisfied by a proportion of the pupils; and the system of financing that rewarded schools for special education for gaining more pupils.

In 1990, the government made the decision to thoroughly reorganize the system, which resulted in the division between schools for general education and schools for LD and MMR being abolished. Driven by changed legislation and finance, elementary schools for general education and special schools for LD and MMR were grouped together into clusters with the aim of sharing, instead of dividing, the responsibility for at-risk children. The finance for special education was made available to the schools in a cluster that, in their turn, financed special education in that cluster. In practice, the existing schools for LD and MMR are retained (though the different labels have disappeared), but the limitation is that no more than 2% of the total number of pupils in a cluster may attend these schools. The available resources per cluster remain the same after the reorganization, although the clusters with a high percentage of attendance must eventually surrender resources.

The philosophy behind this major change can be defined as a redistribution of the available sources of support and the development of a continuum of services. The teacher (the potential referrer) is at the center of this concept, and she or he faces the challenge of developing greater expertise. This challenge has a realistic value in the sense that teachers can only refer now pupils in exceptional circumstances. On the other hand, they can be supported in their work by the expertise and finance that is available within the cluster (the resources initially remain the same per cluster). Moreover, more financial support was made available for each school for the internal counseling of teachers. Within each cluster, a small group of experts are now responsible for the referral policy and for the distribution of expertise. In addition, every school must justify requests for assistance with (documented) educational efforts concerning a pupil. For a more detailed description of the innovation described here, we refer to Stevens & Meijer (1996).

The most important consequence of this change is a shift in focus from the at-risk pupil and his or her characteristics to the quality of the education that he or she receives. This shift implies a change from a focus on (referral) diagnostics to a focus on the educational environment and the correct fit of it with the special needs of the pupil. Another consequence is that the doors to the classroom and to the school have been opened for discussions with colleagues. The teacher must discuss his or her at-risk children with the internal counselor, normally a colleague. The school head must consult with the heads of the other schools in the cluster to discuss the common responsibility for the at-risk pupils in the cluster. In this way a context arises for critical questions to be asked concerning the work of a teacher and of the school.

The changes discussed up to now concern education for children from 4 to 12 years of age. The changes have possibly been even more far-reaching with respect to special secondary education for LD and MMR pupils. The schools have the obligation to integrate general secondary education. This has led to changes in the curriculum in two ways. In the first, extra support is offered in the general program to pupils who have been shown to require this support. In the second, pupils are prepared for simple responsibilities in employment, on the assumption that they will not be able to complete their education with a diploma, even at the lowest level. This assumption must be documented in advance as plausible for every pupil concerned. In both cases the problem of diagnostic criteria exists. Because of the recent nature of the change, an adequate answer to this problem has not yet been formulated. The government wants to see strict criteria out of fear of an increasing demand for resources. The resulting tension has recently led to the return of the IQ as a distinguishing measure. The general opinion is that this measure will have a short life in this context, but the warning that it gives cannot be neglected: As long as the expertise in educational practice cannot formulate an adequate answer with respect to the educational needs of pupils, the government will try to control the flow of pupils using financial measures. From the pedagogic viewpoint we are back to where we started, at least for this moment.

The Dutch government seems really concerned with the development of the quality of education, however critically at least some of its motives are viewed. These developments are expressed in various ways in the Netherlands. For our discussion in this respect the term *adaptive education* is important: that is the correct fit between the needs of the pupils and the characteristics of the educational environment. This was the justification of the major changes discussed above. The first thorough evaluation (Peschar & Meijer, 1997) reported extremely modest results for the development of the adaptive character of education in the clusters over four years. Their conclusion is that the level of educational renewal requires more time and more effort than is often thought and hoped, and that renewal is difficult for central government to control. The recommendations address attention for the qualification of schools team, the development of verifiable models of adaptive education, and breaking away from homogenous grouping of pupils.

Although the evaluation took place very soon after the changes, the results and recommendations were not unexpected. The educational system with its standardization is still intact. In principle, there is no increase in operational space for the individual teacher. Moreover, the crucial question regarding the perceptions of the teacher about him or herself as a teacher, his or her work (and the changes asked for), and his or her pupils has not been asked, while it may be assumed that these perceptions no less than before are linked to the characteristics of the educational system (Stevens, 1997). The results correspond strikingly well to the results of the analysis of the background of the growth of special education in the Netherlands, which was referred to earlier. The suggestion that the real efforts still have to be made does not appear to be unjustified. These efforts must be made where the system must "learn" how to deal with the individual differences between people in talent, tempo, and temperament.

REFERENCES

Bakker, D. J. (1971). *Temporal order in disturbed reading.* Rotterdam: Rotterdam University Press.
Bakker, D. J. (1986). *Zijdelings* (Sideways). Lisse: Swets & Zeitlinger.
Been, P. H. (1994). Dyslexia and irregular dynamics of the visual system. In K. P. van den Bos, L. S. Siegel, D. J. Bakker, & D. L. Share (Eds.), *Current Directions in Dyslexia Research* (pp. 126–140). Lisse: Swets & Zeitlinger.
Been, P. H., & Zwarts, F. (1996). Dyslexie: vroege ontwikkeling en biologische aspecten (Dyslexia: Early development and biological aspects). In K. P. van den Bos & D. P. van Peer (Eds.), *Dyslexie '96* (pp. 153–166). Leuven/Apeldoorn: Garant.

Bladergroen, W. J. (1952). Over diagnostiek en therapie van leesstoornissen (About assesment and treatment of reading disorders). In F. Grewel (Ed.), *Leeszwakke kinderen* (pp. 10–23). Purmerend: Muusses.

Borghouts-van Erp, J. W. M. (1978). *Rekenproblemen: opsporen en oplossen* (Problems with math: Identification and solution). Groningen: Wolters Noordhoff.

Bus, A. G. (1995). *Geletterde peuters en kleuters* (Literacy with toddlers and pre-school children). Amsterdam/Meppel: Boom.

Bus, A. G., & Oostendorp, H. van. (1996). Leesproblemen in het perspectief van ontluikende geletterdheid (Reading problems in the perspective of growing literacy). In K. P. van den Bos & D. R. van Peer (Eds.), *Dyslexie '96* (pp. 31–42). Leuven/Apeldoorn: Garant.

Cruickshank, W. M. (1970). *Buitenbeentjes. Kinderen met hersenbeschadigingen, thuis, op school en in de groep* (Outsiders. The brain injured child in home, school and community). Rotterdam: Lemniscaat.

Doornbos, K., & Stevens, L. M. (1987). *De groei van het speciaal onderwijs* (The growth of special education). Den Haag: Staatsuitgeverij.

Dumont, J. J. (1971). *Leerstoornissen. Oorzaken en behandelingsmethoden* (Learning disabilities. Causes and treatment). Rotterdam: Lemniscaat.

Dumont, J. J., & Kok, J. F. W. (1970). *Curriculum Schoolrijpheid. Vol. 1* (Curriculum Schoolreadiness). Den Bosch: Malmberg.

Dumont, J. J. (1976). *Leerstoornissent 1: Theorie en Model*. Rotterdam: Lemniscaat.

Franken, M. L. O. (1977). *Psychomotorische theorieën en trainingsprogramma's* (Psycho-motor theories and programs for training). Groningen: Wolters Noordhoff.

Gersons-Wolfensberger, D. C. M., & Ruijssenaars, A. J. J. M. (1997). Definition and treatment of dyslexia: A report of the committee on dyslexia of the Health Council of the Netherlands. *Journal of Learning Disabilities, 30,* 209–213.

Hamers, J. H. L. (1994). Leergeschiktheid en leertests: terug- en vooruitblik. In W. H. J. van Bon, E. C. D. M. van Lieshout, & J. T. A. Bakker (Eds.), *Gewoon, Ongewoon, Buitengewoon* (pp. 70–89). Rotterdam: Lemniscaat.

Hamers, J. H. M., & Overtoom, M. Th. (1997). Stimulering van het denken (Enhancement of thinking). *Tijdschrift voor Orthopedagogiek, 36,* 258–266.

Hamers, J. H. M., & Ruijssenaars, A. J. J. M. (1984). *Leergeschiktheid en leertests* (Learning potential and learning potential tests). Harlingen: Flevodruk.

Hamers, J. H. M., Sijtsma, K., & Ruijssenaars, A. J. J. M. (Eds.). (1993). *Learning potential assessment*. Lisse: Swets & Zeitlinger.

Hessels, M. G. P. (1993). *Leertests voor etnische minderheden* (Learning potential tests for ethnic minorities). Rotterdam: RISBO.

In den Kleef, H. M. Th. (1975). *Curriculum Schoolrijpheid. Deel 2A. Auditieve training* (Curriculum Schoolreadiness. Vol. 2A. Auditory training). Den Bosch: Malmberg.

Kalverboer, A. F. (1975). *A neuro-behavioral study in pre-school children*. London: Spastic International Medical Publications.

Kappers, E. J. (1995). Behandeling van dyslexie is maatwerk: een neuropsychologische benadering (Treatment of dyslexia is taylor-made: a neuropsychological approach). In A. J. J. M. Ruijssenaars & R. Kleinen (Eds.), *Dyslexie* (pp. 91–114). Leuven: Acco.

Myklebust, H. R. (1968). *Progress in learning disabilities. Vol. 1*. New York: Grune & Stratton.

Myklebust, H. R. (1971). *Progress in learning disabilities. Vol. 2*. New York: Grune & Stratton.

Peschar, J. L., & Meijer, C. J. W. (1997). *WSNS op weg: de evaluatie van het 'Weer Samen Naar School' beleid* (Evaluation of the inclusion policy). Groningen: Wolters Noordhoff.

Pijl, Y. J. (1997). Verblijfsduur als verklaring voor de groei van het speciaal onderwijs (Length of stay as an explanation of the increasing numbers of children in special education). *Tijdschrift voor Orthopedagogiek, 36,* 226–234.

Reitsma, P. (1995). *Schrift in gebruik* (Script in use). Amsterdam/Duivendrecht: Paedologisch Instituut.

Rispens, J. (1974). *Auditieve aspecten van leesmoeilijkheden* (Auditory aspects of problems in reading). Dissertation. Utrecht University.

Ruijssenaars, A. J. J. M. (1992). *Rekenproblemen* (Problems in math). Rotterdam: Lemniscaat.

Ruijssenaars, A. J. J. M. (1994). Kunnen leerstoornissen vroegtijdig worden onderkend (Learning disabilities, can they be identified early)? In W. H. J. van Bon, E. C. D. M. van Lieshout, & J. T. A. Bakker (Eds.), *Gewoon, Ongewoon, Buitengewoon* (pp. 50–69). Rotterdam: Lemniscaat.

Ruijssenaars, A. J. J. M. (1995). *Behandeling in de orthopedagogiek: kiezen en delen* (Treatment in special education: Choosing and sharing). Inaugural lecture. Leiden: Leiden University.

Ruijssenaars, A. J. J. M., & Gersons-Wolfensberger, D. C. M. (1995). Dyslexie. Afbakening en behandeling (Dyslexia. Delineation and treatment). *Tijdschrif voor Orthopedagogiek, 34,* 561–569.

Stevens, L. M. (1975). *Curriculum Schoolrijpheid. Deel 3. Een evaluatie studie* (Curriculum School-readiness. Vol 3. An evaluation study). Den Bosch: Malmberg.

Stevens, L. M. (1994). Naar een meer geïntegreerde benadering van leerstoornissen, met bijzondere aandacht voor het motivationele aspect (Toward a more integrated approach of learning disabilities, with particular attention to the motivational aspect). In W. H. J. van Bon, E. C. D. M. van Lieshout, & J. T. A. Bakker (Eds.), *Gewoon, Ongewoon, Buitengewoon* (pp. 275–297). Rotterdam: Lemniscaat.

Stevens, L. M. (1997). *Overdenken en doen* (Reflection and action). Den Haag: Procesmanagement Primair Onderwijs.

Stevens, L. M., & Meijer, C. J. W. (1996). Inclusion in The Netherlands: From special education schools to integration to school reform ? *Thalamus, 15,* 38–48.

Stevens, L. M., Werkhoven, W. van., & Castelijns, J. H. M. (1997). Reclaiming Motivattion. *Educattional Leadersship, 54,* 60–63.

Struiksma, A. J. C. (1998). Afscheid van de taak-analyse (Leaving task-analysis)? *Tijdschrift voor Orthopedagogiek, 37,* 18–24.

Tissink, J. (1993). *De constructie van leertests met curriculum(on)gebonden taken* (Learning potential test construction with curriculum associated and nonassociated tasks). Dissertation. Utrecht Universiteit.

Van Bon, W. H. J. (1993). *Spellingproblemen* (Spelling problems). Rotterdam: Lemniscaat.

Van Bon, W. H. J. (1994). Fonemische segmentatie (Phonemic segmentation). In W. H. J. van Bon, E. C. D. M. van Lieshout, & J. T. A. Bakker (Eds.), *Gewoon, Ongewoon, Buitengewoon* (pp. 218–236). Rotterdam: Lemniscaat.

Van Luit, J. E. H. (1994). Een overzicht van een orthopedagogische onderzoekprogrammalijn naar oorzaken en behandelingsmogelijkheden van rekenproblemen (A research program on causes and interventions with respect to problems in math). In W. H. J. van Bon, E. C. D. M. van Lieshout., & J. T. A. Bakker (Eds.), *Gewoon, Ongewoon, Buitengewoon* (pp. 119–146). Rotterdam: Lemniscaat.

Van Luit, J. E. H., & Ruijssenaars, A. J. J. M. (1996). Rekenen en rekenproblemen (Math and math problems). *Tijdschrift voor Orthopedagogiek, 35,* 215–233.

Van den Bos, K. P. (1995). Definitie en aard van dyslexie (Definition and the nature of Dyslexia). In A. J. J. M. Ruijssenaars & R. Kleinen (Eds.), *Dyslexie* (pp. 23–36). Leuven: Acco.

Van den Broeck, W. (1997). *De rol van fonologische verwerking bij het automatiseren van de leesvaardigheid* (The role of phonological processing with automatization of reading skills). Dissertation. Leiden University.

Van der Laan, H. (1973). *Leren lezen, schrijven en rekenen* (Learning to read, write and calculate). Groningen: Tjeenk Willink.

Van der Leij, A. (1982). *De kijk- en luister methode* (The look and listen method). Gorinchem: de Ruyter.

Van der Leij, A. (1983). *Ernstige leesproblemen (Serious problems in learning to read).* Lisse: Swets & Zeitlinger.

Van der Leij, A. (1996). Tien jaar congressen dyslexie in Nederland (Ten years of congresses on dyslexia in the Netherlands). In A. J. J. M. Ruijssenaars & R. Kleinen (Eds.), *Dyslexie* (pp. 9–11). Leuven/Amersfoort: Acco.

Verhoeven, L. (1996). Omgaan met verscheidenheid in leren (Coping with diversity in learning). *Tijdschrift voor Orthopedagogiek, 35,* 321–337.

Verhoeven, L., & Ven, H. van de. (1997). Vroegtijdige interventie van leesproblemen met nadruk op metacognitie en leesmotivatie (Early intervention with reading problems, emphasizing the interest of metacognition and motivation to read). *Tijdschrift voor Orthopedagogiek, 36,* 118–130.

Wedell, K. (1973). *Learning and Perceptuo-motor Disabilities in Children.* London: Wiley.

Chapter 17

Reading Disabilities in Scandinavia

Ingvar Lundberg
Göteborg University, Sweden

Torleiv Höien
Foundation of Dyslexia Research Stavanger, Norway

The Scandinavian countries Denmark, Norway, Sweden, and Finland are often perceived as a homogeneous group of nations, unified not only by their geographical neighborhood in the northern periphery of Europe but also by similar languages, common historical and cultural traditions, similar political patterns, high priorities for social welfare systems, and high egalitarian ambitions.

The school systems of the Scandinavian countries are fairly similar and the provisions made for students with learning disabilities are also similar. The process of decentralizing the school system has advanced rapidly over the past decade in all Scandinavian countries. It is now the primary responsibility of local authorities to guarantee that students with special needs get appropriate provisions. Because the variation between communities is considerable, it is difficult to describe the prevailing practices in Scandinavia. Instead, in this chapter we focus more on the ongoing research activities, especially in the field of reading disabilities in which most resources are allocated. First, however, some current practical and terminological issues will be brought up.

The term *learning disabilities* has no equivalent in Scandinavia. Instead, more specific concepts are used, like specific reading disability or dyslexia, specific difficulties with mathematics or dyscalculia, specific language impairment, attention deficit disorder or DAMP (deficits in attention, motor control, and perception), mental retardation, and autism—all conditions that usually interfere with the learning process in school. The official policy is to de-emphasize the individual disability and diagnostic labels and, instead, speak of complex learning situations in which it is equally important to take the shortcomings of the school into account. One implication of this system-oriented approach to learning disability is that special education is mostly a support given within the framework of ordinary classroom activities. Integration and inclusion are key words, and the goal is a school for all. A typical trend in Scandinavia over the past decades has been the abolishment of special schools for children with learning disabilities and handicaps. With the support of personal assistants, even seriously handicapped children, such as the blind or deaf, are attending ordinary schools.

It has been estimated that close to 10% of the cohort of school beginners is in need of special support provisions (Landgren, 1999). Although socioemotional problems, immaturity, and sometimes disturbing acting-out behavior are the most visible problems, often calling for immediate action, it eventually becomes clear that a majority of the problems that students present to special educators are reading and spelling difficulties. The high societal demands for well-developed literacy skills have forced increased attention on reading problems in our schools. Also research efforts have primarily been focused on these problems. Of particular concern has been the condition termed *developmental dyslexia,* in which a constitutional or genetic origin often has been assumed. In Denmark the term has often been the equivalent to *word blindness,* but it seems as if dyslexia is the commonly used concept in the other Scandinavian countries. In the main part of the present chapter we will focus on reading disability/dyslexia and the contributions of Scandinavian researchers to that field,

READING INSTRUCTION IN SCANDINAVIA

A more thorough review of reading instruction is presented in Lundberg (1999a). The relatively shallow orthographies of the Scandinavian countries have led to the inclusion of phonics elements in early reading instruction. In all these countries, attempts are made to keep a balance between analytic and synthetic methods. Listening, speaking, reading, and writing are integrated from the start, which is in contrast to many other countries where writing is typically introduced later in the program. In Scandinavia, writing is supposed to support the acquisition of reading and facilitate the task of breaking the alphabetic code. The majority of teachers emphasize early phonemic segmentation and sound blending. A whole language approach has inspired many teachers, but they still insist on giving explicit instruction in the alphabetic principle.

HOW IS DYSLEXIA DEFINED IN SCANDINAVIA?

There is no officially adopted or accepted definition of dyslexia in Scandinavia. The practice varies from completely denying the existence of the condition to overuse of the label. Medical doctors and psychologists tend to depend on *DSM IV*. In particular, they emphasize the discrepancy definition in which dyslexia is defined as a marked (not specified) discrepancy between IQ (instrument not specified) and reading achievement (neither instrument nor aspect of reading specified). Some psychologists defend this practice, asserting that only psychologists have the right to assess IQ and thus only psychologists are qualified to diagnose dyslexia.

On the other hand, more and more practitioners and researchers in Scandinavia have come to realize the basic shortcomings of the discrepancy definition. They have assimilated the message from Linda Siegel, Keith Stanovich, Jack Fletcher, and others concerning the limited validity of a discrepancy definition of dyslexia (Fletcher et al., 1994; Lundberg, 1999b; Siegel, 1989; Stanovich & Siegel, 1994). They have also been influenced by our Norwegian–Swedish textbook on dyslexia (Höien & Lundberg, 1991) in which we suggested a definition of dyslexia very similar to the one proposed by the International Dyslexia Association several years later. We emphasized word identification as the core problem in dyslexia, a problem in most cases based on poor phonological processing.

> Dyslexia is a disturbance in certain linguistic functions which are important for using the alphabetic principle in the decoding of language. The disturbance first appears as a difficulty in obtaining automatic word decoding in the reading process. The disturbance is also revealed in poor writing ability. The dyslexic disturbance is generally passed on in families and one can suppose that a genetic disposition underlies the condition. Another characteristic of dyslexia is that the disturbance is persistent. Even though reading ability can eventually reach an acceptable performance level, poor writing skills most often remain. With a more thorough testing of the phonological abilities, one finds that the weakness in this area often persists into adulthood. (Höien & Lundberg, in press)

One example of practical implications of our definition of dyslexia

The definitional issue is not only of purely academic interest. It can have important practical consequences for the individual. Access to certain compensatory tools, like taped books, computer aids, or personal assistance, are often easier to obtain when the formal diagnosis of dyslexia has been given. In Sweden, a scholastic aptitude test can offer a way into attractive programs in higher education. Dyslexic students may then be given extra testing time so that they can prove their actual competence without undue interference by slow and inaccurate reading.

Recently, the central national agency for higher education in Sweden has adopted guidelines for diagnosis of dyslexia, which will allow the student extra testing time at the university entrance examination. This diagnosis is not primarily meant to provide directives for accommodations or provisions once the dyslexic student has started his university program. Rather it is a limited diagnosis only yielding the basis for deciding whether the student is entitled to take tests under adjusted conditions.

The Swedish Dyslexia Foundation has recommended testing procedures based on our dyslexia definition and has also specified a list of professional people who are qualified to handle the assessment according to the guidelines. The majority of the people included in the list are experienced teachers in special education with extensive in-service training; some are speech and language pathologists or some psychologists, and a few are medical doctors, mainly pediatricians, psychiatrists, and neurologists.

Guidelines for assessment include the following dimensions: *Word identification, phonological skills, reading speed,* and *reading comprehension.* Although poor spelling may be a strong indicator of dyslexia, a spelling test is not required because the university entrance test does not involve any writing requirements. Limited vocabulary and problems with second language learning may also be characteristics of dyslexia. However, word knowledge and English reading comprehension are regarded as critical skills for academic success and are thus included in the entrance examination test itself.

Word recognition is often assessed with the Wordchains test in which chains of three words are presented without space between separate words. The student's task is simply to mark the interword spaces (Jacobson, 1995). The number of correctly marked chains within a specific time period indicates performance. This simple test has proved to be very reliable and valid. It is well standardized for all school grades as well as for adults, and is used now also in Norway and the UK (Höien & Tönnesen, 1998; Miller Guron, 1999).

Phonological processing is assessed with a nonword reading task in which the time taken to read the nonwords is recorded. Phonological choice tasks are also used. One word in a triplet of nonwords sounds like a real word when it is pronounced, and the task is to select this alternative. The number of correct choices within a specific time period is the index of phonological skill (see also Olson et al., 1994). Spoonerism-tasks and word-generation tasks have also been used (Lundberg, 1999b). Unfortunately, there are no well-standardized tests available on reading speed and reading comprehension. Here we have to rely on the experience and judgment of the diagnosticians.

A computer-based diagnostic tool is now used in many places in Scandinavia. Designed by Höien in cooperation with Lundberg, it is called KOAS, which is a Norwegian acronym to indicate Assessment of Strategies for Word Identification. KOAS is based on an elaboration of the classical dual-rote model for word recognition (Höien & Lundberg, 1999). The various strategies assumed to be involved in the word reading process are assessed with high accuracy. Important elements are control of exposure times and careful recording of reaction times. This instrument also provides directives for remedial measures.

THE PREVALENCE OF DYSLEXIA IN SCANDINAVIA

Because professionals have used the concept of dyslexia in different ways, it is not possible to estimate the prevalence of dyslexia in a reliable way. If we restrict the term to serious reading and spelling problems based on difficulties at the word level, often caused by phonological problems, many Scandinavian experts agree on an estimate of 4%–8% of the school population. On the average, then, you would find one or two cases of clear dyslexia in each school class.

For adults, the estimation is even more difficult. In the Swedish part of the International Adult Literacy Study (IALS; OECD, 1996) the self-reported incidence of dyslexia amounted to only 1.5%, which probably reflects underreporting. The proportion of Swedes who only reached the lowest proficiency level was much higher than 1.5%. In fact, only 18% of the group reaching the lowest literacy level reported dyslexic problems. The low proportion of self-reported dyslexia might reflect compliance or social desirability but also the fact that a high proportion of low-achieving Swedes has immigrant status. Norway, Denmark, and Finland have also participated in the IALS but in a later round than Sweden. Thus, we now have additional data on self-reported dyslexia only from Norway, where 1% of the respondents reported that they were dyslexic, which is even lower than the low rate reported in Sweden. In international comparison, the Swedish and Norwegian self-reported dyslexia rates are much lower than in any country so far (see also Vogel's chapter 19 in this volume). This intriguing finding certainly deserves further analysis.

When discussing the prevalence of dyslexia we should remember that a low level of literacy does not in itself necessarily reflect dyslexic problems. Linguistic, cultural, social, motivational, and instructional factors may be important causes of low achievement. The manifest problems of comprehending a text might thus be caused by a number of factors.

Poor motivation, poor cognitive functioning, limited vocabulary, and limited world knowledge are not necessarily basic dyslexic factors. As our definition suggests, the current conception of dyslexia, rather, points at word decoding and phonological problems as the core symptoms of dyslexia. However, this does not prevent secondary effects occurring at other levels of processing. Thus, it might sometimes be difficult to isolate dyslexia as such; it may well co-occur with a large number of other functional disturbances, such as ADHD, general cognitive problems, specific language impairments, sensory handicaps, emotional disturbances, and social and cultural deprivation (see also Samuelsson et al., 2000).

In Scandinavian societies the vast majority of people grow up in environments where there is at least a potential of rich literacy stimulation (environmental print, preschool settings, literate adult models, newspapers, magazines, books, libraries, etc.). Children, almost regardless of social background, live in a society in which literacy skills have been highly valued historically (see Lundberg, 1991). However, children with a less favorable genetic disposition may not take advantage of the benefits of rich environmental stimulation. Thus, in highly literate societies with well-developed educational systems like the Scandinavian countries, individual differences in literacy skills may be more related to genetic factors than to lack of opportunity to learn.

SCANDINAVIAN RESEARCH ON DYSLEXIA

Scandinavian research on dyslexia is rather well-coordinated in functional networks with centers or nodes in Copenhagen (Denmark), Stavanger, Oslo (Norway), Umeå, Göteborg, Linköping (Sweden), and Turku, Jyväskylä (Finland). In Norway, Torleiv Höien is the founder of a well-recognized Center for Reading Research in Stavanger. He is now director of the Foundation of Dyslexia Research. Bente Hagtvet, Jörgen Frost, and Sol Lyster all carry out active and inspiring research in Oslo. Carsten Elbro, the first real professor of reading in Scandinavia, has established a very active Center for Research on Reading Disability in Copenhagen. The Swedish scene was earlier dominated by the Umeå group under the leadership of Ingvar Lundberg. After his move to Göteborg a new group is under development there. Åke Olofsson became his successor in Umeå. Stefan Samuelsson in Linköping is another important contributor to the Scandinavian network. In Finland, Turku is a vital center with Pekka Niemi as the most prominent coordinator. He has organized a university clinic for learning disabled children, which has guided teachers and parents as well as generated interesting research. Recently, Jyväskylä has become increasingly important especially with Heikki Lyytinen's strong group on the neuropsychology of reading disability.

Phonological awareness and reading disability

The conception of dyslexia as a phonological deficit has guided much of Scandinavian dyslexia research. The strong relationship between phonological awareness and later success in reading acquisition was demonstrated quite early by Lundberg, Olofsson, & Wall (1980). Their results have been replicated over and over again across languages, ages, and tasks used to measure phonological awareness (Höien & Lundberg, 2000, for a review).

A distinctive advantage in doing research on the relationship between phonological awareness and reading in Scandinavia is the late school start. Until recently most children did not enter school before the age of seven. Thus, one can find perfectly healthy and cognitively well-developed children who, by the age of seven, know only a few letters and cannot read a single word (except for a few logographs). The main reason for this state of affairs is the simple fact that they have not yet enjoyed the benefit of explicit reading instruction. This situation makes it possible to avoid the confounding effects of reading skill and reading instruction when the critical role of phonological awareness is examined. It is also possible to clarify the role of general cognitive development.

Reading disability can be predicted and prevented

In our research we have attempted to answer a number of questions discussed in the current literature on the relationship between phonological awareness, reading acquisition, and dyslexia. A commonly held view is that reading instruction is necessary for the development of phonemic awareness. However, we have demonstrated that phonemic awareness can be developed among Scandinavian preschoolers outside the context of formal reading instruction without the use of letters or other elements of early reading instruction. Lundberg, Frost, and Petersen (1988) designed a Danish program that required daily games and exercises in group settings over a full preschool year. The program included listening games, listening to rhymes and ditties, playing with sentences and words, discovering the initial sounds of words, and finally, carrying out full segmentation of words into phonemes. (An American version of this program is now available; Adams et al., 1998.)

The effects of this program were very specific. There were modest or even no effects on general cognitive functions, on language comprehension, vocabulary and rhyming and syllable segmentation, but rather dramatic effects on phonemic skills. Thus, it was concluded that phonemic awareness could be developed among preschoolers by training, without introducing letters or written text. A more crucial element seems to be the *explicit* guidance of children when they are trying to access, attend to, and extract the elusive, abstract, and implicit segments of language.

Earlier, we had demonstrated the remarkable predictive power of phonological awareness in preschool for later reading achievement in school (Lundberg, Olofsson, & Wall, 1980). What develops later in time (reading) can hardly be the cause of something preceding it. Thus, the longitudinal research has brought us a step closer to an understanding of the causal relationship. The crucial question now is whether explicit training in preschool also facilitates later reading and spelling acquisition in school. The preschool children studied by Lundberg, Frost, & Petersen (1988) were followed over four school years, and reading and spelling were assessed on several occasions. The trained group outperformed the control group on each of 12 points of measurement, indicating the beneficial effect of the preschool program.

Lundberg (1995) presented data from children in preschool with a high risk of developing reading disability as revealed on a pretest of phonological awareness and general language development. At-risk children who were involved in the training program had fairly normal reading and spelling development, whereas the control children showed the expected poor literacy development. Thus, it seems to be possible to prevent the development of reading and spelling disabilities in school by implementing a carefully designed preschool program that brings the children to a level of phonological awareness that is sufficiently high to meet the demands involved in the alphabetic system. The at-risk children who did not enjoy the benefit of such training seemed to face serious obstacles on their way to literacy.

Several other Scandinavian studies have also demonstrated the remedial and facilitating power of phonological awareness training in preschool or school as part of regular teaching or as an important element in special education (Elbro, 1996; Gustafson, Samuelsson, & Rönnberg, 2000; Lie, 1991; Lyster, 1996; Poskiparta, Vauras, & Niemi, 1998).

A study by Höien et al. (1995) supported the view that there are different components of phonological awareness corresponding to the different levels of language analysis required by the task. More than 1,500 children in preschool and grade one in Stavanger were tested with a battery of tasks including rhyme recognition, syllable counting, initial phoneme identification, phoneme deletion, phoneme synthesis, and phoneme counting. Three basic factors were extracted in a principal component analysis: a phoneme factor, a syllable factor, and a rhyme factor. We found that the three components of phonological awareness were separate predictors of early word reading ability, with the syllable factor as the weakest predictor. Not unexpectedly, the phoneme factor proved to be the most powerful predictor of early reading acquisition. Among the various phonemic tasks, the phoneme identification tasks explained the highest proportion of unique variance.

Olofsson (1999) followed up on a group of students 20 years after their first diagnosis as dyslexics at the age of eight. In comparison with a control group, they had clear and persisting problems in tasks involving phonological processing demands, although their reading comprehension was not significantly inferior to the control subjects.

Frost (1999) has reported on a series of studies in which he compared in great detail the reading and spelling development of children with low phonological awareness in kindergarten to those of children with high phonological awareness. As expected, the course of development was very different in these groups. The critical foundation period, when the code is broken and the alphabetic insight is developed, was much shorter for the children with high phonological awareness. They were equipped with a useful instrument for self-teaching as they encountered environmental print. A long foundation period, on the other hand, seems to prevent the powerful self-teaching from developing. The fine-grained analysis of the first critical stages in reading acquisition conducted by Frost is a rather unique achievement, which not only gives us a deeper understanding of what happens in this exciting phase, but also gives us practical guidelines for helping vulnerable children to overcome initial obstacles in reading acquisition.

In another longitudinal study, Jacobson & Lundberg (in press) followed the reading development of 90 dyslexic students from grade two to grade nine and analyzed their growth curves. Twenty-five percent of the variance of the individual slopes could be explained in a multiple regression in which intelligence and phonological factors gave significant contributions. This kind of analysis deserves more attention because it can answer the critical question of which factors determine individual success. Knowledge of these factors would have important implications for remedial work in special education.

Borström & Elbro (1997) demonstrated in an ingenious study how dyslexic problems can be prevented even before most children learn how to read. They examined children of parents with documented reading disability. On good grounds they assumed that these children were at high risk for developing dyslexia in school. The strong inheritance actually suggests that about 40% of the at-risk children will be dyslexic. Now, these children were divided on different conditions, in which one group enjoyed the benefit of intense phonological stimulation before they entered school. The training was clearly effective, reducing the risk of developing dyslexia later in school from 40% to 17%.

The same logic that was applied by Borström and Elbro (1997) is also being used in an ongoing longitudinal study in Jyväskylä (Lyytinen, 1997). More than 4,000 parents of newborn children have been screened for reading problems. Very early signs among the at-risk babies have been examined by electro-physiological measures. Because the children have not yet started school it is too early to evaluate the findings, although Borström and Elbro have observed some suggestive differences between at-risk children and controls.

Examples of Scandinavian research on the remediation of dyslexia are provided by Elbro, Rasmussen, and Spelling (1996), Lundberg and Olofsson (1993), and Poskiparta, Vauras, and Niemi (1998). They have demonstrated that computer-based programs with synthetic speech feedback have beneficial effects on the word recognition and spelling skills of children with early signs of dyslexia. Arnbak and Elbro (1998) have also demonstrated that training in morphological awareness is beneficial for dyslexic students.

Neurobiological perspectives

A step in the direction of finding a neurological correlate to the phonological problems was taken by Larsen, Höien, Lundberg, and Ödegaard (1990) in a study of 15-year-old dyslexics in Stavanger. Brain scans (MRIs) revealed that the planum temporale tended to be of equal size in the two hemispheres more often among dyslexics than among normal controls. More specifically, however, all dyslexics with severe phonological problems had symmetry of the plana temporale. We still do not know, however, how this deviation from the normal pattern in the language cortex affects the development of phonological coding and other processes necessary for fluent reading.

It would be tempting to look for a clear-cut dyslexia diagnosis by using brain imaging and referring people with symmetric plana to the dyslexic category. Even when disregarding the discouraging costs, such a procedure is not feasible. It will certainly be very difficult to assess reliably the symmetry of individual cases. Individual variability is considerable. One can also find individuals with strong indications of dyslexia based on other criteria but with perfectly normal asymmetry of planum temporale as well as nondyslexic individuals with symmetry.

An interesting case of developmental surface dyslexia has been reported by Samuelsson (2000). The child had very early acquired and well-localized brain damage in the occipital region, which might explain her inability to use an orthographic or logographic strategy in reading and spelling.

Functional MRI studies will certainly reveal more about the neurobiological basis of dyslexia in the near future. Kenneth Hugdahl in Bergen, Martin Ingvar in Stockholm, and Ritta Hari in Helsinki are some of the Scandinavian brain scientists who have already significantly contributed to a deeper neurobiological understanding of dyslexia.

In this context the Rodin Remediation Academy deserves mentioning. It is an international academy of scientists with interests in language impairments and dyslexia. It was founded in 1984 by a Swede, Dr. Per Uddén, and has its executive council located in Stockholm. Among its 100 members there are seven Nobel laureates and an impressive list of other, highly respected scientists from various fields. The primary interest of the academy is to promote research on reading disabilities and language dysfunction. Since its founding, there have been 25 international conferences and seminars organized under the auspices of the Academy in many different countries (the 25th was held in Riken Brain Science Institute in Japan in 1999) attended by distinguished researchers from all over the world. Several of these meetings have been documented by important publications (for example, von Euler, Lundberg, & Lennerstrand, 1989; von Euler, Lundberg, & Llinàs, 1998). The Academy emphasizes the multidisciplinary nature of learning disabilities and has members from a range of different fields including brain sciences, linguistics, psychology, and education.

Psychological and social dimensions of reading disability

The failure of learning an important skill in school, such as reading, has profound effects on an individual, far beyond having reading problems. Niemi et al. (1999) identified children who were particularly hard to teach. These resistant learners showed very slow progress in the training of phonological awareness. Their reading and spelling skills were also far behind. Niemi and colleagues proposed that the underlying cause of the resistance might be a psychological vulnerability affecting the child's ability to cope with the stressful and threatening school situation. Students may become inhibited to reduce emotional stress. Evidence for motivationally based regressive reading careers has been reported by Niemi's group (Salonen et al., 1998). These studies represent a new and very important orientation in the search for explanations of reading disabilities. It is apparently time to go beyond the circumscribed module of phonological processes.

A study of long-term unemployed

A social perspective on reading disabilities is also provided by studies of long-term unemployed, prisoners, and inmates in institutions for juvenile delinquents. Lindgren and Ingvar (1996) found in a study of the population of people who had been unemployed for more than 12 months that at least one out of five had serious reading and spelling problems. The test battery primarily captured manifest reading ability without going beneath the surface and investigating word recognition and phonological processing. Thus, the prevalence of dyslexia in a more restricted sense cannot be estimated. However, the conclusion is important. A strategic measure to be taken for many long-term unemployed individuals must involve intense training of reading and writing skills.

Prison population

Recently, two studies have been conducted in Sweden reporting high frequencies of dyslexic problems in different samples of prison inmates (Alm & Andersson, 1997; Jensen et al., 1998). Alm and Andersson (1997) found that 39 out of 61 prison inmates (64%) exhibited reading and writing skills that were below average for grade six children (12 year olds); they also concluded that 19 out of 61 inmates (31%) in their sample showed reading and writing deficits attributable to dyslexia. Jensen et al. (1998) reported similar findings. They found that 26 out of 63 inmates could be diagnosed as dyslexics (41%) and that an additional 10 cases were borderline dyslexics (10%). However, there are methodological drawbacks associated with these Swedish studies because of high attrition rates, lack of relevant control groups, and controversial assessment methods. Information to distinguish between poor reading caused by lack of educational opportunity versus poor reading caused by phonological coding deficits has not been reported.

Samuelsson et al. (in press) have estimated that about 10% of the prison population suffered from dyslexic problems, that is, just a slightly higher prevalence than in a normal population and far below earlier estimates. The extensive literacy problems observed among the inmates were interpreted as based on social, cultural, and educational deprivation rather than constitutionally based dyslexia.

In a study in progress we have a more extensive battery of tests, questionnaires, and interviews with a total testing time of about four hours for each participant. We also have two comparison groups, one group of younger individuals matched on reading level and one group of adult readers matched on educational level and reading habits.

Institutions for juvenile delinquents

Studies by Svensson, Lundberg, and Jacobson (in press) have attempted to estimate the prevalence of literacy problems in the population of juvenile delinquents in Swedish institutions. The picture turned out to be more complex than had been reported earlier. Literacy problems are certainly common among the inmates, but a surprisingly large number of pupils show adequate reading and spelling skills. In the poorly achieving group (about 25%) immigrant youngsters are highly overrepresented. Immigrant pupils often show adequate word reading ability but fail in text comprehension tasks. Dyslexia in the restricted sense (word recognition problems based on deficit phonological coding) was not more frequent among the inmates than in the normal population (6%–8%).

DYSLEXIA AND CREATIVITY

Our main focus so far has been on dyslexia as a serious handicap in our current knowledge-based society. However, the coin might have another side. It has been suggested that dyslexics sometimes show uncommon gifts, skills, and talents in fields like creative arts, architecture, handicrafts, design, and so on (see West, 1997). Systematic studies of this assumption are few, however. An attempt at clarification has recently been made by Wolff and Lundberg (unpublished). We studied a sample of students in creative arts and photography and compared them with a sample of students in business school. Both types of higher education have very restricted admission policies with about a 10% selection rate. Among the art students, close to 30% showed dyslexic tendencies. In contrast, such tendencies were almost completely absent among the students in business school. Further studies on this issue are under way.

CONCLUSION

The absence of a term covering the meaning of learning disabilities in Scandinavia has forced us to restrict our focus to reading disabilities in our review of the Scandinavian situation. We have deliberately chosen to present research published internationally by Scandinavian researchers. Considering the relatively small populations in the four countries, the internationally oriented research activities must be regarded as quite lively. However, many important fields of learning disabilities deserve more attention. At the beginning of a new century it feels natural, or at least tempting, to speculate a little on what contributions from Scandinavia can be expected in the foreseeable future.

The further development of information and communication technology with improved speech recognition and speech synthesis will certainly be very visible in Scandinavia as a technologically advanced society. The empowerment potential of the new techniques is indeed very promising. Proficiency in foreign languages, especially English, has an obvious survival value in Scandinavia. At the same time, individuals with dyslexia normally have basic problems with foreign language acquisition, which further increases the burden for these individuals. We have reasons to expect strong efforts in Scandinavia to understand these problems better and to find new teaching approaches. One step in this research direction has been taken by Miller Guron and Lundberg (2000). The rapid development within brain science and genetics will also have a strong impact on Scandinavian dyslexia research. One such promising example is Päivi Helenius' dissertation in Helsinki in which she used the new Magnetoencephalographic recording technique (Helenius, 1999). Another example is Torkel Klingberg's recent work in Stockholm on the structure of the white matter of the connections between Broca's and Wernicke's areas in the brain. Molecular genetics is also a hot field, which will influence our understanding of learning disabilities. The relatively homogeneous populations of Scandinavia will probably facilitate the work on locating critical genes involved in learning disabilities. This work might also be important in identifying subgroups of disabilities.

Reading, writing, and mathematics are primarily cultural skills acquired and used in educational, social, and cultural contexts. This indicates that we must direct our research efforts toward the social and cultural dimensions of learning disabilities. We have to understand the conditions under which a functional weakness will develop into a handicap and the conditions where the handicap can be avoided. We also expect more sociologists and philosophers to be involved in the field of learning disabilities. Hidden values and implicit assumptions must be brought to daylight and discussed in the light of substantive knowledge.

The late Dr. William Cruickshank, to whom this volume is a tribute, was our model in this respect. His wisdom, sophistication, and deep knowledge has been a great inspiration to the scientific community.

REFERENCES

Adams, M. J., Foorman, B. R., Lundberg, I., & Beeler, T. (1998). *Phonemic awareness in young children.* Baltimore, MD: Brookes.

Alm, J., & Andersson, J. (1997). A study of literacy in prisons in Uppsala. *Dyslexia, 3,* 245–246.

Arnbak, E., & Elbro, C. (1998). Teaching morphological awareness to dyslexic students. In P. Reitsma & L. Verhoeven (Eds.), *Problems and interventions in literacy development* (pp. 277–290). Dordrecht, Netherlands: Kluwer Academic Publishers.

Borström, I., & Elbro, C. (1997). Prevention of dyslexia in kindergarten: Effects of phoneme awareness training with children of dyslexic parents. In C. Hulme & M. Snowling (Eds.), *Dyslexia. Biology, cognition, and intervention* (pp. 235–253). London: Whurr.

Elbro, C. (1996). Early linguistic abilities and reading development: A review and a hypothesis about distinctness of phonological representations. *Reading and Writing. An Interdisciplinary Journal, 8,* 453–485.

Elbro, C., Rasmussen, I., & Spelling, B. (1996). Teaching reading to disabled readers with language disorders: A controlled evaluation of synthetic speech feedback. *Scandinavian Journal of Psychology, 37,* 140–155.

von Euler, C., Lundberg, I., & Lennerstrand, G. (Eds.). (1989). *Brain and reading.* New York: Stockton Press.

von Euler, C., Lundberg, I., & Llinàs, R. (Eds.). (1998). *Basic mechanisms in cognition and language.* Oxford: Elsevier Science.

Fletcher, J. M., Shaywitz, S. E., Shankweiler, D., Katz, L., Liberman, I., Stuebing, K. K, Francis, D. J., Fowler, A., & Shaywitz, B. A. (1994). Cognitive profiles of reading disability: Comparisons of discrepancy and low achievement definitions. *Journal of Educational Psychology, 86,* 6–23.

Frost, J. (1999). *Initial enabling skills in early reading and spelling.* Ph.D. dissertation. University of Copehagen.

Gustafson, S., Samuelsson, S., & Rönnberg, J. (2000). *Scandinavian Journal of Educational Psychology, 44,* 145–162.

Helenius, P. (1999). *Neuromagnetic and psychoacoustical correlates of impaired reading and abnormal sound sequence processing in developmental dyslexia.* Helsinki: Department of Psychology, Helsinki University.

Höien, T., & Lundberg, I. (1991). *Dysleksi.* Oslo: Gyldendal.

Höien, T., & Lundberg, I. (1999). *KOAS. Kartlegging av Ordavkodingsstrategier.* Stavanger: Foundation of Dyslexia Research.

Höien, T., & Lundberg, I. (2000). *Dyslexia. From theory to intervention.* Dordrecht, NL: Kluwer Academic Publishers.

Höien, T., Lundberg, I., Bjaalid, I. K., & Stanovich, K. E. (1995). Components of phonological awareness. *Reading and Writing. An Interdisciplinary Journal, 7,* 1–18.

Höien, T., & Tönnesen, G. (1998). *Ordkjedetesten.* Stavanger: Foundation of Dyslexia Research.

Jacobson, C. (1995). Word recognition index (WRI) as a quick screening marker of dyslexia. *Irish Journal of Psychology, 16,* 260–266.

Jacobson, C., & Lundberg, I. (In press). Early prediction of individual growth in reading. *Reading and Writing. An Interdisciplinary Journal.*

Jensen, J., Lindgren, M., Wirsén-Meurling, A., Ingvar, D., & Levander, S. (1998). Dyslexia among Swedish prison inmates in relation to neuropsychology and personality. (Submitted paper.)

Landgren, M. (1999). *Deficits in attention, motor control and perception–DAMP.* Doctoral dissertation. Department of Child and Adolescent Psychiatry, Göteborg University.

Larsen, J. P., Höien, T., Lundberg, I., & Ödegaard, H. (1990). MRI evaluation of the size and the symmetry of planum temporale in adolescents with developmental dyslexia. *Brain and Language, 39,* 289–301.

Lie, A. (1991). Effects of a training program for stimulating skills in word analysis in first-grade children. *Reading Research Quarterly, 26,* 234–250.

Lindgren, M., & Ingvar, D. (1996). Reading and writing disabilities in Swedish unemployed adults. Assessment and remediation. (Submitted paper.)

Lundberg, I. (1991). Reading as an individual and social skill. In I. Lundberg & T. Hoien (Eds.), *Literacy in a world of change* (pp. 14–22). Stavanger: Center for Reading Research/UNESCO.

Lundberg, I. (1993). The teaching of reading in the Nordic countries. *Scandinavian Journal of Educational Research, 37,* 43–62.

Lundberg, I. (1995). Reading difficulties can be predicted and prevented: A Scandinavian perspective on phonological awareness and reading. In C. Hulme & M. Snowling (Eds.), *Reading development and dyslexia* (pp. 180–199). London: Whurr.

Lundberg, I. (1999a). Learning to read in Scandinavia. In M. Harris & G. Hatano (Eds.), *Learning to read and write. A cross-linguistic perspectives* (pp. 157–172). Cambridge: Cambridge University Press.

Lundberg, I. (1999b). Towards a sharper definition of dyslexia. In I. Lundberg, F. E. Tönnessen, & I. Austad (Eds.), *Dyslexia: Advances in theory and practice* (pp. 9–29). Dordrecht, NL: Kluwer Academic Publishers.

Lundberg, I., Frost, J., & Petersen, O.-P. (1988). Effects of an extensive program for stimulating phonological awareness in preschool children. *Reading Research Quarterly, 33,* 263–284.

Lundberg, I., & Olofsson, Å. (1993). Can computer speech support comprehension? *Computers in Human Behavior, 9,* 283–293.

Lundberg, I., Olofsson, Å., & Wall, S. (1980). Reading and spelling skills in the first school years predicted from phonemic awareness skills in kindergarten. *Scandinavian Journal of Psychology, 21,* 159–173.

Lyster, S. A. (1996). *Preventing reading and spelling failure.* Doctoral dissertation. University of Oslo, Department of Special Education.

Lyytinen, H. (1997). In search of the precursors of dyslexia: A prospective study of children at risk for reading problems. In C. Hulme & M. Snowling (Eds.), *Dyslexia. Biology, cognition and intervention* (pp. 97–107). London: Whurr.

Miller Guron, L. (1999). *The Wordchains test.* London: NFER Nelson.

Miller Guron, L., & Lundberg, I. (2000). Dyslexia and second language reading. A second bite at the apple. *Reading and Writing. An Interdisciplinary Journal, 12,* 41–61.

Niemi, P., Kinnunen, R., Poskiparta, E., & Vauras, M. (1999). Do pre-school data predict resistance to treatment in phonological awareness, decoding and spelling? In I. Lundberg, F. E. Tönnessen, & I. Austad (Eds.), *Dyslexia: Advances in theory and practice* (pp. 245–254). Dordrecht, NL: Kluwer Academic Publishers.

OECD. (1995). *Literacy, economy and society.* Paris: OECD.

Olofsson, Å. (1999). Early reading problems: A follow up 20 years later. In I. Lundberg, F. E. Tönnessen, & I. Austad (Eds.), *Dyslexia: Advances in theory and practice* (pp. 197–206). Dordrecht, NL: Kluwer Academic Publishers.

Olson, R. K., Forsberg, H., Wise, B., & Rack, J. (1994). Measurement of word recognition, orthographic and phonological skills. In G. R. Lyaonn (Ed.), *Frames of reference for the assessment of learning disabilities: New views on measurement issues* (pp. 243–277). Baltimore, MD: Brookes.

Poskiparta, E., Vauras, M., & Niemi, P. (1998). Prompting word recognition, spelling and reading comprehension skills in a computer-based training program in grade 2. In P. Reitsma & L. Verhoeven (Eds.), *Problems and interventions in literacy development* (pp. 335–348). Dordrecht, NL: Lower Academic Publishers.

Salonen, P., Lepola, J., & Niemi, P. (1998). The development of first-graders' reading skill as a function of pre-school motivational orientation and phonemic awareness. *European Journal of Psychology of Education, 13,* 155–174.

Samuelsson, S. (2000). Converging evidence for the role of occipital regions in orthographic processing: A case of developmental dyslexia. *Neuropsychologia, 38,* 351–362.

Samuelsson, S., Gustavsson, A., Herkner, B., & Lundberg, I. (In press). Is the frequency of dyslexic problems among prison inmates higher than in a normal population. *Reading and Writing: An Interdisciplinary Journal.*

Samuelsson, S., Finnström, O., Leijon, I., & Mård, S. (2000). Phonological and surface profiles of reading difficulties among very low birth weight children: Converging evidence for the developmental lag hypothesis. *Scientific Studies of Reading, 4,* 197–217.

Siegel, L. S. (1989). IQ is irrelevant to the definition of learning disabilities. *Journal of Learning Disabilities, 22,* 469–479.

Stanovich, K. E., & Siegel, L. S. (1994). The phenotypic performance profile of reading-disabled children: A regression-based test of the phonological-core variable-difference model. *Journal of Educational Psychology, 86,* 24–53.

Svensson, I., Lundberg, I., & Jacobson, C. (In press). The prevalence of reading disabilities among inmates at Swedish institutions for juvenile delinquents. *Dyslexia.*

West, T. G. (1997). *In the mind's eye.* New York: Prometheus Books.

Chapter 18

Learning Disabilities Studies in South America

Luis Bravo-Valdivieso, Ph.D.[1]
Neva Milicic Müller, Ph.D.[2]

HISTORICAL BACKGROUND

Interest in special education began in Chile in 1852 with the creation of a school for deaf children, which subsequently added a class for blind children. In 1928 and 1929, another three schools for children with behavior disorders and a school for blind children were opened and in 1945 several schools for mentally retarded (MR) children were established, along with a few special classes for them within the regular schools. In the 1960s special schools annexed to pediatric hospitals were opened that served as diagnostic and rehabilitation centers for learning disabled children and for teacher training as well. These "clinical" special schools were followed in the decades of 1960s and 1970s by a great number of new special schools for learning disabled (LD) and MR children and for "differential groups" inside the schools. In 1980 there was a change in the orientation in the field of public special education toward the creation

[1]Professor, Facultad de Educación y Psicología. Pontificia Universidad Católica de Chile. Correspondence regarding this article should be send to: Escuela de Psicología, Pontifica Universidad Católica de Chile, Avda. Vicuña Mackenna 4860, Macul, Santiago, Chile. Phone (56)(2) 6865905, Fax (56)(2) 6864843, e-mail: abravov@puc.cl

[2]Professor, Escuela de Psicología. Pontificia Universidad Católica de Chile. Correspondence regarding this article should be send to: Escuela de Psicología, Pontificia Universidad Católica de Chile, Avenida Vicuña Mackenna 4860, Macul, Santiago, Chile, Phone: (56-2) 6865905. Fax: (56-2) 6864843. E-mails: nmilicic@puc.cl

of support teams and special classes within the regular schools for LD children. In Venezuela, special types of schools for blind, deaf, mute, and "abnormal" children were founded in 1912, and in 1948 special education classrooms were created in the regular schools (Feldman & Feldman, 1981). Special classes for academically "backward" and mentally retarded children were set up in Uruguay in 1928 (Lorenzo, 1973).

LEARNING DISABILITIES AND CULTURAL DIFFERENCES IN THE SOUTH AMERICAN COUNTRIES

Culturally deprived children are defined in the United States and other developed countries as "subcultural minorities," in comparison to the majority of children who have had sufficient cognitive development and motivation toward academic learning. In those countries, school learning difficulties brought about by poverty affect a minority of children who receive special education in order to compensate their deficiencies. This is not the case in Latin American countries. In our countries, poor children constitute a majority, and they must follow the programs of studies designed for the minority, children from middle or high social–economic status (SES). As a consequence, low SE level show retardation in their cognitive and psycholinguistic development that affects their academic performance and brings about general learning problems for reading, writing, and mathematics. They are "high-risk children." Several studies have shown that verbal and phonological abilities of children from low SES entering public schools are lower than those of children entering private middle-class schools (Bravo-Valdivieso, 1998).

In the South American countries most LDs are not explained by neuropsychological abnormalities in children's development. Instead we find many children with "general learning problems" that arise from their psychological or social immaturity for school learning. These learning problems may be greater in poverty areas than in middle class schools. Among these high-risk children that begin first grade of elementary school, there are many that suffer verbal and cognitive deficiencies and they have not had any pre-school education. Then, it is very important when studying children with L.D. in the S.A. countries, to differentiate children with general learning problems brought about by sociocultural factors from those with "specific learning disabilities" that have their origin in neuro-psychological anomalies in their development .

Therefore, while learning disabilities in the United States "constitute a serious social problem of epidemic proportions"—according to Schonaut and Satz (1983, p. 542) in the South American countries, learning disabilities in low SES children constitute a worse "epidemic problem." It is likely that the percentage of children with learning difficulties in South American countries is greater than in the United States or in European countries, because of poor nutrition, unsanitary conditions, lower cognitive–verbal development, and so forth. In Chile, the rate of prevalence of reading retardation among school children who have had consultations at public Diagnosis Centers was 78% (Bermeosolo and Punto, 1996). Most of these children belonged to low SES schools. Moreover, follow-up studies show that their prognosis in learning to read is poor and there is a strong "effect of initial reading performance" on the following school years (Bravo-Valdivieso, Bermeosolo, Pinto, and Oyarzo, 1994).

The disadvantage in cognitive and psycholinguistic development could be one of the main causes of the high number of children who are held back or who drop out of school in South American countries. These children who have general learning problems need not be taught in special schools, as children with specific learning disabilities do, but they do not receive special educational support within their schools either. The scarcity of school services and the quality of teaching keep many children from the poverty subculture from receiving an adequate education in their own schools. Most of them become illiterate.

An analogous phenomenon can be seen when we measure IQ with some tests that have been validated using the criteria of academic performance. Children from low SES who have learning difficulties do poorly on traditional tests because of their linguistic differences as well. Most of traditional school tests have been designed to measure academic intelligence, which is culturally determined. As many of these tests have been validated with an external criterion of academic performance, children who have learning problems will also receive low scores on them. Then it is frequently assumed that the cause of their learning problems is their low-level intelligence. This is why in the first half of the century the major focus of special education was on mental retardation and not on learning disabilities in socioculturally different children. Moreover, there are a large number of working-class and rural South American children who manifest a type of intelligence that is primarily nonverbal and therefore it will be of little help in a school learning situation.

THE INITIAL CLINICAL SUPPORT

In describing the growth and development of special education for learning disabled children in some South American countries, it is necessary to emphasize the contribution of the child psychiatry and pediatric neurology departments of the public hospitals, and the contribution of the universities for the training of teacher specialists. In Brazil, Chile, Argentina, and Uruguay, the first services that received LD children were *clinical* and the early research was done at the hospitals.

These original clinical contributions to special education included teacher training in some specific learning disabilities and research in subjects such as "minimal brain dysfunction," "specific dyslexia," "epilepsy," and "mental retardation." This work at hospital services was strengthened by some special schools connected to them and by clinical psychologists, who helped teachers understand the neuropsychological and cognitive aspects of learning disabled children. Thus, until the 1960s, most of the teachers who worked in this area were self-taught and received little systematic training. Until 1960 pediatric hospitals bore the complete burden of both diagnosis and rehabilitation of children with developmental disturbances. For instance, in a mental health report published in 1971 in Chile, it was stated that 30% of children who had received consultation in Child Psychiatry Services had been diagnosed as reading disabled ("dyslexics"), and 10% of them were performing poorly in school because of emotional problems.

THE TRAINING OF SPECIAL EDUCATION TEACHERS

One of the main problems presented in our countries for the systematic training of teachers to work with LD children was the lack of awareness among authorities with regard to learning disabilities. Most of them thought that school failures were due to mental retardation or cultural deprivation and that those children did not need help in the schools. This lack of public awareness of this problem caused, as a consequence, a scarcity of specialists and school facilities for LD children.

In Chile during these years, several articles were published referring to the high cost of school failure, the rate of children held back and who dropped out in public schools, caused by children with learning disabilities. Those articles aimed at making the educational authorities aware of the social problems brought about by the high rate of LD children in the schools. As a consequence, the Catholic University of Chile created in 1969 the first graduate programs for training teachers for LD children and to investigate this problem. This was the first Chilean university to begin teacher training and research in the area of LD. Students in these graduate programs were elementary and preschool teachers who became—after the training—"Special Education Teachers." The program lasts three years, is part time, and ends with the opportunity to a practice teach learning disabled children in a public school.

In other countries, this specialization was given to "speech therapists" and "psycho-pedagogists," as in Peru and Argentina. In Venezuela, the government created in 1965 the first institute for educating special teachers, and this training was given in the Venezuelan universities from 1977 (Feldman and Feldman, 1981).

After the 1970s and 1980s, several institutions of higher education created the specialization in psychopedagogy, which trains teachers to work with children with specific learning disabilities. This training of educational specialists in the universities contributed to changing the social emphasis of special education for LD, because until that time the principal preoccupation was centered on mentally retarded and/or sensory or motor handicapped children. Thereafter, the focus of preoccupation began to shift toward learning problems in children without mental retardation or sensory deficits. This new outlook pointed to the need for reevaluating elementary school programs and curriculum in elementary schools, especially in those that received children coming from the subculture of poverty as well. With this aim, in 1974 those establishments supported a National Conference on Special Education that was held in Chile, organized jointly by the Ministry of Education and several universities.

In this conference the need for reforming the national elementary education programs was noted, and a more flexible system of academic advancement was proposed, according to the level of psychological and pedagogical maturity of the children. Moreover, the creation of a special education system that was defined as a differentiated and interdisciplinary specialization of regular education addressed to those children who, whether due to transitory or permanent causes, are prevented from following the regular educational program was proposed. It was stated that special education must not be constituted as a segregated or independent entity apart from the general educational system but must make its principal objective to incorporate the child as quickly as possible into the mainstream of education. Children with physical or psychic deficiencies/handicaps cannot be maintained indefinitely in a segregated educational structure, however perfect that structure might be in itself, because at the end of his school years the student's integration into the social and economic communities will be even harder. It was clearly expressed that special education does not constitute a different educational system; rather, it is a differentiation of regular education, applicable to individual cases as needed. The effectiveness of special education can be seriously compromised if it must receive an overpopulation of children due to inadequacies in the regular education system. This report concluded by stating that the work of special education must be complemented by preventive preschool education. However, in Brazil, special education for LD children began and went on being under a clinical vigilance according to Aratangy et al. (1981).

THE INTEGRATION OF LD CHILDREN IN THE
SETTING OF THE REGULAR SCHOOLS

As we have said, in the 1970s the first differential classes within regular schools were created for LD children, together with diagnostic centers to assist in detection and treatment of specific learning disabilities. At the same time, the recognition and prevalence of specific learning disabilities had increased because those teachers now possessed greater knowledge of educational disabilities. Special education options were planned according to the level of severity of the disabilities. Children with specific learning disabilities and mild educational problems were treated in the differential support room within regular schools. On the other side, children with mild mental retardation, moderate behavioral problems, and/or mild to severe learning disabilities attended segregated special schools. Despite its difficulties and inconveniences, the differential school had the advantage of recognizing the principle of reducibility and the right of every child to receive an education. Its creation was an important step toward the recognition that people with disabilities are capable of learning and developing if they are given support in accordance with their characteristics.

Nevertheless, the creation of parallel educational systems, in spite of providing additional attention to some children with special needs, generated another set of problems that questions their existence. These criticisms say that it is unfair to exclude some children from the regular system, as this segregates them, physically and psychologically, from their peers. Moreover, segregation, is inefficient, since it interrupts professional communication and increases educational costs due to the waste of educational resources that are created by the separation and duplication of services. Diagnoses to classify and place the child in one system or the other have questionable validity and act as labels with no educational value. These labels serve to deny the children access to the services and programs they need to facilitate their development.

In Latin America the problems for integration are basically the same reported by UNESCO (1988) and Ainscow (1995). They relate to rigid administrative systems, little consideration to individual needs, administrative separation between the regular staff and special school with limited communication among them, and limited teacher training with regard to disability topics. In Chile, in spite of regulations for student's mainstreaming, the issues are discouraging (Alvarez, 1999). Children with specific learning disabilities do not constitute a homogeneous group, and by definition, these students have difficulties in processing, organizing, and expressing information (Vaughn, 1985). Children with specific learning disabilities also manifest difficulties in the development of social abilities and the processing of social and affective cues. Hence, deliberate systematic work is needed to assist them in their social development, which in turn, will improve their social interactions and prevent future difficulties (Milicic, 1988).

Nevertheless, concrete actions toward integration of the LD children in the regular schools have been taken during the last five years. Seminars and experimental integration projects at the preschool and elementary levels have been conducted. In addition, feedback is being collected from schools that are to integrate children with disabilities. These include strategies for dealing with parent's needs and with the lack of special services. One consequence of integrating LD children in schools is the need to prepare teachers to work positively in this process. [A training program that has been successful in promoting novel integration alternatives within the classroom.] This program has been implemented since 1988 in several suburbs of Santiago by two Chilean psychologists, A. M. Arón and N. Milicic (1999). The main objective of the program is to train teachers to create interactive learning contexts that promote the development of social abilities and enable children to interact creatively in their social environment, while developing their potential (Arón & Milicic, 1993). Presumably, this model will help children with specific learning disabilities improve their performance in the classroom.

In short, special education for LD children began in several South American countries focusing greater interest on the learning difficulties and in school curriculum. At present the interest is in the integration of LD children into the mainstream of regular education.

EARLY RESEARCH IN LEARNING DISABILITIES

Most of the research in learning disabilities in several South American countries began in the 1950s. At present, however, searching for these papers is difficult and requires hard work, because most of them were published in journals of limited circulation, and it is not easy to find them. Moreover, at the time there was little communication and exchange of research among South American specialists. Most of the early research in these countries was clinical. It originated in the neurological and psychiatric services for children and the authors were not very sophisticated in statistical analyses. The articles mainly described the clinical problems presented by LD children and focused on the study of disabilities such as "minimal brain dysfunction," "hyperactivity," "dyslexia," and "mental retardation." Similar trends can be found in the papers published in Argentina, Chile, Brazil, Venezuela, Uruguay, and Peru.

The earliest published clinical studies about LD, were conducted by Quirós in Argentina, Olea and Bravo-Valdivieso in Chile, Mendilarhasu and Rebollo in Uruguay, and Sardi de Selle in Venezuela. In these same countries, the first studies of reading and writing difficulties appeared, done by Carbonell and Tuana in Uruguay, Condemarín in Chile, Braslawsky in Argentina, and Santana de Salazar in Venezuela. Studies of intelligence, memory, and mental development were done in Peru by Alarcón and Blumenfeld. Quirós published in 1959, 1965, and 1968 several papers about dyslexia. In 1965 he published a book titled *Childhood dyslexia (La Dislexia en la niñez)* where he describes dyslexia as "a perturbation of language that disturbs learning and development reading and writing" (p. 12). According to Quirós, severe dyslexia would be a type of childhood aphasia that is different of in reading and writing delay brought about by environmental or educational factors.

In this same period, Olea and Moyano (1962, Olea, 1966, 1970) in Chile published several papers regarding clinical research on dyslexic children. He associated dyslexia with minimal brain dysfunction (MBD) and believed that dyslexia is caused by deficits in visual perception, spatial orientation, and rhythm and psychomotor development. He developed a test for diagnosing dyslexia in children and to evaluate the integrity of the brain basic processes for learning to read (1979). Bravo-Valdivieso (1968) published one of the first psychological studies of a group of children diagnosed as MBD and learning disabled. Condemarín and Blomquist (1970) published the first book in Chile on dyslexia and its diagnosis and treatment. This book was aimed at teachers working with reading retarded children in schools. This book was followed some years later by another book on reading comprehension and psycholinguistics abilities (Alliende & Condemarín, 1982).

Research in Uruguay began with the work of Carbonell, who studied LD from an educational perspective. In 1965 she did a study about laterality and learning to read in a group of first grades. She found that children who had more difficulties in learning were impaired in spatial orientation. In 1968 Carbonell published another article about writing and spelling difficulties in Spanish-speaking children and their relationship with the phonological segmentation in the spoken language, and in 1969 she conducted a study on children who could write better than they could read. She found that in the group of Spanish-speaking children, spelling mistakes were largely of visual and not auditory origin. She said that it would be of interest to compare the reading difficulties of Spanish-French-, English- and German-speaking children. In another study, Carbonell and colleagues (1972) tested the Boder's Diseidetic and Dysphonetic subtypes of dyslexia in Spanish-speaking Uruguayan dyslexic children, but they did not find the dysphonetic variety among those children.

The Dyslexia Society of the Uruguay was created in the 1960s and in 1968 the Interamerican Institute for Children (OEA) published a book in Uruguay containing the papers presented at the 1967 III Seminary of Dyslexia. Most of these papers are descriptive pedagogical and clinic studies of groups of dyslexic children. Santana de Salazar (1969) has worked in Venezuela on the diagnosis and reeducation of children with severe reading disabilities who had repeated the same grade for several years in learning to read. She associated their failure with intelligence and perceptual abilities and with the socioeconomic level.

The research in LD done in these countries culminated with the First Hispano American Congress on Reading and Writing Disabilities, held in Chile, in 1971. This Congress showed an important concern for learning disabilities in reading difficulties in low socioeconomic level children. It is interesting to mention that the most cited authors in the Latin American publications in this decade were Ajuriaguerra and Zazzo from France, Piaget from Switzerland, and Strauss, Myklebust and Cruickshank from the United States.

RESEARCH IN THE YEARS TO FOLLOW

In 1972 in Uruguay, a series of books entitled *Neuro-psychological Studies* were published in which the neurological and psychological traits of dyslexia were analyzed. Mendilaharsu (1972), a neurologist, with other collaborators published a study of dyslexic children, applying a battery of psychological tests. The aim was to study their intelligence, visual perceptual and spatial abilities, and their language. Among the findings of this study, they report that dyslexic children had more difficulties rehearsing spoken sentences because they were slower in processing sequences and rhythms than children without reading problems. Moreover, dyslexic children at the beginning of the reading applied a "passive" and "receptive" strategy for decoding, without doing an active inference on meaning. Mendilaharsu (1981), as Quirós and Della Cella, (1965) had previously done, associated dyslexia with children with dysphasia.

In Venezuela, Sardi de Selle, Feldman, and Eskenazi (1971) studied children with scholastic retardation attending a public school. They concluded that their school retardation was due to the delay in the initiation of schooling, repetition of the first grade because of reading disabilities, and cultural deprivation. In this same country, Fierro de Ascanio (1974) analyzed the vocabulary of children with academic retardation that came from an environment of social disadvantage. The children had a passive vocabulary, but they were not capable of using it for learning at school.

In Argentina, during the same period, Azcoaga (1969) studied LD from a neuro-psychological clinical point of view. He followed the work af Pavlov, Luria, Vigostky, and Ajuriaguerra as theoretical models for his work. He associated reading acquisition and dyslexic's deficiencies with the children's level of neuropsychological development. He preferred to use a descriptive clinical model of research instead of a quantitative one. Azcoaga and his associates described three types of pathology regarding higher cortical processes that may cause different types of dyslexia: "anorthic, gnostic-praxical, aphasic" pathologies (Azcoaga, 1979). Azcoaga has been one of the main leaders Latin American neuro-psychological research, and one of the founders of the Latin American Neuro-psychological Society (SLAN).

In Peru, research began in 1947 with studies of intelligence and mental retardation related to performance in the schools. The most important Peruvian researcher in LD and in MR has been A. Majluf (1993), who since 1970 has published several studies on the socioculturally deprived Peruvian children coming from low social–economic backgrounds. She found that many LD children presented chronic malnutrition that affected their school performance and that interacted with the severe deficiencies in teaching that she found in the schools. The teachers did not adequately know their methodologies to help those children from very deprived environments, and they were not appropriately trained for this work. In 1976 she followed up low-class and middle-class Peruvian children, using Piagetian scales to asses their spatial organization, conservation, and construction abilities. She found a clear developmental progression in both groups. Nevertheless, by seven and a half years old, middle-class children were significantly more advanced than low class children in these cognitive abilities.

In Chile, Bravo-Valdivieso (1973) published a book based on a neuro-psychological study done on a group of children with normal IQ who had been diagnosed as having "minimal brain dysfunction" and compared them with normal children. The main difficulties of the MBD children were related to learning to read and write. This research was done following a clinical and psychometric methodology, and showed that those MBD children presented deficits in the development of higher cognitive processes like the organization of thinking, reasoning, and abstraction, as well as in perceptual and psychomotor abilities.

In the early 1980s two experimental studies were conducted to provide help to LD children in their homes or in their schools, in order to increase the supply of specialized teachers. Chadwick and Tarky trained low SES mothers to help their preschool children in logical mathematical thinking. They showed that it is possible to help low SES children by training mothers to teach them at home. Milicic (1982) did another study in a tutorial development program for children at high risk of having reading disorders in the first grade. Several eighth-grade students in the same schools completed this tutorial program. The differences with a control group were significant in the reading tests. Psychological advantages were found in the tutors as well.

Another Chilean study was presented at the IARLD meeting at Utrecht in 1981 by Bravo-Valdivieso (1982). The aim of this research was to identify some traits in Spanish-speaking dyslexic children, according to the type of errors—visual or phonemic—that they showed during decoding aloud. This study found several discriminating differences between phonemic and visual subtypes of dyslexic children in verbal tests, although both subgroups had no IQ differences measured by the WISC. This study supported the hypothesis that there may be at least two types of reading problems in Spanish-speaking children produced by visual and by phonological deficiencies during decoding aloud.

In 1979, The Children with Learning Difficulties, an international symposium, sponsored by UNICEF, was held at the Catholic University of Chile. Specialists from Argentina, Uruguay, Colombia, and the United States attended this meeting to discuss the subject in a Latin American context. From the United States Frank Vellutino, Kenneth S. Goodman and Yetta Goodman, and Pauline Kernberg participated. This meeting emphasized the psycholinguistic strategies study, and diagnostic and treatment of reading disabilities in psycholinguistic strategies. In 1981 and 1984, there were two other international symposia, at the same University and also sponsored by UNICEF, that analyzed reading comprehension problems and mathematical disabilities. In 1983, William Cruickshank and L. Bravo-Valdivieso attended an InterAmerican Seminar held in Cali, Colombia, in which the topics of learning disabilities and minimal brain dysfunction in children were discussed. Cruickshank presented his experiences with cerebral palsy and attentional deficit. This seminar had a clinical and educational approach to LD for the Colombian specialists.

SOME TESTS AND TESTING PROBLEMS

A main problem of performing LD research in our countries has been the scarcity of standardized tests. The cultural and linguistic differences with North American children are real and make difficult the plain translation of the American tests for the assessment of South American children. As a consequence, we have had to create new tests validated for these children. The following describes some of these tests.

Basic Functions Test (Berdicewski and Milicic, 1978)

This instrument was devised to be used with children in their last year of preschool or with those about to start first grade. Its specific purpose is to identify children with high risk for failure in reading and writing during first grade. The test is made up of 58 paper-and-pencil items of a multiple choice type, administered to groups of children between five and a half and seven and a half years of age. With three subtests it measures the following functions: visual-motor coordination, auditory discrimination, and language. These and other tests are usually applied in research and in diagnosing in several South American countries.

Pre-Calculus Test (Milicic-Schmidt, 1978)

The purpose of this test is the evaluation of mathematical reasoning in children between 4 and 7 years of age. More specifically it is designed to detect those who are subject to a high risk of failure in this area. The test itself is made up of 10 subtests, which cover different areas: basic concepts, visual perception, matching (one-to-one correspondence), ordinal numbers, recognition of geometric figures, reproduction and sequencing of figures, numbers, cardinality, problems, and conservation.

Specific Dyslexia Test (Condemarin and Blomquist, 1970)

This test aims at locating the child's reading level through the use of increasingly complex syllables as well as inquiring into whatever specific errors may be present, such as letter confusions or inversions. It was standardized for use in Chile by Berdicewski, Milicic, and Orellana (1983). It consists of an individual paper-and-pencil test, of easy correction, made up of two parts: reading level (100 items) and specific errors (71 items). The former allows appreciation of the degree to which the child is able to cope with syllable difficulty in reading, while the latter detects any specific dyslexia type of errors the child makes. This test requires that the child has already been introduced to reading, since he or she is required to read and recognize the sounds of letters, syllables, and words.

PRESENT TRENDS IN RESEARCH

Presently we find an increase in LD research. Most of this research is published in Spanish-language journals. Several researchers have focused their work on studying the reading disabilities in Spanish-speaking children, and their differences with English-speaking reading disabled children. Both languages have different grammatical features. Spanish has a regular "transparent" orthographic decoding, in comparison with English, and several of these studies have documented that there are differences between the reading difficulties presented by children in these two languages.

In Argentina Borzone de Manrique and Signorini (1994, 1998) studied the relationship between phonological awareness, and spelling and reading abilities in a group of first grade skilled and less-skilled readers. Results showed that less-skilled readers had better performance on spelling than on reading. No association was found between phoneme segmentation and word reading. The less-skilled readers could spell many words they could not read. Certain characteristics of Spanish phonetic structure—a small number of vowels, simple syllabic structure—and the relative transparency of its orthography may account for the early development of phonemic segmentation skills and allow the mastery of sound–letter correspondence rules that is reflected in spelling performance. In another publication Borzone de Manrique and Signorini (1998) studied the variations in early writing forms in Spanish and the relationship between phonological awareness and writing tasks in a group of kindergarten children. Their results suggest that in the process of writing acquisition, children move back and forth across forms of writing. The relationship between the writing forms and phonological awareness showed that children might be using several ways to write, from a nonanalytic approach to print to an analytic phonological mechanism. The pattern of variation observed in the children reflected the interplay among different types and levels of knowledge of print, the phonological structure of words, the sound–letter correspondences, and the cognitive demands of the tasks.

In recent work, Signorini and Piacente (in press) studied the word processing skills of Spanish-speaking beginning readers and the nature of the mechanisms underlying early word reading skills, exploring the possible effects of a regular orthography on the development of those skills. They examined the word processing skills of beginning readers and found that logographic reading was of limited importance in these children. Early word reading in Spanish-speaking children was strongly biased toward the phonological recoding of letter strings. The familiarity and lexicality effects could be pointing to the use of a lexical model described as orthographic reading. Accordingly, in the process of becoming a reader, Spanish-speaking children's knowledge of letter–sound correspondences establishes the connections linking the letters to the pronunciations. Beginners read short familiar words by forming complete connections between written forms and their pronunciations.

Another trend in the research has been the study of LD in children coming from low SES. Research in learning disabled children from low social–economic status (SES) presents some methodological problems. Most of those children have been handicapped by several environmental deficiencies other than their learning difficulties. As a consequence, they lag behind in the development of the cognitive and verbal abilities necessaries for school learning. Therefore, it is difficult for researchers to delimit in the samples the children with general learning problems, as a consequence of their disadvantageous social–economic background, from the children with specific learning disabilities brought about by neuro-psychological developmental anomalies.

On the other hand, the American definition of LD precludes children from low SES from being considered learning disabled. Moreover, the widely known definition of dyslexia, proposed by the World Federation of Neurology, says that dyslexia can be diagnosed in the presence of "sociocultural opportunity," that is to say, discarding the sociocultural underdevelopment of deprivation (Chritchley, 1970). One consequence of this definition has been that most researchers in dyslexia and/or in specific reading retardation from developed countries have been careful not to include children with sociocultural deprivation in their samples. That is why Senf (1986) has pointed out that learning disabilities have "gained the reputation of being a white, middle class disorder." However, though this definition implies that the environmental and sociocultural factors do not play a causal role in LD and dyslexia, it does not deny that they could not play an important role in its variability and in its prevalence. And Rutter (1978) ironically says that "there is not ground for supposing that social disadvantage protects children from dyslexia," and he adds that it is very likely that children with constitutional reading difficulties will make less progress if they belong to disadvantaged homes or if they attend poor schools.

Therefore, to discard socially disadvantaged children in the research on LD would not be adequate for a Latin American educational context, where most of these problems are intrinsically mixed. In the Latin American studies in LD it would be particularly difficult to consider children with low SES as a category of exclusion, because poverty appears as a permanent and pervasive social–cultural influence for school learning. South American subcultural "majorities" should not be excluded from the studies of learning disabilities and their environmental variables should be taken into account in the research.

A way to cope with the methodological problems of studying the learning disabled among low SES children has been to compare matched groups of low SES children, with and without learning disabilities, belonging to the same schools and social environments, in order to decrease the interference of unknown independent socioeconomic variables. This way it may be supposed that both groups experienced similar environmental influences. This methodological approach would show which are the cognitive traits that discriminate between learning disabled and normal low SES children.

In Chile, research was done on two groups of children that came from similar low-income families and schools, with the aim of looking for some neuro-psychological and cognitive variables that discriminate between a group of low socioeconomic level children who learned to read normally (NR) and another group of severe reading retarded schoolmates (RR). Their differences in learning could not be imputed to differences in their social–economic origins (Bravo-Valdivieso,1995). They were all Spanish-speaking children and both groups (RR and NR) were equivalent in age, grade, gender, and SES. The results showed cognitive and verbal deficits in children with severe reading retardation, within the low SES children, though they had the same IQ (WISC-R). The greatest differences between them were in the tasks of processing the phonological information, in the memory of visually sequenced letters, in auditory comprehension, and in verbal abstraction of similarities. The results confirmed the hypothesis that severe reading retardation may appear as a learning disability independent of SES and IQ. It is very likely that sociocultural and economic deprivations had a negative effect on children's development, which increases their difficulties, but the social deprivation did not appear to be the cause of their learning disabilities. In spite of their cultural and economic deprivation, the neuro-psychological characteristics of this group of severe reading retarded, low SES, Latin American children appeared very similar to those found in LD children from more developed countries.

FUTURE NEEDS

In South American countries there is only a small group of researchers, most of them found at universities, whose work is not enough to promote a real change in the situation of children with learning disabilities. There is not enough transfer of the results of research to the school context (teachers, parents, and children). Moreover, it is necessary to promote links between national researchers and the international community in seminars and congresses held in the Spanish language. One of the major limitations in the research in these countries is the scarcity of appropriate instruments for the assessment of children. It is necessary to develop appropriate instruments or adapt and standardize tests for the South American cultural context. Finally, it is necessary to carry out research concerning the efficacy of treatment strategies used to integrate children with learning disabilities in the regular classroom, and to assess the effectiveness of educational strategies for children with LD as well.

REFERENCES

Aaron, A. M., & Milicic, N. (1993). *Vivir con otros. Programa de desarrollo de las habilidades sociales.* Santiago de Chile. Edit. Universitaria.

Aaron, A. M., & Milicic, N. (1999). *Clima Social Escolar y Desarrollo personal.* Santiago de Chile. edit. Andres bello.

Ainscow, M. (1995). *Necesidades especiales en el aula.* Madrid: Narcea Ediciones.

Alliende, F., & Condemarín, M. (1982). *La lectura: Teoría, evaluación y desarrollo.* Santiago de Chile: Ed. Andres Bello.

Alvarez, C. (1999). *Integración de niños y niñas con necesidades educativas especiales a la Educación parvularia en la Fundación Integra y en la JUNJI.* Seminario para Licenciatura en Educación de Párvulos, Universidad Metropolitana de Ciencias de la Educación.

Aratangy, L. R., Bastos, C., Goulart, M., Lerner, B. R., Paulino, M., Rosenberg, L., & Swartzman, J. S. (1981). Learning disabilities in Brazil. In L. Tarnopol & M. Tarnopol (eds.), *Comparative reading and learning difficulties* (pp. 241–256). Massachusetts Toronto Lexington Books.

Azcoaga, J. E. (1969). *¿Qué es la dislexia escolar?* Rosario, Argentina: Edit. Biblioteca.

Azcoaga, J. E. (1979). *Aprendizaje fisiológico y aprendizaje pedagógico.* Buenos Aires: El Ateneo.

Azcoaga, J. E., Derman, B., & Iglesias, P. A. (1979). *Alteraciones del aprendizaje escolar.* Buenos Aires: Edit Paidos.

Berdicewski, O., & Milicic, N. (1978). *Manual del Test de Funciones Básicas.* Santiago de Chile: Ed. Galdoc.

Berdicewski, O., Milicic, N., & Orellana, E. (1983). *Elaboración de normas para la Prueba de Dislexia Específica de Condemarín-Blonquist.* Santiago de Chile: Universidad Católica.

Bermeosolo, J., & Punto, A. (1996). Caracterización de una muestra de alumnos asistentes a Grupo Diferencial. *Boletín de Investigación Educacional,* II, 369–392.

Borzone de Manrique, A. M., & Signorini, A. (1994). Phonological awareness, spelling and reading abilities in Spanish-speaking children. *British Journal of Educational Psychology, 64,* 429–439.

Borzone de Manrique, A. M., & Signorini, A. (1998). Emergent writing forms in Spanish, *Reading and Writing: An Interdisciplinary Journal, 10,* 499–517.

Bravo-Valdivieso, L. (1968). Trastornos del desarrollo psicológico en niños con daño cerebral mínimo. *Revista Chilena de Pediatría, 39,* 369–380.

Bravo-Valdivieso, L. (1973). *Trastorno del aprendizaje y de la conducta escolar.* Santiago de Chile: Edit. Nueva Universidad.

Bravo-Valdivieso, L. (1982). Psychological correlatives of reading retardation for different aged children. *Thalamus, 2,* 15–29.

Bravo-Valdivieso, L. (1995). A four year follow-up study of low socioeconomic status Latinamerican children with reading dificulties. *International Journal of Disabilitiy, Develoment and Education, 42,* 189–202.

Bravo-Valdivieso, L. (1998). *Lenguaje y dislexias.* México: Ed. Alfa Omega.

Bravo-Valdivieso, L., Bermeosolo, J., Pinto, A., & Oyarzo, E. (1994). El "Efecto lectura Inicial" y rendimiento escolar básico. *Boletín de Investigación Educacional, 9,* 7–20.

Carbonell, M. (1968). Ortografía y disortografía española. En Instituto Interamericano del Niño: *Dislexia escolar.* pp. 210–251. O.E.A.

Carbonell, M. et al. (1972). *Tamiz diagnóstico de dificultades de lecto-escritura de Helena Boder.* Segundas Jornadas. Sociedad de Dislexia de Uruguay.

Chritchley, M. (1970). *The Dyslexic Child.* London: Charles Thomas.

Condemarín, M., & Blomquist, M. (1970). *La Dislexia. Manual de lectura correctiva.* Santiago: Edit. Universitaria.

Echeita, G., Dı̈k, C., & Blanco, R. (1995). Necesidades especiales en el aula. Formación docente en el ámbito de la integración escolar. *Boletín "Proyecto principal de educación en América Latina y el Caribe" N° 36,* 51–56.

Feldman, N., & Feldman, M. (1981). Reading and learning disabilities in Venezuela. In L. Tarnopol & M. Tarnopol (Eds.), *Comparative Reading and Learning Difficulties* (pp. 497–518). Messachusetts Toranto Lexington Books.

Fierro de Ascanio, J. (1974). Aporte al estudio del vocabulario en niños retardados escolares. *Revista de Psicología, 1, 1.* (Venezuela)

Lorenzo, E. G. E de. (1973). Historical development of Special Education. Uruguay. In UNESCO, *The present situation and trends of research in the field of Special Education.* Paris: UNESCO.

Majluf, A. (1993). *Marginalidad, inteligencia y rendimiento escolar.* Lima, Peru: Ed. Brandon.

Mendilarhasu, C. (1972). Estudio de la dislexia de evolución. *Acta Neurológica Latinoamericana, 18,* 299–317.

Mendilarhasu, C. (1981). *Estudios Neuropsicológicos.* Montevideo, Uruguay: Edit. Delta.

Milicic, N. (1982). *The design and evaluation of a compensatory programme for psychosocially deprived children in Chile.* Unpublished doctoral dissertation, University College of Wales, Cardiff.

Milicic, N. (1983). Un programa de Tutoría para la enseñanaza de la lectura inicial. *Lectura y Vida, 4,* 15–24.

Milicic, N. (1988). *Algunas estrategias para desarrollar habilidades sociales en niños con trastornos de aprendizaje* [Strategies to develop social skills in children with learning disabilities]. Conferencia presentada en el Congreso de la Sociedad de Dislexia de Uruguay, Montevideo, Uruguay.

Milicic, N., & Schmidt, S. (1978). *Test de Precálculo.* Santiago, Chile: Editorial Galdoc.

Olea, R. (1966). Daño cerebral mínimo. *Revista Chilena de Neuropsiquiatría, 5,* 34–38.

Olea, R. (1970). Disfunción cerebral mínima, daño o déficit cerebral del niño. *Revista Chilena de Pediatría, 41,* 318–323.

Olea, R. (1979). Batería de Integración cerebral funcional básica. *El Niño Limitado.* Número especial.

Olea, R., & Moyano, H. S. (1962). Acerca de las bases neurológicas de la dislexia de evolución. *Fonoaudiología, 8.*

Orellana, E. (1994). Una experiencia con lenguaje escrito en el nivel preescolar. *Boletín de Investigación Educacional, 9,* 118–133.

Orellana, E. (1995). Instrumento de Evaluación ELEA. Fundamentos teóricos y análisis estadísticos. *Boletín de Investigación Educacional, 10,* 163–180.

Quirós, J. B. (1959). La Dislexia como síntoma y como síndrome. *Acta Neuropsiquiátrica Argentina, 5,* 178–193.

Quirós, J. B. (1968). Dislexia y lenguaje. En, Instituto Interamericano del Niño: *Dislexia escolar* (pp. 40–45). O.E.A. Montevideo.

Quirós, J. B., & della Cella, M. (1965). *La Dislexia en la niñez.* B. Aires: Paidós.

Rutter, M. (1978). Prevalence and types of Dyslexia. In A. L. Benton & D. Pearl (Eds.), *Dyslexia* (pp. xx–xx). New York: Oxford Univ. Press.

Santana de Salazar, H. (1969). *Análisis y tratamiento de un grupo de niños con dificultades para la lectura.* Thesis. Central University, Venezuela.

Sardi de Selle, H., Feldman, N., & Eskenazi, S. (1971). *Consideraciones generales acerca del estudio de un grupo de niños con retardo pedagógico.* Ministerio de Educación Primaria y Normal. Venezuela.

Schonaut, S., & Satz, P. (1983). Prognosis for children with learning disabilities: A review of follow-up studies. In M. Rutter (Ed.), *Developmental Neuropsychiatry* (pp. xx–xx). New York: Guilford Press.

Senf, G. (1986). Learning Disabilities research in sociological and scientific perspective. En Torgessen y Wong (Eds.), *Psychological and educational perspective on learning disabilities* (pp. xx–xx). London: Academic Press.

Signorini, A., & Piacente. (In press).

Tarnopol, L., & Tarnopol, M. (1981). *Comparative Reading and Learning Difficulties.* Massachusetts Toronto. Lexington Books.

Tuana, E., Carbonell, M., & Lluch, E. (1980). Diez años de investigación ortográfica. *Lectura y Vida, 1,* 16–19.

UNESCO (1988). United Nations Education, Scientific and Cultural organization. *Review of the present situation in special education.* Paris

Vaughn, S. (1985). Why teach social skills to learning disabled students? *Journal of Learning Disabilities, 18,* 588–591.

Vernon, Ph. (1972). *Intelligence and cultural environment.* London: Methuen.

Chapter 19

The Challenge of International Research in Learning Disabilities

Susan A. Vogel, Ph.D.
Northern Illinois University

INTRODUCTION

This volume was conceived and written to honor the memory and to celebrate the life and contributions of Bill Cruickshank, a visionary thinker, well ahead of his time, and a fearless spokesperson on behalf of individuals with learning disabilities (LD). Bill was interested early on in the contributions of medicine to our understanding of learning disabilities (e.g., neurology, psychiatry, neonatology, and genetics, to mention only a few), in teacher preparation (Cruickshank, 1966, 1981), in the creation of facilitative educational settings (Cruickshank, 1966, 1981, 1985), in screening and assessment especially in the early childhood years, and in the transition to adulthood and the factors that contributed to successful outcomes. But perhaps the area in which Bill painted with the broadest brush strokes was his endeavors to raise awareness of learning disabilities among a wide array of professionals not only in North and South America, but also in Western Europe, the then Eastern bloc countries, and Africa and Asia. In his worldwide travels and consultations, he became aware of the need to facilitate interchange of ideas and share knowledge about LD. The awareness of this need resulted in his founding the International Academy for Research in Learning Disabilities (IARLD) in 1976. As a result of the publication of Bill's writings in translation, formal IARLD conferences and congresses in North America, the

United Kingdom, and Europe, and informal meetings, there was a significant increase in awareness of learning disabilities globally.

HISTORICAL OVERVIEW OF LEARNING DISABILITIES
FROM AN INTERNATIONAL PERSPECTIVE

The first step in conducting international research in the field of learning disabilities was to learn about the history of learning disabilities in North America, Europe, Africa, and Asia. To this end, colleagues in various countries took it upon themselves to publish overviews of the field of learning disabilities (or reading disabilities/dyslexia) in their respective countries, including discussion of terminology and definitional issues, public policy and education law, identification/assessment, special education services, history of parent and professional learning disabilities organizations, and teacher preparation (Chapman, 1992; da Fonesca, 1996; Fabbro & Masutto, 1994; Fletcher & Klinger Kaufman de Lopez, 1995; Jimenez Gonzalez & Hernandez Valle, 1999; Opp, 1992; Salter & Smythe, 1997; Wiener & Siegel, 1992). In reviewing this literature, it is clear that there are many similarities in the early history of learning disabilities such as in the definition of LD in the United States and the Netherlands in that both initially included the exclusion clause and provision of intervention in self-contained classrooms or special schools. But there are also many differences in the understanding of learning disabilities from one country to another.

One way to understand cross-national research findings is to try to understand the differences in the cultural paradigms of disability including medical, social, political, and pluralistic alternatives and their impact on education, intervention, and outcomes. The underlying assumption is that the dominant paradigm in each country will determine the definition, public policies, education law, identification/assessment, teacher preparation, and special education services in each country.

Public Policy, Cultural, and Societal Differences

Canada is a good case in point. In Wiener and Siegel's (1992) seminal article, they identified five factors in Canada that influenced the development of special education services for Canadian children with learning disabilities. The first factor related to the autonomy of the various provinces within the Canadian federal political system. The next three factors considered the complex linguistic and cultural differences within the Canadian population, for example, the bilingual (French and English), multicultural, and native communities in Canada. These three factors emphasized the importance of differentiating between cultural differences, language differences, and language-based LD in the diagnostic process. The fifth factor related to the societal expectation that the government will meet the population's health, education, and social service needs. Included under this umbrella was also meeting the needs of those with LD for special education services.

Differences in Special Education Intervention

Other factors have also been identified that impact on the understanding of LD in different countries. One of them is the history of availability of special education at the provincial, state, or national level. The type and intensity of special education services, the setting in which these services are delivered (Soto & Hetzroni, 1993), and preparation of LD teachers must all be taken into account in the interpretation of cross-national comparative research. When and how special education is provided for students with learning disabilities will also change over time (Lindgren, De Renzi, & Richman, 1985; see chapters 13 and 16 regarding Germany and the Netherlands in this volume) and has to be considered in the interpretation of research findings.

Definitional Issues

One of the first challenges faced by those conducting cross-national comparative research is to identify the target population, namely, individuals in each country who have learning disabilities. What we learned from descriptive and historical publications is that the concept of learning disabilities not only varies from one country to another, but within each country the definition varies over time. For example, in the 1970s and 1980s in Germany learning disabilities was defined as mild mental retardation (see chapter 13 by Opp in this volume), while in the Netherlands it included the comorbid condition of behavior disorders (see chapter 16 by Stevens and Werkhoven). Alternatives in definition must, therefore, be considered within a national context as well as an historical perspective in which the definition and its purpose are taken into consideration. Moreover, the identified differences need to be considered in sample identification in order to conduct cross-national comparative research and in the interpretation of findings.

In some countries, a different challenge presents itself. For example, in New Zealand, Italy, and Scandinavia, learning disabilities are not recognized in federal legislation as a disability category. In New Zealand, for example, parents have unsuccessfully lobbied the legislature for recognition and services for children with learning disabilities, an

effort spearheaded by the national parent/professional organization
(i.e., The New Zealand Federation of Learning Disabilities Associations).
In other countries, professionals have preferred to use the terms *dyslexia*
or *reading disability* (Gersons-Wolfensberger & Ruijssenaars, 1997; Leong,
1999; Lingren, De Renzi, & Richman, 1985; Niemi, Porpodas, &
Tonnessen, 1999; Wimmer & Goswami, 1994, and see Lundberg &
Hoien's chapter 17 in this volume).

Even when the terminology is the same, we have also learned that
definitions may vary. Not only will definitions vary from one country to
another, but also within a single country there may be several definitions
of learning disabilities in use simultaneously. The United States (and the
Netherlands, as can be seen in Stevens and Werkhoven's chapter 16 in
this volume) are good cases in point. In the United States, for example,
the earliest and then widely accepted definition of LD is the one that still
appears in the federal law and exists side by side with the later definition of the National Joint Committee on Learning Disabilities and with
the Rehabilitation Services Agency's definition of learning disabilities
developed to provide assistance to adults with disabilities preparing for
or encountering difficulties in employment (Vogel, 1989).

COST A8 COLLABORATIVE INTERNATIONAL RESEARCH

The first area to receive systematic cross-national attention in learning disabilities/dyslexia was a multinational coordinated research effort
among 17 countries in which 15 languages were spoken (referred to as
the COST A8 countries). It was coordinated by the European Cooperation in the Field of Scientific and Technical Research (Murray, Kirsch, &
Jenkins, 1998; Niemi, Porpodas, & Tonnessen, 1999; Organization for
Economic Cooperation and Development, & Human Resources Development in Canada, 1995, 1997). The COST A8 group identified several
topics of interest including comparative linguistic studies and the impact of identified differences on those with reading disabilities, as well
as large-scale studies on early language development and reading intervention (Landerl, Wimmer, & Frith, 1997; Leong & Joshi, 1997; Olufs-
son & Stromquist, 1998). In addition, COST A8 nations were among
the small, but growing number of nations where comparative linguistics research has focused on the impact of differences in orthographic
transparency, for example, in English and German (Landerl, Wimmer, &
Frith, 1997).

To date, there has been only one other large-scale international comparative research initiative referred to by the name of the measure
(i.e., The International Adult Literacy Scale, or the IALS Collaborative

Project). The IALS was a modification of the National Adult Literacy Survey (NALS) administered in the United States in the early 1990s to a national, representative population of adults ages 16 and older. The unique feature of the NALS was that it included questions about disability status in the background questionnaire. A national sample of adults with self-reported learning disabilities was thus identified and compared to the general population (see Reder, 1995; Reder & Vogel, 1997; Vogel, 1998; and Vogel & Reder, 1998a; 1998b; 1998c for an overview of findings).

THE INTERNATIONAL ADULT LITERACY SURVEY

With the availability of the IALS, a uniform method and instrumentation became available in a multitude of languages to assist in understanding the similarities and differences among those with learning disabilities in different nations. The IALS was designed to measure the literacy skills of the total population and to identify the proportion who were functionally literate. In addition, the IALS was intended to contribute to education and labor market policy and societal programs designed to raise the competence of the citizens in participating countries.

The IALS is coordinated by Statistics Canada, the Educational Testing Service of Princeton, New Jersey, and the Paris-based Organization of Economic and Cultural Development (Murray, Kirsch, & Jenkins, 1998; Organisation for Economic Co-Operation and Development, & Human Resources Canada, 1995; 1997). A first round of data collection in 12 nations took place between 1994 and 1996 and included Belgium, Canada, Germany, Great Britain, Ireland, New Zealand, the Netherlands, Switzerland (French-speaking), and the United States. A second wave of data was collected from an additional 10 nations two years later that included Chile, the Czech Republic, Denmark, Finland, Hungary, Italy, Norway, Portugal, Slovenia, and Switzerland (Italian-speaking). Nine out of the 12 countries in the first wave asked a series of disability status questions. (Until such time as the data are released, we cannot be sure how many countries in the second round asked the disability questions, however, we do know that the Scandinavian countries and Denmark agreed to ask the disability questions and used the term *dyslexia*, rather than *learning disability*.) The questions addressed to participants were: (1) Did they have a disability; (2) If so, did they have a learning disability (or dyslexia); (3) If so, did they have this problem while they were in primary or secondary school; and (4) Do they still have this problem.

After the interviewers asked the participants background questions regarding literacy practices at home and at work, literacy self-assessment and self-reliance, educational attainment, employment history and present status, financial and disability status, they asked them to read three kinds of passages: prose, document, and quantitative literacy. After reading, they had to respond to a series of questions requiring an exact response (not multiple choice). The items were divided into five levels of difficulty: Level 1 required the participants to make a literal match, level 2 required low-level inferences, level 3 required global comprehension, level 4 required high-level inferences, and level 5 required the creation of hypertext (e.g., to compare one or more texts).

Anticipated Outcomes of the IALS International Comparative Research Project

The purpose of the IALS' collaboration is to determine the prevalence of LD in the general population ages 16–65, their literacy proficiency, and educational attainment of individuals with LD/D. Second, we plan to compare these findings cross-linguistically and cross-nationally in light of the shared and unique features of the participating nations. The long-term goal of this project is to develop a series of internationally endorsed recommendations to increase awareness and early identification of LD/D, to identify effective reading instructional strategies for children, youth, and adults with LD/D, and to recommend public policy that will mandate provision special education services.

One of the anticipated outcomes of this research is to gain a perspective on our own standing in comparison to other nations regarding the prevalence of LD/D, the educational outcomes for those with LD/D, their literacy proficiency, and adult outcomes. Second, we anticipate that this research will provide a more in-depth understanding of learning disabilities/dyslexia in our own countries by identifying the factors that seem to have influenced achievement of more positive outcome in other countries. By learning how other nations have solved similar problems, it is our hope that each nation will be able to enhance the literacy acquisition and life outcomes of those with learning disabilities/dyslexia in their own countries.

WHY BILL CRUICKSHANK WAS RIGHT IN ESTABLISHING THE IARLD

If Bill Cruickshank were here now, it is our guess that he would gain great satisfaction in reading this volume. He would rest easier knowing that the U.S. National Institutes of Health under Reid Lyon's leadership funded large-scale epidemiological and longitudinal research programs. He would be able to observe the beginnings of large-scale international research projects that hold promise to move us toward an increase in our knowledge and understanding of the magnitude and complexity of the problem of LD/D globally and to understand its impact on long-term outcomes. He would be the first to acknowledge the many remarkable accomplishments of the last 25 years, but he would also be the first to exhort us all to work harder in our research, teaching, and clinical work and to enhance our international collaborations in order to understand better the complexities of learning disabilities and ultimately enhance the life satisfaction and outcomes for those with learning disabilities.

REFERENCES

Chapman, J. W. (1992). Learning disabilities in New Zealand: Where Kiwis and kids with LD can't fly. *Journal of Learning Disabilities, 25,* 362–370.

Cruickshank, W. (1966). *The teacher of brain-injured children.* Syracuse, NY: Syracuse University Press.

Cruickshank, W. (1977). Myths and realities of learning disabilities. *Journal of Learning Disabilities, 5*(7), 57–64.

Cruickshank, W. (1981). A new perspective in teacher education. The neuro-educator. *Journal of Learning Disabilities, 14,* 337–341.

Cruickshank, W. (1985). Learning disabilities: A series of challenges. *Learning Disabilities Focus, 1*(1), 5–8.

da Fonseca, V. (1996). Assessment and treatment of learning disabilities in Portugal. *Journal of Learning Disabilities, 29,* 114–117.

Fabbro, F., & Masutto, C. (1994). An Italian perspective on learning disabilities. *Journal of Learning Disabilities, 27,* 138–141.

Fletcher, T. V., & Klinger Kaufman de Lopez, C. (1995). A Mexican perspective on learning disabilities. *Journal of Learning Disabilities, 28,* 530–534, 544.

Gersons-Wolfensberger, D. C. M., & Ruijssenaars, W. A. J. J. M. (1997). Definition and treatment of dyslexia: A report by the committee on dyslexia of the Health Council of the Netherlands. *Journal of Learning Disabilities, 30,* 209–213.

Jimenez Gonzalez, J. E., & Hernandez Valle, I. (1999). A Spanish perspective on LD. *Journal of Learning Disabilities, 32,* 267–275.

Landerl, K., Wimmer, H., & Frith, U. (1997). The impact of orthographic consistency on dyslexia: A German-English comparison. *Cognition, 63,* 315–334.

Leong, C. K. (1999). What can we learn from dyslexia in Chinese? In I. Lundberg, F. E. Tonnessen, & I. Anstad (Eds.), *Dyslexia: Advances in theory and practice* (pp. 117–139). Dordrecht: Kluwer Academic Publishers.

Leong, C. K., & Joshi, R. M. (1997). Relating phonologic and orthographic processing to learning to read and spell. In C. K. Leong & R. M. Joshi (Eds.), *Cross-language studies of learning to read and spell* (pp. 1–29). The Netherlands: Kluwer Academic Publishers.

Lindgren, S. D., De Renzi, E., & Richman, L. C. (1985). Cross-national comparisons of dyslexia in Italy and the United States. *Child Development, 56,* 1404–1417.

Murray, S., Kirsch, I., & Jenkins, L. (1998). *Adult literacy in OECD countries: Technical report on the First International Adult Literacy Survey.* Washington, DC: U. S. Department of Education, National Center for Educational Statistics.

Niemi, P., Porpodas, C., Tonnessen, F. (1999). Reading disorders and their treatment in Europe: Introduction to the special series. *Journal of Learning Disabilities, 32,* 384–385, 393.

Opp, G. (1992). A German perspective on learning disabilities. *Journal of Learning Disabilities, 25,* 351–360.

Organisation for Economic Co-Operation and Development, & Human Resources Canada. (1995). *Literacy, economy and society: Results of the First International Adult Literacy Survey.* Paris: Author.

Organisation for Economic Co-Operation and Development, & Human Resources Canada. (1997). *Literacy skills for the knowledge society: Further results from the International Adult Literacy Survey.* Paris: Author.

Reder, S. (1995). *Literacy, education and learning disabilities.* Portland, OR: Northwest Regional Educational Laboratory.

Reder, S., & Vogel, S. A. (1997). Lifespan employment and economic outcomes for adults with self-reported learning disabilities. In P. Gerber & D. Brown (Eds.), *Learning disabilities and employment* (pp. 371–394). Austin, TX: Pro-Ed.

Salter, R., & Smythe, I. (1997). *International Book of Dyslexia.* London: World Dyslexia Network Foundation.

Soto, G., & Hetzroni, O. (1993). Special education/integration in Spain: Highlighting similarities and differences with mainstreaming in the USA. *International Journal of Disability, Development, and Education, 40,* 181–192.

Stahl, N. A., Higginson, B. C., & King, J. R. (1993). Appropriate use of comparative literacy research in the 1990s. *Journal of Reading, 37,* 2–12.

van den Bos, K. P., Siegel, L. S., Bakker, D. J., & Share, D. L. (1994). *Current directions in dyslexia research.* Lisse, Netherlands: Swets & Zeitlinger.

Vogel, S. A., (1989). Adults with language learning disabilities: Definition, diagnosis, and determination of eligibility for postsecndary and vocational rehabilitation services. *Rehabilitation Education, 3,* 77–90.

Vogel, S. A. (1998). Adults with learning disabilities: What learning disabilities specialists, adult literacy educators, and other service providers want and need to know. In S. A. Vogel and S. Reder (Eds.), *Learning disabilities, literacy, and adult education* (pp. 5–28). Baltimore, MD: Paul H. Brookes.

Vogel, S. A., & Reder, S. (1998a). Educational attainment of adults with learning disabilities. In S. A. Vogel & S. Reder (Eds.), *Learning disabilities, literacy, and adult education* (pp. 43–68). Baltimore, MD: Paul H. Brookes Co.

Vogel, S. A., & Reder, S. (1998b). *Learning disabilities, literacy, and adult education.* Baltimore, MD: Paul H. Brookes Publishing Co.

Vogel, S. A., & Reder, S. (1998c). Literacy proficiency of adults with self-reported learning disabilities. In M. C. Smith (Ed.), *Literacy for the 21st century: Research, policy, practices, and the National Adult Literacy Survey* (pp. 159–171). Westport, CT: Greenwood Press.

Wiener, J., & Siegel, L. (1992). A Canadian perspective on learning disabilities. *Journal of Learning Disabilities, 25,* 340–350, 371.

Wimmer, H., & Goswami, U. (1994). The influence of orthographic consistency on reading development: Word recognition in English and German children. *Cognition, 51,* 91–103.

Author Index

Subject Index